The Destruction and Creation of Michael Jackson

The Destruction and Creation of Michael Jackson

Ellis Cashmore

BLOOMSBURY ACADEMIC
NEW YORK · LONDON · OXFORD · NEW DELHI · SYDNEY

BLOOMSBURY ACADEMIC
Bloomsbury Publishing Inc
1385 Broadway, New York, NY 10018, USA
50 Bedford Square, London, WC1B 3DP, UK
29 Earlsfort Terrace, Dublin 2, Ireland

BLOOMSBURY, BLOOMSBURY ACADEMIC and the Diana logo are trademarks of
Bloomsbury Publishing Plc

First published in the United States of America 2022

Cover design by Eleanor Rose
Cover image: Michael Jackson arrives at the Santa Barbara County Courthouse for the second
day of the defense's case in his child molestation trial May 6, 2005 in Santa Maria, California.
Photo © Carlo Allegri / Getty Images

Library of Congress Cataloging-in-Publication Data
Names: Cashmore, Ellis, author.
Title: The destruction and creation of Michael Jackson / Ellis Cashmore.
Description: New York : Bloomsbury Academic, 2022. | Includes bibliographical
references and index. |
Summary: "However people remember Jackson, no one can deny that, in cultural terms,
Jackson remains a compelling subject: an icon of the late 20th century, he reflects not only
the changes in the circumstances of the African American population, but changes in white
America. Jackson was idolized, perhaps even objectified into an extraordinary being for whom
there were no established reference points in whites' conceptions. This book posits that
Jackson was a creation of, at first, American and, later, global culture at a time when
it seemed desirable, if not necessary to exalt a Black person on merit. America had
become a society in which someone of Jackson's indisputable genius not only can,
but must, rise to the top"– Provided by publisher.
Identifiers: LCCN 2021053251 (print) | LCCN 2021053252 (ebook) | ISBN 9781501363580
(hardback) | ISBN 9781501363573 (paperback) | ISBN 9781501363566 (epub) |
ISBN 9781501363634 (pdf) | ISBN 9781501363559
Subjects: LCSH: Jackson, Michael, 1958-2009. | Singers–United States–Biography. |
Rock musicians–United States–Biography. | Fame–Social aspects. |
African American celebrities. | LCGFT: Biographies.
Classification: LCC ML420.J175 C38 2022 (print) | LCC ML420.J175 (ebook) |
DDC 782.42166092 [B]–dc23
LC record available at https://lccn.loc.gov/2021053251
LC ebook record available at https://lccn.loc.gov/2021053252

ISBN: HB: 978-1-5013-6358-0
ePDF: 978-1-5013-6363-4
eBook: 978-1-5013-6356-6

Typeset by Deanta Global Publishing Services, Chennai, India
Printed and bound in Great Britain

To find out more about our authors and books visit www.bloomsbury.com and
sign up for our newsletters.

Mike will forever be, as almost all the girls say, "so cute."
Ben Fong-Torres, *Rolling Stone*, April 29, 1971

He is an innocent man who does not intend to have his career and his life destroyed by rumors and innuendo.
Johnnie Cochran Jr., quoted in the *Los Angeles Times*, January 26, 1994

I don't think Michael Jackson obsesses most of the American people anymore. He is, to a certain extent, yesterday's news.
Jeffrey Toobin, senior legal analyst for CNN, January 16, 2004

Michael Jackson's death was much like his life—a circus of rabid fans, family, opportunists and media members, who were in a frenzy Thursday trying to confirm yet another rumor about one of the strangest and most high-flying celebrity lives on record.
Pat Saperstein, *Variety*, June 25, 2009

CONTENTS

Destruction and Creation: TimeLine

Michael Jackson, born Gary, Indiana, August 29, 1958;
died Los Angeles, California, June 25, 2009

DESTRUCTIVE IMPACT

CREATIVE SURGE

MILESTONE EVENT IN THE BLACK EXPERIENCE

LAWSUIT BROUGHT BY WADE ROBSON AND JAMES SAFECHUCK

PUBLISHING DEALS

2022

FEBRUARY *MJ: The Musical* opens on Broadway; Variety's reporter is removed for asking questions about sex abuse.

2021

DECEMBER Investigation into the murder of Emmett Till is closed by US Justice Department unresolved; the case had been reopened in 2018. (See **1955**)

MAY A longrunning dispute concludes when an LA judge declares MJ's assets at the time of his death were worth $111 million; in 2013 IRS audited the estate and estimated assets at $482 million, leading to a $700 million tax bill. Also in dispute were his music publishing assets (including his 50 percent stake in Sony/ATV); IRS estimated these at $320 million, but the ruling reduces the figure to $107 million at the time of death.

APRIL An LA judge rules that Wade Robson, now thirty-eight, can't sue Jackson's businesses over the childhood sexual abuse he allegedly suffered; same judge ruled against James Safechuck on similar grounds in November 2020. LAW

2020

DECEMBER US appeals court rules MJ's estate can take action against HBO over *Leaving Neverland* and allegations he sexually abused two boys; the estate sues the network for $100 million, arguing the documentary violated a non-disparagement clause in a 27-year-old contract (see **1992**).

DECEMBER Neverland, MJ's amusement park-themed property in Los Olivos, near Santa Barbara is sold for $22 million (£16 million) after being on the market for five years; its initial asking price was $100 million, suggesting the premium usually associated with property belonging to a beloved celebrity wasn't a factor; *Forbes* values the estate at $28 million.

NOVEMBER *Forbes* calculates MJ has more posthumous earnings than any other dead entertainer, with $48 million from his music, publishing ,and other interests in the previous twelve months; he is the highest earner every year since his death in 2009, with about 70 percent of his income coming from music publishing (see 2016, 2015, 2012, 1995, 1980); Britain's *Sun* newspaper reports MJ has generated $2 billion/£1.5 billion since his death.

NOVEMBER A Los Angeles court dismisses a claim by James Safechuck that MJ's companies, MJJ Productions and MJJ Ventures, had a fiduciary duty to him as a child working for the pop star; Safechuck's lawsuit alleges that Jackson abused him hundreds of times in the late 1980s and early 1990s, and claims that "the thinly-veiled, covert second purpose of (MJ's) businesses was to operate as a child sexual abuse operation, designed to locate, attract, lure and seduce child sexual abuse victims." LAW

SEPTEMBER MJ's cousin auctions an IV drip she retrieved from his bedroom shortly after his death.

MAY California appeals court overturns 2017 jury verdict awarding Quincy Jones $9.4 million in royalties and fees from the Michael Jackson estate over the use of material in the concert film *Michael Jackson's This Is It* and two Cirque du Soleil shows.

JANUARY A California law comes into effect that allows victims of childhood sexual abuse until the age of forty to file civil law suits, making them able to sue third parties, who either knew, or should have known, that abuse was happening, or failed to take reasonable steps to prevent the abuse; it also extends the statute of limitations. This overrules a 2017 ruling that denied James Safechuck and Wade Robson the right to sue. LAW

2019

MARCH Radio stations around the world, including in New Zealand and Canada, begin to ban MJ's songs.

FEBRUARY Jackson estate sues HBO, claiming that, in 1992, the network agreed to air an MJ concert and that the contract included a non-disparagement clause; HBO screens *Leaving Neverland* on March 3 and 4.

JANUARY *Leaving Neverland* debuts at Sundance Film Festival, later airs on HBO and Channel 4. DESTRUCTIVE IMPACT

2018

JULY Quincy Jones is awarded $9.4 million in royalties and production fees from the Jackson estate after a four-year legal case; Jones sought $30 million; trial centers on definitions of terms in the two contracts Jackson and Jones signed in 1978 and 1985; the verdict is overturned in 2020.

JUNE Joe Jackson (b. 1928) dies from pancreatic cancer, age eighty-nine.

2017

JANUARY British broadcaster Sky pulls episode of its *Urban Myths* drama series, in which white actor Joseph Fiennes played MJ, after complaints from the Jackson family; the episode focuses on a purported road trip of MJ, Elizabeth Taylor, and Marlon Brando (see 2001).

DECEMBER A California judge dismisses a lawsuit brought by Wade Robson, now thirty-five, who sought to sue two MJ-owned corporations; the judge finds that the corporations are not liable for Robson's exposure to MJ but does not rule on the credibility of Robson's accusations (see March 2021).

2016

MARCH Sony strikes a $750 million deal with Jackson's estate to acquire the 50 percent stake it does not own in Sony/ATV, the music publishing group (see 1995; 1985). PUB

2015

OCTOBER Sony triggers the buy-sell process with the Jackson estate that allows it to buy out MJ's stake in 750,000-song Sony/ATV catalog that now includes Adele, Taylor Swift, and Lady Gaga. PUB

2014

NOVEMBER James Safechuck sues, alleging MJ abused him on over 100 occasions between 1988 and 1992, after the pair met when Safechuck appeared in a Pepsi commercial (see 1986). LAW

2013

MAY Wade Robson takes legal action against the Jackson estate, alleging that Michael Jackson molested him over a seven-year period between the ages of seven and fourteen; this starts a law suit that continues till March 2021. LAW

AUGUST Internal Revenue Service (IRS) states MJ's estate owes $702 million in federal taxes, plus penalties, based on its evaluation of his assets at the time of his death; this initiates a dispute that will continue until 2021.

2012

AUGUST Sony/ATV Music Publishing agree to administer the Mijac Music catalog, though Mijac is still owned by the Jackson estate; John Branca reports MJ's total posthumous sales have now exceeded 40 million albums. PUB

JUNE Group led by Sony/ATV and the Jackson estate (among others) complete a $2.2 billion deal for the purchase of EMI Music Publishing. `PUB`

MARCH 100 North Carolwood Drive, Beverly Hills, LA, the home where MJ died, is listed on the market for $23.9 million.

2011

NOVEMBER California jury finds Dr. Conrad Murray guilty of involuntary manslaughter of MJ.

2010

AUGUST Katherine Jackson files for divorce after sixty years of marriage; she and husband Joe have been estranged for two years; it is the second time she has filed (see 1973).

JUNE *Billboard* estimates that MJ's estate has generated more than $1 billion in revenues in the year after his death from various sources including the sale of 33 million albums globally, 26.5 million track downloads, merchandising, and income from the concert film, *This Is It.*

2009

DECEMBER *Thriller* is named by the US Library of Congress' National Film Registry as one of twenty-five "culturally, historically or aesthetically significant" films to be preserved for all time; among the other films selected are *Dog Day Afternoon* (1975), *Once Upon a Time in the West* (1968), and *The Incredible Shrinking Man* (1957).

JULY Footage of MJ's accident while shooting Pepsi ad in 1984 is released.

JULY Public memorial for MJ held at LA's Staples Center.

JULY 422,000 copies of MJ's albums sold in United States in the first week after his death (forty times previous week's total).

JUNE Katherine is granted temporary custody of MJ's children.

JUNE 25 MJ dies, age fifty.

MARCH MJ announces series of concerts at London's O2 Arena.

MARCH Debbie Rowe reveals, "I offered him [MJ] my womb."

2008

NOVEMBER MJ settles a dispute with Sheikh Abdullah bin Hamad al-Khalifa, son of the king of Bahrain, out of court (see 2005).

NOVEMBER Reports that MJ converts to Islam and changes name to Mikaeel.

2006

DECEMBER James Brown dies, aged seventy-three.

MARCH Johnny Jackson, who played drums with the Jackson 5 in the mid-1960s, is stabbed to death in a house in Gary; he is aged fifty-four.

2005

AUGUST Hurricane Katrina leaves New Orleans devastated; African Americans comprise 67 percent of the city's population; there are over 1,800 fatalities.

JULY MJ and his children travel to Bahrain as guests of the royal family following the acquittal; they stay here for several months.

JUNE MJ is acquitted of all charges.

FEBRUARY MJ stands trial; jury is told he abused a thirteen-year-old boy, exposing him to "strange sexual behavior" during visits to his Neverland ranch; witnesses for the defense include Wade Robson (who says MJ did not molest him—see 2017, 2021) and Macaulay Culkin. DESTRUCTIVE IMPACT

2004

FEBRUARY Janet Jackson has a "wardrobe malfunction" during the Super Bowl halftime show in Houston, Texas.

MARCH–APRIL A nineteen-member grand jury convenes to hear evidence to MJ's case; grand jury indicts MJ on April 21 but charges not made public.

2003

DECEMBER The Nation of Islam restrict access to MJ and make decisions for him related to the media, his business affairs and legal strategy, according to the *New York Times* (December 30).

DECEMBER MJ is formally charged with committing lewd and lascivious acts with a child under the age of fourteen.

NOVEMBER 20 MJ is booked and released on $3 million bond; authorities state he will be charged with "multiple counts of lewd and lascivious acts with a child under the age of 14."

NOVEMBER 18 Police raid Neverland; MJ is not present.

JUNE Lee Myung-ho, a Korean lawyer, reaches an out-of-court settlement with MJ after filing a $12 million civil suit; Lee claims in the lawsuit that MJ is on the brink of bankruptcy; if the case had gone to trial, it threatened to cause embarrassment to the now-reclusive MJ.

APRIL Michael Jordan retires for the third and final time.

FEBRUARY *Living with Michael Jackson*, a documentary fronted by the British journalist Martin Bashir, includes footage of MJ discussing regularly having sleepovers with children, including Gavin Arvizo. *New York Times* describes MJ as "creepy, but almost touching in his delusional naïveté." DESTRUCTIVE IMPACT

FEBRUARY MJ fires his attorney John Branca after ten years.

2002

NOVEMBER MJ dangles his third son, nine-month-old Prince Michael II (Blanket), from a Berlin hotel balcony. *Chicago Tribune* (November 27) records, "That Michael Jackson has become increasingly paranoid and out of touch with reality is not news. Besides, his strangeness is so familiar we hardly notice." DESTRUCTIVE IMPACT

JULY MJ accuses Sony and recording industry of neglecting black artists and singles out Tommy Mottola for particular criticism; Al Sharpton accompanies him at a media conference to publicize his criticism.

FEBRUARY Prince Michael Jackson II, aka Blanket, is born; his mother is not known.

2001

OCTOBER *Invincible* is released; "Jackson has enlisted enough co-writers to fill a city bus, but they haven't helped him recapture the vitality and command that made the highlights of his work with Quincy Jones," reports the *LA Times*.

SEPTEMBER Improbable story circulates about MJ, Elizabeth Taylor, and Marlon Brando in a road trip in aftermath of 9/11.

MARCH MJ speaks at the Oxford Union.

2000

AUGUST MJ meets Gavin Arvizo, a ten-year-old boy with cancer.

1999

FEBRUARY Amadou Diallo is shot and killed by four NYPD officers. MILESTONE

1998

APRIL Paris Jackson, MJ's daughter is born.

1997

MAY *Blood on the Dance Floor: HIStory in the Mix* is mainly a remix album but with five new tracks.

FEBRUARY Michael Joseph "Prince" Jackson Jr. is born.

1996

NOVEMBER MJ marries Debbie Rowe in Australia.

JULY MJ performs at the fiftieth birthday party of the Sultan of Brunei (on the northwestern coast of Borneo); 60,000 people watch the concert, for which MJ is paid a reported $17 million.

JANUARY Lisa Marie Presley divorces MJ.

1995

NOVEMBER Diana's interview with Martin Bashir draws almost 23 million viewers in the UK; her marriage to Charles is in ruins and she says, "There were three of us in this marriage," in reference to the Duchess of Cornwall (then Camilla Parker Bowles); the interview is a catalyst for divorce proceedings. The interview opens doors for Bashir, who goes on to interview MJ in 2003, but who is, in 2020, accused of having used fraudulent means to secure the Diana interview.

OCTOBER Million Man March is a procession of hundreds of thousands of African American men to Washington, DC, in an attempt to put black issues back on the government agenda. MILESTONE

JUNE 14 Lisa Marie Presley and MJ appear on ABC News' *Primetime Live*; 60 million viewers watch.

JUNE 20 *HIStory: Past, Present and Future, Book I* is released; *LA Times* reports, "The skin-deep lyrics themselves may not take us too far into his [MJ's] thinking, but the downbeat tone does."

MAY "Scream," a duet with January, angrily addresses media coverage of sexual abuse allegations against MJ.

MARCH ATV Music Publishing, controlled by MJ, merges with Sony's music publishing arm to form Sony/ATV. PUB

1994

SEPTEMBER After two grand juries fail to indict and Jordan Chandler tells authorities he will not testify in court, LA and Santa Barbara district attorneys end their investigation.

MAY MJ marries Lisa Marie Presley.

JANUARY 25 MJ settles contested sexual abuse allegation out of court; lawyer Johnnie Cochran Jr. says, "The resolution of this case is in no way an admission of guilt by Michael Jackson."

JANUARY 24 LA county district attorney's office announces it will not bring extortion charges against Evan Chandler.

1993

DECEMBER MJ states on video: "I am not guilty of these allegations, but if I am guilty of anything it is of giving all that I have to give to help children all over the world."

NOVEMBER *Dangerous* tour is aborted.

SEPTEMBER 14 Lawsuit from the Chandler family alleges sexual abuse by Jackson and seeks $30 million.

SEPTEMBER 16 Janet appears shirtless on front cover of *Rolling Stone*.

AUGUST 27 *Los Angeles Times* publishes story headlined: POLICE SAY SEIZED TAPES DO NOT INCRIMINATE JACKSON.

AUGUST 24 Anthony Pellicano, MJ's pi, states, "A demand for $20 million was made and presented. It was flatly and consistently refused."

AUGUST 17 LAPD investigation begins after Jordan Chandler accusations; Jackson had met the twelve-year-old boy the previous year. DESTRUCTIVE IMPACT

AUGUST Teenagers Brett Barnes and Wade Robson hold a press conference stating that they shared a bed with Jackson on many occasions, but nothing sexual had happened.

JULY An unnamed boy tells a therapist and then social workers that MJ had abused him over a four-month period.

MAY *National Enquirer* runs story headlined: MICHAEL JACKSON'S SECRET FAMILY — A MILLIONAIRE'S WIFE AND HER TWO KIDS; this prompts suspicions of untowardness. DESTRUCTIVE IMPACT

FEBRUARY Michael reveals to Oprah on tv he had been abused by his father and that he has a vitiligo, a skin condition; it is the most-watched television interview in history with a global audience of 90 million.

1992

OCTOBER *Dangerous* tour concert in Bucharest, Romania, is broadcast on HBO; the contract for this contains a clause which becomes a source of legal contention in 2020 when the Jackson estate sues the media company for $100 million (see December 2020).

MAY MJ meets twelve-year-old Jordan Chandler; he later becomes friends with the boy.

APRIL Riots sparked by acquittal of LAPD officers charged with beating Rodney King.

1991

NOVEMBER *Dangerous* is released; *LA Times* calls it "Relatively tame, and wildly unfocused."

OCTOBER Elizabeth Taylor marries Larry Fortensky at a lavish ceremony at Neverland.

MARCH Rodney King is arrested and severely beaten by LAPD officers. MILESTONE

FEBRUARY LaToya's book *Growing Up in the Jackson Family* is published.

1989

NOVEMBER Sammy Davis Jr.'s sixtieth birthday celebration; MJ sings an unreleased co-composition in tribute.

SEPTEMBER Janet's *Rhythm Nation 1814* is released.

APRIL Central Park Jogger case; four black and one Latino men charged and imprisoned; their convictions are vacated in 2002. MILESTONE

FEBRUARY MJ fires his manager Frank Dileo after five years.

1988

JUNE Berry Gordy sells Motown to MCA Records for $61 million.

FEBRUARY MJ's book, *Moonwalk*, is published.

JANUARY CBS sells its recording division to the Sony; it is renamed Sony Music Entertainment in 1991.

1987

DECEMBER MJ buys 2,700-acre Sycamore Valley Ranch, in Los Olivos, California (about 30 miles from Santa Barbara), and builds a home, complete with its own amusement park rides; he names it Neverland (it is eventually sold in 2020).

AUGUST *Bad*, MJ's seventh studio album, is released nearly five years after his previous studio album; it sells 35 million copies. CREATIVE SURGE

1986

DECEMBER Jackson meets ten-year-old James Safechuck onset of a Pepsi commercial; Safechuck becomes a frequent traveling companion of Jackson's, sometimes accompanying him on tour. See May 2014.

JUNE MJ agrees to make three commercial videos for Pepsi for $15 million; contract stipulates that he will not, in the two commercials he appears in, be seen clasping a can of Pepsi (he drinks only fruit juice and Evian).

SEPTEMBER MJ is reported to claim, "I can tell the press anything about me and they'll buy it";

National Enquirer publishes story headlined "Michael Jackson's Secret Plan to Live to 150" with picture of MJ in a hyperbaric (oxygen) chamber.

SEPTEMBER *Captain EO*, the 3D sci-fi film, opens at Walt Disney World.

SEPTEMBER *The Oprah Winfrey Show* launches; it runs until 2011.

FEBRUARY Janet's *Control* is released.

1985

OCTOBER MJ acquires ATV Music Publishing for $41.5 million; attorney John Branca is instrumental in the deal. PUB

SEPTEMBER Oprah Winfrey's talk show changes its name to *The Oprah Winfrey Show*.

MARCH "We Are the World," written by MJ and Lionel Richie and sung by several artists known collectively as US For Africa, is released as a single, with all royalties going to charities.

1984

DECEMBER Bernard Goetz shoots four black teenagers he believed were menacing him on a New York subway, leaving one paralyzed; Goetz becomes a folk hero, "the Subway Vigilante"; he is convicted of carrying an unlicensed firearm and serves eight months of a one-year sentence.

DECEMBER *Beverly Hills Cop,* with Eddie Murphy, is released.

July *Victory* album; Don King promotes tour to accompany album; PepsiCo sponsors tour in deal reputed to be the biggest deal of its kind ($6 million); MJ announces he will not tour with band again after tour.

SEPTEMBER MJ releases press statement denying he uses hormones or has had plastic surgery and will sue publications that spread false rumors; in the same release, he confirms "I love children . . . I would like to continue to keep their respect."

SEPTEMBER *The Cosby Show* starts on NBC; it will run until April 1992.

SEPTEMBER Michael Jordan signs for Chicago Bulls.

MAY Prince's "When Doves Cry" is released.

JANUARY MJ burnt in accident while shooting Pepsi ad.

JANUARY Oprah Winfrey starts presenting *A.M. Chicago*, a morning talk show airing on WLS-TV.

1983

JANUARY David Bowie points out, "There are so few artists featured on it [MTV]. Why is that?"

DECEMBER *Michael Jackson's Thriller*, the John Landis-directed video, is premiered. CREATIVE SURGE

NOVEMBER MJ and brothers sign $5 million deal with PepsiCo that shatters record for celebrity endorsement deals. CREATIVE SURGE

OCTOBER *Say, Say, Say* video is released; it is one of several collaborative efforts with MJ and Paul McCartney (there are several mixes, including a seven-minute vinyl reissue in 2015).

MAY NBC broadcast *Motown 25: Yesterday, Today, Forever*, a concert featuring MJ's performance of "Billie Jean," in which he moonwalked on stage.

MARCH "Billie Jean" and "Beat It" are shown on MTV; *Guardian* calls this the start of "the Jackson era" and it lasts roughly till 1989. CREATIVE SURGE

FEBRUARY Epic releases "Billie Jean."

1982

NOVEMBER *Thriller*, MJ's sixth studio album, is released; the accompanying video is screened over a year later.

1981

AUGUST MTV launches; the cable tv network features 24-hour music videos.

July *Triumph* tour of North America starts.

1980

OCTOBER *Triumph*, the Jacksons' fourteenth studio album, is released; BBC will later describe it as, "the second of the trio of albums that marked Michael's all-conquering phase."

MJ starts his personal publishing company, Mijac Music (by 2010 *Billboard* estimates the value of Mijac has risen to $150 million). PUB

1979

POSSIBLY SEPTEMBER Michael dismisses father Joe as his manager.

AUGUST MJ's first solo album for Epic is released; "A triumph for producer Quincy Jones as well as for Michael Jackson, *Off the Wall* represents discofied post-Motown glamour at its classiest," concludes *Rolling Stone*; it includes "Girlfriend," written by Paul McCartney. CREATIVE SURGE

JULY "Disco Sucks" campaign reaches culmination at Chicago's Comiskey Park where 48,000 gather to smash disco records; the campaign, ostensibly against disco music, has racist and homophobic undertones; the episode is known as Disco Demolition.

MJ has first surgery on his nose after an accident.

JANUARY *Destiny* world tour starts.

1978

DECEMBER *Destiny* album revives the Jacksons' sagging musical career.

DECEMBER Recording begins for *Off the Wall*.

OCTOBER *The Wiz*, a reimagining of *The Wizard Of Oz* with Diana Ross as Dorothy and MJ as the Scarecrow is released; music for the film is composed by Quincy Jones, who goes on to work with Jackson on a three-album run: *Off the Wall*, *Thriller* and *Bad*. Jones signs first of two contracts (another in 1985), which become the subject of a legal contest (see **2017**; **2020**).

JUNE Affirmative action is affirmed after case of *Regents of the University of California v. Bakke*. MILESTONE

1977

AUGUST Elvis Presley dies; his daughter Lisa Marie is nine.

JULY MJ goes to New York to play in *The Wiz*.

1976

NOVEMBER *The Jacksons* is the first album for CBS/Epic under the name "The Jacksons."

1975

JULY Jackson 5 announces the intention to leave Motown and move to CBS's Epic Records (later owned by Sony); "We left Motown because we look forward to selling a lot of albums," Tito Jackson is quoted by the *New Yorker*, "Motown sells a lot of singles. Epic sells a lot of albums"; "We thought it was time for us to start writing some of our own songs," Jackie tells the *FT*; Jermaine remains at Motown.

1974

APRIL Jackson 5 appear at MGM Grand Hotel, Las Vegas; Janet and LaToya make guest appearances.

1973

APRIL Third solo album *Music and Me* is released.

MARCH Katherine Jackson files for divorce but rescinds the divorce papers at the urging of her church.

1972

JUNE/JULY Motown leaves Detroit and relocates to LA; releases (in March) Stevie Wonder's *Music of My Mind* (first album under a new contract).

JANUARY "Got to Be There," MJ's first solo album, is released by Motown.

1971

OCTOBER MJ launches solo career with first single "Got to Be There" (solo album of same name is released January 1972). CREATIVE SURGE

SEPTEMBER *Jackson 5ive*, an animated series (Michael voiced by Donald Fullilove) starts on ABC tv and runs for twenty-three (thirty minutes) episodes until 1973.

AUGUST Second album *Ben*; title track is first solo number one single for MJ.

JULY Donny Osmond's single "Sweet and Innocent" is released.

1970

NOVEMBER Average age of Jackson 5 is nearly fifteen; (MJ, ten; Marlon, thirteen; Jermaine, fifteen; Tito, seventeen; Jackie, nineteen) when band appears at NY's Madison Square Garden; *Rolling Stone* reports, "The average age of the Garden crowd seemed about the same, giving rise to an identification so total that half the audience seemed dazed."

NOVEMBER The Osmonds (see 1962) release "One Bad Apple," a song originally offered to and rejected by the Jacksons; the band has four more hit singles and is marketed as a white equivalent of the Jackson 5.

OCTOBER SCLC's Operation Breadbasket protest Jackson 5 concerts in Texas because their promoter Dick Clark is white; Gordy responds, "Black, white. What the hell's the difference as long as we all make money . . . The Jackson 5 are bigger than any race issue"; three concerts are canceled.

1969

DECEMBER The band appears on the influential Ed Sullivan Show.

NOVEMBER First Motown single, "I Want You Back," is released; it is the first of four consecutive singles to go to number one in charts. CREATIVE SURGE

JULY Elvis kick starts the final phase of his career with a residency in Las Vegas; over the next few years, he divorces his wife, puts on weight, and starts using tranquilizers, barbiturates, and amphetamines.

MARCH Jackson family moves to California.

1968

AUGUST Berry Gordy signs the brothers and Diana Ross introduces the Jackson Five at a Beverly Hills club.

AUGUST James Brown releases his "Say It Loud—I'm Black and I'm Proud." MILESTONE

JUNE Elvis's "68 Comeback Special" is an hour-long NBC broadcast featuring the 33-year-old's return from exile in Hollywood, where he'd spent years making mediocre films while the Beatles and other bands eclipsed him.

JUNE Bobby Taylor, a Motown artist, is impressed by the Jacksons' stage performance and recommends them to Suzanne de Passe, an assistant to Motown owner Berry Gordy.

MAY "Jackson Five," as the band is billed, appear at Harlem's Apollo Theatre on same bill as Etta James.

APRIL Martin Luther King is assassinated in Memphis, Tennessee.

FEBRUARY Frankie Lymon dies.

JANUARY "Big Boy (aka I'm a Big Boy Now)" is Jackson 5's first single release on Steeltown Records.

1967

JUNE Otis Redding's appearance at the Monterey Pop Festival, California, is seen as a symbolic crossover moment when a black artist who was popular with African Americans, played to a nearly all-white audience of 200,000 (over 3 days); Redding dies 6 months later.

MARCH Aretha Franklin's million-selling single "I Never Loved a Man (the Way I Love You)" is released.

FEBRUARY Jackson 5 win amateur night at the Apollo Theatre; other winners include Billie Holiday, Ella Fitzgerald, Jimi Hendrix, and the Isley Brothers.

Motown is the biggest black-owned business in the United States, with revenues of almost $30 million.

1966

POSSIBLY JUNE Joe Jackson forms the Jackson 5, adding Marlon and Michael to band previously called Jackson Brothers; Johnny Porter, or Johnny Jackson as he is better known, becomes drummer (he is stabbed to death in 2006); sometimes the band is advertised as the Jackson Five Plus Johnny.

MAY Janet Jackson is born.

"Black Power" is in popular use; Black Panthers are formed in Oakland, California.

1965

AUGUST The Voting Rights Act is passed; it aims to remove all barriers that have prevented African Americans exercising their rights to vote. MILESTONE

MARCH MLK leads a March of 25,000, 50 miles (80 km), from Selma, Alabama, to Montgomery; it is a landmark event in the civil rights struggle. MILESTONE

(February) Malcolm X is shot to death. MILESTONE

1964

DECEMBER Sam Cooke is shot to death in LA in mysterious circumstances.

JULY "Dancing in the Streets" by Martha and the Vandellas is released by Motown.

JULY Civil Rights Act is passed. MILESTONE

JUNE Malcolm X declares, "We will get our rights by any means necessary."

FEBRUARY Muhammad Ali discards his former name Cassius Clay shortly after becoming heavyweight champion of the world, and announces he is a follower of the Nation of Islam, often known as Black Muslims.

1963

Joe Jackson forms the Jackson Brothers, with sons Tito, Jackie, and Jermaine and their friends Ronnie Rancifer and Milford Hite. Five-year-old Michael is allowed to watch them practice.

1962

DECEMBER Alan, Wayne, Merrill, and Jay Osmond appear on tv's Andy Williams' Show.

1961

JANUARY Sammy Davis Jr. does not sing at US president John F. Kennedy's inauguration despite having campaigned for JFK; later Davis's daughter claims it was because Davis married a white woman.

1960

APRIL Student Nonviolent Coordinating Committee (SNCC) is formed in Raleigh, North Carolina, and starts Freedom Rides. MILESTONE

SEPTEMBER Ray Charles's "Georgia on My Mind" single becomes a best seller, establishing Charles, then a predominantly gospel and country singer as a major presence in entertainment.

1959

JANUARY Tamla Records starts operations in Detroit; the name Motown is added a year later. MILESTONE

1958

AUGUST 29 Michael Jackson born in Gary, Indiana.

1956

APRIL Nat King Cole is attacked by whites on stage in Birmingham, Alabama. MILESTONE

JANUARY Frankie Lymon and the Teenagers' "Why Do Fools Fall in Love" is released.

1955

DECEMBER Bus boycott in Montgomery, Mississippi, after Rosa Parks refuses to give up her seat on a segregated bus; this is an historic moment in the civil rights movement. MILESTONE

AUGUST Emmett Till is lynched in Money, Mississippi. MILESTONE

1954

MAY *Brown vs Board of Education* case legally ends racial segregation; verdict reverses the "separate but equal" that had been in force since 1896. MILESTONE

1949

NOVEMBER Joe Jackson marries Katherine Scruse; he is nineteen, she seventeen.

1947

MAY Billie Holiday, thirty-two, is arrested for drugs possession and serves ten months in a federal prison; she is arrested, again on narcotics charges, in 1959, on her deathbed.

1946

Joe Jackson moves from Oakland, California, to East Chicago.

Proximate Deaths

2018

Joe Jackson, father, dies from cancer, aged eighty-nine.

2015

Arnold Klein, dermatologist, dies, who treated Jackson; cause of death undisclosed.

2014

Thomas Sneddon, DA who twice sought to try Jackson, dies from cancer.

2011

Elizabeth Taylor, friend and confidante, dies of congestive heart failure, aged seventy-nine.

2009

Evan Chandler, father of Jackson's accuser, kills himself.

2006

Johnny Porter Jackson, early drummer with the Jackson band, stabbed to death.

Jackson's Career Earnings Year by Year, 1979–2014

Forbes May 28, 2014: https://bit.ly/31qJNcH

No entertainer in history had ever faced a reckoning like it. The full force of it wasn't felt until after his death. If it was payback, it was the most perverse and diabolical in history.

1

Pact with the Devil

It was a warm spring night in 1930s Mississippi and nineteen-year-old Robert Johnson sat at his table, mesmerized by the music of delta blues artist Son House. He was in a juke joint—a bar featuring music, mostly on a jukebox, but sometimes from live acts. Johnson must have been inspired by Son's raw, unlacquered music and, when the occasion arose, picked up a guitar and started playing. He was an aspiring bluesman himself and presumably considered this an opportunity to showcase his talents. He was wrong; and the juke joint's owner summarily relieved him of the guitar and showed him to the door.

Nothing was seen of Johnson for about a year, but, one night, he reappeared in the Magnolia state, Gibson acoustic guitar slung across his back, and wandered into an establishment. "Mind if I play?" he asked the bartender after ordering a soda (Prohibition ended in 1933, but Mississippi didn't legalize liquor sales until 1966). "Go ahead," said the bartender, his eyes lighting up when he noticed the peculiar seventh string on Johnson's instrument. "What's that for?" Johnson smiled cunningly. "You'll find out."

Within seconds, the crowd quieted and everyone turned to see who was bending notes in ways they'd never heard. The blend of harmonic depth and rhythmic thrust bordered on the magical. And when he sang, there was a steely center to Johnson's wispy tonal palette. He delivered some of the most bewitching blues ever heard. Surely this wasn't the same guy. As news got round, people began to wonder how the well-meaning but heavy-handed teenager had improved in such a short time; in fact, how could anyone improve so much in a single lifetime? Johnson had gone from being a maladroit amateur to a virtuoso in little over a year.

A story grew: it supposed that, once ejected from the juke joint a year before, Johnson, embarrassed and demoralized but not defeated, drifted aimlessly till he came to an intersection of dirt rounds. Crossroads have a special meaning to some, who believe they define a place where two worlds meet and are often populated by supernatural spirits. Here, Johnson dropped to his knees and summoned help from the dark side. And so, blues' eerie version of the Faustian myth emerged. Johnson, it was thought, had made a deal with the devil, receiving wondrous musical gifts in exchange for his soul. He became one of the most acclaimed bluesmen of his generation, with his "Cross Road Blues," released in 1937 by Vocalion Records, still regarded as a blues classic.

Johnson died in Greenwood, Mississippi, on August 16, 1938, the victim of poisoning by the enraged husband of a woman with whom he was having an intimate relationship. That too could have been part of his myth: other, less sensational accounts suggest he died of syphilis, or aneurism caused by drinking the illicitly distilled liquor known as moonshine. He was twenty-seven. (Greenwood is about ten miles south of Money, where, in 1955, black teenager Emmett Till was lynched after allegedly addressing a white woman as "baby.")

There's no comparable myth surrounding Michael Jackson. But there might well have been. Like Johnson, Jackson was a young man blessed with uncommon artistry. The source of his preternatural talent wasn't evident: his parents had no known musical prowess, and his brothers and sisters, though adept and, in sister Janet's case, formidable musically, occupied a level below his stratosphere. His uncanny aptitude was known well before his lifechanging encounter with producer Quincy Jones in the late 1970s, but, after, Jackson's expressiveness became a source of amazement. For a decade or more, he was untouchable. Like Elvis and Sinatra before him and his contemporary Madonna, Jackson defined an epoch.

But there was a price to pay: as Faust surrendered his soul and Johnson his life, Jackson had his own reckoning; it was an exceptional one. No entertainer in history had ever faced a reckoning like it. The full force of it wasn't felt until after his death. If it was payback—and don't forget we are still in the hazy realm of myths—it was the most perverse and diabolical in history. Over a period of sixteen years before his death in 2009, Jackson faced an incessant rumbling of whispers, cryptic admonishments, and outright accusations about his sexual habits. After his death, the rumbling became crashing thunder and the incriminations, for the first time, began to stick. Some argued, in death, Jackson was unable to defend himself against the allegations of sexual impropriety. His accusers claimed personal experience of Jackson's crimes and, of course, they went uncontested legally. There was no one else alive who could challenge the claims of sexual abuse. If Jackson had surrendered his soul to the devil, he was in hell or purgatory. This wasn't like Johnson's pact: it had posthumous clauses.

Jackson's life is like a great many others. It is also unlike any other. The entertainment industry heaves with stories of child stars gifted with incredible talents, some of whom navigated a transition to adulthood relatively unscathed, while others foundered on rocks and sunk to oblivion. Jackson, at first, seemed to be one of the former. That was a deception: he was never unscathed. He was damaged pretty much from the start. In fact, if Jackson himself is to be believed, the joy and lightheartedness typically associated with childhood were largely missing from his life. "My father beat me. It was difficult to take being beaten and then going onstage," he told Oprah Winfrey in full view of a tv audience, in 1993. Joe Jackson, his dad, "was strict; very hard and stern." The special gifts supposedly possessed by young Jackson were not courtesy of the devil—unless, of course, you believe in a devil-in-disguise. Father Joe made his child practice relentlessly, honing his singing and dancing skills for hours at a time. His perfectionism was eventually shared by his son. Perfectionism is not a good quality: it is a refusal to accept any standard short of perfection and that can—and usually does—have unhealthy effects.

Yet, when he stepped out onstage, all audiences saw and heard was a sweet, multitalented prodigy and, later, a self-possessed young man with the world at his feet. I'm not about to try to convince you that Jackson was tortured, tormented, and afflicted by the agonies heaped on him by a fanatical father who lived vicariously through his children and, by displacing his own ambitions onto them, turned them into beasts of burden. Nor will I argue that Jackson's headlong surge to stardom left him no space or time to mature as other kids do, leaving him as a young man without the usual coordinates most people acquire as they grow up. I won't even argue that having every imaginable luxury is a form of deprivation (no one would believe me anyway). Jackson never wanted for any material item. He had the money to buy everything that was buyable. And, he probably assumed everything he wanted actually was buyable. But I repeat: I won't argue this.

Jackson was an entertainer who should have been buried at least ten years before he died—under an avalanche of bad publicity. True, he was cleared by courts of law. And true, he rigorously maintained his innocence, pointing out the absence of proof. Yet, he also did some extraordinarily odd things and, even more extraordinarily, talked about them openly. The fact that he wasn't buried all those years ago tells us more about ourselves than it does Jackson. We didn't absolve, forgive him, or hand him a free pass. Even in a culture that affords celebrities nine lives, Jackson somehow managed to survive, his reputation not exactly intact, but not in shreds. The tearing into shreds came nearly ten years after his death. Even then, Jackson remained a paradoxical character, by which I mean someone who is popularly seen as riven with contradictions and inconsistencies, who seems to think and behave confusingly and in a way that defies all expectations. In other words, bewildering. His devotees stood firm and continued to love him. His detractors damned him. And between the two groups, people shook their heads and asked themselves, "Was he dazzling, or was he dirty?" and "Could he be both?"

*   *   *

Readers may have heard the old story about the drunk scrambling about on hands and knees under a streetlight. A police officer approaches and asks what the drunk is doing. "Looking for my keys." "I'll help you," says the officer. After a minute or so of searching in vain, the police officer pauses and enquires, "Are you sure this is where you dropped them?" "No," says the drunk. "I dropped them in the park. But the light is better here."

You might feel like you're looking for the keys when you start reading and discover that this story of Michael Jackson's life starts in the present day and proceeds backward. But its goal is not to find someone. Jackson's life has been pored over in a dozen or more different ways, each intending to capture the essence of a figure who was odd, when he was alive, but, in death, has become mystifying. I can't claim reversing the conventional timeline and telling his life story backward will reveal hidden secrets about Jackson. But there is light here and it shines not only on a man but on all sorts of other people, including us. Jackson's story is his audience's. I don't believe it's possible to understand anyone's significance without looking all around them, the circumstances in which they were born and matured, the events, moods, and ideas that formed their milieu, the people who helped shape them.

Everyone knows the outcome of Jackson's life, so I hardly spoil the surprise by firing time's arrow backward. But not everyone, or possibly anyone, knows the causes: what gave rise to the actions, events, and circumstances. I'll drag readers backward and sideward from Southern California and Bahrain to Singapore and the American Midwest and beyond, looking for clues.

If you want to learn the innermost secrets of a popstar, you'd be better off re-reading the many biographies. *The Destruction and Creation of Michael Jackson* is a lens for dispersing the light of the streetlamp. It shines mostly and most brightly on the man himself. But who wants another biography of Jackson? His life was too perplexing to be chronicled as a life story. Writers who strive to capture the "true Michael Jackson" leave readers asking the question: Was there one at all? It seems to elude everyone who searches for him, or it.

Be forewarned: I approach Jackson much as other writers have approached the question: "Did Shakespeare write all his own plays?" Was it just him, or him and several other uncredited playwrights? Did Jackson scale the heights and become the illustrious, towering, preeminent yet scandalous, deplorable, and iniquitous entertainer of the late twentieth century because he was exceptional? Or because audiences pushed him to those heights, then dragged him down? Readers will not get pat answers, though they might get a few more glib analogies like the Shakespeare one. Jackson's life was extraordinary; so were his times. My task has been to see one in terms of the other without making either ordinary. I haven't straightened Jackson's life into a linear account any more than I've unkinked the crooked, knotty period from the 1960s to the present day. Jackson remains a perplexing, indeterminate, even spectral figure full of intricacy and entanglements. This is how I've approached him, his life, and his times: as three inseparable entities. The story of Jackson's life has been told several times, though I believe not like this. He was a bewilderingly complex character and I've tried to do him justice with a book that is complex, but I hope not bewildering.

I segue readers into landscapes, some of them historical. In Chapter 8, for example, I trace key incidents that have repeatedly affected the lives of black Americans: I'm referring to the pattern that reached global attention with the killing of George Floyd in 2020. The pattern has no starting point, though I begin the chapter with the murder of Emmett Till in 1955. The victims are a million miles away from Jackson, you might think. But are they? After all, they, along with all the other casualties I cover in this chapter and the many others I don't, were black. Jackson's experience was affected by what was going on around him, not just in the same period of time, but in the decades before he was born.

Two women who had a major impact on Jackson's life come into focus in Chapter 9. Debbie Rowie's impact was close and immediate: she was mother of two of Jackson's three children. Princess Diana's impact was less tangible, but no less real: she helped cultivate a world in which the public were mesmerized by people they didn't know, probably had never seen and with whom they might not even have shared the same land mass. Jackson knew Diana and maintained a friendship at distance: they both became quarry, each eventually involved in a desperate attempt to escape the very thing that had helped them in their early careers. Michael's sister Janet also occupies a chapter of her own (Chapter 11). Often eclipsed by her more exalted brother, Janet had a formidable and winding career and was, for a while, a preeminent performer to rival Madonna.

I have created space for characters who were co-stars in the Jackson drama. The cast could almost be a who's who of late-twentieth-century cultural figures. So, the reader will run into Elizabeth Taylor, the Reverend Al Sharpton, Paul McCartney, Whitney Houston, O. J. Simpson, Elvis, Princess Diana, Madonna, Spike Lee, Bill Cosby, Don King, Oprah, Michael Jordan, Ronald Reagan, Berry Gordy, Diana Ross, and many other notables whose actions or sheer presence impacted to some extent on Jackson. The reader will also learn about the influence, however indirect, of historical characters, such as Frankie Lymon (1942–68), who was a Jackson-like figure in the 1950s and 1960s, and Roscoe "Fatty" Arbuckle (1887–1933), a major silent screen star whose career was derailed by a sex scandal. Nat "King" Cole (1919–65), the first African American to have his own series on radio and then television, will come into view in the final chapter. All these people played key roles in Jackson's life and indeed in the cultural moods he lived through.

I've added a "Destruction and Creation: TimeLine" section, which readers will have already noticed. It runs from today back to 1946, when Joe Jackson moved to East Chicago. The spine of the chronology is Jackson's life, though, as with the rest of the book, context is everything. So I've included significant events that, in their own, ways signpost cultural changes. I've assigned labels to major events that hastened either the destruction or creation of Jackson, and also to a couple of developments that recur in the book. Namely, Jackson's acquisition of song publishing rights, and a lawsuit brought by Wade Robson and James Safechuck.

For readers who like linearity and chronological order and who don't wish to read the book back-to-front, I'll break down the chapters into time periods at the end of this chapter, but remember: there are many overlaps and some time-shuttling, so don't expect a precise timecode. And do expect a narrative closer to that of the Christopher Nolan film from 2000 *Memento*, or Duncan Jones's 2011 film with Jake Gyllenhaal *Source Code*.

Following the final chapter, there is a collection of over forty Key Players, these being people who have, for some reason, shaped Jackson's fortunes, for better or for worse, sometimes from afar. They all appear in the text of the book, but this is a shorthand guide with a paragraph on each. At the end of the book, readers will find a comprehensive bibliography of all sources either quoted or cited in the book, together with urls and the date when accessed, where appropriate.

Readers will notice there are dozens of songs mentioned in the text. I've listed them at the end of the book and created a Spotify playlist for those who want to listen. There are just three tracks not available on Spotify, two of them can be heard on YouTube Music, the other on regular YouTube. The playlist can be found at: https://spoti.fi/3wji2C3.

As promised a couple of paragraphs ago, here's a chapter timecode.

Chapter 1. Present. The introduction provides an overview and establishes the context.

Chapter 2. 2009–20. Deciding Jackson's place in recent history.

Chapter 3. 2008–19. His stunning death and the surprising aftermath.

Chapter 4. 2006–8. Jackson's time in Bahrain and other parts of the Mideast.

Chapter 5. 2003–5. The criminal charges against Jackson, the trial and acquittal.

Chapter 6. 2003. The lead-up to and initial fallout from the Bashir documentary.

Chapter 7. 2000–2. How the Jackson narrative began to spiral out of control.

Chapter 8. 1955–2021. The history of violence against African Americans from Emmett Till.

Chapter 9. 1993–9. Debbie Rowe, Princess Diana, and their impact on Jackson.

Chapter 10. 1993–8. Chandler affair, drugs confession, and the marriage to Lisa Marie Presley.

Chapter 11. 1966–2021. Was Janet Jackson the most culturally significant female artist of the 1980s?

Chapter 12. 1990–2. How the seeds of MJ's ultimate destruction were sown.

Chapter 13. 1986–9. When the *National Enquirer*'s bizarre stories added to the Jackson mystique.

Chapter 14. 1983–5. Why Jackson didn't get along with Don King, but did get along with Arnold Klein.

Chapter 15. 1964–2018. Bill Cosby's role in landscaping culture in the late twentieth century.

Chapter 16. 1983–4. How MTV and the video age boosted Jackson's status.

Chapter 17. 1984. The importance of Michael Jordan, Oprah, and other black symbols of the 1980s.

Chapter 18. 1983–5 Why people started to analyze Jackson and, in Paul McCartney's case, reinterpret him.

Chapter 19. 1978–82. Quincy Jones and the gamechanging *Off the Wall* album.

Chapter 20. 1969–77. The rise of Motown as a cultural force.

Chapter 21. 1949–68. The Jackson family origins and a prehistory of the band.

Chapter 22. 2009–present. Who created Michael Jackson and what would have happened if he'd lived?

My longtime friend Rick Bayles has given me a good deal of detail about the music industry and I am grateful to him.

"The Jackson family was large, intact, vibrant, successful and seemingly happy, giving America an idealized image of domestic bliss," wrote Rolling Stone's Touré.

2

Ticket to Ride

"There is virtually no one Michael Jackson knows who does not view him as some sort of big-bucks ticket to ride," wrote Anne Orth for *Vanity Fair* in 1994. "Certainly in his own twisted family, he has from an early age been leaned on—the adorable little sensitive, effeminate one with the most talent, taught to manipulate the press, even lie about his age as an eight-year-old."

It wasn't just his family. He was a ticket for everyone. We all felt we had a certain right to travel with him and participate in Jackson's life. That's what a ticket does: entitle the holder to enter places that might otherwise be restricted. Certainly, as Orth pointed out, there was a coterie of family members, friends, and miscellaneous sycophants who sought the "big bucks," and plenty who got them. But most went along with the ride because of the sheer entertainment it offered. And education too.

Jackson was public property from the get-go. Performing practically since he was old enough to stand, he soon became a market commodity and stayed that way. Since the early 1970s, the Jackson 5, as the brothers were called, were sold to America and indeed the world as a wholesome assembly of God-fearing boys reared by God-fearing parents. And, unlike the popular racist conception of black families, they were not, it seemed, dysfunctional. Only later, did audiences savor the irony. Once the show-stealing Michael drew attention to himself and the unorthodox manners that were to define much of his adult life, the family dynamic was harshly exposed. Later the world was treated to further Jackson bizarreries: we all witnessed the transformation of a human popstar to a cultural artifact.

Jackson's life could be an allegory of a violent, divided, tribal, conflict-torn America still trying to rid itself of its most obdurate demon. Jackson was a singer, a dancer, an idiosyncratic collector, a quirky obsessive, a sexual enigma, and many other things besides. He didn't fight or assuage racism or position himself as an icon of black struggle. In later life, he and we were unsure whether he was black at all. He didn't go into politics or even encourage African Americans to vote. But Jackson was such a uniquely divisive, yet historically significant figure, that he will continue to command argument in much the same way as Muhammad Ali, Billie Holiday, and Martin Luther King Jr. inspire discussion. In many senses, Jackson was a presence as relevant and challenging as any African American. Or was he?

Anybody with even a passing familiarity with popular culture over the past half-century will know Michael Jackson was a dominating presence for much of the 1980s and 1990s. He continued to cast a spell in the twenty-first century. He was someone who could not be ignored: the fascination was worldwide and inexhaustible. Yet, considering he began appearing regularly in the media in 1968, and, from then, enticed countless writers to make sense of him, we know relatively little about him.

We probably learned more about Jackson in the ten years after his death than we thought we'd learned during the fifty years he delighted or enraged us. Or, at least, we *think* we learned. Perhaps we'll never know. But we know for sure he was a grown man who fashioned his 2,700-acre ranch in Santa Barbara County, California, into a children's playground, not just any old playground either: a wonderworld, complete with rollercoaster, Ferris wheel, amusement arcade, and menagerie where pets were kept. We also knew he enjoyed the company of many young boys and girls, whom he supplied with copious candy and, occasionally, according to some, alcohol. These weren't children he secreted away: he paraded them publicly, often with their parents' consent—puzzlingly, perhaps. Even more puzzlingly, some parents allowed their children to sleep in the same bed as Jackson. And remember: Jackson was acquitted of sexual molestation in 2005.

We know there are countless theories, schools of thought, and deep-seated suspicions about Jackson. There's also a continuum of characterizations: at the one end, pedophile and at the other genius. They are not mutually exclusive, but readers will see my point: between the two there are a bewildering number of representations. I am not going to offer yet another. There isn't going to be damnation, even with faint praise; there's been enough evisceration for one lifetime. Nor am I about to swoon over Jackson's virtuosity. I acknowledge his flair, his technique, his brilliance even. But I am always aware Jackson was surrounded by producers, co-writers, choreographers, and a minor industry of people who turned his music and his theatricality into extraordinary forms of entertainment. I could say the same thing about any performer, of course.

For a long while Jackson comported himself and was revered a popstar without equals. All that talent; all that public fascination. All that magic. He seemed made for the late twentieth century, a time when America still struggled with the torment of post-civil rights. It was a time when the nation rid itself of the most bedeviling issues in its near-400 year history (Jamestown was established in Virginia in 1607), only to see it reappear in different guises. Jackson was, in many ways, an emblem: a prodigious upstart, born if not in poverty in modest circumstances, who humanized the American dream more exquisitely than anyone in history: a black man who rose over historical, social, cultural, economic, and every other kind of barrier to become the most luminous entertainer of his time. Some readers might find this description excessive and perhaps tasteless. This is how I intend to approach Jackson and I trust they will understand my logic as I progress.

Like him or loathe him, we have all been part of Jackson's life. When I write "life," I should use quotation marks because there is more than one, just as there is more than one Michael Jackson. There is what we might call the life lived by the flesh-and-blood mortal who succumbed to a lethal cocktail of prescription drugs in 2009. But there is another life that exists beyond time and space, a life of the imagination—our imagination.

"Michael Jackson's life was a long, fascinating soap opera that included not only his success but also his tiffs with his family, his erratic behavior, his plastic surgeries, his bizarre marriages, his masked children, his brushes with the law, his alleged drug use, and finally his mysterious death," wrote Neal Gabler in *Newsweek* just after Jackson's death in 2009. Jackson's life, like that of Princess Diana, O. J. Simpson, Elizabeth Taylor, Harry and Meghan, and several others, is not just his own. They are all ours too. Gabler calls them narratives, presumably meaning unbroken accounts, consisting of incidents and people that connect to form an overall story. The story may be a chronicle, or a history to record events and it may incorporate elements of a fable in the sense that it conveys a moral or lesson.

Jackson's life was all these and more: it was entertainment. Callous as it seems to call someone whose days ended so tragically entertainment, that's exactly what it was: a performance that provided the world with enjoyment and amusement as well as learning. As a child, Jackson was encouraged to provide thrills and satisfy audiences; as a young man, he probably realized he could do this without actually trying; as a middle-aged man, he found that he couldn't stop entertaining, even when he wanted to. *If* he ever wanted to.

* * *

In the 1970s and 1980s, post-civil rights America came of age. The segregation and institutional racism that had denied anything resembling equality of opportunity to about 13 percent of the population had been formally vanquished in 1964 and 1965. But like a captive habituated to a Stockholm syndrome-like confinement, the nation was slow to escape its past. There was no miraculous transformation, but rather a labored and reluctant traipse from history. The pace wasn't fast enough for many African Americans, who embraced what was called Black Power, a movement that strove for the civil rights technically provided by the 1964 legislation.

Newly desegregated and formally committed to equality, America couldn't convince anyone that the land of opportunity was for real. "This is the land of the free and home of the brave," someone might have reminded black Americans. It sounded hollow. "Skin color, race, or whatever you want to call it doesn't matter any more. Anybody can go as far as their talent, commitment and capacity for hard work will take them."

The riot that swept through Watts, Los Angeles, for six days in the summer of 1965 left 34 dead, over a thousand injured and 4,000 arrested. Fire and deliberate destruction left many homeless. The Watts neighborhood was home to mostly African American citizens and, while the uprising was started after a relatively nondescript traffic stop, the underlying cause was later identified as "white racism," particularly in the dragnets practiced by the police, that is, the systematic stop-and-searches. The Watts conflict triggered a chain of similar episodes for the next two years, African Americans, forcing racism to the fore of the American agenda. Blacks, though now ostensibly enjoying civil rights, were structurally excluded from what President Lyndon Johnson had called the Great Society.

Over the next two years, 163 riots broke out across the United States, the final conflagration being in Detroit where forty-three died in what *Time* magazine (August 4, 1967) called "the bloodiest uprising in half a century and the costliest in terms of property damage in U.S. history." Detroit, in the 1960s, was often held up as a perfect example of a progressive city: it has a thriving black bourgeoisie and a local government that invested in programs to alleviate poverty. In common with a great many other American cities, Detroit had a deep history of segregation, with African American populations living and often working physically away from whites. White-dominated assemblies typically governed cities. Detroit had been losing jobs for at least a decade and African Americans tended to experience the worst of the consequences.

The Black Power movement advanced a forceful radical critique of American society than many politicians and liberal analysts had been willing to accept. It demanded the restoration of black identity through ethnic unity. The Nation of Islam, though not affiliated to the broader movement, insisted that America's racism was endemic and probably irremovable. Only by physically segregating and establishing self-sufficiency could African Americans survive and prosper. Muhammad Ali was the nation's most celebrated adherent. Another radical organization but one that opposed segregation, the Black Panthers urged black people to arm themselves to defend against white attackers. All agreed that wholesale changes rather than piecemeal changes were needed: prison reform, welfare rights, constraints on the police, robust antipoverty programs, and enhanced job opportunities for blacks were necessary.

Added to this combustible racial disorder in the cities was a growing opposition to the war in Vietnam and reluctance to believe the political rhetoric that this was still a winnable military struggle. The Tet Offensive launched by the Vietcong and North Vietnamese Army in January 1968 was a surprise attack on South Vietnamese cities, notably Saigon. It was eventually repulsed, though shook American confidence and hastened the withdrawal of US forces. It also undermined any public hope that the war was near an end, despite nearly four years of fighting.

The advance toward dystopia continued in April 1968 when civil rights leader and Nobel Peace Prize winner (1964) Martin Luther King Junior went to Memphis, Tennessee, to lend his support to the city's striking sanitation workers and was assassinated on the balcony of his hotel room. Rallies, protests, and violent uprisings in over a hundred cities followed.

And then *shazam!* Six months after the King assassination "I Want You Back" jumped to the number-one-singles spot. A group of five black brothers from the then emerging Detroit-based Motown organization appeared. They were either serious anomalies or actual African Americans who had bought into all that land of the free stuff and made it to the top of the charts. They hadn't been held back by their blackness, nor opted to run riot, nor even complained about the persistence of discrimination. They didn't even mention Dr. King. They just sang and danced their way to the top. And remember: they were brothers. And *brothers*.

* * *

The Negro Family—The Case for National Action, completed in March 1965, became one of the most controversial documents of the twentieth century. Best known as the "Moynihan Report," after its principal author, Daniel Moynihan, it postulated that civil rights legislation alone would not produce equality across all ethnic groups. Moynihan's decision to analyze America's inequalities primarily in terms of family structure drew criticism, but the report has to be understood in context. In the mid-1960s, the focus on the broken African American family as a source of all kinds of problems was not exceptional.

The Jacksons were not products of a pathological, ghetto-dwelling family of addicts and they didn't live off welfare. As the *Rolling Stone* writer Touré put it in 2014, "The Jackson family was large, intact, vibrant, successful and seemingly happy, giving America an idealized image of domestic bliss" (June 26). They didn't use their newfound fame as a platform to berate America. In fact, America was nothing like the hellhole described by the likes of Huey P. Newtown, Eldridge Cleaver, or other social critics. It was actually a pretty decent place. And the Jacksons were living proof that aptitude and hard work were the only constituents you needed to succeed.

Managed by their dad, the brothers seemed positively wholesome, a family unit quite unlike popular stereotypes, with none of the instabilities usually associated with blacks. In fact, they looked like the kind of boys who could easily integrate into the new post-civil rights America. They didn't disturb, challenge, or incite any kind of animosity; they diligently promoted harmony, stability, and a satisfaction with how things were. The Jackson brothers were clean and offered a confection that was unlikely to be confused with that presented by many other black artists, many of them still associated with the so-called jungle music that emerged in the 1950s. Others, like Sam Cooke and Marvin Gaye, had died in unsavory circumstances (in 1964 and 1984, respectively). And others, like James Brown, had served time in prison, or, like Ray Charles, been arrested on drug charges. There were dozens of African American musicians, many of the highest caliber, but they were mostly flawed in one way or another.

By contrast, the Jacksons were flawless; in a way, they had been sanitized by Motown, the Detroit-based record company started in 1959 by Berry Gordy. The band wasn't just a commercially well-packaged commodity prepared and wrapped for general consumption: the Jacksons appeared as a kind of fulfillment of the American dream. Here was a family that was black yet untainted by the disparagement typically aimed at black people. The sense of democracy felt by America after the civil rights legislation was hypothetical but not yet palpable. Black sports stars never really counted. Even from slave days, African descended prizefighters distinguished themselves with their physical prowess. There were any number of baseball, basketball, and football players who qualified as all-time greats. They were allowed to have flaws; they were just there to perform athletically and be enjoyed by audiences. Black musicians were different: they were primarily for the delectation of whites, but they were allowed to have personalities, characters, and tastes though probably not opinions. The brothers were not just entertaining: they were valuable. I mean valuable in an ideological sense—they made an ideal seem real and authentic.

In time, the Jackson 5 would insinuate themselves not only into America's culture, but the world's. But Michael was something else. He instigated change, not only at a cultural level but at the level of consciousness; he affected the way people thought. Assumptions, expectations, judgments, inferences, and conjectures were all changed as a result of Jackson's life. "Why can't all blacks be like Michael Jackson?" white Americans must have asked themselves when they saw the irrepressibly cute young virtuoso: well-behaved, neatly dressed, impeccably mannered, and, best of all, noticeably manageable.

If the way the Jacksons sprang to prominence in the late 1960s was random and spontaneous there was surely something fateful about the way America framed and developed them, in particular Michael, for successive decades.

The force behind the band was the father. A cruel patriarch with ambitions greater than his ability, who lived, it seems, vicariously through his sons, Joe Jackson, who died in 2018, pushed Michael and his other children, often waking them in the early hours to rehearse or perform. He'd scare and punish them in an effort to make them one of the world's most garlanded acts. In this respect, his initial project was successful. The Jackson 5 did become one of the most vaunted acts of the late twentieth century. But at considerable cost.

Joe Jackson knew, perhaps intuitively, that America was not so much ready, but in need of an African American family that it could love; and in a miracle of inspiration, he shaped his own family into exactly that. The young Michael added sweetness and delicacy. "They were the people who represented black America," Orth quoted ABC News *Day One* correspondent Michel McQueen. More accurately, the Jacksons were the people that America wanted to believe represented black America.

There's a difference. A huge difference. By the time Orth was writing in 1994, the Jacksons' disguise was beginning to look exactly like that—a disguise. Maybe they were truly representative after all. If so, America was in trouble: greed, recklessness, malice, tension, and internecine hatred were the hallmarks. Jackson's meltdown was not just his.

*   *   *

In April 2003, again in *Vanity Fair*, Orth wrote: "The crazier Jackson appears, the more he is indulged and excused and not judged as a middle-aged man with serious obligations and responsibilities." She was referring to Jackson's appearance in a Santa Maria, California, courtroom: he turned up four hours late, as a defendant in a $21.2 million civil lawsuit brought against him by European concert promoter Marcel Avram, wearing a black wig and a prosthesis that served as a tip for his nose. His face was caked with makeup. When on the stand ready to testify, Jackson bobbed his head as if listening to music, tapped the court's mic and asked, "Can I have another Jolly Rancher, please?" (Jolly Rancher is fruit-flavored candy.) It was, as Orth pointed out, "behavior one would expect of a 12-year-old." But: "This bizarre behavior often works to his advantage," added Orth. Often.

By then, the satisfaction audiences took from Jackson's life had changed. Dizzyingly so. Jackson appeared to have transformed from a gifted Peter Pan-like adolescent with tireless joie de vivre into a curious human package of eccentricities. In the mid-1980s, he began wearing a surgical mask in public. No big deal: celebrities wear all manner of accessories, usually just to draw attention to themselves. Elton John did this kind of thing all the time: outlandish glasses and clothes were almost trademarks. David Bowie wore an eyepatch for a while in the 1970s. Grace Jones never appeared without wearing something worthy of disbelief. And, as for Madonna, corsets, chokers, chains, handcuffs, and assorted S&M gear were standard issue for a while.

The mask might not have warranted a mention, unless a rumor hadn't nudged it into the foreground. Jackson, it was said, had taken to sleeping in a hyperbaric chamber. This is a sealed vessel in which the flow of breathing air can be adjusted. The enclosed environment can be rich in oxygen. Athletes use the chambers, as do patients suffering from decompression sickness, as well as cancer patients who have tissue injury after radiotherapy. Jackson was neither an athlete nor a patient, at least as far as anyone knew. On September 16, 1986, the tabloid *National Enquirer* published a picture of Jackson apparently sleeping in a chamber and an accompanying story that started: "Michael Jackson has embarked on a plan he believes will keep him alive until at least 150. The plan, according to the story included, in addition to sleeping in the chamber, receiving electric shocks and taking 50 vitamin pills every day." The writer Charles Montgomery revealed that Jackson had first seen one such chamber at the burns clinic of the Brotman Medical Center in Southern California. Jackson financed the burns unit. He had been treated for burns in 1984, when his hair caught fire during the filming of a Pepsi advertisement. The Michael Jackson Burn Center closed in August 1987 due to financial problems.

The *Enquirer* article didn't start the gossip about Jackson's apparent oddities and, it's at least possible that he initiated the oxygen chamber story just to keep up his public profile. But, combined with the mask and his by-then well-known penchant for traveling with a pet chimpanzee named Bubbles, it probably prompted many fans and distant observers alike to ask: "What exactly is happening to Michael Jackson? Is he being willfully ridiculous, or is he genuinely becoming weird?" Over the next couple of decades, we got some answers. Speculations bled into hearsay and hearsay into downright lies. But truth didn't matter; the Jackson mystique went into production and it accommodated every conceivable belief.

Over the next several years, in fact till Jackson's death, the screws turned on Jackson: what were initially seen as foibles became creepy eccentricities and, as self-professed victims came forward, even devotees started to wonder whether there was something sinister about the once-glowing performer. A different figure was emerging as the 1980s closed. Jackson himself must have felt besieged.

The title of Orth's story I quoted at the start of this chapter was "Nightmare in Neverland," Neverland being the name of Jackson's estate. Nightmares probably make more sense as troubling, disjointed, haphazard descents into inescapable situations. At the time Orth was writing, Jackson, or rather his public image was fracturing and he seemed to be trapped.

*   *   *

In August 1993, the Los Angeles Police Department opened a criminal investigation into Jackson after a private investigator working for Jackson claimed he had refused to pay extortion money. Police searched Jackson's two homes in Southern California, according to the pi, Anthony Pellicano. What the police were seeking and whether anything was recovered from either home was not clear at that time. But the *Los Angeles Times* reported,

"The allegations against Jackson were made by a woman who claims that her child was abused at one of the entertainer's homes" (August 24, 1993). After news broke on KNBC Channel 4 on August 23, 1993, at 5:00 p.m. eastern, there followed a worldwide surge of publicity that opened up Jackson's hitherto private life to scrutiny.

That scrutiny ultimately revealed a kind of Rorschach inkblot: people looked at the same splotch, but saw different things. And they'd react differently: while some might have offered to kiss the ground Jackson walked on, others would have gladly buried him in that ground. The former saw a springy charmer, an impossibly gentle manchild, a stylish star who lit up any stage he graced and an artist of infinite talent whose album *Thriller* sold more than any record in history. The latter saw an obsessive and despicable child abuser who concealed his evil intent with a deep wackiness.

There was what seemed a relentless assault, Jackson's reputation assailed by mischievous accusations and incriminatory condemnations. The media competed for tasty scraps like hungry animals at feeding time. It was if the world was demanding a rethink of the previous decades. "It was difficult to imagine how things could get much worse for Michael Jackson in the fall of 1993," wrote his biographer J. Randy Taraborrelli. "In just a matter of months he had without a doubt experienced the 'swift and sudden fall from grace', he would later write about" (pages 517–18). Taraborrelli was referring to Jackson's 1997 song "Stranger in Moscow." As we now know, they got significantly worse.

In November 1993, Jackson abruptly canceled the remaining dates of a world tour, announcing "horrifying" allegations of child molestation had caused him to become dependent on painkillers and left him "physically and emotionally exhausted." He also insisted that he was at the center of an extortion attempt. Then he vanished. Remember Orth's point ten years later: bizarre behavior often worked to his advantage. But not always. Within a month of the cancellation, Jackson's sister LaToya Jackson told reporters that she could no longer "be a silent collaborator of his crimes against small, innocent children." It was an incredible, damning statement, the first denunciation from a member of the family. As such, it was influential. This was Jackson's own sister seeming to echo the emerging opinion of many across the world. "I love Michael very dearly, but I feel even more sorry for these children because they don't have a life anymore."

LaToya was estranged from the family and, as such, maybe bore a grudge. Even so, she was Michael's older sister and actually disclosed she had seen checks made out to the parents of children who claimed they had been abused. It was a potent criticism and one that almost guaranteed Jackson would live out his last sixteen years in a way that would become myth and history. LaToya apparently charged between $25,000 and $40,000 per interview. In this respect, she wasn't alone: everyone who knew something, however inconsequential, about Jackson had a scale of charges for the media. Even the Jackson family. He was, to repeat Orth's term, the ticket to ride.

NBC planned a $6 million television special featuring Michael himself and designed, perversely, to exploit the unfolding drama. "The TV special was to be the launch of their [the Jackson family's] latest moneymaking plan," wrote Orth. "A series of franchises to market clothes and cartoon taking advantage of Michael's relationship with children." Today it seems barely believable that any television network would be interested, if not on grounds of taste, because they wouldn't have a viewing audience. Although, it's also possible that anything, literally anything featuring Jackson, or something or somebody associated with him would excite the interest of a TV company somewhere.

So, why did he continue to mesmerize audiences? After all, once the boyish, cleancut symbol of the new black America had morphed into an altogether more unpleasant character, what further use was he? Admiring Jackson was fine; damning him was better. Here was a black man who had everything: abundant talent, global adulation, and more money than he could ever hope to spend (although he did manage to), Jackson, for a while, in the 1970s and 1980s, had the world at his dexterous feet. And yet he eventually succumbed and became a casualty, just like so many other African Americans. Drug dependencies were but one of collection of shortcomings that suggested that, beneath one Michael Jackson, there was another, perhaps others, all of them seriously flawed.

The flaws didn't make him less captivating. Quite the opposite. Audiences were awed by a black man with gifts; they were comforted by his deficiencies. Reassured perhaps that the reason why black people didn't make progress was not because of racism or in the way history had dealt them a poor hand, but because of themselves. Even the most talented were liable to self-destruct.

While he was cleared of the charges, the innuendo followed him to his death like a stray puppy. When Jackson died suddenly and unexpectedly in 2009, it was as if someone had shooed away the pup and brought in Kerberos, the ferocious three-headed hound that prevented the dead from leaving Hades.

*   *   *

Great presences rarely provide answers: they ask questions. We then try to fathom them out. Jackson never stopped asking questions, but not just about himself. Jackson was a consummate self-dramatist: he provided the media with an endless source of raw material that could be processed into tabloidy stories. Whether his life was reality or commercial entertainment didn't make much difference. Audiences did the necessary deliberation. It was a hyper-dramatic life, more sensationalistic than Madonna's or even his friend Elizabeth Taylor's.

Even allowing for a degree of design in his more exotic behavior and perhaps an element of self-aware manipulation in influencing the media, Jackson packed a disarming amount of scandal, wrongdoing, and all-round transgression into his fifty years. No one could have provoked more outrage, disapproval, and disgust, while at the same time commanding godlike exaltation. Did he have a rare ability to incite judgmental reactions? Or did audiences simply enjoy reacting judgmentally? Maybe a studiedly cynical media with an appetite for calumny deliberately misrepresented him, knowing how audiences would respond. Perhaps there was just an accident of time, place, and person, all three colliding to produce a story that would sound far-fetched were it not true.

Jackson's lifespan, 1958–2009, coincides with a change in the way we made sense of the world. Commercial entertainment was nothing new; but the manner in which it pervaded social life and provided everyone with a scope, or a way of looking at the world, was. The media, from the 1970s, perhaps before, began to treat politics, crime, religion, war, policy, and everything else that mattered in the world as if it were entertainment. And, we—like Jackson—are products of a particular kind of culture.

I quoted Neal Gabler earlier in the chapter. In 1998, he wrote the book *Life: The Movie* in which he documented a cultural revolution in which entertainment became "a cosmology that had governed American life with increasing vigor since at least the turn of the [twentieth] century" (pg. 56). It's an intriguing choice of words, cosmology meaning an account or theory of the universe's origins and development. I believe he means that we— consumers, the audience—drew our knowledge and understanding of the world (rather than the whole universe) through popular entertainment, at first radio, then film, and, from the late 1950s, television. While Gabler's book was written in 1998, just before the digital revolution had gathered momentum, he would have surely included social media in the new cosmological order that directs modern life. Jackson was part of the kind of cosmology Gabler has in mind: a real living person, he was also a prism through which everyone could look at a society in the throes of change.

Jackson's musical virtuosity is undeniable. But there is much more that makes him a compelling character. For more than forty years, he forced us to take notice, perhaps without even wanting to. His life offered a vista wide enough for us to understand a cultural chasm that has fissured America since before his birth and beyond his death.

Kehinde Wiley's painting depicts Jackson as a seventeenth-century monarch in a suit of armor, sitting proudly on a white stallion. Ludovic Hunter-Tilney, of the Financial Times, *believes the painting "reveals the megalomaniac side of the King of Pop's personality."*

3

Nothing Strange about Your Daddy

At the time of his death, Jackson was midway through sittings for a huge (128" x 112") painting by the naturalistic American painter Kehinde Wiley, which depicts Jackson as a seventeenth-century monarch in a suit of armor, sitting proudly on a white stallion. Cherubs hover above, showering him with laurels. Its composition and title *Equestrian Portrait of King Philip II (Michael Jackson)* make its inspiration clear: it is modeled on Peter Paul Rubens' *Philip II on Horseback* (*c.*1630), which is a staple of European art history. Jackson's motivation in commissioning the work is far from obvious. But whenever was his motivation obvious? Wiley's painting inserts Jackson, an African American subject, into a position occupied by a white European prince. Ludovic Hunter-Tilney, of the *Financial Times*, believes the painting "reveals the megalomaniac side of the King of Pop's personality."

Hunter-Tilney points out that Jackson's reckless spending rivaled that of the Habsburgs, one of the dominant dynasties in Europe from medieval to modern times, famed for their extravagance. Jackson was also an exceptional humanitarian, recorded in the famous Guinness book as the pop star who had contributed to most charities. But, as Hunter-Tilney adds: "By the time Wiley's overblown portrait was being painted Jackson's public image had been shredded by child abuse claims." So perhaps the commission does reveal Jackson's vainglorious attempt, however futile, to recover some pomp and regality, albeit through a work of art. Jackson might have sensed his reputation was being torn to pieces by disparaging insinuations, but he couldn't have known how his death would occasion arguably the most vicious, unremitting posthumous character onslaught in history.

* * *

In February 2008, it emerged Jackson's Neverland estate in California was going into foreclosure to settle debts of $25 million against it. Jackson's finances were, it seemed, in disarray. Ten years before, Jackson's yearly earnings for 1998 totaled $18 million, according to *Forbes*' Zack O'Malley Greenburg. Ten years before that, an especially bounteous 1988 yielded $125 million. Jackson's lifetime earnings at that stage were calculated as $1.1 billion.

Jackson's creditors were paid off by Thomas Barrack, a billionaire casino investor. The deeds to Neverland transferred to a company called Colony Capital. At this stage, Jackson lived mainly away from Neverland, in a relatively modest gated community in Las Vegas. The property was intended for his mother when he bought it about twenty years before. Katherine was in her late eighties when her son and his three children, Michael Junior, Paris, and Prince Michael Jackson II, aka Blanket, moved in with her. All of them apart from Katherine routinely wore surgical masks like their father.

A year before, in the December 2007 edition on the magazine *Ebony*, Jackson asked rhetorically: "Who wants mortality? . . . I give all in my work because I want it to live." Presuming he meant immortality not "mortality," this might have been read as determined promise to leave the world with a lasting legacy. But, in the same article, the Reverend Jesse Jackson dismissed the idea that he would persist in performing for as long as he possibly could. "He just doesn't want to go out like that," wrote Joy T. Bennett paraphrasing the reverend, before quoting the civil rights leader directly: "Not the way James Brown did or Jackie Wilson did . . . they just kept going, running, killing themselves."

Self-styled "hardest working man in showbusiness," Brown died with congestive heart failure in 2006, age seventy-three. Jackie Wilson died from pneumonia in 1984, age forty-nine. Both were still performing at the time of their deaths. It might have struck Reverend Jackson and a great many more that Michael Jackson did not wish to prolong his theatrical career right to the end of his life. In fact, Jackson had given several indications that he wasn't especially interested in appearing in public, let alone on stage. In Bennett's story, he expressed a hitherto unknown ambition: "I see myself more productive in film . . . a concert is the most fleeting thing in the world . . . with film, you stop time."

But, around the time of the *Ebony* article, a close circle of Jackson's business associates, led by his lawyer Peter Lopez, revealed that they were in negotiations for a series of Michael Jackson concerts. The other party in the negotiations was AEG Live, a company that owned the O2 Arena in London. The venue holds 20,000 people. No firm deal had been announced at that stage. There was also talk of a Jackson comeback under the guidance of British impresario Simon Fuller and rumors of an appearance at the Grammys, but nothing materialized and Jackson continued to live in relative seclusion in Vegas with sidetrips to the Persian Gulf state, Bahrain, where he enjoyed the hospitality of the king's son, Sheikh Abdullah bin Hamad al-Khalifa. Here, he circulated without being recognized, mainly because he wore an *abaya*, a full-length, sleeveless outergarment. There was no sign of new recordings and only whispers of concerts. Whatever the state of his finances, Jackson's lack of productivity would not have helped. Nor would his prodigality.

Since his career peak earnings period, the late 1980s and early 1990s, Jackson's outgoings were estimated to be a prodigious $35 million per year. Much of this went on expensive hotel suites, if not entire floors, and Jackson's habit of scattergun spending in expensive stores. Viewers of a television documentary in 2003 would have seen him in stores literally pointing indiscriminately at items and buying them. Jackson's formidable backcatalog and his ownership of publishing rights to music, including over 250 Beatles songs, guaranteed him a fabulous income. But, when his supposed friend al-Khalifa took him to court in an effort to recoup $7 million Jackson apparently owed him, the unbelievable truth seemed to be that Jackson was in financial trouble. The case was set to be heard in London, though Jackson never appeared. His legal team announced an out-of-court settlement, but without further explication.

Still murmurs of concerts continued. Brother Jermaine Jackson's suggestion that "the whole family would be reforming" was denied by Michael. "My brothers and sisters have my full love and support, and we've certainly shared many great experiences, but at this time I have no plans to record or tour with them," Rosie Swash, of Britain's *Guardian* newspaper, quoted him on March 3, 2009.

And then, when stories of his demise seemed to be misguided or belated rather than premature, Jackson released news of a "special announcement" that he'd make at 4:00 p.m. on Thursday, March 5, 2009. He hadn't toured since 1997 and had not even performed on stage at all since he was cleared of child abuse charges in 2005. The special announcement was that Jackson would perform ten straight shows at the O2 Arena and these would be his "final curtain call," presumably meaning his last ever series of concerts. He shouted, "This is it! This is it!" to the 2,000-strong crowd, which had anticipated the news. Jackson then left the podium with, "I'll see you in July."

Within days, the ten-concert residency had been extended fivefold to fifty and, when tickets went on sale at 7:00 a.m., March 13, they sold at warp-speed. The promoters AEG Live confirmed that all 750,000 seats were sold within four hours. According to AEG Live's president, Randy Phillips, Jackson would earn between £50 and £100 million from the concerts. Jackson would take a three-month rest between October and December. But there were doubts about Jackson's physical fitness. Remember, he was fifty.

Other performers are inveterate tourists: Madonna and Cher both toured when over sixty. Elton John did a 300-date tour that spanned five continents, in his seventies. Others, like David Bowie, were more cautious: a heath scare in 2004 when he was a nimble fifty-seven and exercised regularly convinced Bowie that he should stop touring; he eventually died in 2016, two days after his sixty-ninth birthday. So Jackson's age alone shouldn't have been a problem. Prince had done twenty-one nights at the O2 in 2007 as he approached his fiftieth. Kate Bush came out of a 35-year withdrawal to perform twenty-two dates in London in 2014, when fifty-seven. So fifty concerts with an intervening period for recuperation, while onerous, should not have been unmanageable. At least, not if Jackson had something resembling a beneficial lifestyle. Phillips tried to assuage doubts over his health by reminding ticket holders that Jackson was obliged to undergo a four-hour medical assessment and passed "with flying colors."

Jackson, though, was a renowned perfectionist, an artist who had been schooled and disciplined—often brutally—to refuse any standard short of perfection on stage. Any time he stepped out in front of an audience, every move, every mannerism, every gesture, every twitch—not only his but his troupe's—had to be exquisitely choreographed. This pedantry had served him well over the years. His shows were never anything less than spectacularly precise. This required hours and days and weeks of sheer physical work. The 2009 movie *Michael Jackson's This Is It* is directed by Jackson's principal choreographer Kenny Ortega and is pretty much unembellished rehearsal footage: Jackson appears in decent physical shape and holds back on vocals to save his voice for much of the time, but the grueling physical aspect of his work is apparent.

Jackson probably never knew for sure whether he would end his day on a high—or on gurney. The exhausting, punishing, and possibly debilitating rehearsals he put himself through must surely have been taking their toll. He demanded a lot of his dance troupe and he led by example. But at his age and with his lifestyle, it must have been an unpredictable schedule. Would he return home every night and slip into a blissful, restorative slumber? Or would he be wheeled pell-mell across a hospital's emergency room?

*   *   *

Phillips and his AEG Live colleagues probably didn't need too much persuading when Jackson requested a personal physician on an honorarium to take care of him in the run-up to and during the concert run. They might have balked at the generosity of the honorarium, which was $150,000 per month, but the principle of having a qualified medical practitioner on board was sensible. Or so it seemed.

Jackson appointed Dr. Conrad Murray, a cardiologist he'd known since 2006, when he asked him to examine one of the children while in Las Vegas. Murray ran a clinic nearby. Jackson must have liked Murray and stayed in touch. It appears Murray treated Jackson periodically for insomnia.

This seemed plausible: showbusiness performers keep irregular hours and, sometimes, steady sleep patterns elude them. Elvis, Prince, and Tom Petty were regular users of narcotic analgesics.

Murray was born on the Caribbean island Grenada and moved to study in the United States in 1980. He was brought up by his mother and didn't meet his absentee father until he was twenty-five. His father worked as a physician in Texas, where Murray studied pre-medicine and biological sciences. He continued his studies in Nashville and did graduate training in Minnesota. He practiced at first in California and then in Las Vegas.

Whatever his merits as a medical practitioner, his financial acumen appears to have been slight: he ran up $400,000 in court judgments and, in 2008, was ordered to settle $3,700 in unpaid child support. After Jackson's death it was discovered that Murray's debts were more than $780,000. So the decision to commit himself to the lucrative arrangement with Jackson must have made itself.

Whether Murray's professional expertise was the clincher for Jackson is uncertain. It's possible that the medic's preparedness to administer unconventional preparations might have been a factor. Jackson relied on various combinations of drugs to facilitate sleep. Murray, or Jackson, favored an anesthetic (that induces insensitivity to pain) rather than a hypnotic (that induces sleep) drug. Jackson was presumably satisfied with his treatment. Propofol was, it seems, his and Murray's anesthetic of choice. Murray administered it via an intravenous drip. As a qualified medical practitioner, he was presumably aware of the addictive properties of the drug. There's evidence that Methadone (an analgesic), Fentanyl (a synthetic opiate), Percocet (oxycodone and acetaminophen), Dilaudid (an opioid used to treat moderate to severe pain), and Vicodin (an analgesic) were also prescribed. According *Vanity Fair's* Mark Seal, Frank Cascio, a friend and personal assistant of Jackson since 1984, had become concerned that the performer was exhibiting symptoms that indicated "addiction to the narcotic pain medication" as early as 2000—before he knew Murray.

Jackson was rehearsing for the O2 shows in Los Angeles; on June 24, he left shortly before midnight after a characteristically arduous day. Murray was waiting for him when he arrived at his home in the Holmby Hills neighborhood at about 12:30 a.m.; he'd been administering propofol for sixty consecutive nights until June 22, when he started to try to wean Jackson off. Murray remembered he gave Jackson sedatives, but he had difficulty dropping off and, according to Murray, grown anxious about the looming London dates. "I must be ready for the show in England," he told Murray and, according to the doctor's account, specifically asked for "the milk"—this being "milk of amnesia," as propofol, a white emulsion, is sometimes known.

As it was then about 10:00 a.m. Pacific Time and Jackson showed no signs of sleepiness. The likely scenario is that Murray hooked up the drip and administered propofol; he presumably favored this method because it infused the drug continuously and thus ensured the effects did not wear off quickly; it would have effectively left Jackson anesthetized. The drug can trigger potentially fatal cardio-respiratory effects, so Jackson required vigilant observation. Murray recalled that he had the equipment to monitor Jackson's oxygen levels and heart rate and stayed with Jackson for a while before going to the bathroom.

While Murray was visiting the bathroom, he took time to make several phonecalls, including one to Sade Anding, "a woman he'd been pursuing romantically," as an ABC News team led by Ashleigh Banfield put it. Anding later testified that she was in conversation with Murray when he suddenly stopped talking. "I just remember saying, 'Hello, hello, hello! Are you there?'" Anding told an LA court in 2011. She then heard "a commotion as if the phone was in a pocket or something" followed by coughing and "mumbling of voices."

What she heard was Murray returning from the bathroom to find Jackson was not breathing. Murray found a weak pulse and immediately started cardiopulmonary resuscitation (CPR); executing this emergency procedure effectively prevented him from calling 911. He called out and his cries were heard, it seems, by, among others, the chef, Jackson's oldest son Prince and security guard Alberto Alvarez, who ran to Jackson's room to find him lying on his back, his eyes and mouth open. Murray was at his side, performing CPR. "He had a bad reaction," Murray told Alvarez, instructing him to remove the intravenous bag of propofol and call 911.

The call was made and recorded at 12:21. Later, phone records showed that for forty-seven minutes—after Murray said Jackson stopped breathing—Murray made three calls: one at 11:18 a.m. to his Vegas medical clinic, for approximately thirty-two minutes; one to a patient whom he called to talk about test results; and at 11:51 a.m. to a friend in Houston, for eleven minutes. When paramedics arrived, they took over the resuscitation compressing Jackson's chest and delivering mouth-to-mouth ventilation before rushing him to the Ronald Reagan UCLA Medical Center in Westwood, about 2.7 miles from Jackson's home. A fire truck also arrived, soon followed by several paparazzi, who trailed the emergency vehicle to the hospital only to be thwarted by Jackson's bodyguards. At the hospital crowds had already gathered by the time the fleet arrived. Chants of "Michael, Michael" could be heard as Jackson was whisked into theater.

Murray told the physician in charge of the emergency department that he'd given him two separate doses of Lorazepam, branded as Ativan, to treat his anxiety, but failed to disclose the propofol treatment. This was to prove a crucial omission. Subsequent investigations showed that FedEx had delivered a cumulative total of more than four gallons of propofol in seven packages over a period of time to an address in Santa Monica, where a Nicole Alvarez lived. She was a close friend of Murray's, having met him in 2005 when he was a customer at a Las Vegas "gentlemen's club," where she worked. He later started to pay her $2,300 per month rent. Having advised hospital doctors, Murray left the hospital before police officers arrived. By then local and national TV stations had sent crews to stake out the hospital and the skies above the Westwood area thrummed with the sound of helicopter propellers. Fans gathered at various locations, including the Hollywood Walk of Fame, where Jackson had a star.

About an hour and a half after he'd been admitted, Jackson's brother Jermaine Jackson addressed the media. "My brother, the legendary King of Pop, Michael Jackson, passed away on Thursday, June 25, 2009 at 2:26 pm . . . It is believed he suffered cardiac arrest in his home."

The cause of death was changed after further examination and on August 27, 2009, the Los Angeles coroner's office ruled Jackson's death a homicide, the cause being "acute Propofol intoxication with benzodiazepine effect," according to the coroner's report ("benzodiazepine" referred to the sedative Ativan). On February 2, 2010, Murray was charged with involuntary manslaughter. He pled not guilty. In November 2011, Murray was sentenced to four years' imprisonment. A change in California law allowed his time in jail to be significantly reduced. He served two years and was released from a prison in Los Angeles at 12.01 a.m., on October 27, 2013. His medical license was revoked and he remained on parole.

During Murray's trail, his lawyers' defense was that Jackson injected himself with the lethal dose and that Murray had been trying to dissuade Jackson from using propofol. He prescribed it, lawyers argued, to combat Jackson's insomnia, which, the defense claimed, was a side effect of Jackson's prior dependence on Demerol. This is the trademark for pethidine, the compound used as a painkilling drug. The judge concluded it was "not relevant." No Demerol was found in Jackson's body after his death. But, in the August 11, 2011, edition of *Rolling Stone*, Matthew Perpetua raised the possibility that Jackson did have a dependency on this drug in the months before his death.

Murray repeatedly insisted on his innocence and maintained that Jackson's death was due, at least in part, to Demerol withdrawal. Jackson, he argued throughout, didn't divulge a Demerol dependency to him. So Jackson must have accessed the opiate from another undisclosed source. In his 2016 self-published book *This Is It!* Murray claimed he safeguarded Jackson. "In me Michael Jackson found a protective father figure (though I was not old enough to be his dad) with whom he felt utterly safe."

Recall Maureen Orth's observation I used to open Chapter 2. "There is virtually no one Michael Jackson knows who does not view him as some sort of big-bucks ticket to ride." Eleven years after his death, Jackson's cousin Marsha Stewart revealed that, shortly after Jackson died, she went to his house: "I was able to go in and go to the bedroom. When I went in the bedroom there was a bed there with some juice, it looked like a sandwich . . . and I noticed this . . . what I did was took it and put it in my purse." "This" was the blood-stained IV drip Murray used to administer propofol to Jackson. In September 2020, the drip was put up for auction. The story was recounted by the *Daily Mirror*'s Mark Jeffries.

*   *   *

Surely no man has been eulogized and condemned so immoderately in the aftermath of their death. Love and hate gushed in roughly equal proportions. Those who loved Jackson pointed out that not a single allegation against him was ever proved; if anything, he was a victim of tabloid culture, its voyeurism and its distorted attachments to anyone capable of provoking strong emotions. Detractors seized on every new revelation and, of course, these redoubled in the absence of Jackson. He was unable to defend himself, of course.

"I want his three children to know: wasn't nothing strange about your daddy," pronounced Al Sharpton at Jackson's funeral. "It was strange what your daddy had to deal with." It was an oblique reference either to the media's tenacious pursuit, or perhaps to white racism.

The two-hour memorial service at Los Angeles' Staples Center drew 18,000 mourners. It was a showbusiness affair, A-listers from entertainment and sports, including Mariah Carey, Stevie Wonder, Jennifer Hudson, and Usher, gathered, perhaps not yet grasping the depth of hatred felt by many toward Jackson and certainly not able to anticipate how the ferocity would build over the next ten years. Berry Gordy may have been alluding to Jackson's ill-judged associations with children when he said: "Sure there was some sad times and maybe some questionable decisions on his part." Or this might just have been sour grapes: Jackson's early success was with Gordy's Motown label, but he later left Motown and signed with CBS.

More than 31 million Americans watched the two-hour memorial service live, well below the number of people who viewed the funeral of Princess Diana, in 1997, and the burial of President Ronald Reagan, in 2004; though both these events were before the internet had become an alternative to traditional television. So many more probably watched the service on other platforms.

The interest in Jackson took a palpable commercial form when consumers rushed to retail and online outlets to buy albums. By the end of June 2009, the three best-selling albums in the United States were *Thriller*, *Number Ones*, and *The Essential Michael Jackson*, selling a collective 422,000 copies—forty times the week prior to his death. According to the *New York Times*' Ben Sisario, many retailers ran out of stock. The online sales were staggeringly high considering the year was 2009. This was long before online sales passed store sales. Fifty-seven percent of Jackson's album sales were digital downloads. "In the five years that SoundScan has tracked downloads, no artist has sold more than 1 million tracks in one week," wrote Sisario. In the days following his death, Jackson sold 2.3 million downloads, separate from album sales. Jackson occupied the top nine spots on *Billboard*'s catalog chart, as a solo artist or with the Jackson 5. His music was released by Epic/Legacy, a division of Sony; and the Jackson 5 albums were released by Motown.

Sisario quoted *Billboard*'s director of charts: "The level of dominance by Michael Jackson on the top pop catalog albums chart is unlike anything we've seen on any *Billboard* chart, regardless if it occurred pre- or post-death."

This was reflected on radio: "Billie Jean" was played 4,500 times following his death, compared to only 94 plays in the 3 days before. Immediately after the announcement of his death, many radio stations played Michael Jackson continuously. Jackson's past and the innuendo surrounding him had probably deterred many stations from playing his music. But his death removed any prohibitions.

Spikes in sales often follow the death of an artist. Nirvana sales surged 150 percent following Kurt Cobain's suicide in 1994. When the rapper Notorious BIG was killed in 1997, his grimly prescient album *Life After Death* was just about to be released; it sold 689,000 copies in its first week. Even so, Jackson's post-death sales were gargantuan.

Record sales, radio play, and music video marathons in the weeks following his death opened up unexpectedly lucrative revenue streams for Jackson. As often happens, the entertainer earned much more posthumously than in life. Jackson had considerable assets, including the Neverland ranch and other homes, plus his royalties from record, film, and merchandise sales, all of which contributed to his net worth of about $350 million. But remember, he was mired in liability. He couldn't pay his phone, water or legal bills and had to figure out a way of repaying a $300 million bank loan, or lose half of his prized catalog of Beatles music (I'll cover Jackson's accumulation and disposal of music publishing assets over the course of the book). *Forbes* had estimated in 2009 that Jackson was in debt "for at least $200 million." This changed dramatically.

For the ten years after his death, Jackson was the highest earning deceased performer in the world. It isn't unusual for artists to have a longterm upswing in fortunes after dying (if this doesn't sound too crass): Elvis Presley and Elizabeth Taylor both became richer in the afterlife. Creator of the Peanuts cartoon Charles Schulz also continued to earn amply (about $30 million per year) after his death in 2000. But Jackson's postmortem earning were higher than anyone's every year for a decade, proceeds from streaming and his music publishing catalog boosted by royalties from movies and a Vegas show. In 2019 alone, he earned $60 million. The year before, his estate sold his stake in EMI Music Publishing to Sony, bringing the 2018 total to $400 million. *Forbes* calculated Jackson's earnings for the ten years following his death to be $2.1 billion (inflation-adjusted; for comparison that's the same price Google paid for the smartwatch company Fitbit in 2019).

Jackson was the subject of a staged concert, *Thriller Live*, which played for a decade in London. The Cirque du Soleil show *Michael Jackson ONE* ran for several years in Las Vegas. The film documentary *Michael Jackson's This Is It* (director, Kenny Ortega) came out in 2009, grossing $261 million worldwide. Do we understand why so many fans bought records (that they probably already possessed), or merchandise, went to movies and shows that featured the dead, but still pulsing artist? Re-purchasing records is probably a way of validating a relationship; demonstrating or confirming strong feelings of affection or loyalty. Many fans obviously took great interest in and pleasure from Jackson's output: they were captivated by him and experienced the kind of enthrallment that escapes outsiders. Concerts and films featuring Jackson or facsimiles were ways of not so much of remembering him as watching the nearest technology could offer to the real thing.

There were probably several pragmatists too. Fans who bought tickets for the sell-out O2 shows from agencies or directly from the venue were entitled to a full refund, following Jackson's death, though as music memorabilia specialist Tim Terry told the *Financial Times*, "Anyone who has held on to their Michael Jackson, 'This Is It' tour tickets rather than claiming a refund have also made a sound investment. They are sure to be collectables in the future" (January 19, 2011). At the time of writing, they were fetching about 200 dollars on eBay. Michael Jackson impersonators, of which there were thousands, were already around when Jackson was alive, though their business no doubt picked up after his death. A warrantable Michael Jackson industry sprang up after his death.

Reactions to Jackson's death serve to remind how popular Jackson remained even while doubts about his proclivities clustered.

Crass as it sounds, the adage "death is a good career move," which came into currency after Elvis's death in 1977, has too much traction to be dismissed as morbid humor. Sales of posthumous records, books, and films often surge, but, in some cases, the dead figure becomes canonized, his or her artistic body of work afforded greater significance than it had during the artist's life.

Professionally, his career was flagging at the time of his death, but in the years following, it surged again. The on-average $60 million a year was filtered through record labels, promoters, agents, and various other channels, but ultimately the money came from consumers—people who identified in some way with or enthused over Jackson.

Popular entertainers are not like valuable gems. The value of diamonds, for example, is determined by their clarity, which is diminished by their flaws—imperfections, spots, chips, and so on, especially near the center of the gem. Entertainers can have all manner of deficiency. Flaws are often constituent parts of their personae. No one on earth can have been unaware that, for all Jackson's undoubted musical brilliance, there were many aspects of his character and lifestyle that were questionable. Even those devotees who literally worshiped Jackson in life and death were aware of the unsavory insinuations; they were prepared either to ignore them or dismiss them as part of some sort of conspiracy. Or they honestly believed the sworn testimonies of people, young men, who affirmed Jackson had not abused them. Men like Wade Robson who steadfastly maintained Jackson's innocence while he was alive.

At the time of his death, the flaws in Jackson's diamond were apparent rather than real. He faced two accusations of sexual abuse during his lifetime, one that was settled out of court in 1994, and another of which he was cleared at a trial in 2005. Robson was at that trial defending Jackson. He was one of five boys the prosecution alleged Jackson had molested. All denied that anything inappropriate happened. Robson was five when he met Jackson after winning a dance competition in his hometown of Brisbane, Australia. He and his mother moved to the United States after Jackson's grandiose promises. In court, he told how he spent plenty of times with Jackson at the Neverland ranch and beyond and even performed on stage with Jackson. The now-infamous sleepovers did happen.

When Jackson was accused of abusing Gavin Arvizo in 2005, Robson had been a key witness for Jackson's defense. By then a 22-year-old choreographer, he replied unambiguously "No," when asked if Jackson had ever touched him inappropriately. Same answer when asked if Jackson had ever kissed him on the lips. Prosecutors may have suspected he was lying, but the unequivocal manner of his responses proved influential. And, of course, he was under oath when he denied any wrongdoing. But crucially, Robson told the court that Jackson had not abused him. Jurors presumably found his testimony credible. Years later, in 2019, a decade after Jackson's death, Robson amended his original submission. Jackson was "one of the most kind, loving, gentle, caring people I know," reflected Robson. "He also sexually abused me for seven years."

* * *

Robson made the statement in *Leaving Neverland,* a four-hour documentary directed by Dan Reed, broadcast by HBO in the United States and Channel 4 in the United Kingdom in March 2019. Robson was by then thirty-six. He and James Safechuck, forty-one, were the two foci of the program that advanced the most incriminatory argument against Jackson to date. After the transmission, Jackson's legacy was re-evaluated.

Safechuck had been a child actor in a Pepsi advertisement when he first met Jackson in 1986. Then aged ten, he toured with Jackson, with the blessing of his mother. The mothers of both boys were, it seems, comfortable about their children sharing so much time with Jackson, often in privacy. It appeared in the documentary that they were swept up by Jackson's extravagant generosity and his not inconsiderable charm. They may also have been starstruck, that is, fascinated or impressed by a celebrity of Jackson's stature.

Safechuck provided testimony during the 1993–4 Jordan Chandler case, but wouldn't take the stand during the 2005 case, a decision he believed annoyed Jackson and effectively ended of their relationship. "In Paris he introduced me to masturbation and that's how it started," said Safechuck in the documentary, adding, "I don't have any unpleasant memories."

Both he and Robson detailed how Jackson gently persuaded them into a code of silence, telling them they would go to prison if anyone discovered the truth of their secret encounters and that parents, especially women, were not to be trusted. Both men disclosed how they were eventually replaced by younger boys: according to their accounts, Macaulay Culkin (of *Home Alone* fame) was preferred to Robson in the *Black or White* video (1991). Culkin himself insisted there was never any impropriety in his friendship with Jackson.

Robson and Safechuck met with aggressive incredulity from most Jackson loyalists and many jumped to the same conclusion as the Jackson family, that both men were pursuing some form of compensation. When director Reed gave a talk at the Edinburgh Festival, Jackson fans protested. The Jackson estate sought $100 million (£77 million) damages from HBO over the documentary, claiming the film breached a non-disparagement clause in a 27-year-old contract (about which I'll write more in Chapter 12). The legal dispute centered on a concert broadcast from Jackson's *Dangerous* tour when he was at or very near the height of his global popularity. "HBO profited off the *Dangerous* World Tour by airing a concert from the tour and promoting Michael Jackson's talents," the estate's suit claimed, according to *Rolling Stone*'s Jon Blistein. "Now, HBO is profiting off the *Dangerous* World Tour by airing a 'documentary' that falsely claims Michael Jackson was abusing children on the same tour." HBO responded: "Our plans remain unchanged . . . This will allow everyone the opportunity to assess the film and the claims in it for themselves."

After the transmission of *Leaving Neverland*, there was almost exactly the opposite reaction to Jackson's death: radio stations stopped playing Jackson's music; the Jackson songs heard in gyms, retail areas, and other public spaces were silenced and tv clips of Jackson's performances became scarce. Jackson's estate canceled the Chicago run of a jukebox musical about Jackson three weeks after a one-time screening of Reed's film at the Sundance Film Festival and weeks before its HBO premiere. The producers of a musical, *Don't Stop 'Til You Get Enough*, cited scheduling difficulties caused by a labor dispute as the reason for dropping it. Television specials to commemorate ten years after his death were axed. An episode of *The Simpsons* featuring the voice of Jackson was pulled from streaming services and streaming channel.

Reed's documentary offered a persuasive and irrefutable narrative. Irrefutable because Jackson was dead and obviously unable to contest any of the arguments, as he had done on previous occasions. Members of the Jackson family went on the attack, describing the documentary as "another lurid production in an outrageous and pathetic attempt to exploit and cash in on Michael Jackson." The family was quoted by Nicole Sperling, of

Vanity Fair, in 2019: "This so-called 'documentary' is just another rehash of dated and discredited allegations." Both Robson and Safechuck made clear they were never offered any compensation for participating in *Leaving Neverland*. Robson had in fact sued the Jackson estate in 2015, but a judge ruled that too much time had passed. He tried again in 2017, but again unsuccessfully: Jackson alone was responsible for his actions, it was decided, not his companies. The legal case went on till 2021, when an LA judge ruled that Robson, by then thirty-eight, couldn't sue Jackson's businesses over the childhood sexual abuse he allegedly suffered; the same judge had ruled against James Safechuck on similar grounds in November 2020.

The versions of events Robson gave at the 2005 trial and in *Leaving Neverland* contrasted starkly. If he was being honest in Reed's documentary, why had he lied under oath earlier? Or was he being truthful then? "I want to speak the truth as loud as I spoke the lie," said Robson in the documentary. Of course, if Robson had given his later testimony fourteen years earlier, Jackson would have been sent on a very different time-space tangent: the probability is that he would have been given a prison sentence and thus denied access to the various prescription drugs he took habitually and which ultimately proved fatal. Prison life would no doubt not have suited Jackson and it's possible that he could have perished. Equally, he could well have rehabilitated himself, in which case the probability is that he would still be alive, possibly still behind bars.

Frank Dileo (left), Jackson's manager from 1984 to 1989, believed most people associated with Jackson were self-serving. "All they were interested in was what they were getting," he reflected. "And they killed the golden goose."

4

Prisoner of all Those around Him

"Michael Jackson has been living in the tiny nation of Bahrain for almost a year. Possibly as a crossdresser, a drug addict, a Muslim, or at least a still weird human being," Devin Friedman reported in the May 2006 edition of *GQ*. Bahrain is a sheikdom comprising a cluster of islands in the Persian Gulf, its official language being Arabic. "After his acquittal last June, he vacated Neverland, flew east, and disappeared into the desert, presumably to escape an entire nation that no longer loved him."

It's doubtful that an *entire* nation ever loved him. But a good proportion of the world still felt affectionate or, at least, tender enough to buy his products and sustain his considerable income. His outgoings were more than considerable. The suite in the sail-shaped, seven-star Burj al Arab hotel in Dubai—about 300 miles across the Gulf from Bahrain—was $9,000 a night in 2006; today about $26,000. Beneath the group of people gathered at the 1,053-foot (321 meters) tall hotel, the teeming population of the prosperous emirate busied themselves, few of them aware that Michael Jackson was above. So were two senior executives from Sony, owner of his record label. Jackson had his own retinue of representatives present. He was a partner, with Sony, of a profitable music publishing business that had over 250 Beatles songs in its catalog.

Were Jackson still magicking up albums like a sorcerer, there would have been no meeting in Dubai. If an album sells 20 million units and you have a sweet royalty deal, there is no reason in the world you should ever have to worry about paying bills. Trouble was that Jackson's bills were not the kind you, reader, or I would rack up. Unless you stay regularly at the Burj and other comparably lavish hostelries of course. Jackson did. And he wasn't making albums, anyway. *Invincible* was released by Sony's Epic label in 2001. There had been nothing since. And live performances were literally history: the *HIStory* tour was 1996–7 and there were appearances in September and October 2001.

Sony was concerned because Jackson was the company's partner in a lucrative music publishing business that included songs by the Beatles and other musicians. Jackson, who had acquired the ATV publishing company for $47.5 million from South Africa-born, Australia-based billionaire Robert Holmes à Court, (1937–90), had been an estimable business partner. His astute acquisition of the company in 1985 had angered his erstwhile friend Paul McCartney, and was a sound investment. As a Sony artist himself, he was satisfied when the global corporation became his partner. During his fallow phase after 2005, Jackson relied on the income from the publishing catalog. But, when he used his stake plus the copyrights to his own songs as collateral for about $270 million in bank loans, it was like baring his throat in the presence of wolves. He faced what ten years before would have seemed a laughably preposterous predicament: he was deep in debt.

It was in Sony's interest to keep him afloat. If Jackson became insolvent, his 50 percent stake in the business would go up for sale, thus exposing the multinational conglomerate corporation to the possibility that it could become the partner of the highest bidder. Sony would then have to confront the uncomfortable possibility that it would be forced into a new, unpredictable partnership not of its own choosing. So it offered to help Jackson find a bank prepared to lend him more than $300 million to pay off his debts. In exchange Jackson would probably have to forfeit a portion of his half of the Beatles catalog. Sony had the right of first refusal if Jackson sold his half of the Sony/ATV catalog, as it was known.

Promoters are not by nature cautious and certainly not moralistic; so there would have been no shortage of them if Jackson ever showed a spark of interest in gracing a stage. No one was going to take notice of the scandal engulfing his personal life. Or perhaps more accurately, *everybody* was going to take notice of the scandal, but that wouldn't put them off buying concert tickets. The question was: for how long? Later rather than sooner, even devout fans run out of hope and accept the likelihood that there will never be another live appearance. Ensconced on the Mideast island, Jackson looked set for a long retreat from public view, maybe forever.

There were plenty of exemplars of child stars who faded in maturity. Macaulay Culkin, Jackson's friend whom I mentioned in the previous chapter, was an international movie sensation at ten in 1990. The *Home Alone* movies are still re-running on television. Culkin became a jobbing actor, mainly in tv roles, and doing voiceovers. Haley Joel Osment was eleven when he mesmerized audiences in M. Night Shayamalan's *The Sixth Sense* ("I see dead people") in 1999. Twins Mary-Kate and Ashley Olsen created a business empire around their early 1990s sitcom *Full House*. Then the roles dried up.

Jackson, who had been performing since he was seven, already had an extensive career in showbusiness terms. He was forty-seven. Perhaps he was hoping to enjoy a career arc somewhat like his friend Elizabeth Taylor's. She arrived in Hollywood from England and picked up a few film parts before making a major impact as the twelve-year-old star of *National Velvet* in 1944. She remained at the top for the rest of her life. Taylor though was schooled in the Hollywood jungle and adapted in order to survive: she acquired acumen when it came to contract-negotiation and died how she lived—a rich woman. Jackson seemed to have grasped the cutthroat reality of showbusiness when he brokered a sound deal with CBS in 1975: the $750,000 bonus he received on signature was a princely sum, unheard of in the music industry at that point. But, on reflection, someone else, like his father, could have hammered out the terms and just left Jackson to enjoy the proceeds.

Jackson later became estranged from his father (whom he dismissed as his manager in 1979) and became otherworldly. As he did, he probably relied on financial advice from pliant yet self-interested people. Frank Dileo, who was Jackson's manager from 1984 to 1989, told Timothy L. O'Brien, of the *New York Times*, "Some people can go to a person like Michael and say, 'Listen, this is out of hand.' Other people would much rather say, 'Whatever you want,' and they don't care," Dileo believed that the majority fell into the latter camp. "All they were interested in was what they were getting. And they killed the golden goose."

* * *

The sides of reality seem to have become slippery for Jackson in the late 1980s. His mystifying bid for the skeleton of the Victorian Englishman Joseph Merrick, better known as the Elephant Man, for a breathtaking $1 million was the first of a series of barely comprehensible acts. One of the more comprehensible was the purchase of the property in Los Olivos, California, about 30 miles from Santa Barbara. Not cheap at $17 million (some say it was over $19 million), it was still California real estate and so tangible property, even if it was expensive to maintain: about $2 million per year. That was in late 1987 and Jackson was in rude health financially, having grossed over $35 million from the *Bad* tour. Jackson might have been quirky; but when you make that kind of money, you can afford to be. In others, some of the behaviors exhibited by Jackson at this time might have been interpreted as signposts en route to a mental health condition. But quirky is not the same as troubled. Money serves as a bulwark.

If Jackson was given to sudden and unaccountable changes of mind and action that was probably because he wasn't ordinary: he had all the gifts. So, when he sunk money into exorbitant projects, like videos, even his personal finance advisers didn't seem to care and perhaps the ones who did were cut loose. This probably explains Jackson's penchant for rotating through teams of advisers. This is not to suggest Jackson was ignorant of budgets or not savvy enough to make crucial decisions. The $22 million (approximately) settlement of what could have been a career-ending molestation case in 1994, in retrospect, looked an astute decision. And his sale of half of the previously mentioned publishing catalog to Sony in 1995 brought him an impressive $100 million, which seemed like good business.

The outlandish projects kept coming. Some estimate Jackson splurged $65 million of video projects alone. "He's a millionaire who lives like a billionaire," wrote Alison Boshoff, of Britain's *Daily Mail*. It was a simple but probably accurate way of summarizing Jackson's rush toward financial ruin. "He was spending between £13million and £20million a year more than he was earning," estimated Boshoff. That's between $17 million and $26 million every year.

According to O'Brien, Myung-Ho Lee, a South Korean, was a "central figure" in Jackson's debt accumulation. He was one of a number of business advisers retained by Jackson, in his case between 1998 and 2001. As early as 1998, Jackson had taken out a $90 million bank loan, spent it and then let Myung-Ho Lee arrange a $140 million loan from Bank of America, using the ATV publishing business as collateral. Jackson blew the $140 million in months, then took a further $30 million line of credit from the same bank. There followed a slew of actions against Jackson from former lawyers, managers, and advisers over deals gone south and unpaid invoices.

Myung-Ho Lee later claimed that he was appointed specifically to put the Jackson's finances in order, but was ignored when he urged Jackson to curb his profligate spending. The relationship deteriorated to the point where Myung-Ho Lee took Jackson to court for failing to pay him.

In 2003, when Jackson was forty-four, he reached a $12 million out-of-court settlement with Myung-Ho Lee. In the court papers, Myung-Ho Lee called Jackson as a "ticking financial time bomb waiting to explode" who owed banks hundreds of millions of dollars in loans. Jackson's countersuit alleged Myung-Ho Lee and his company Union Finance fleeced him for millions and destroyed financial records. The following year, Myung-Ho Lee was quoted in *Vanity Fair*: "He has a lot of skeletons in his closet," Lee said of Jackson. "Some are real and some are in his mind, which makes him a prisoner of all those around him."

By the time of his Dubai meeting with Sony, his debt had probably reached anything between $178 million (lowest estimate) and $270 million (highest). Commonsense tells you that even the most reckless extravagance and irresponsible wastefulness isn't likely to take an individual into this kind of financial abyss (even a fully pimped-up Gulfstream G650ER will only set you back $66.5 million, less in 2006). Jackson must have had several deeply unwise investments that have remained undisclosed. And, of course, his debts had to be serviced—probably at unfavorable rates of interest. O'Brien wrote, "Jackson was making monthly payments of about $4.5 million in 2005," *Monthly* payments.

So, it's possible to understand why the Sony people were expecting some sort of financial apocalypse unless Jackson really could work magic. He showed no inclination to do anything resembling productive work, had no plans for theatrical projects, and, as far as anyone knew, had written no new material. Add to this the uncertainty over whether the recent court case had hurt—or benefited—his boxoffice appeal.

Complicating matters slightly was the fact that Jackson, a couple of years before in 2003, sold his debts to a New York investment group called Fortress Investment. When someone "sells" a debt, it means they transfer responsibility for the debt or debts to a third party and, from then on, pay the new owner at agreed-upon terms. The interest rates are typically high. Sony negotiated a deal with Fortress to reduce interest rates and brought in Citibank to offer Jackson a new loan, but on one condition: that Jackson sell Sony half of his 50 percent stake at a future date for a figure thought to be about $250 million. This would keep Jackson afloat and provide Sony with a buttress and Citigroup with a precautionary fallback resolution. The final deal involved Citigroup's provision of a $25 million mortgage on Neverland. Jackson lost a chunk of his music publishing investment, but he had enough breathing space to continue pursuing a lifestyle to which he'd grown accustomed over the years. As for the future, all Jackson needed to do was work in some capacity. This was something he'd signally not done in recent years. It took another unexpected episode to concentrate his mind.

*   *   *

"Michael wants to lead a normal life and does not want to be hounded by the media. He does not want to be misquoted or falsely portrayed, and he wants to make sure that his children are not under public pressure." Jackson must have been crossing his fingers behind his back; or maybe he was already being misquoted. But this is how *Gulf News* reported his presence in the oil-rich islands, once ruled by Portuguese, then Persians before becoming a British protectorate. Habib Toumi, the publication's bureau chief, was writing in January 2006, six months after Jackson's arrival on a private plane as a guest of the Al Gosaibis, one of the kingdom's richest and most prominent merchant families (which was in 2011 involved in a financial crisis that left 100 banks including Deutsche Bank, HSBC, and Societe Generale owed an estimated $22 billion).

Ostensibly, Jackson was in the territory as a consultant for AAJ Holding, a company owned by Ahmad Abu Bakr Janahi, which planned to build an amusement park and entertainment center in Oman, a country in the eastern corner of the Arabian peninsula. But he was also there at the behest of Sheikh Abdullah bin Hamad al-Khalifa, the prince of Bahrain, who was, it seems, a friend of Michael's brother Jermaine and an aspiring songwriter himself. Jermaine had apparently visited Bahrain in 1989 and reportedly converted to Islam.

According to William Lee Adams, of *Time* magazine, "the two men moved into the same palace to collaborate on music together." The Sheikh paid $30,000 in utilities bills at the Neverland ranch. Jackson apparently could not afford to pay them. There were more bills, including legal fees totaling about $2.2 million that the Sheikh settled for Jackson. Whether or not this was a gift or a loan later became a matter of contention. Jackson appears to have assumed the former and behaved as a royal guest. He cruised around Bahrain in a red Ferrari he had shipped in from the United States, went shopping for children's toys, and, in one notable incident, was sighted in a women's bathroom in a shopping mall in Dubai. This is less shocking in today's gender fluid climate than it would have been in the binary 2000s, even in one of the most liberal of the Islamic Mideast states.

Jackson was still news, but, without court cases to sensationalize or concerts to rhapsodize over, the occasional contretemps in public bathrooms was tame. *GQ*'s Friedman reported that Jackson hired someone to reconnoiter places he wanted to visit, either alone or with his children. She would plot a course, including an escape route in the event of a media encroachment, and alert cinema and store staff that Jackson would appear and should not be approached, less still touched.

At first Jackson dressed in his usual, flamboyant style, but the penny must have dropped quickly: if he were to blend to the point where he could venture out without the recon, he would need alternative garb. The *abaya* was traditionally a woman's garment, but it had the advantage of being full length and could coordinate with head covering, making it serviceable for when Jackson wanted to go out incognito. Of course, the silvery right glove was a bit of a giveaway.

Jackson's intentions have never been transparent. Initially, he stayed with the Al Gosaibi family, but, according to *Gulf News*, moved into a mansion in Sanad, about 10 km (6 miles) south of Manama (Bahrain's capital). He reportedly paid $8 million. If the reported figure was correct—and he couldn't afford it, though this never seemed to stop him—then it would appear Jackson intended to stay in seclusion. But how would he sustain his lifestyle and, for that matter, his children's? Remember, the Sheikh had musical ambitions, not only for himself but, it was later revealed, for Jackson. Al-Khalifa owned a record label called 2 Seas and planned to revive Jackson's career by releasing a new album. The album never materialized; Jackson never delivered any work. Al-Khalifa also envisaged a biography of Jackson and a stage play, in which Jackson would be involved. Jackson, who had been in showbusiness practically his whole life, must surely have permitted himself a few moments of clarity and realized the generosity of his host was indexed to this project and that, as with many other arrangements, there was a *quid pro quo*.

If the illogicality that passed for logic in Jackson's head was dominant for his initial period in the tranquility of the Persian Sea, it was jolted after eleven months when the Sheikh's patience and benevolence wore out. By then, he'd decided Jackson was not going to record the mooted album, nor do anything else of practical significance. Jackson was uprooted from his Mideast hideaway and returned to Los Angeles in May 2006. Separated from his would-be music partner, al-Khalifa must have grown aggrieved and instructed his lawyers to pursue Jackson for the money he'd given him during his unproductive stay in Bahrain. He claimed Jackson owed him $7 million and took him to London's High Court in an effort to recover what he insisted was a business loan. Jackson instructed his lawyers to reply that there had been a mistake, a misrepresentation and, interestingly, "undue influence."

Jackson's defense planned to demonstrate that the Sheikh had exploited their client's vulnerability and lack of business sense. It seemed a tall order. At least, in one sense: after all Jackson had been in the entertainment industry for over four decades and surely had some insight into its commercial machinations. And Jackson had shown forethought when he transferred the deeds to Neverland to private investment firm Colony Capital for $22.5 million when he was in default on a loan, as noted in the previous chapter. Colony Capital managed the 2,700-acre property in Los Olivos, California, where Jackson lived for more than fifteen years up to 2005, and put it on the market in 2015 for $100 million.

Presumably feeling the name Neverland was forever tainted, the company changed the identity to Sycamore Valley Ranch. It still didn't sell and was discounted to $67 million two years later. It was relisted again in 2019 for $31 million, and then pulled off the market. Jackson's decision to hand over to Colony Capital and thus to a company in which he retained an interest may have been in anticipation of losing the court case to the Sheikh. In this eventuality, Jackson would have protected his prized property. If this was the motivation, or one of several behind the deal, it suggests his lawyers' argument about his lack of business sense was flimsy.

But, in another sense, he had grown from childhood in a kind of cocoon, enveloped and protected by any number of people who were keen to prolong the wellbeing of, as Frank Dileo put it, the golden goose, or the "ticket to ride," as Anne Orth described Jackson in Chapter 2. As for vulnerability, Jackson specialized in creating imagined worlds and was probably trying to do the same in Bahrain; he usually had a fey, or dreamy look that could be interpreted as vulnerability. Jackson had arrived in Bahrain after four months in a Santa Maria courtroom and was not in the best of health.

Essentially, Jackson countered the Sheikh's claims by insisting there was no legally binding contract and that the money he'd been given (he didn't dispute the amount) was a gift. This included a new $120,000 Rolls-Royce. Jackson's financial problems had been well documented over the previous three years, so it's unlikely the Sheikh assumed Jackson could actually pay him back, apart from with records. While a London High Court battle over money didn't register as much interest as a sex case, Jackson was still news, so there must have been disappointment among the media when he didn't show. Nor did the Sheikh. As Alison Boshoff wrote, "It would have been a fascinating case, giving an insight into Jackson's life of extreme luxury, matched in scale only by eccentricity and reckless spending."

In November 2008, their respective lawyers confirmed that the two parties had signed an out-of-court agreement in settlement of the dispute. The sum involved was not disclosed. A handful of fans were at court to hear the lawyers' twenty-second address, even though they knew neither party was due to appear. Jackson, meanwhile, was in Southern California, or possibly Nevada. He was seven months away from his death.

* * *

Jackson probably didn't see them, but, around the time he was preparing to return to the United States, American tabloids were featuring pictures of a bathroom described as Whitney Houston's. Empty beer cans, crack pipes, spoons encrusted with what looked like cocaine residue, and miscellaneous garbage covered all surfaces. The photographs were sold to magazines by Houston's sister-in-law who also provided commentary on Houston's various damaging habits, including self-harming. Five years later in 2011, police were called to Houston's suite in the Beverly Hilton in Los Angeles to find her facedown in the bath, dead. She was forty-eight.

There was an elemental symmetry between Houston's and Jackson's lives. And deaths. Houston had been urged into showbusiness and overbearingly coached by a parent, in her case Cissy Houston, who had been a backing singer, but never a solo star. She was the cousin of Dionne Warwick, and the goddaughter of Aretha Franklin. Whitney Houston sold over 120 million records; she was the first American singer to score seven consecutive number one singles; her 1992 single "I Will Always Love You" remains the highest selling single by a female artist in history. She was an African American who had an impact beyond music. There were other black female singers, but none more globally popular or international feted as Houston. After the release of her movie *The Bodyguard* in 1992, she had probably eclipsed Madonna as the world's preeminent woman artist. Madonna, as we now know, had enough resilience to bounce back.

Houston followed up with another film in 1995, *Waiting to Exhale* (based on Terry McMillan's novel). But then her public appearances became more erratic and there were rumors of drug and alcohol use. In 2001, Houston appeared with Jackson on a tribute concert to commemorate his thirtieth birthday at New York's Madison Square Garden. Joal Ryan, of *E! News* thought she looked "a tad on the scrawny side." It was no secret that

Houston was struggling. With what, no one knew for sure. Drugs? Alcohol? Anorexia? Physical abuse from her husband? All of the above?

In 2002, Houston talked on television about her historical use of drugs, illicit, and prescription, as well as alcohol, but denied having an eating disorder. She also denied using crack cocaine, which, in the 1990s was circulating. "I don't do crack . . . crack is whack," she confirmed to Diane Sawyer, of ABC's *Primetime* show.

Her tempestuous marriage to singer Bobby Brown seemed to be taking an unpleasant turn. In 2003, police responded to a domestic violence emergency call and found Houston with a bruised cheek and a cut lip. Brown subsequently turned himself in and was charged with misdemeanor battery for hitting his wife and reportedly threatening to "beat her ass."

Even if he hadn't seen the tabloid images of Houston's bathroom, Jackson would have heard about her apparent meltdown when he got back to the States in Spring 2006. We'll never know his reaction, but a mixture of dismay and empathy is probably not wide of the mark. Houston, like Jackson, was an African American who had, without asking, been consecrated by blacks before alienating large sections of the black population. By 1989, when she was twenty-six, she had already won eleven American Music Awards, two Grammys, and boasted the biggest-selling debut album by a female artist in history. Yet she was jeered and booed at the prestigious Soul Train Awards. Houston's rise might have been hailed by blacks, but her success in the mainstream led many to conclude she was no longer black. Reverend Al Sharpton derided her as "Whitey Houston." This was the late 1980s, remember. Today, African American music dominates the musical landscape, so it's hard to imagine how Houston's success represented a kind of "white-out." Black artists, or at least spectacularly successful black artists, like Houston and Jackson, were expected to be standard bearers, not just for themselves but for black people and their shared history of suffering.

Celebrities aren't just admired: pity, disapproval, or revulsion are powerful responses that keep audiences rapt. It might have been hard to believe that someone with Houston's looks and voice could ever lose her balance and teeter toward the cliff edge. But her unsteady wobble made for compelling viewing. And Houston didn't seem to mind the glare: in 2009, she appeared on Oprah Winfrey's tv show. Then a 46-year-old mother, and with two spells in rehab behind her, she talked with a disarming innocence about her use of drugs and her marriage, which had ended a year before. "Something happens to a man when a woman has that much fame," she surmised on *Oprah*.

People couldn't stop gawping as Houston teetered ever closer to the edge. In February 2010, she made a horrifying comeback. Once considered in the same class as Judy Garland and Barbra Streisand, Houston sounded unmelodious and raspy. "If they expected to hear the Whitney of 20 years ago, go buy a CD," her tour manager said after a disastrous concert in

Brisbane, Australia (quoted by the *Guardian*'s Dave Simpson, in 2010). It was a fair point. People didn't criticize late career Bob Dylan, Johnny Cash, or Rod Stewart. Her tour manager's remark was slightly premonitory because eight years after her death a holographic Houston embarked on a European tour; holographic recreations of Jackson, as well as Tupac Shakur, Frank Sinatra, and Maria Callas had also appeared in concert.

Every success she'd enjoyed in her pomp found a perfect counterpoint in her downfall. Jackson wasn't around to witness the final two years of her ravaged decline, which bore resemblance to his own drug-induced deterioration. And his ascent. Houston must have seen parallels: when she appeared at the O2 in 2010, she included a long tribute to Jackson, which suggested identification. "I'm here I'll take his place," she told the audience with a morbid prescience. Both Jackson and Houston were obsessives, driven to ever-higher levels of theatrical perfection and rewarded not just with money, but the adulation of audiences. Both were idolized, then pilloried by African Americans. And both were monitored, not just as they rose but as they fell. Houston's dizzying fortunes captivated the media, which seized on any morsel, good or bad. Not because the media took cruel pleasure from her misadventure; but because they acted as audiences' proxies; they represented as well as guided the tastes, sensibilities, feelings, and interests of audiences. They still do.

*   *   *

In November 2006, seven months after his exit from Bahrain, Jackson went to London to World Music Awards, where he picked up two awards. He gave a brief acceptance speech, sang a couple of lines and left to boos from a half-empty Earl's Court arena. The crowd's expectation was that he would sing at least one number. Jackson showed up in Tokyo in March 2007, again to appear rather than sing: guests paid $3,500 per head to spend time with Jackson at a kind of party. He granted a rare interview to *Ebony* for its November 2007 issue (referred to in the previous chapter), but revealed nothing tangible about his future, or much about his present state of mind.

There were also stories that a remixed *Thriller* was in the works, but the twenty-fifth anniversary passed without sign of the rumored remix, less still any new material. Surprisingly, the British national radio station BBC6 Music reported that Jermaine Jackson had suggested that Michael and his other brothers had discussed concert dates that could happen "sometime in 2008." Jackson himself had not performed on a concert stage since 1996/97, when he played eighty-two shows in fifty-eight cities as part of the *HIStory* tour. Plans for collaborations with will.i.am, Akon, and Kanye West surfaced, but yielded nothing. Jackson's most recent studio album was *Invincible*, seven years before.

The usual Jackson tittle-tattle continued to bubble: he was buying a castle in Ireland for $20 million; he was having more work done to remove wrinkles from his face; he'd contracted an MRSA-type skin infection during plastic surgery to reconstruct his nose; he was being sued by a woman calling herself Billie Jean Jackson, who claimed to be the mother of his youngest child, Prince Michael II, aka Blanket, and wanted joint custody. Perhaps the most unusual story to surface concerned a fifty-foot Michael Jackson robot that would stand in Las Vegas and be released to roam the desert firing laser beams that would be visible from airplanes.

As he turned fifty, in August 2008, Jackson went on ABC television's *Good Morning America* and pronounced his musical career still active. "I am writing all the time . . . I love composing." There was no evidence of his compositions, nor any promise to end his reclusiveness. Meanwhile, his finances continued to flounder and, as we've seen, he narrowly avoided foreclosure on the abandoned Neverland. The gates of the ranch were opened in December, but only for an auction of 2,000 of Jackson's items, including his socks and gloves. There was still no indication whether or not Jackson would ever perform again. Even as evidence of his financial predicament crystallized, no one knew how he intended to get himself out of debt, or even if that was his intention. One clue arrived when it was announced that Jackson had struck a deal for a stage production based on *Thriller*. This was met with a sharp response from film director John Landis, who argued Jackson didn't have adequate proprietorial rights. Landis directed the original *Thriller* video.

And then, on March 5, 2009, Jackson took everyone by surprise, making a five-minute appearance in the mall-like atrium of London's O2 Arena to announce an upcoming series of concerts. The concerts were to be promoted by AEG Live whose chief executive Randy Phillips later increased the initial ten concerts to a total of fifty. "We knew this was show business history," Phillips told the BBC, "but this is a cultural phenomenon." It was an accurate description of the doomed project.

Jackson's lead attorney at his child molestation trial was Thomas Mesereau, seen here accompanying him to the Santa Barbara County Courthouse on March 25, 2005. Mesereau's strategy proved a masterstroke.

5

Yesterday's News

In November 2003, Jackson, then forty-five, flew into Santa Barbara, California, on a private Gulf Stream G-4 jet and went straight to the county jail to surrender. He was booked under suspicion of child molestation. He posted a $3 million bond and was released in less than an hour. The media were assembled as Jackson left. Holding out his hand with the palm showing and two fingers extended to signify peace, Jackson acknowledged journalists and blew kisses before flying back to Las Vegas. Jackson's family issued a statement, dismissing what they called the "vicious allegation" against him as a "big lie." Jermaine Jackson compared the accusation to "a modern-day lynching" of a man whose life has been "about peace."

Jackson had given an interview on television to British journalist Martin Bashir nine months earlier in February. Bashir filmed the documentary titled *Living with Michael Jackson* between late 2002 and early 2003 and was granted the kind of access often denied other journalists. Bashir had, in 1995, pulled off something of a media coup when he interviewed Princess Diana for the BBC program *Panorama*; it is still regarded as the most revealing interview she ever gave and enhanced her reputation as the injured party in a loveless marriage. Jackson's reputation, on the other hand, suffered irreparable damage after his Bashir interview.

In Bashir's program, Jackson was shown holding the hand of a boy named Gavin Arvizo, who was later disclosed as his accuser. Arvizo was diagnosed with cancer in 2000. Jackson learned of Arvizo's condition, sent him a basket full of toys, and later invited him and his family to Neverland. Arvizo visited the ranch many times, often accompanied by members of his family. Jackson giggled when he said on camera that he and the boy had slept in his bedroom but in separate beds. "It's not sexual, we're going to sleep," Jackson assured Bashir when he probed into his unusual friendship.

With a barely believable ingenuousness, Jackson submitted, "The most loving thing to do is to share your bed with someone. It's a beautiful thing.

It's very right." Predictably, the tv interview elicited an excited reaction over the propriety of Jackson's relationship with Arvizo and prompted memories from a decade before. Santa Barbara district attorney Thomas W. Sneddon (1941–2014) had been investigating Jackson since 1993, when Jackson was first accused of molesting a thirteen-year-old boy. That witness and his family accepted a civil settlement of a reported $20 million and this closed the official criminal investigation. Sneddon's suspicions lingered and the Bashir interview gave them fresh impetus. Sneddon sent forty police vehicles to Jackson's Neverland ranch. Law enforcement officers searched the ranch for about thirteen hours; search warrants were served on two other locations in Southern California where some items were seized but there was no evidence of any illegal activities. The subsequent investigation went on for two years.

Together with the Santa Barbara Sheriff's Department, Sneddon decided to interview Arvizo, alongside his mother Janet, father David, and brother Star. The process took place over July and August but yielded no specific allegations. Then, in November 2003, Gavin Arvizo told police that Jackson had molested him serially between February 21 and March 12, 2003. During this time, Jackson, said Janet Arvizo, held the family against their will at Neverland. On December 18, Jackson was formally charged with seven felony counts of child molestation and two counts claiming he administered an "intoxicating agent"—alleged to be wine—to a young cancer patient at his Neverland ranch.

The ten charges were:

1. Conspiracy involving child abduction, false imprisonment, and extortion, including twenty-eight specific acts between February 1 and March 31, 2003.

2–5. Lewd act upon a child under the age of fourteen, between February 20 and March 12, 2003.

6. Attempt to get a child under age fourteen to commit a lewd act upon Jackson between February 20 and March 12, 2003.

7–10. Administering an intoxicating agent—alcohol—to assist in the commission of child molestation.

A criminal defendant can't be convicted unless guilt has been proven beyond a reasonable doubt (civil cases are proved by lower standards of proof such as "the preponderance of the evidence," meaning basically the likelihood that something happened). So the accused bears no burden to prove innocence. Jackson pled not guilty to all charges in January 2004. Crowds of supporters waited for hours until Jackson turned up at the Santa Maria, California, courthouse, 200 miles north of Los Angeles. Jackson was twenty minutes late for the arraignment. Lots were drawn and sixty fans were allowed to watch the proceedings from the public gallery. Each time a member of the

Jackson family entered the courtroom, there were applause—in defiance of courtroom officials who had forbidden such expressions of approval. CNN's senior legal analyst Jeffrey Toobin was in the courtroom and reasoned that the "several hundred" Jackson fans who had waited at the courthouse were a "core" rather than representative of the general population. "He [Jackson] is, to a certain extent, yesterday's news" (quoted in CNN.com, January 16, 2004). It was a grievous misjudgment.

In January 2005, the world's media laid siege to the Santa Barbara courtroom, while another congregation of media camped about 30 miles away outside the Neverland ranch. "About 2,200 members of the media from around the world received credentials to cover it—more than the O.J. Simpson and Scott Peterson murder trials combined," wrote *Esquire*'s Kate Storey. (Peterson was convicted of the first-degree murder of his pregnant wife in 2004, after a five-month trial.) More than thirty countries sent media representatives. Glossies, newspapers, tv channels, websites, and chatrooms were all trying to satisfy their consumers' appetite for daily, or minute-by-minute updates and trivia about Jackson.

Most performers who have starved audiences of records, concerts, or movies for prolonged periods would have faded from public view. Jackson was different: his trial was the most globally fascinating since 1994–5, when O. J. Simpson was cleared of murdering his ex-wife. The former football player and actor Simpson, an African American who strenuously tried to avoid being identified as black, was accused and later cleared of murder. In 1995, a CBS poll showed a disparity: only 22 percent of blacks polled thought Simpson was guilty, while 76 percent of whites had formed the conclusion that he was. Polls are notoriously misleading but figures like this are at least indicative: more blacks were likely to believe Jackson was guilty than they were of Simpson. Writing in 2017, over two decades after the trial, Rory Carroll, of the *Guardian*, quoted the writer Earl Ofari Hutchinson, "OJ will always, till the end of time, be a symbol not only of racial division and polarization but of how the justice system deals with African Americans. He's an eternal symbol." He made no mention of Jackson.

In the period before Jackson's trial, 62 percent believed the allegations against him were true, according to a CNN/*USA Today*/Gallup poll. More Americans moved to an unsure or neutral stance by mid-December, only 54 percent believing Jackson was guilty, though Gallup's News' Jeffrey M. Jones added the rider, "blacks are much more likely to view Jackson favorably than are whites, and also to believe the allegations against Jackson are untrue." Even so, more blacks thought Jackson guilty than thought O. J. Simpson had killed his ex-wife in the 1990s.

People of the State of California v. Michael Joseph Jackson, like *People of the State of California v. Orenthal James Simpson*, had constituents that were media-intimate rather than just media-friendly: race, fame, sex, possibly pedophilia, and a few odd elements that no one could anticipate.

Rodney Melville, who presided over the Jackson trial, banned cameras from the courtroom, but allowed television audiences a replay of the "action" with actors reading from court transcripts every day. This was part of his plan to stop his trial turning into another Simpson experience in which there was the flamboyant judge Lance Ito and a group of lawyers and witnesses whose theatrics earned them posttrial careers as authors, broadcasters, and self-styled legal experts. Judge Ito in particular was extensively parodied on comedy and talk shows as he appeared to lose control of the case in full view of television audiences. Melville, perhaps mindful of this, reminded participants that they should not disclose any information pertinent to the Jackson case outside the courthouse walls. In other words, they were gagged.

The Jackson case was, like Simpson's, deluged by hype bordering on hysteria, but the trial was not televised. Sky's ingenious, if inadequate, response was to restage the case as it progressed, using actors to recreate the daily proceedings in the Los Angeles studios of E! Entertainment. Sky News was then available in 40 countries, and E! in 120, meaning that the "trial" was being seen across the globe. Most media crews were obliged to remain outside the courtroom in close proximity to gawping fans. A kind of sub-narrative to the trial developed as relations between the media and mistrustful Jackson fans became strained. Even to the present day, Jackson acolytes believe he is—and always has been—unjustifiably maligned.

Whether it was testament to Judge Melville's discipline or the media and their audience's insatiability, the only scraps of knowledge to escape the courtroom were inconsequential. A fan outside the courthouse holding a placard affixed with a bag of what appeared to be feces, for example, made news. But just when it seemed this was set to be the antithesis of the colorful Simpson trial, Jackson intervened. Hours before jury selection started, Jackson—ever, the supreme self-publicist—released a video statement in which he simply asked audiences to "keep an open mind and let me have my day in court." It was a tidbit, but one that quickly circled the world, thanks to the internet. The Simpson trial took place at a time before the value of the net had even been glimpsed let alone realized.

"The internet upstarts barely in the picture 10 years ago when Mr Simpson was on trial emerged as formidable opponents for newspapers and broadcasters constrained by common decency and the rules of their trade," wrote Christopher Parkes, of the *Financial Times*, highlighting a trend that would continue for years. Social media was in its infancy at the time of the Jackson trial, and, while no one knew it at the time, the tendency to conflate reality with rumor, half-truth, and what we now call "fake news" was probably emerging.

*   *   *

"The 15-week trial that began on 28 February 2005 was an immersive and clamorous multimedia spectacle," advised Margo Jefferson. "Everything Jackson owned, from his penis to his art collection, was examined and photographed by the Santa Barbara police department." She was writing in the *Guardian* thirteen years after her laudatory book *On Michael Jackson*.

Even before the trial had officially opened, there was a clash of tropes ready to wear for the media: the cunning, predatory child molester taking advantage of starstruck fans versus the grasping mother, manipulating her son to extort money from a world-renowned celebrity. Prosecutors tried to convince the twelve jurors (eight women and four men) that Michael Jackson charmed and isolated children and put their families off the scent by lavishing them with gifts. The defense responded by targeting the mother of the child, questioning why a responsible parent would willingly allow her child to sleep with a grown man unless there was an ulterior motive. "When the family found out that they were not going to live at Neverland forever, they realized that they weren't going to get rich, that's when their story changed and the accusations began," Jackson's attorney Thomas Mesereau opened his defense. Mesereau, then forty-nine, his white hair worn like a member of a progrock band, vied with Jackson as the most conspicuous character in court.

It seemed an unusual start, but Mesereau had taken the advice of a private investigator he had hired. The pi was Scott Ross, who had worked on the defense of actor Robert Blake, successfully disclosing information about his murdered wife, who had, it was argued, a habit of sending letters and nude photos of herself to famous men and had trapped Blake into marrying her by becoming pregnant. Blake was acquitted of murder in March, 2005. Mesereau (who would represent Bill Cosby in 2018) argued that Arvizo's mother was the prime mover of the whole case. He contended that Arvizo had dreamt up the molestation incidents at the urging of his mother. Jackson was just another celebrity target she sought to fleece.

He was answering a prosecution that claimed Jackson manipulated the then thirteen-year-old Arvizo (fifteen when he appeared in court), exposed him to "strange sexual behavior," and plied him with alcohol. Sneddon depicted Jackson as a resourceful deviant who enclosed himself in what he called "the private world of Michael Jackson." The culture Jackson created at Neverland, Sneddon suggested, was conducive to the sexual molestation that allegedly occurred. Sneddon repeatedly referred to the Martin Bashir documentary— which the jury was shown—underlining how damaging the program became to Jackson's reputation and, ultimately, to Jackson himself. The prosecution's case rested almost solely on the evidence provided by the Arvizos.

False imprisonment was one of the charges leveled against Jackson; Janet Arvizo claimed Jackson had kept her at Neverland against her will. Effectively, this broadened the scope of the case: rather than argue a narrower case against Jackson that would turn only on the testimony of Gavin Arvizo, Sneddon included a conspiracy charge that centered on the claim that Jackson's accomplices had conspired to kidnap the child's mother and keep her at Neverland. This allowed Mesereau, when conducting his defense, to put Janet Arvizo on the stand and reveal the information Ross had discovered about her past. That information included welfare fraud as well as a previous civil suit in which she was found to have lied. There was also a minor error that had major repercussions: it was established that she had left Neverland to have her legs waxed at precisely the time she later claimed she was being held at the ranch against her will. In other words, Mesereau attacked her credibility, at one point presenting a dossier that caused her to invoke her fifth amendment against self-incrimination if questioned about her welfare fraud case.

Wade Robson was the leadoff witness for the Jackson defense. Jackson's housekeeper testified for the prosecution that she'd actually seen Robson in bed with Jackson. Then ten years old, Robson was, said the housekeeper, naked from the waist up. She believed Robson and Jackson had showered together. When Robson himself took the stand in May 2005, when he was twenty-two, he bluntly responded: "Nothing ever happened." Fourteen years later, Robson would recant his testimony on television: "Michael told me that I had to lie and that's what I did," said Robson in *Leaving Neverland*. "I lied."

Robson confirmed that he was only five years old when he went on stage to dance at a Jackson concert in Australia. He stood up for Jackson when he was first accused of abuse by Jordy Chandler in the early 1990s. The irony of Robson's attestation didn't become clear until years later, but he was a persuasive witness for the defense, steadfastly refuting all arguments about Jackson's inappropriate behavior. His testimony, as Kate Story put it, "changed the direction of the trial."

Over the next three months, dozens of witnesses were called to testify. These included showbusiness celebrities, the first of which was Macaulay Culkin who had visited Jackson's ranch, stayed with him and denied all suggestions that he had behaved improperly (he is godfather to Jackson's daughter, Paris). Years later in 2020, Culkin told *Esquire*'s Ryan D'Agostino, "He [Jackson] never did anything to me. I never *saw* him do anything. And especially at this flash point in time, I'd have no reason to hold anything back."

Culkin's and, indeed, Robson's evidence contrasted sharply with Arvizo's and his younger brother's: they claimed Jackson had masturbated in their presence and molested them many times. Jackson's defense pointed out inconsistencies in their accounts that there was no DNA evidence to link Jackson to the alleged abuses.

Perhaps the most surprising aspect of the defense's argument was its agreement that Jackson shared his bed with boys. Presumably, Mesereau thought this fact had been so well established, there was little point in denying it. What he denied was that any improper behavior transpired in bed. It was a stretch, but remember: everyone is presumed to be innocent and no one may be convicted of an offense unless each element of the offense is proved beyond a reasonable doubt. This was key in the Simpson case. Even if jurors think there is a good chance that someone indicted actually did the deed, they must consider whether there is room for uncertainty. In other words, Jackson may well have shared his bed with others, but the question was not "did he have sex with them?" It was, "might he not have?"

As if almost to remind the jury and everyone else watching that this was no ordinary trial with an ordinary defendant, Jackson, on March 9, decided not to appear in court. His attorney explained to Judge Melville that Jackson was at the hospital after complaining of back pain. Melville, perhaps sensing the first glimpse of grandstanding, threatened to issue a warrant for Jackson's arrest and forfeited bail. When Jackson arrived at court, he was wearing pajama pants and slippers.

*　*　*

The trial kept people guessing and the verdict kept them thinking. The jury of eight women and four men deliberated for seven days. At 2:12 p.m. on June 13, 2005, the clerk of the court began reading out the verdicts of "not guilty" of all ten counts. Whoops went up around the courtroom. Jackson turned to the jury and mouthed "Thank you." He looked frail and unwell as he reached for a tissue and wept as the clerk finished reading the verdicts. Thinner than he was at the start of the trial four months before, and nothing like the hale and healthy figure who had moonwalked on top of his SUV barely a year before. The court session lasted twenty minutes, after which Jackson walked free, greeted by screams and cheers by about a hundred fans outside the courthouse. Jackson blew a kiss and climbed into a waiting car. There was no showboating or celebratory speeches.

At forty-six, he remained a free man, cleared of all child molestation and conspiracy charges. The jury had considered the testimonies of 140 witnesses and 600 pieces of evidence. Had Jackson been convicted of all ten counts, he could have faced a minimum of three years and a maximum of eight years in prison on each count.

Later, there was a posttrial press conference at which jurors explained how crucial Janet Arvizo had been to their decision-making. Mesereau's strategy had proved a masterstroke. "She [Arvizo] never took her eyes off us," said one juror. "I was uncomfortable with that." When asked whether they accepted Mesereau's portrayal of the family as scam artists, one juror replied, "The thought was definitely there." Within months of the trial, prosecutors charged Janet Arvizo with fraud and perjury related to materials brought up during the trial. She faced more than seven years imprisonment for failing to disclose when applying for welfare that she'd been paid tens of thousands of dollars from a civil lawsuit. In 2006, she accepted a plea bargain, agreeing to pay more than $8,600 in restitution to Los Angeles County and perform 150 hours of community service.

Jury foreman, Paul Rodriguez, used the expression "very troubled" to describe how jurors felt about Jackson's overnight sleepovers with children in his bed. Mesereau, remember, had not denied that these took place. Jurors were instructed by the judge to base their verdicts on the facts of the case, not, as Rodriguez put it, "our beliefs or our own personal thoughts." While it wasn't germane to the trial, Rodriguez expressed the collective desire of the jury. "We would hope . . . that he doesn't sleep with children anymore," he told CNN News (June 15, 2005).

Twelve years after the trial in 2017, four of the twelve jurors reflected on the dynamics of the jury deliberations. Initially, the jury was split: nine choosing an acquittal, three convinced Jackson was guilty. While doubts about Janet Arvizo's credibility were uppermost in the minds of jurors in the immediate aftermath, the jurors assembled years later remembered how the child himself was an implausible victim. "He didn't seem as distraught as you would think somebody who'd been molested would be," recalled Paulina Coccoz. Another juror Melissa Herard asked fellow jurors to look closely at Arvizo's face: he seemed to be smirking (quoted by Chris Jancelewicz, of Global News).

Jackson's legal costs were never revealed but BBC's Matthew Davies estimated $5 million. Mesereau himself wouldn't have come cheap: $500 per hour, maybe more. Of course, Jackson's freedom was priceless. The case was evidence for critics of the US justice system who have argued for years that the ability of only the affluent to afford the best lawyers leads to systemic inequalities at law. Would someone facing Jackson's charges, but without the resources to find $5 million for a legal team have been able to construct such a sturdy and successful defense? The question remained hypothetical.

*   *   *

Jackson was not seen in public in the United States after climbing into the car that sped him away from the Santa Maria courtroom. Two weeks after the verdict, Jackson flew by private jet to Bahrain. His brother Jermaine had ties to the country's royal family after he and the king's son Sheikh Abdullah bin Hamad al-Khalifa made plans to release a family song. In fact Jermaine had visited much earlier in 1989 and had converted to Islam some time later. Details had been announced six months before. Within a month, reports were circulating that Jackson was the guest of senior figures in Bahrain and was buying a fourteen-acre property near the Sheikh's palace. There were other reports that Jackson was considering buying property in Berlin.

Mesereau confirmed that Jackson would not be returning to Neverland. "He's living permanently in Bahrain. He has friends there who have been very loyal and helpful to him in a difficult period of his life," Mesereau told the Los Angeles Times' Hector Becerra in October 2005. And news filtered out of Bahrain. "He [Jackson] is being accompanied in Bahrain by none other than his 20-year-old 'ward,' Omer Bhatti," reported Roger Friedman, of *Fox News* in August 2005. "Michael Jackson has officially announced that he has been following the five tenets of Islam and intends to convert to Islam, according to a report by on the website of Arab-Israeli newspaper *Panorama*," Rose Nahmias, of YNetNews.com divulged in October. "The Anti-Defamation League has demanded an apology from Michael Jackson after a US TV network aired what was said to be a telephone answering machine message in which the pop star referred to Jews as "leeches," the *Sydney Morning Herald* stated on November 24. "Jackson's family is planning to trip to Bahrain to stage a drug intervention. . . . The family is in a state of emergency. They consider it a life-or-death situation," reported UPI News Service via the *New York Daily News* on December 7. Toward the start of the trial, CNN's Jeffrey Toobin reckoned Jackson was "yesterday's news," but, after it, stories from the Mideast suggested anything but.

* * *

Can we take pleasure from the art of someone we know has committed deeds we find despicable and disgusting? And, even if that artist is legally innocent, can we ignore the grist of innuendo the rumor mill has ground out for two decades? Even if a jury of twelve peers sits, listens, and deliberates for seven days and returns a verdict of not guilty, does it necessarily follow that the accused hasn't transgressed and mistreated people, who, for various reasons, have chosen not to come forward? These were among the soul-searching questions the world had to ask when Jackson stood accused of sexual molestation in 2005.

Jackson wasn't the first pop or rock artist to force audiences to wrestle with the apparent paradox. In 1958, Jerry Lee Lewis arrived in England with a wife who also happened to be his thirteen-year-old cousin. In 1959, Chuck Berry was convicted of transporting a fourteen-year-old girl across state lines for "immoral purposes" and convicted under the Mann Act (originally intended to combat prostitution). He was sentenced to five years' imprisonment and given a $5,000 fine; the verdict was vacated because the judge made racist comments, but Berry was retried and ended up serving almost two years in prison. Led Zeppelin's Jimmy Page allegedly had a relationship with a fourteen-year-old girl in the early 1970s. For more than two decades from the early 1990s, R&B singer R. Kelly faced allegations of sexual abuse. Tupac Shakur and James Brown were both known to have assaulted their female partners.

Popular music and transgressive behavior have a history. Vandalism, violence, drugs use, sexual deviance, and ostentatious displays of wanton eccentricity: the rest of society may frown on most of these. But one or more of these is almost obligatory for any pop star who wants to make the cut. Audiences don't just forgive them their trespasses; they sometimes want them to trespass some more. Who would want Ozzy Osbourne to apologize for mutilating live animals and start campaigning for Peta?

Outside music but still in the entertainment industry Roman Polanski, Woody Allen, and Bill Cosby have been among the many men (they are always men) who have challenged audiences to answer whether artists can be separated from their art or whether their oeuvre is necessarily contaminated by their errant behavior. Time may be a factor: for example, the operatic legacy left by Richard Wagner (1813–83) remains so sacred that we often erase thoughts of his associations with Nazism.

When well-known, perhaps respected, even loved celebrities are accused of an egregious abuse of the power, privilege and advantage their status confers, we're all obliged to rethink: Can we ever appreciate their music, acting, or any other aspect of their performance again? Or will evocations of their misdeeds intrude on our sensitivity?

Once the most idolized pop star on the planet, Jackson was made to defend himself against the claim of a teenager whom he had befriended and accepted as a houseguest, but who later accused him of heinous acts. This made him more disorienting than any of the other transgressing artists. He played havoc with audiences' expectations. Jackson's alleged iniquities didn't involve vulnerable women or men, but children. There was no category for this: hugely successful pop singers with money and status to spare just didn't abuse children. Incredible as it seemed, there was enough evidence to get Jackson to court.

In sexual abuse cases, the odds are typically stacked against the accusers: they're notoriously difficult to prove because of the paucity of evidence. Frequently, they come down to a battle of credibility: Do jurors believe the accuser or the defendant? Jackson's trial was complicated because the boy he supposedly molested maintained friendly relations with him even after the alleged abuse. In a sense, argued his defense, Jackson was the victim. Counterbalancing this was the shadow of doubt that had been cast across Jackson for a number of years before.

Western systems of justice are ostensibly predicated on the principle that we are all innocent until proven guilty. That presumption of innocence has been a casualty of circumstance. Since the Harvey Weinstein exposé in 2017 and the #MeToo movement that followed, singers and other performers have been dropped, canceled, expunged, and replaced on the whiff of wrongdoing. Jackson was an innocent man and would remain that way until his death. At least, in a technical sense. Were his trial today, we all know what would happen, regardless of the verdict. An acquittal would make no difference. You can be sure you would never hear "Billie Jean" or any other Jackson nor even Jackson 5 song on public airwaves ever again.

Jackson's trial in 2005 may have changed the way some parts of his audience engaged with him. Those who grew up listening to albums like *Destiny* (1978), *Off the Wall* (1979), and *Thriller* (1982) would have probably recognized a familiar process: black man rises and achieves remarkable success in unlikely surroundings before malevolent powers combine with fate and lamentable decision-making to ravage him. For Michael Jackson, read O. J. Simpson or Mike Tyson. Every time an African American man steps into mainstream, he must be as prepared as Theseus in the labyrinth; at some point, he is going to run into the Minotaur. Some have beaten the monster. Jackson wasn't one of them.

For many, Jackson *was* the monster.

Two people on Jackson's hit list were Uri Geller, seen here on the right, and Rabbi Shmuley Boteach, on Jackson's right. But in 2001, they were all friends and assembled at the Oxford Debating Union, where Jackson appeared.

6

Through the Eyes of a Child

Hit lists are endlessly interesting. An inventory of people to be killed either for revenge, financial gain, or some other reason is one of those stock motifs in film and literature. From *Kind Hearts and Coronets*, Robert Hamer's 1949 classic about a poor relative of an English Duke who plots to inherit the title by murdering the eight other heirs who stand ahead of him in the line of succession, to Steven Spielberg's *Munich*, about a Mossad assassin's elimination of the five men responsible for the Munich massacre during the 1972 Olympics, hit lists have featured in film. Richard M. Nixon had an "opponents list," compiled by an aide charged with identifying the thirty-seventh president's most dangerous political enemies and how to "screw" them. The list was revealed during the Watergate hearings, which led to Nixon's resignation in 1974. Stuart Wood's *Hit List* (2020) is one of dozens of books bearing the same title and similar narratives: people keep getting bumped off because they have something in common.

What's this got to do with Michael Jackson? You may well ask. In 2003, it was revealed that he had his own hit list: twenty-five people he had earmarked as enemies, including David Geffen, owner of DGC Records in 1990 and DreamWorks Pictures, and the previously mentioned Spielberg, who apparently refused to give Jackson the role of Peter Pan in his 1991 film *Hook*. These and twenty-three other people who had, for various reasons, upset Jackson were cataloged for death. And it wasn't just a theoretical list. A ritual involving the slaughter of dozens of cows, sheep, and chickens; a witch doctor from Mali; and a mysterious Egyptian woman claiming links to the ruling elite of Saudi Arabia were involved in an effort to exterminate Jackson's adversaries.

Admittedly, the article in which this lurid story was disclosed appeared in the April 1, 2003, edition of *Vanity Fair*. But it was written by Maureen Orth, who had written several other serious pieces on Jackson and, on reflection, it was probably not the freakiest story about Jackson anyway.

Practically anything anyone could dream up about him was likely to be considered before either being rejected as hokum or conditionally accepted as within the realms of possibility. This was nearer to the latter. In the story, Jackson told his then business adviser, Myung-Ho Lee, to wire $150,000 to a bank in Mali for a voodoo chief named Baba, who then had forty-two cows ritually sacrificed for a ceremony. The execution of the constituent members of the hit list would then commence. The source of the weird tale remains unknown, though Orth wondered, "if Jackson is as crazy as he seems—or a cool manipulator of his own fame." (Whether Myung-Ho Lee executed the request is unlikely, particularly, as we'll discover later in the chapter he was heading for a major dispute with Jackson.)

Much of the rest of Orth's article seemed well grounded: Jackson was besieged by debt totaling $24 million and incapable of restricting himself to a manageable budget. This meant he spent about a million every month. Orth reported a $10,000 monthly debit from a Beverly Hills drug store. She quoted one of Jackson's maids who said he bleached his skin "because he does not like being black and he feels that blacks are not liked as much as people of other races." While this was part of an affidavit, we should take it as opinion and be aware that Jackson was diagnosed with vitiligo, a condition in which the skin's pigment is lost from some areas of the skin, leaving whitish patches, the condition often has no obvious cause.

Whether or not members of the hit list were marked for death is a matter of doubt, though the actual existence of a list of enemies seems certain. Jackson believed some people were out to destroy him. In addition to the Hollywood moguls, those people included Uri Geller, a self-proclaimed psychic who seemed to have telekinetic and possibly telepathic powers. Born in Israel, Geller became a prominent television and stage performer in the 1970s, suggesting his supposedly paranormal gifts were granted to him by extraterrestrials. The kind of man, you might imagine, who would appeal to Jackson. In fact, they were good friends for a while, Jackson being the best man at Geller's renewal of his wedding vows in 2001. Other people on the list included Thomas Sneddon who prosecuted Jackson at the 2005 trial, and Tommy Mottola, formerly chair of Sony Music Entertainment, whom I will come to in Chapter 7.

Jackson got to know Geller after calling Mohammed Al Fayed at his home in Sussex, England. The purpose of the call and the reason he knew Al Fayed—then owner of Harrod's of London—is not clear. But, according to Lynn Barber, of the *Observer*, Al Fayed said to Jackson, "Guess who I've got with me? Uri Geller" and Jackson asked to talk with him. Jackson suggested Geller, then famed for his parapsychic activities, stop by next time he was in the United States. When Geller visited Jackson, he was working on a new album and asked Geller to compose a meditation script that would calm him. Jackson later told Geller he'd met the Dalai Lama but remained unimpressed. Geller countered that he knew a man of god he'd like Jackson to meet. He was Rabbi Shmuley Boteach (later to appear on Jackson's hit list), co-author, with Geller, of *Confessions of a Rabbi and a Psychic*. The rabbi visited Jackson and took him to a synagogue in New York.

Boteach had an affiliation to Oxford University and invited Jackson to talk at the Oxford Union (the prestigious debating society with members mainly from University of Oxford). Jackson agreed and Geller seized the opportunity to procure his services as best man at the renewal of his wedding vows. Geller had married the same woman twice before, but this was to be a Jewish service. Jackson was a Jehovah's Witness. He arrived two hours late, on crutches. Some, like Barber, thought, "it looks like exploitation, to turn a wedding into a publicity stunt," though Geller claimed the money he received from magazines would go to sick children. Geller planned to take Jackson on a "peace mission" in the Middle East, though there is no evidence that this materialized. But Jackson warmed to Geller and the two men became friends; in fact, Geller became something of a confidante and adviser. So when British journalist Martin Bashir became interested in Jackson as a subject for a planned television documentary, he made Geller his first contact.

On Geller's account, Bashir sent him a private letter from Princess Diana in an effort to persuade him. Geller had known Jackson for five years. He would have been familiar with Bashir's acclaimed interview with Princess Diana in 1995. The letter presented to Geller would have presumably served as a recommendation; it was written to Bashir after the interview, which is still acknowledged as rehabilitating Diana's reputation; in it she claimed she was treated by the royal family as "unstable," suffering from an eating disorder, and afforded little scope for personal growth; she also talked about her loveless marriage. She emerged triumphant from the interview, though, years later, it was discovered that Bashir secured the precious interview by breaching journalists' guidelines—which might make skeptics wonder about the provenance of the letter.

Diana was a beautiful, yet lonely princess imprisoned in a loveless marriage with a prince, whose suspected infidelity with an older and less attractive woman was the talk of the court. Trapped and with no apparent escape route, she seemed defenseless against a powerful and uncaring royal family. Diana made an enchanting victim, a vision of mistreated womanhood smiling serenely at her millions of faithful followers. Her popularity seemed to grow in inverse proportion to that of her husband. Diana threw herself into charitable work and aligned herself with great causes, visiting people living with Aids, children in hospitals, and other groups, all of whom responded empathically. People from everywhere were drawn to Diana, who seemed somehow to speak for everyone—even when she was silent.

In one way, Diana personified glamor, elegance, and dignity; in another she captured a culture of misogyny in which abuse of women was not necessarily visible, nor restricted to one social class: any woman, no matter how privileged, was susceptible to cruel and painful treatment. Gaslit into thinking her best course of action was to maintain dignity and keep her composure, Diana took a calculated risk and colluded with the media, the same media that had both elevated and tormented her. So, when she talked to Bashir, she was a princess, but no fairytale princess. Diana had married Prince Charles in 1981. She was divorced in 1996, the year before her death. Her interview with Bashir birthed the now-famous line, "there were three of us in this marriage."

If Jackson allowed Geller to convince him that Bashir could present him in a way that evoked empathy—and I'm using the word properly: an ability to understand and share feelings—he was deluded. Quite unlike Diana, who could, when the occasion demanded, present herself as an Everywoman, Jackson had few properties, affairs, foibles, or circumstances to which others could relate. His autocratic father and turbulent childhood was a start, but, in adulthood, he grew more remote. It might have been different if he'd been spurned by a heartless lover, or even indulged in nasty habits, as Whitney had done. Viewers might then have felt sympathy for or identified with him. But how could they connect with someone who insulated himself inside a gigantic children's playground complete with oxygen tent and pet chimpanzee and chilled out, not with the likes of Beyoncé or Halle Berry, but teenage boys? And who surrounded himself with sycophants masquerading as friends? Even Diana had friends, like Rosa Monckton, who were prepared to warn her when they felt she was being exploited.

Diana's metamorphosis from a publicly humiliated object of pity into the beloved spirit of the 1990s was helped dramatically by her conversation with Bashir. Jackson, however, needed different sorcery.

*   *   *

Bashir was a Londoner with Pakistani parents. He worked for BBC on documentaries before the celebrated interview with Diana. In 1999, he moved to the UK's principal commercial channel ITV. After that, his status was such that he could cherry-pick his interviewees: he was the only journalist to interview the au pair Louise Woodward, found guilty of the involuntary manslaughter of a baby in Boston, for example. Jackson rarely gave interviews, so Geller must have convinced him of the value of a one-on-one with Bashir; there were in fact a series of interviews. In addition, Bashir was allowed to take a camera crew into Neverland and the shooting took place over eight months. Jackson was forty-four at the time, Bashir thirty-nine. Geller told Louis Theroux, another British journalist seeking an interview to Jackson, that he favored Bashir over him. He also told Theroux that David Frost wanted to interview Jackson. Geller was speaking in *Louis, Martin & Michael*, a 2003 documentary on BBC television (details in the bibliography).

Geller must have presented a compelling case: Bashir was granted permission to start filming in April 2002. The documentary *Living with Michael Jackson* aired in February 2003. Uri Geller was thanked in the closing credits.

Years later in 2013, Rabbi Boteach added a prologue. "One of Mr. Bashir's producers had initially contacted me in about 2000 to pitch a documentary about Michael's life," he wrote for *Observer Media*. Boteach presented Jackson the kind of wisdom a security adviser might offer a racehorse owner the day after a Kentucky Derby favorite has bolted through an open door: "Your life's not ready to be opened to the public." The documentary went ahead, anyway. According to Boteach, "Mr Bashir had gone through a different friend of Michael's who had introduced the two and a deal was made." Geller was, presumably, the "different friend." Boteach remained critical of Bashir, whose "intention was to enhance his own reputation by burying Michael's." Or so Boteach suspected. "A weird Michael Jackson was going to be a lot more saleable than a mostly normal yet highly eccentric performer." How come Geller didn't know this? After all, he claimed psychic powers.

History might have been different had Jackson heard about the fraudulent means Bashir employed to procure his career-defining interview with Diana. In 1996, the Diana interview was investigated internally by BBC, which found Bashir had commissioned fake statements. His action was a lapse and nothing more, it concluded. On the twenty-fifth anniversary of the interview, BBC launched a fresh enquiry, which decided Bashir was "unreliable," "devious," and "dishonest." Had Jackson known this, the chances of his agreeing to what became a pivotal event in his destruction would have been remote.

That's supposition. In actuality, the Jackson/Bashir interview went ahead and the tv program itself was either a tour-de-force or a calamity, depending on perspective. It commanded huge viewing audiences and press coverage to rival the 1977 miniseries *Roots*, which was one of the most discussed tv shows in history (based on Alex Haley's novel). As an exposé—a report of something discreditable—it worked like a charm; as a reputation-embellishing portrait, it worked like a curse.

"I felt he wasn't being entirely honest," confessed Bashir—with a straight face, I presume—in voiceover after Jackson had denied stories about his extensive and heroic plastic surgery over the years. Was Jackson being honest about anything? From the outset of the documentary *Living with Michael Jackson*, Bashir appeared to have struck up an amiable relationship with his subject: they were seen chatting, dancing, and driving dodgem cars at Neverland. The ranch appeared as a wonderworld—for a child. But what attractions did it hold for a grown man. Jackson explained: "I am Peter Pan. I'm Peter Pan in my heart." Peter Pan is the name of J. M. Barrie's 1940 play about the eponymous boy with magical powers who never grew up and who lives in Neverland. "Peter Pan represents something that's very special in my heart. Youth, childhood, never growing up, magic, flying, everything that I think children in wonderment and magic is what it's all about." (Readers might ponder whether there's a difference between "never growing up" and never being willing to grow up.)

Bashir's gentle probing elicited less-than-shocking responses, at least initially. By 2005, most people suspected Jackson was a kind of manchild, an adult, who by default or design remained in a relatively immature state of mind, with commensurate tastes and sensibilities. His prodigious ability in music and dance made him appear a savant—someone with an extraordinary "island of genius," that contrasted with an overall disability. Jackson pulled this apparent incongruity together by showing Bashir his "giving tree," which he climbed. "I've been writing so many of my songs in this tree," said Jackson, as if the tree was his inspiration. Maybe it was. Or maybe he was playing with Bashir.

The camera followed Jackson to an antique store where he jabbed his finger seemingly, buying items indiscriminately. These included a gold chess set at $80,000. Again, the oddities fitted the popular conception: Jackson's Caligula-like extravagance was as well known as his eccentricities; in fact, they were part of the same thing. Why would he want a gold chess set? Did he even play chess? The spree ended up costing Jackson an estimated $6 million. Again, he could have been having fun by showing off to Bashir.

The subject of transmogrification came and went without resolution: Bashir asked about his talked-about plastic surgery and apparent attempt to look like someone else and Jackson just refused to get drawn beyond a denial. Bashir may not have believed him. But Jackson would not relent and, despite Bashir's obvious interest in this aspect of Jackson, there was little if any enlightenment.

When the subject of Jackson's interest in children came up, it must have struck most viewers as if someone was describing how they'd committed a heinous offense without even a hazy awareness of why their behavior was considered odious by others, nor even that it was a violation of what's considered right or natural. "Why can't you share your bed? That's the most loving thing to do, to share your bed with someone," asked Jackson rhetorically. Except that the question was far from rhetorical: he might have asked it to engender agreement from viewers, but, if so, he betrayed a staggering disconnect. Jackson had seemingly broken away from the conception of reality shared by mostly everyone else.

So when Jackson pronounced, "I would never harm any child," viewers were probably left wondering, "What does he mean by 'harm'? Deliberately inflicted physical injury? Material damage to a human being? Because, if so, Jackson is not mature nor sophisticated enough to realize that harm can be invisible: it can mean potential ill effects that are not immediately available to the senses and manifest years later. That's also harm. Or was he just lying, as he might have been about plastic surgery?"

While Jackson described his relationship with a thirteen-year-old Gavin Arvizo as "not sexual," footage of them holding hands seemed to suggest something different. Or did they? "Kids want to be loved, they want to be touched, they want to be held," said Jackson who also disclosed that he sometimes slept on the floor while giving the children his bed, describing this arrangement as a "beautiful thing." This was arguably the most astonishing, perplexing, and incriminating passage of the documentary. Jackson's disclosures were "alarming," wrote Rupert Smith of the *Guardian*. The 14 million viewers in the United Kingdom and 38 million in the United States must have gasped as they would if watching someone put their head in a lion's mouth, having interrupted the king of beasts during mating season.

But was it so astonishing, considering this was Jackson, who lived in an almost make-believe world at Neverland, and, according to media reports, was berserk with idiosyncrasies? And was it really so perplexing given his limitless appetite for publicity and his proficiency in, to use Orth's term, manipulating his own fame—and, in this instance, infamy. A well-chosen phrase such as this was almost guaranteed to make it into the news. If that was Jackson's motive, then the admission becomes more intelligible. And, as for incriminating, well, as subsequent events proved: it wasn't.

* * *

Living with Michael Jackson was broadcast on Britain's ITV channel on Monday, February 3, 2003. The documentary's US transmission was three days later and US media were given previews. In contrast to the British media reaction, which was mostly critical of Jackson, American reviewers savaged Bashir. Alessandro Stanley, of the *New York Times,* for example, considered Jackson "creepy, but almost touching in his delusional naïveté: a victim of an abusive father, of his own psyche and also of his interviewer's callous self-interest masked as sympathy." *USA Today* thought Bashir's interview approach "unduly intrusive." This was 2003, remember.

By Friday, Jackson's lawyers had lodged an official complaint to the independent television commission (ITC) and the broadcasting standards commission (BSC), claiming Jackson had been "unfairly treated" and had his privacy infringed, even though Jackson himself had granted Bashir unusually open access. Voiceovers, editing, and the questions raised sought "to infer sexual impropriety," according to the complaint. Jackson's lawyers argued that there was "clear innuendo." It sounded like carping in 2003. In 2021, it would have sounded much more like legitimate grievance, given the remodeling of Bashir's reputation.

"Michael is a controversial figure with many critics. It's not surprising that a film about him, which is open and revealing, draws some hostile reaction and comment about him," announced the program's producers Granada Television, which sold the show to the ITV network, adding, "It's regrettable that Michael should feel devastated as a result of that, but perhaps inevitable" (as reported by Jason Deans of the *Guardian* on February 6, 2003).

Legal proceedings against Granada, alleging breach of contracts, were initiated. Jackson's lawyers also sought to ban Granada from cashing in on additional footage it held. Three days after legal action was mounted, Granada agreed not to show any unseen footage until a ruling. (Although Granada approached an out-of-court settlement with Jackson's company, MJJ Productions Inc., the case was put on hold when Jackson was arrested.)

Jackson prepared a video statement in which he explained: "Martin Bashir persuaded me to trust him that his would be an honest and fair portrayal of my life, and told me he was 'the man that turned Diana's life around'." And, in what seemed an act of retaliation, Jackson sold footage of himself shot by one of his own cameras and featuring himself and Bashir chatting. Fox in the United States and Sky in the United Kingdom were both controlled by media mogul Rupert Murdoch at the time. While Jackson had not charged Granada, he took $2 million for the footage, which was then turned into a program called *The Michael Jackson Interview: The Footage You Were Never Meant to See* and shown on Murdoch's channels. Fox insisted that, while it had access to his footage, Jackson had no editorial control over the show.

Jeff Anderson, Granada's controller of current affairs, told David Lister of the *Independent*: "We have made this [the Bashir] film entirely on our own terms. No money has been paid and no areas of the singer's career or personal life have been off- limits." This meant that the Fox money was Jackson's sole remuneration for the exercise, an exercise which, of course, proved to be the most self-destructive of his professional life.

Bashir's glimpse into Jackson's soul was scary: he not only disclosed the immature man everyone thought they knew and many knew they loved but also showed an unfamiliar and somewhat sinister eccentric barely perceptible as the smooth artist who had charmed the world for over twenty years. Bashir's obliquely understated exploration showed Jackson stuck tormentedly between fame and privacy, known to millions as a superstar, but suspected of harboring secrets. Now those secrets were a matter of public record. Jackson may have objected to the style of his portrayal, the light in which he had been seen, but there was no denying it was him. He wasn't just playing a creep: he genuinely came across as creepy.

Watching a grown man holding a child's hand and talking, without the slightest recognition of his own wrongdoing, about sleeping with him, challenged the most open minds to harmonize the conflict. Even if he felt intimate and affectionate yet—as he repeatedly stressed—nonsexual bonds with young boys, how could he not realize how incredulous the world would be when he spoke about it? And, if he were using platonic friendships as a ruse to camouflage his predilections, how could he think anybody would believe him? The responses ranged from "No Michael, keep your feelings to yourself 'cause no one will understand" to "Does this sicko think anybody is buying any of this?" Not many would have thought, "This just isn't true."

"What we saw later in Bashir's film was frightening and surreal," wrote Roger Friedman, of Fox News on February 7, 2003, "How can California authorities not investigate this situation?" As we now know, they did exactly that.

Bashir was inundated with hate mail and pulled out of an engagement to present an award at the Brits, the British Phonographic Industry's annual popular music awards in London. Some fellow artists attacked Bashir. Justin Timberlake, for example, "That guy is despicable. He had better keep out of my way. Michael is a really nice guy who looks at the world through the eyes of a child" (in the *Sydney Morning Herald*, February 21, 2003).

While some American reviewers assailed Bashir, ABC tv was impressed enough with his work to offer him a job as a reporter on its *Nightline* show. In 2008, he was suspended after describing some of the participants at an Asian American journalists' convention in Chicago as "Asian babes." He apologized for what he called his "tasteless remark." Two years later, he joined MSNBC. He criticized presidential candidate Sarah Palin as "America's dunce," and a "world class idiot." Palin bizarrely compared the United States' federal debt to slavery and, in response, Bashir suggested Palin should endure the treatment of slaves, including having someone defecate in her mouth. Bashir resigned from MSNBC in 2013. In 2016, Bashir returned to the BBC as a religious affairs correspondence. While known as a journalist, Bashir also harbored aspirations to be a singer. In 2010, he released an album of reggae tunes called *Bass Lion*. And, in 2019, he appeared on the British *The X Factor*, but was eliminated. He resigned from the BBC in 2021.

Geller, who, on his own account, was instrumental in making the program happen, was not excused by Jackson. "My friendship toward him still stands, but I think that his friendship towards me tarnished a little bit," Geller told MTV News' Jennifer Vineyard on November 26, 2003. "It is impossible for me to believe Michael would abuse a child with cancer. And I would be shocked to the core, my belief system will be shattered." Geller is a psychic, remember. Whether Jackson ever spoke to him again is doubtful. As I wrote earlier, Geller together with his spiritual guide Boteach apparently ended up on Jackson's hit list.

As for Rabbi Boteach, he ended up on the hit list though, it seems, he absolved himself for the collateral damage. In 2019, Jordan Hoffman for the *Times of Israel* interviewed him. "A very charismatic and sharp fella," thought Hoffman. "His website claims that he is "America's Rabbi" and his bio reminds readers that he was, at one time, a spiritual leader to Michael Jackson. Should we credit him for not obscuring past truths, or is this just an incredibly tone-deaf boast?" Boteach hosted radio shows and wrote on spiritual matters.

*   *   *

"Society's fascination with Michael Jackson may be unhealthy, but it is hardly baffling. Like junk bonds or fen-phen, Mr. Jackson is one of those phenomena that seem destined to be yanked from the public at any minute but are irresistible while they last," wrote Alessandra Stanley of the *New York Times*, summoning comparisons between public attractions to highrisk methods of making plenty of money quickly (junk bonds) and for losing weight, again quickly (fen-phen was a dieting concoction popular in the 2000s). Stanley made the legitimate point that "most celebrities have at least one disgrace that can win them a spot on a television magazine show."

She was writing in 2003, just after the Bashir documentary's transmission and a few months after 21.3 million television viewers watched Whitney Houston tell Diane Sawyer about her drug preferences. Stanley had no access to a crystal ball, so couldn't see how Houston's life would spiral downward until her death eight years later; nor could she have foreseen how the one-disgrace allowance wouldn't work for Jackson. He would be charged with child molestation in December, ten months after the *Living with Michael Jackson* documentary first aired.

In between, as Stanley claimed, society's fascination with Jackson, however unhealthy she believed it was, continued. As often happens, when the media scents shifts in popular tastes, it both reflects and shapes them. Crudely put, the shift was from appreciating Jackson's artistry to denouncing his predilections. So news about his misfortunes and tribulations was likely to make it into the media. Four months after the television documentary's transmission, reports filtered out that Jackson and his former financial manager Myung-Ho Lee settled their $12 million breach-of-contract lawsuit. It was a confidential agreement and, as such, put the lid on any possibility that Jackson's current financial state would be exposed in court.

As we saw in Chapter 4, Myung-Ho Lee described Jackson as a "ticking time bomb waiting to explode" in court papers. In his suit, Myung-Ho Lee submitted that Jackson had appointed him in 1998 to put his finances in good order. Consider the irony. Part of Lee's advice was to curb his reckless spending. He also revealed that, instead of heeding his advice, Jackson relied instead on the counsel of "charlatans" and "hucksters." He didn't mention names.

As the settlement notice was being filed in an LA court, Jackson was in his birthplace, Gary, Indiana, where thousands of fans watched his multi-vehicle motorcade to the City Hall, where he received the keys to the city. Reports also suggested that he visited his former high school to receive an honorary award. It seemed so Jackson-like to be basking in glory, seemingly oblivious to the adversity that was engulfing him. Perhaps he'd become anesthetized to trouble: by some accounts, he'd received around 1,500 lawsuits during his near-four decades in showbusiness. He shrugged many of them off. As Duncan Campbell and Tania Branigan detected in May 2003: "Many of the lawsuits have been brought by people who know that sometimes it is simpler and cheaper to settle an action than go through the long and publicity-fuelled process of fighting it in court."

Intuitively, you might think that, as a celebrity becomes more successful, their status strengthens and the lawsuits would multiply. But, as Campbell and Branigan pointed out, "The more vulnerable someone seems in the public eye, the more allegations and lawsuits they tend to attract." Jackson, in mid-2003, was at his most vulnerable. Stricken by allegations, condemned by many sections of the media and their audiences and, if the new contention was to be believed, heading full tilt toward bankruptcy. And, even then, all these seemed mere stumbling blocks when compared to the problem that lay ahead.

Hailed by some as a messianic leader, derided by others as a crass opportunist who appealed to base prejudices, the Reverend Al Sharpton was an undeniably effective orator who espoused the cause of black Americans. In July 2002, Jackson recruited his support when accusing record companies of racism.

7

With Walt Disney or Michelangelo

No other celebrity in the modern age attracted more newsprint, airtime, or memes than Jackson. Elizabeth Taylor might have edged him earlier in the twentieth century and Kim Kardashian would depose him in recent years. But, in the years either side of the millennium, Jackson was peerless. Where there wasn't a new best-selling album or concert tour, there was some sort of rumor about nose jobs, pet chimps, oxygen chambers, or surrogate mothers. And where there wasn't an actual real-life event worth reporting, there were stories, real or imaginary. Jackson rarely denied them either. He was very much a creator of his own ever-enlarging legend.

Jackson's life was probably less dramatic than everyone supposed. But he must have known how the world devoured tittle-tattle about him. By the end of the twentieth century, Jackson wasn't a star in the traditional sense: he was a media spectacle. So when sales of his albums slid from the record-breaking heights of the 1980s and 1990s, he knew his accidental career diversification offered a way to sustain his legend. So, there was never a denial of a report that seeped out of New York and gradually to the rest of the world that typified Jackson's unfathomable life and which, to no one's surprise, was never confirmed nor refuted.

It started on September 7, 2001. The audience filled New York's Madison Square Garden, paying up to $2,500 a ticket to see Jackson's first performances since 1989 in the continental United States (his world tour included Hawaii in 1997). It was nominally thirty years after he separated from his brothers to make his first solo single, so it was billed as a "30th Anniversary Celebration." More on this shortly.

The day after the second performance, the cataclysmic attacks on New York's World Trade Center ignited widespread panic in the city. There was also a lockdown on all flights, meaning no passengers could fly in or out of New York City. Jackson considered an evacuation via a private plane, but even this was grounded. He, Elizabeth Taylor, and Marlon Brando were all intent on heading west to the presumed safety of their California homes. Tim Mendelson, Taylor's former personal assistant, told *Vanity Fair*'s Sam Kashner how the three improvised by renting a car. They dispensed with their usual luggage and personal assistants, squeezed into the rental car and headed 500 miles west to Ohio where they boarded a plane. It isn't clear who was behind the wheel, or whether they took turns.

Brando, then seventy-seven, and at his most corpulent; Jackson, straight from his concerts, probably exhausted and possibly self-medicating; and Taylor, no doubt discomforted by having to travel in something other than a private jet or the backseat of a Rolls-Royce. Brando, on Mendelson's account, aggravated his fellow riders by intermittently stalling at KFCs and other fast food outlets. It is a delicious story and one that intuitively everybody wants to believe.

All the same, Dan P. Lee of *New York* magazine in 2011 quoted Brando's lawyer: "That story's all bullshit." He suggests instead: "Like everyone else, the three indeed found themselves temporarily stranded in Manhattan. Taylor evidently decided to stay on, busying herself with charity work, while Brando and Jackson flew later, separately, on private jets to Los Angeles."

Kashner also pours cold water on the tale, quoting an anonymous aide of Taylor's who reckoned she did not join her two companions and instead went to church and then to Ground Zero, where she talked to reporters. This is a more plausible rendition of events, or at least it would be were there any newspaper stories to corroborate it. It is difficult to imagine any editor spiking a story on Elizabeth Taylor's impromptu visit to the scene of the catastrophe in the aftermath of 9/11. The apocryphal story, like so many other Jackson stories, became part of the folklore that surrounds him; exactly the same could be said about Taylor; and, to a more limited extent, Brando.

"It was during and after the crisis that Elizabeth's relationship with Michael—whom she already adored—deepened," wrote Kashner, who added an aperçu about Taylor's regular visits to the Neverland ranch. Jackson had hosted her wedding in 1991. Taylor learned that Brando's son Miko, who worked as a bodyguard for Jackson, was rounding up children for sleepovers at the ranch. "She knew it wasn't right," wrote Kashner. "Even if they *were* the innocent little sleepovers Michael claimed, he was still on dangerous ground."

It was a strange and implausible story, but one which kept people agreeably occupied, if only for the images it evoked. And the story had legs. Fifteen years later, Sky TV decided to dramatize the event for a television movie. The casting director's choice for the role of Michael Jackson was Joseph Fiennes. Fiennes had played celebrated artists before: he'd portrayed the Bard in the film *Shakespeare in Love*. Shakespeare was, of course, a white man. As was Fiennes. Stockard Channing played Taylor and Brian Cox Brando. "We were casting Michael Jackson in 2001 and that obviously is a challenge in terms of the physical resemblance," director Ben Palmer told Hannah Ellis-Petersen. But the decision to cast a white man as Jackson even in a film based on supposed rather than factual events meant that the tale, like Jackson, would take on an afterlife. The series in which the drama featured was called *Urban Myths*.

Many cited Jackson's own reaction to the possibility that a white actor could portray him: in 1993, he'd been asked by Oprah if it was true that he wanted a white child actor to play him in a tv advertisement. Jackson answered, "It's the most ridiculous, horrifying story I've ever heard." Indignant at the suggestion, he asked Oprah, "Why would I want a white child to play me? I'm a black American. I'm proud to be a black American. I'm proud of my race. I'm proud of who I am." It was an untypical outburst from Jackson. But his view was shared by his daughter Paris who said the prospect of having a white actor play her father "makes me want to vomit" (quoted by Roison O'Connor, of the *Independent*, January 16, 2017).

* * *

Invincible. What did it mean? That Jackson was too powerful for the massed forces of the media that, as he saw it, wanted to finish him? Or that he was invulnerable to the endless gossip and cruel innuendo that seemed to follow him? Or that he was just going through a lull in a showbusiness career that was so far unrivaled and, given historic record sales, was unlikely ever to be matched. Or could it have meant that at forty, Jackson wanted to remind the world he was still around and had an indomitable will to climb back to the top? Whatever it meant, it was the title of one of the most expensively produced records ever. *Invincible* was reported to have cost $30 million. Jackson spent five years making his first entirely new album since 1995's *HIStory: Past, Present and Future*, which had been poorly received.

Due for release in October 2001, Jackson even teamed up with his brothers to promote it. He hadn't performed as part of the group in sixteen years, during which time he'd shown no interest at all in anything but his solo career. The immodestly title Tribute to Michael Jackson concert— well, there were two, actually—was at New York City's Madison Square Garden. Among the audience were Muhammad Ali, Sean Connery, and Marlon Brando, with whom Jackson was to feature in an apocryphal but unforgettable story, of course. The lineup of artists included Eminem and Destiny's Child led by Beyoncé.

Jackson probably had one eye on Elvis Presley's '68 Comeback Special: this was an NBC television concert that heralded Presley's return to theatrical performances after a fallow period of seven years, in which he appeared only in nondescript movies. A soundtrack of the fifty-minute concert, officially known as *Elvis*, was released on record and became a best seller. Presley was thirty-three and went on to enjoy a renaissance until his death almost nine years later. The concert revitalized Elvis's career by introducing him to a new audience. The following year, he took a four-week residence in Las Vegas. Many thought he might not be able to deliver onstage over a sustained spell, but he did exactly that. Jackson's association with the Presley family was through Elvis's daughter Lisa Marie, to whom he was married for two years from 1994. Over the next 7 years, Elvis performed over 600 shows in Las Vegas.

Jackson's other eye might have been on Madonna who, in the 1980s, vied with him as the world's preeminent pop star and who, not coincidentally, was also never far from a scandal. In her case, the scandal always seemed to owe more to design than accident. Jackson's scandals were like multiple collisions. Whereas Jackson had foundered, Madonna had made a stately transcendence into the 1990s, hand-picking the world's most current producers and writers and refreshing her music for each succeeding generation. She's still doing it, of course. Also, Madonna, like a bullfighter, felt kinship with her audiences. She barely stopped touring. Unlike Jackson, who practically vanished in a vapor trail, leaving fans with videos, which were admittedly brilliant, but no naked exposure on stage. Until September 2001.

The show was described as Jackson's "30th Anniversary Celebration," this marking thirty years (nominally) since he split from his brothers to make his first solo single. It wasn't a concert, at least not in the conventional sense: it was, like Elvis's comeback, a television special, with long breaks between songs and video montage. Before the show, Jackson walked among his audience, his face concealed by a scarf, surrounded by bodyguards. An hour later he appeared again, this time to watch others such as Whitney Houston, Liza Minnelli, and Usher perform his songs in tribute. There were videos and encomiums from the likes of Chris Tucker, Samuel L. Jackson, and Elizabeth Taylor, who described Jackson as "my closest friend." Taylor herself had not been on stage since her appearance in the Noël Coward play *Private Lives* in 1991. Brando sat onstage in an armchair and delivered a puzzling lecture about "children hacked to death by a machete." There was a second performance on September 10. The timing was less-than-perfect.

When Jackson sang, "his voice was shaky and faltered repeatedly," according to the *New York Times* review. Jackson's "combination of superhuman skills and vulnerability endeared him to the world in the 1980's, and even his rising bitterness and tabloid headlines in the 1990's have not entirely erased the sympathy he seems to crave," discerned Jon Pareles. But was Jackson really yearning for sympathy? Couldn't he just have been promoting an album and faced, with a paucity of well-rehearsed material, resorted to padding out a few live numbers with guest appearances?

Alexis Petridis speculated that there was a subtext to the *Invincible* album. Jackson, he believed, was "an utterly unique figure" even in the hyper-transgressive environment of popular music where oddities are the norm rather than the exception. By 2001, he had ceased to be just a hugely successful and fabulously wealthy oddball "and become a rather sinister, twilit figure." Petridis thought that Jackson had, at this point, realized his public image was out of control. "Almost every aspect of Invincible stresses that—despite all evidence to the contrary—Michael Jackson is just a normal guy."

Petridis corroborates his argument by noting that six (of sixteen) tracks had input from producer du jour Rodney Jerkins, who had risen fame for his work with Whitney Houston and Mary J. Blige among others. "His very presence attempts to recontextualise Jackson," reasoned Petridis. "Instead of soul music's own Citizen Kane, closeted in his Neverland mansion, Jackson is merely another R&B singer queuing for Jerkins's magic touch." On this account, Jackson was trying to normalize himself through his music. For Petridis this proved to be his undoing: the music was "utterly anodyne," with no track remotely approaching the levels of Jackson's previous work.

Rolling Stone's James Hunter was in broad agreement and no more enthusiastic. The listener, wrote Hunter, is "placed squarely in Michael Jacksonland, a bizarre place where every sparkling street is computer-generated, every edifice is larger than life and every song is full of grandiose desperation."

* * *

Invincible was released on October 30 and entered the *Billboard* chart at number one, with sales of 366,000. This was only slightly less than sales of his previous album *HIStory*, when it was released in 1995. But the album's initial success faded quickly and it dropped out of the top ten after only four weeks. Even the New York concerts, which were shown as a two-hour CBS special, didn't translate into sales. Yet 25.6 million viewers watched the tv show, suggesting that Jackson's appeal was still very active. After three decades as a solo artist, "Jackson remains an object of fascination," wrote Edna Gundersen, of *USA Today*, who interviewed Jackson in the weeks following the concerts.

"How do you respond to inaccurate articles about you?" asked Gundersen. To which Jackson replied predictably, though probably not candidly, "I don't pay any attention." Gundersen pressed further. "Do these rumors persist because you don't refute them?" "No," said Jackson. "[The media] tend to want to twist what you say and judge you.... If I could stand face to face with Walt Disney or Michelangelo, would I care what they do in their private life? I want to know about their art."

It was an enlightening answer and not just because it revealed where on the pantheon Jackson thought he stood (between the creator of Mickey Mouse and the decorator of Sistine Chapel's ceiling). Jackson hadn't grasped how, in the late twentieth century, audience sensibilities had changed dramatically and the private lives he spoke of were actually not private at all. If we traveled along a time/space warp and took today's audience to the early twentieth or sixteenth centuries, they would want to know whether Disney dabbled in cryogenics and whether that church ceiling in Rome filled with images of naked men embodied the leading figure of the High Renaissance's sexual identity as well as his admiration of male beauty.

Asked how he was able to "shield" himself from the criticism, Jackson solved the problem I set earlier. "Expecting it, knowing it's going to happen and being invincible, being what I was always taught to be. You stand strong with an iron fist, no matter what the situation." Perhaps his father Joe's strongarm parenting equipped him well in the long run.

It's hard to believe Jackson, an arch manipulator of the media who had been brought up in the public gaze and learnt to survive and prosper in the unforgiving environment of showbusiness, was unaware of the demands of modern audiences. It's doubtful if anyone in or out of showbusiness failed to hear the chimes. When Neal Gabler wrote in 2009, a "celebrity is a celebrity only so long as he or she is living out an interesting narrative, or at least one the media find interesting," he might have had Jackson in mind. Jackson was a performer par excellence, but his music alone wasn't the reason for his longevity in entertainment: audiences found his personal activities spellbinding long after they'd grown tired of his music. Not that *Invincible* was a flop: it was Jackson's fastest-ever selling album, moving units more quickly than even *Thriller*. By 2020, it had sold over 13 million copies globally. The first single from the album was "You Rock My World" and this was a top ten success, spending twenty weeks in the *Billboard* Hot 100 chart. It was to be Jackson's last album of new material during his lifetime and became one of the most notable recordings. Again, not because of music alone.

"*Invincible* is just as good or better than *Thriller*, in my true, humble opinion," Jackson told Edna Gundersen. He considered his album artistically on par with *Thriller* and expected sales to be commensurate. In Jackson's eyes, it was a classic. "When *The Nutcracker Suite* was first introduced to the world, it totally bombed." There is truth in this: critics didn't rhapsodize over Tchaikovsky's ballet when it opened in St Petersburg in 1892; appreciation came over time.

When it became clear that the album wouldn't reach the commercial heights of the other two, Jackson questioned the record label rather than his own material. Initially, he argued that Sony had not put enough effort into promoting the album. In addition to the cost of making the album ($30 million), Sony committed $25 million to promoting it. Two more singles were spun off the album and there was a video of "You Rock My World." Artists typically arrange concert tours to coincide with the release of an album and boost sales. Jackson did not; his televised New York gigs were his contribution. Disappointed with the initial sales of the album, Jackson blamed Sony. Absolutely not himself. In response to Gundersen's query, "Did you have doubts about your current relevance?" Jackson snapped,

"Never. I have confidence in my abilities. I have real perseverance. Nothing can stop me when I put my mind to it."

He then broadened the critique. "The recording companies really, really do conspire against the artists—they steal, they cheat, they do everything they can," claimed Jackson. It was an unusual, even unprecedented evaluation. Jackson left Motown in 1977, but largely because his father sensed the company wasn't realizing the Jackson 5's potential. Motown was owned by Berry Gordy, himself an African American. The chief executive of Sony Music was Tommy Mottola, a white man.

* * *

On July 6, 2002, Reverend Al Sharpton addressed a gathering of his organization, the National Action Network, in Harlem. His theme was record companies, which, he declared, were wracked with injustice. Sammy Davis Jr. died broke, he told his audience. James Brown and Little Richard were also exploited. The pattern in the music industry reflected that of the rest of society. It was vintage Sharpton, a preacher from the age of four, ordained at nine and a lifelong activist who campaigned on practically any issue in which he believed racism was present. Hailed by some as a messianic leader, derided by others as a crass opportunist who appealed to base prejudices, Sharpton was an undeniably effective orator who espoused the cause of black Americans. As such, he was a thorn in the side of every political party, corporation, or individual who was or even just appeared unfriendly to African Americans. (Sammy Davis Jr. died of throat cancer in 1990; his estate was valued at over $4 million, though he left a tax debt of nearly $5 million that, with interest and penalties, came to $7 million. He had signed recording contracts on less than favorable terms).

It wasn't Sharpton's first encounter with Jackson. "I worked closely with the Jackson family on the Victory Tour in 1984," he wrote in his book *The Rejected Stone: Al Sharpton & the Path to American Leadership*. "I heard that some of the black concert promoters who had invested in the Jacksons earlier in their careers couldn't get any dates on the tour." He appealed to the family. The family retained him as a community affairs director for a $500,000 fee, according to Eric Fettmann. "After the tour, Michael and I became very close friends. He leaned on me for counsel, for spiritual guidance, and for friendship," wrote Sharpton.

Jackson had no history of engagement with political causes. Not that he was detached from the big humanitarian issues of the late twentieth century. But he wasn't a natural confederate of the firebrand Sharpton. But, standing alongside the reverend on the podium, Jackson seemed to harden. "Throughout the years, black artists have been taken advantage-of," announced Jackson, "these artists are always on tour because if they stopped touring, they'd go broke." Jackson pulled no punches and, if the audience thought this was un-

Jackson-like, they had another shock when Jackson weighed-in with, "When you fight for me, you're fighting for all black people. Dead and alive."

African Americans had probably waited for years, perhaps decades, to hear Jackson, the evidently born-again black man, align himself with black people. Or more accurately enjoin black people to align themselves with him. It was hard to picture him as a smoldering civil rights hero. For long, many suspected he wanted to rid himself of his blackness: the plastic surgery, the hair-straightening, the mysterious blanching of his facial skin all suggested he wanted to dismember himself from the African American population. He denied this and, on occasion, pronounced a primal bond with black people. But Jackson was a friend of children first and foremost and it didn't matter what ethnic group they communed with. Now, he seemed to have left his magical kingdom and was north of 96th Street in Northeast Manhattan, where in the 1920s and 1930s black music, at least in the way we know it, took shape.

Jackson reminded the audience of Otis Blackwell (1931–2002), who wrote "Don't Be Cruel" and "All Shook Up," both successes for Elvis Presley, and several other songs, without becoming stupendously successful. It was a slightly odd reference because Blackwell had been inducted into the Nashville Songwriters' Hall of Fame in 1986 and, in 1994, received a Pioneer Award from the Rhythm & Blues Foundation. He didn't die penniless, but suffered a stroke in 1991 and had poor health from then till his death in 2002, age seventy. Historically, there have been a great many other talented but impecunious black artists who have died in poverty.

If Jackson had pitched his attack on the record industry and left it at that level, he would have probably earned admiration for a bracing assessment. But the motive for his attack became clearer when he identified Tommy Mottola as "mean, a racist and he's very, very, very devilish." Mottola, said Jackson, had called one unidentified artist a "fat black nigga." In his biography, *Hitmaker*, Mottola recalled how, in 1991, when Sony renewed his recording contract, Jackson insisted that the company issue a press release stating that the deal was worth $1 billion, even though the actual advance royalty paid by Sony was $35 million—still a substantial sum of money, but 3.5 percent of what Jackson wanted everyone to think he was getting.

The episode illustrated Jackson's unusual disposition. Presumably, he wished to exaggerate his value to the record company and perhaps provide his own self-evaluation. When it came to *Invincible*, Jackson wanted Mottola to put his money where his mouth was, and the production and promotion budget suggested Mottola was prepared to do just that. (There is no evidence, actual or inferred, that Mottola uttered the racist statement.) Sony issued a statement describing Jackson's comments about Mottola "ludicrous, spiteful and hurtful."

Sharpton later distanced himself from Jackson's remarks about Mottola, who was known to many as supportive of black artists. He was married to

Mariah Carey between 1993 and 1998. "I have known Tommy for 15 or 20 years, and never once have I known him to say or do anything that would be considered racist," Sharpton told the *New York Post*'s Jeane Macintosh (July 8, 2002). "I didn't know that Michael planned to personally attack Tommy—but nobody tells Michael Jackson what to do."

The origins of the personal dispute lay in Jackson's request for complete ownership of his masters, these being the original recordings from which copies are taken (Sammy Davis Jr. often signed recording contracts without securing legal ownership of masters of his own songs). When Mottola was reluctant to release them, Jackson came to the conclusion that he was a sort of despot who exploited black artists and this must have prompted him to think more deeply about the manner in which the record industry has treated African Americans. Sharpton shared this aspect of Jackson's argument and continued to address industry concerns over contracts and royalties.

Jackson, though, was immersed in his particular struggle. He took the uncharacteristic step of traveling by bus to Sony's midtown Manhattan offices and appeared holding a poster of Mottola, doctored with horns and forked tail. He had a picket sign that read, "Sony Music Kills." *Invincible* had sold about 4 million copies at this point. (Comparisons with today's market are complicated by the mix of physical and digital sales that surged after 2007, before vinyl started its comeback around 2016; but 4 million represents about the same global sales figure as, say, Katy Perry's 2010 *Teenage Dreams.*)

Jackson's social conscience as well as his animosity toward Mottola seemed to dissipate after the Harlem meeting. He never made another album of new material for Sony or any other company. Mottola left Sony the following year after a disagreement over a possible deal with Apple. As we know, he made it onto Jackson's hitlist. (Years later, in 2020, Ye— then known as Kanye West—appeared to implicate Mottola and Sony in Jackson's death when he tweeted, "MJ told you about Tommy before they killed him," though there was no explication of "they.")

Jackson was far from alone in disputing the terms of his recording contract. George Michael lost his case to Sony in 1992. Prince had a public clash with Warner in 1993 and marked "SLAVE" on his face to dramatize the way he felt about his relationship with the label. In 2019, Taylor Swift had a contractual wrangle with her record label, Big Machine, that, for a while, appeared to mean she wouldn't be able to sing some of her own material. So artists, black and white, have had disagreements with their record companies.

(Ownership of master recordings gives artists creative control over their own material and prevents labels, for example, releasing compilations without consent. While it wasn't as important in the early years of the century as it is today, ownership of masters provides the artist with control of licensing, which is crucial to sampling. Historically, many artists signed away their ownership of masters either for a period of time or indefinitely, often in return for advance royalties; but these deals limited the artists' ability to use their own material.)

* * *

A few months before the Harlem assembly, Prince Michael II, Jackson's third child, was born amid great secrecy. The existence of the baby was not made public until August 2002 when he was thought to be seven months old, but the mother's identity was concealed; and remained so. Jackson's other two children were aged four and five; their mother was Debbie Rowe. *People* magazine's Rachel F. Elson reported the new baby was conceived "the natural way" (November 20). Seven years later, this was contradicted by a Mexican nurse known only as Helena who declared she was the surrogate mother and had been paid $20,000 for her services; the baby was fertilized in vitro, using Jackson's sperm and the ova of a woman, whose identity was unknown, but who thought to have been paid $3,500. According to Ryan Parry of the British newspaper *The Mirror*, which broke the story in 2009, the baby, who became known as Blanket, was born at the Sharp Grossmont Hospital in La Mesa, near San Diego. As surrogate, Helena carried the baby; the biological mother is still not known. The newspaper's story suggested Jackson was not present at the birth, but the newborn was taken to Neverland, presumably wrapped in a blanket—the paper didn't specify, but the nickname must have come from somewhere. (He later changed his name to Bigi.)

Jackson presented his child to the public in a most inexplicable manner: honored in Berlin for his philanthropic work on behalf of children, he accepted his lifetime Bambi entertainment award and issued his familiar plea for world peace. During the visit, Jackson appeared on the fourth floor balcony of his Adlon Hotel suite to acknowledge hundreds of acolytes gathered to revere him. They were made to gasp in horror as he briefly dangled the child over the balcony. There seemed no rhyme nor reason to the action and Jackson later called it a "terrible mistake." Berlin police initially said they were exploring the possibility of opening an investigation, but nothing developed. "Mr. Jackson . . . seems to be on the verge of unraveling," asserted the *New York Times* (November 22, 2002). "Is Michael Jackson out of control?" asked CNN.com (November 21). "Going over the edge" is how *Time* magazine described Jackson's destination (November 19). Even in the context of his multiple bizarreries, needlessly endangering the life of his own baby, even if for only a few seconds, was aberrant, especially considering that the dimension of his life that seemed relatively unaffected by his extremities was his dedication to the care of children. "I got caught up in the excitement of the moment," explained Jackson without clarifying anything.

Uri Geller, at the time a friend (though soon to join Mottola on the hitlist, of course) told BBC, "He [Jackson] probably did it because he was overwhelmed emotionally by the fans," though he may have been closer to the truth when he suggested the "baby" was not Blanket at all, but a fake of some kind, possibly a doll. That in itself seems to require an explanation. One was never forthcoming and Jackson left Germany having nourished the media with a meaty, if discomforting, scandal. No celebrated person is scandal-proof, even or—in Jackson's case—*especially* after death. But no one has ever solicited scandal as winningly as Jackson. Even where the prospects of action regarded as morally and possibly legally wrong and liable to cause public outrage were not good, Jackson could outsource an unforgiveable offense from his own child.

Although no one knew it at the time, the Rodney King riots were the start of a new narrative that would take shape over the next three decades. "This is America" screamed many in disbelief: the 1992 uprisings were the first meaningful signs of racial unrest since civil rights.

8

A Nightmare

"If you had to choose a time to be, in the words of Lorraine Hansberry, *young, gifted, and black* in America, you would choose right now," Barack Obama told a graduating class at Howard University in Washington, DC, drawing attention to Hansberry's 1996 collection of plays, interviews, and letters, which bore a similar title to the 1970 hit record by Bob and Marcia (written by Nina Simone and Weldon Irvine). It was 2016 and the then president of the United States advised that the country was, by every criterion, better than when he was a student in the 1960s—a period when the equal rights and social justice movements emerged in the modern era.

Obama may well have been speaking from the heart, but it was hard to square with actual events. Two months after his speech, five police officers in Dallas were killed in response to two incidents in which black men were shot dead by police. Any rational analysis of race relations in the United States in the mid-1960s would have concluded that the crucial and inimical role racism had played in the history of America for the previous 400 years or more was bound to diminish. And Obama was probably right in a sense: it had diminished since the enactment of laws in 1964 and 1965, which outlawed discrimination. But racism had not disappeared; there were many loose ends left to untangle.

America has a long history of white resentment. Resentment, that is, of what most people regard as progress, advancement, illumination, awakening, sophistication, and open-mindedness. This might have been intelligible in 1955, when Emmett Till, a fourteen-year-old, was killed by white men who spotted him talking to a white woman and responded by beating him, gouging out an eye, shooting him in the head, tying a cotton gin around his neck with barbed wire, and throwing him in the Tallahatchie River, in Money, Mississippi (a place that features in Bobbie Gentry's song "Ode to Billie Joe"). Monstrous, but intelligible: America was racially segregated and bigotry was real, remorseless and easily reconcilable with the way of life in the South. But the specter of Emmett Till loomed large and didn't vanish with the onset of civil rights: it continued to haunt the modern era.

If any single incident offered a powerful and elucidating image of a nation divided by race since the onset of civil rights, it was the Central Park Jogger case. On April 19, 1989—a full quarter-century after the key legislation, remember—a 28-year-old white woman named Trisha Meili went for her early evening exercise run through New York's Central Park when she was apparently bustled out of her stride by a group of loud and hostile men. After that, the exact sequence of events is uncertain. But Meili was raped, beaten to the head with a rock, dragged about forty feet, and left for dead. Discovered unconscious at 1:00 a.m., suffering from blood loss and hypothermia, she was not expected to survive and remained in a coma for a week. She suffered several lacerations and a fractured skull; her left eye socket had been crushed.

By April 20, 1989, five young men, four African American and one Latino, who had been swept up with about fifty teenagers, were accused of the violent crime. It was swift remedial justice and served to restore a semblance of stillness to the agitated city. Four of the young men were sentenced to five to ten years in a youth correctional facility, and the fifth five to fifteen years in an adult prison. They were known as "the Central Park Five." All protested their innocence and claimed they had been coerced into making false confessions by the New York police.

At the time, the potent crystallized form of cocaine known as crack had recently appeared on the streets. The Central Park Five were thought to be "wilding," a term that came into currency in the period and referred to the activities of youths going on a protracted and violent rampage in public spaces, attacking people at random. While wilding wasn't the exclusive preserve of blacks, it was coded as a predominantly black pursuit.

The forensic evidence suggested a miscarriage of justice: DNA found at the crime scene didn't match any of the accused. But the media was more concerned with parables of good and evil to pay too much attention. And it was distracted by a *dehumanizing* image to the point where it overlooked the incompetence and waste in some of its key public agencies. I take the term from Brent Staples, who argued a "process of dehumanization often leads Americans to view African-American men as larger and more fearsome than they are." Writing for the *New York Times* about the disparate treatment in the criminal justice system when black people are confronted by law enforcement, Staples discerned how terms such as "savages," "brutes," or "beasts" are readily associated with black defendants.

The image was never more apparent: the marauding gang was urban terror incarnate—black, bestial, out-of-control, probably on crack, and ready to wreak havoc on anyone or anything. Whether the gang actually existed was of secondary importance: it was a potent image. The question remained unanswered: Why didn't the forensic evidence match?

An entrepreneur not widely known outside New York used the case as an occasion to make his first mark on civic affairs. "You better believe that I hate the people who took this girl and raped her brutally," proclaimed Donald J. Trump at a standing room-only press conference. Trump was moved to run a series of his own advertisements in the media under the headline, "Bring Back the Death Penalty." The case also foregrounded Reverend Al Sharpton, who was a regular at the demonstrations outside the courthouse where the young men were tried. The demonstrators sensed the Five were getting rough justice. Others took an opposing view and called for castration.

The real rapist was a serial offender who went free—and committed more crimes—until he was arrested after another rape. He was sentenced to ten years. It took until 2002 before he confessed to the Central Park rape, while serving time for another crime, raping three women, in addition to raping and killing a pregnant woman; he said he was the sole attacker and always acted alone. The five men recanted their confessions and stressed they were made under coercion. It's worth wondering how many confessions have been forced from accused men and women over the years before the DNA era made many redundant. (DNA testing was actually first used in 1987 to convict a rapist in Florida, but even in 1995 there were doubts about its reliability: O. J. Simpson was cleared, in part, because of doubts about the dependability of evidence based on blood found at the murder scene). The five men's convictions were vacated in 2002, and the city paid $41 million in 2014 to settle their civil rights lawsuit. They had spent between six to thirteen years in prison.

"The racial tropes of our past were not abandoned in ancient boneyards, but were poured into the concrete that modern America was built on," wrote Jim Dwyer, of the *New York Times*. The Central Park Jogger case "was big enough, terrible enough, to electrify a city grown numb to its own badness."

Ava DuVernay's four-part series *When They See Us* (2019) is a dramatization of the case and its aftermath.

* * *

A couple of years after the Central Park rape, on a March night in 1991, four Los Angeles policemen were filmed by an unseen onlooker brutally beating a man pulled over for a traffic violation. The police officers were white, while Rodney King, was African American. It was probably the kind of incident that happened routinely in this and many other parts of the United States. But the presence of an unseen third party weaponized with a video camera transformed this into something unexpected. (The actual footage is still viewable at: https://abcn.ws/3b1zFuZ.)

When, in April 1992, the case against the police went to court, the judge ordered an unusual change of venue for the trial to a predominantly white suburb. The officers were cleared on all but one charge by a jury comprising ten whites, one Asian and one Latino, no African American. Violent protest against the apparent lack of justice spread across the nation for four days. The Rodney King riots, as they became known, left the United States stunned, though not changed forever.

Although no one knew it at the time, the Rodney King riots were the start of a new narrative that would take shape over the next three decades. "This is America" screamed many in disbelief: the 1992 uprisings were the first meaningful signs of racial unrest since civil rights. But it was only a start. Only two months after the rioting, a 35-year-old black motorist Malice Green was beaten by Detroit police officers and later died from the injuries. Two police officers were convicted of second-degree murder, both later reduced to the less serious charge, of involuntary manslaughter. In 1997, Abner Louima, a 33-year-old Haitian immigrant, was arrested for interfering with officers trying to break up a fight. Police officers were charged and convicted of beating and torturing him and, later, for obstructing justice by covering up the crime.

But perhaps the most extraordinary exposé of violence and racial injustice came on February 4, 1999, when a 23-year-old West African immigrant street trader named Amadou Diallo stepped out from his South Bronx apartment in the Bronx. His death said all anyone needed to know about how cosmetic the so-called colorblind society actually was.

Diallo encountered four plainclothes members of New York Police Department's roving Special Crimes Unit, who were searching for a rape suspect. The Unit had been accused of stopping and frisking young black men without cause, a practice we now call racial profiling. Diallo reached inside his pocket and one of the police officers, Sean Carroll, shouted, "Gun!" At that point, another officer Edward McMellon apparently tripped and stumbled backward giving the impression to the others that he might have been shot. The officers, all of them white, later said they feared Diallo was going for a gun. The officers, who carried nine-millimeter semiautomatic weapons, opened fire discharging forty-one shots and killing Diallo instantly. Diallo fell and Carroll approached him, looking to where he thought the gun would be. "I grabbed it, and it felt soft," he said. "It was just a wallet."

Robert Johnson, the district attorney for the Bronx, admitted, "I cannot recall any homicide in which 41 shots were fired at the deceased." "Even an execution squad would not have fired so many shots," said the Reverend Al Sharpton. "Are we talking about policing or are we talking about a firing squad?"

The sheer quantity of gunfire turned what would have been a controversial case into a major media spectacle. In the days following the killing, there were demonstrations outside the Supreme Court in the Bronx, where the four police officers pled not guilty to the charges. About 400 protestors claimed that the police policy of routinely frisking people, most of them black or Latino, created police brutality. But, perhaps the most significant event in helping raise awareness of the killing was a song by Bruce Springsteen, who wrote "American Skin (41 shots)" specifically about the Diallo case and sang it at a number of concerts. It included the line, "You can get killed just for living in your American skin." Diallo's parents praised Springsteen for keeping the memory of their son alive, but the police and the Mayor denounced him.

The charges laid against the police officers were for second-degree murder, a charge that required the prosecution to prove that the killing was intentional and/or committed with depraved indifference to human life. It carries a sentence of fifteen years to life. It is a notoriously difficult charge to prove; to succeed the prosecution needed to demonstrate that the officers' *intention* was to kill. There were forty-one shots fired, after all; and post mortem examinations suggested several of the bullets hit Diallo while he lay prostrate on the ground.

New City's hardline on crime had resulted in a 70 percent drop in crime in the previous five years but complaints against the police had risen by nearly 40 percent. Howard Safir, the city's police commissioner held up New York as a model for urban policing. In March, Safir announced changes to the Secret Crimes Unit, including the requirement that the previously plainclothes officer wear uniforms. He explained that he was responding to the concerns of community leaders.

The trial was moved from the Bronx to Albany, about 130 miles north, because of the pretrial publicity; the media feasted on the case. Jury selection began on January 31, 2000. The prosecutor Eric Warner stopped short of explicitly accusing the NYPD officers of racism, but cited officer Carroll's testimony that he wanted to stop Diallo on a "hunch" that he might be a wanted rapist or robber. On February 25, all four officers were acquitted of all charges.

Los Angeles Times' John J. Goldman described the scene after the decision: "Standing under umbrellas in the rain outside the gray stone courthouse afterward, Diallo's mother and the Reverend Al Sharpton made appeals for peace." Sharpton promised, "This is not the end, this is only the beginning." Was he right? The officers involved were not retried and, while three left the NYPD, the remaining officer Kenneth Boss was promoted to sergeant in 2015—much to the ire of the mother of the slain Diallo. Sharpton too was critical. "It's an ugly and wrong message to send from the police department," he said. In contrast New York's mayor Rudolph Giuliani considered it "an eminently fair verdict under the circumstances." Giuliani wouldn't condemn Diallo's killers and, at one point, defended the police officers who, he said, had "gone through a nightmare."

From that moment, Sharpton began attacking, forcing a public examination of how New York's police conduct their business. While Giuliani reeled off statistics to show that police shootings declined during his period in office, Sharpton pointed out that civilian complaints against the police has risen nearly 40 percent. Out of 45,000 people stopped-and-searched, 37,000 were released without charge.

I earlier described the Diallo killing as "extraordinary" and, in a great many ways, including the amount of gunfire, the initially non-confrontational scene and final exculpation of the police officers, it was. Yet in another way, it was very ordinary. Chameleons are extraordinary animals because they can change color to suit their environments; in Northern Europe they would be even more extraordinary; in Sub-Saharan Africa less so. It depends on context: time, place, climate, and surrounding circumstances.

The death of Diallo was only one item in an inventory of killings or perversions of justice involving black people, usually men. The names read like a grim index of American history. As well as the cases already mentioned there were, this century alone, those of James Brisette (2005), Sean Bell (2006), Trayvon Martin (2012), Tamir Rice (2014), Alton Sterling (2014), Freddie Gray (2015), Laquan McDonald (2015), Philando Castile (2016) and Antwon Rose II (2018). The list of casualties was long but consistent: they were all black.

Two cases in particular, those of Eric Garner and Michael Brown in 2014, rattled America and sparked disturbances not only in the United States but beyond. The decision not to charge white police officers for the killing of unarmed black men outraged the world. Sharpton was at the fore of a huge "Justice for All March" in Washington, DC, and there were similar protests elsewhere in 2014. Garner had been killed in New York by a police officer who employed a chokehold; Brown was shot dead in Ferguson, Mississippi; the deaths were within weeks of each other and in neither case were there prosecutions.

The Garner and Brown cases became the focal point for national and international debate on race and racism. They gave rise to what's now called #BlackLivesMatter. The movement existed before, principally in response to the Trayvon Martin death (his shooter George Zimmerman was acquitted), but the deaths of Garner and Brown gave the movement fresh impetus and augmented by social media, it became a global *cause célèbre*.

Garner's dying gasp, "I can't breathe," became a slogan for protestors in much the same was as "Burn, baby, burn" was for the dissidents in Watts in 1965, though the Garner protestors marched rather than rioted. Amnesty International came up with its own slogan to capture the long, repetitive history, "Another Year, Another Unarmed Black Man Killed by Police." It used this as its headline for a report on the anniversary funeral of Oscar Grant, who was killed by police officers in Oakland, California, in 2009. But it was Garner's grim last words that remained in the popular imagination and returned hauntingly in 2020, when George Floyd was killed by Minneapolis police officer Derek Chauvin in a confrontation captured on video.

In 2021, a twelve-member jury swiftly and unanimously found Chauvin guilty of three counts, including murder. A rare verdict against a police officer was a milestone in the fraught history of America and a rebuke of law enforcement's historical treatment of blacks. The case, as every reader will know, started a global chain reaction that spread to schools, sports, and practically every other sphere of society. Pledges to oppose racism in its every form followed. Much of the gesturing was probably just that—for show and performed in the knowledge that it would have little effect. But breaking curfews and defying national guard troops, over six days and across nearly forty American cities suggested that the case was certainly the most explosive since that of Rodney King and potentially the most pivotal.

Black Lives Matter morphed from a social movement, principally an online movement, to a credo—a statement of beliefs that guide actions. Many of the world's leading commercial brands, including Levi's, Puma, and H&M, aligned themselves with #BLM. Gestures took place before many sports events. Society as a whole introspected, examining the way racism had sometimes crept surreptitiously into its day-to-day operations, without individuals even noticing—a process known as institutional racism. The Floyd case of 2020, or more accurately, its aftermath was distinct enough to suggest it was a harbinger of change. In April 2021, almost eleven months after Floyd's death and about ten miles from where it occurred, police fatally shot a black man, Daunte Wright, during a traffic stop.

* * *

Jennifer Carlson, a professor of sociology, in 2016, offered a way of understanding the various cases in terms of what she called a "moral breach." She argued that, after the 1960s, the United States was in the process of transitioning from a segregated to a postracial, or colorblind society, the popular assumption being that the goals of the civil rights movement had been substantially achieved and that overt forms of discrimination were consigned to America's history. This presented a paradox: black politics—which Carlson doesn't define but we'll presume is the collective effort of people of African descent to gain power and influence in the processes and institutions of government—was replaced by a universal colorblind approach that urged unity and cooperation.

Carlson points out that, the world over, there are moral panics, these being instances of public alarm and anxiety in response to a problem regarded as threatening to the moral standards of society. Specific groups are typically identified as the threat and the media usually exaggerate or amplify the extent and severity of their menace. But, where the danger is collective or amorphous (that is, without a clear definition), everyone in society is meant to feel obliged to react, if only because of the prevalence of the risk. Carlson called this moral regulation: it's a way of encouraging us all to buy into a threat that we can't always see, but we trust is all around us. A virus, for example. But Carlson interpreted the series of killings after the King riots of

1992 as an instance of what she called a moral breach, which she describes a moment of moral concern where this is a clash of "conflicting values systems."

In contrast to moral panics which are oriented to "recentering normal orders"—restoring the state of being usual—moral breaches tend to "pivot the center." In other words, the moral breach challenges and destabilizes affairs, sometimes forcing people to question the source and distribution of blame for groups, individuals, or practically anything identified as blameworthy. Carlson wrote about "a panic about a panic" and she illustrated this with two episodes, the Trayvon Martin killing and another case I haven't yet mentioned, that of Bernhard Goetz, a white man who, in 1984, shot four black youths on a New York subway; in both cases self-defense was alleged to justify the killings. The men Goetz shot were no goody-two-shoes: one of them had demanded money from Goetz. At his eventual criminal trial, the jury found that he'd acted in self-defense and was guilty only of carrying an unlicensed firearm.

Carlson's careful scrutiny of the media coverage reveals that the men Goetz shot stood for "a faceless, nameless, racialized threat" that was widespread in the 1980s. "Racialized folk devils" is how she characterized the figures and all those who resembled them. Twenty-eight years later, "coverage portrayed Trayvon Martin as a victim" and his "death represents a nightmare faced not by all Americans but by those at risk of being racially profiled as criminals."

The Civil Rights Act of 1964 and the Voting Rights Act of 1965 were the culmination of years of protest that began with Rosa Parks's refusal to give up her seat on a segregated bus in Montgomery, Alabama, in 1955. The "black criminal trope," as Carlson calls it, was still very much alive at the time of the Goetz case—in this instance, a trope is a recurrent theme, a motif. Black criminality was a cause of panic, a prolonged panic, but a persistent concern nonetheless, however ill founded. The black criminal was a central figure in a wider social breakdown and, while Carlson didn't link it to the mid-1960s legislation, there was surely an implicit association with the effects of desegregation. For many, desegregation removed a grotesque but sturdy control apparatus and unleashed a black criminality onto a society unprepared or unwilling to deal with the threat.

Carlson's argument complements that of Brent Staples, which I covered earlier in this chapter: his term "dehumanization" sums up the way whites were processing the aftermath of civil rights. Both writers seem to be suggesting that white America reacted by denying there could be a consensual end to segregation, nor closure at the end of centuries of racist oppression. Instead there was the new horror of maverick foes, armed with primal urges, unpredictable and unrestrained.

The Goetz and Martin cases, like those of Diallo, King, and the other victims referenced in this chapter were not random, nor accidental, rather were parts of a pattern. Some might say an inevitable pattern—inevitable because trying to collapse an asymmetrical structure that had been in place since the early seventeenth century and had proved uncommonly resistant to change was bound to provoke pushback. It was as if Newton's Third Law was being tested on a whole society. For every action, there is an equal and opposite—and in this instance, usually horrendous—reaction.

In his book *White on Black: Images of Africa and Blacks in Western Popular Culture*, Jan Nederveen Pieterse summarized the reaction, "The American complex about race is geared chiefly to suppressing black males." The suppression takes many forms. Whether you're an iconic athlete who charges millions to display your talent or a street vendor like Diallo who ekes out a living selling cutprice trinkets, the fact remains, as far as Pieterse is concerned: you will be contained, restrained, or else crushed. The links between the likes of Diallo, Martin, and all the other black men written of in this chapter are not as tenuous as they might appear.

* * *

Savagery, bestiality, and primitiveness: attributes such as these sustain an unbridgeable difference between blacks and whites in America. Forget how bogus and antiquated the attributes may seem. They live and draw subsistence every timed a black person does or is just thought to have done something that might be seen as vaguely negative. All the cases I've considered in this chapter serve as evidence, however misshapen. Now think of some of the attributes ascribed to Jackson. Let's start with the good ones: talented, brilliant, gifted, touched by genius. Then the less generous: odd, weird, strange, peculiar. And the bad: degenerate, debauched, perverted, pedophilic.

Jackson had no template. He was conspicuously not part of the menacing, brutish population of black men who habitually terrorized urban America and had to be controlled or laid to waste by upstanding white police officers. He didn't share the athletic virtues of people like Muhammad Ali, Jesse Owens, Michael Jordan, or the numberless other black virtuosos of sport. Where did he fit in, then? Jackson often acknowledged Diana Ross as both his muse and guiding light. She was part of a tradition of illustrious blacks who distinguished themselves in popular entertainment. Before her were Lena Horne, Ray Charles, Nat King Cole, and the wondrously accomplished dancers, the Nicholas Brothers, among others. Pieterse argues that the fame was a form of imprisonment. Imprisonment in the six-star Burj al Arab's penthouse suite, maybe; but the fame was still a form of confinement.

Pieterse argues that white society accepted, even rejoiced in the brilliance of these abundantly gifted performers and other blacks. But only on the condition that they didn't challenge the paternity of white society that produced them and gave them their big chance. So, for example, when Paul

Robeson (1898–1976) expressed communist sympathies, he was denounced and frozen out of parts. It was as if the contract that enabled him to cross over into the mainstream film and music markets stipulated that he should express no political views, refrain from challenging the status quo, and remain deferential.

Even after desegregation had made it possible for blacks to stay in the same hotels, eat in the same restaurants, and live in the same neighborhoods as whites, there was still a sense in which black people were confined, even the ones who had distinguished themselves in art and sports. These were both areas in which the performers carried out their tasks principally for the delectation of white audiences.

In many senses, Jackson was an emblem of postracial America. An unwitting emblem perhaps, but no less commanding: acclaimed and respected as a character who stood out because he represented a new kind of society, in which race and racism were unimportant, if not entirely irrelevant. After the turmoil of the 1950s and 1960s, the injustice, tragedies, and violence of history were reminders, but only that—reminders of how life once was. While she didn't have Jackson in mind when she wrote of "the dream of democracy," Jean Elshtain might well have been alluding to his popular representation, "nurtured by the presumption that none of us is stuck inside our own skins, that our identity and our ideas are not finally reducible to our membership in a race, an ethnic group, a sex." Elshtain, a professor of social and political ethics, was addressing a symposium on "Race and Racism: American Dilemmas Revisited" (and published in the journal *Salmagundi* in Fall, 1994–5).

In 1992, around the time of the Rodney King riots, Jackson was at the pinnacle of his global supra-popularity. But he was losing the putative racial characteristics that had defined every other black entertainer in history. His vanity and insufferable narcissism made what used to be admired as perfectionism now appear just anal. Yet he was still expected to be lovable, most of the time, at least, and voiceless on issues other than music. At times, he did give the impression that he was as domesticated as Bubbles, his chimpanzee.

At other times, he somehow succeeded in being transgressive, though not in the way Robeson had been more than a half-century before. Jackson broke the frame Pieterse described: there was a disorienting novelty about the way he simultaneously identified with and denied blackness. David Brackett, a professor of musicology, compared Jackson with another transgressive artist who attracted criticism and, in the process, prompted arguments. "Like Elvis, Michael Jackson became a lightning rod for discussions about race, gender, and sexuality."

It might not seem a convincing comparison, given Elvis's career trajectory, which landed him in Vegas, but, in the 1950s, he was considered one of the most dangerous performers in America, if not the world, a purveyor of frightening primitivism that threatened to strip young audiences of their civilized values and reveal their base instincts. Jackson was never suspected of having that effect on humankind; though the two figures resonate at distance—the exquisiteness of their music, the mania they seemed to inspire in their followers, the delirium they occasioned among critics, and the sexuality they expressed.

Jackson was licensed liberties no other black artist in history had been permitted. The conditions of success Pieterse regarded as crucial were flouted by Jackson, principally because, as I suggested earlier, he was emblematic of an age in which *change* prevailed. He too changed, sometimes inexplicably, at other times in a way that seemed to validate his domesticity. Jackson was, after all, a black man, born near Chicago to a working family; he shared much in common with the other men whose conflicts with the police and self-appointed white guardians I have described in this chapter. But he was also very different from them. In later life he may have been less conspicuously black in both appearance and attitude, but he remained an obvious counterpoint—a pleasing and notable contrast to the less pleasant and often feral figures who featured in that terrible decades-long fresco that decorated modern America.

Themes of race and identity seemed intertwined in Jackson. No one, it seemed, ever worked them out. Not even him. But in a period when America's most persistent and irresolvable social problem maintained a sinister energy that kept it active despite all official attempts to kill it, Jackson presented America with a different type of black man; a puzzling yet marvelous human being who could divert attention away from gun victims.

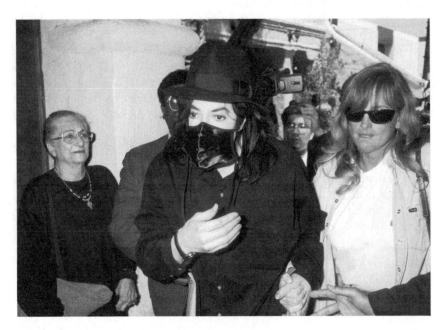

It was an inspired idea: a natural, full-term pregnancy, micro-managed by the best obstetricians money could buy. Debbie Rowe became pregnant in 1996 and married Jackson later in the same year. She was thirty-seven, he was thirty-eight.

9

Aladdin's Cave

"Of all the rumors whispered and speculation spread, of all the questions left unanswered surrounding the death and life of Michael Jackson, perhaps most intriguing of all is how the most famous man in the world married and started a family with a cipher who worked in his dermatologist's office," wrote Richard Gerdau and Lee Hoffman, of *ABC News*, in 2009.

She wasn't love-struck, swept along on a romantic tsunami. In fact, she married with her eyes wide open, probably like someone closing the sale of prime property. She had little in common with her husband and she probably knew the chances of the marriage lasting beyond a few of years were remote. So Gerdau and Hoffman's description of her as a cipher, a person of no importance, seems harsh.

Debbie Rowe was working as a nursing assistant for cosmetic dermatologist Dr. Arnold Klein when she met Jackson. It was April 1993 and Klein had been recommended to Jackson by Elizabeth Taylor. Rowe liked drinking and riding a Harley-Davidson; she was probably a Jackson fan too. Rowe and Jackson grew to know and, presumably, liked each other. When he was prescribed medication for his various skin conditions he asked specifically for Rowe to administer them. In fact, she accompanied him on several of his trips, serving as his personal nurse.

At some point the pair came up with an inspired idea: a natural, full-term pregnancy, micro-managed by the best obstetricians money could buy. Rowe became pregnant in 1996 and married Jackson later in the same year. She was thirty-seven, he was thirty-eight. Jackson and his first wife had divorced only weeks before after a nineteen-month marriage.

The wedding was not a typical Jackson extravaganza: it took place in the relative obscurity of the Sheraton on the Park hotel (now Sheraton Grand Sydney Hyde Park) in Sydney, Australia. At the wedding, Jackson's best man was an eight-year-old boy described as Jackson's nephew. Rowe wore a highly untraditional black wedding dress. An unusual wedding. Well, unusual for most; not for Jackson. That was October 1996. Months earlier, Rowe, on her own account had been artificially inseminated by an anonymous donor and became what she described as a "thoroughbred," an allusion to purebred racehorses. "They impregnated me. . . . I got paid for it," she was quoted by Marissa Calligeros in 2009 (that is, after Jackson's death; Rowe did not discuss details of the process by which she became pregnant before then). The following February, Rowe gave birth to a boy, Michael Joseph Jackson Jr., who became known as Prince.

A surrogate mother bears a child either from her own egg (ovum) fertilized by a man or from the implantation in her uterus of a fertilized egg of another woman. In the first case, she is artificially inseminated with a man's sperm, then carries the baby, delivers it, and becomes the baby's biological mother. The second case involves *in vitro* fertilization (IVF), which means that the fertilization takes place outside the body and the embryo is placed into the uterus of what's known as a gestational surrogate, who then carries the baby until birth. In this case, she has no genetic ties to the child. Often, she is called the birth mother, but this doesn't mean she is the biological mother—that's the woman whose ova were fertilized. It isn't completely transparent which of these kinds of surrogates Rowe became: the former is most likely. There are uncertainties about who provided the sperm. As with almost everything Jackson did (or perhaps didn't do), there were rumors: Marlon Brando was among the putative candidates, along with Macaulay Culkin, Corey Feldman, and Uri Geller. Arnold Klein, the former employer of Rowe, dismissed media reports alleging that *he* fathered Prince through a sperm donation; though, in 2013, two years before he died, he tweeted an image of himself and Prince with the tag, "Hmmmm . . ."

Rowe had no meaningful experience of motherhood, at least not in the accepted sense of the word: the state of being a mother. She had almost no contact with her child and chose to live apart from Jackson. She maintained Jackson "wanted to pretend that we were a family," but he never really wanted to live with her. "That's why he bought me a house." Theirs was not a marriage made in heaven. Again, not in the accepted sense. But, in a way, it *was*: she had blue eyes, fair skin, and blonde hair and was willing to carry a baby; he wanted a blue-eyed, fair-skinned child with blonde (or blond, if we stick with a gendered adjective) hair and sought a willing bearer.

Rowe was prepared to talk openly about the delivery. Jackson apparently held her hand for much of the 23-hour labor. Rowe's maternal instincts weren't immediately obvious. "Michael was definitely more excited than I was," she reflected. "And that's what made it wonderful for me was to see the look on his face," said Rowe, describing the baby as "a gift" to her husband. "I didn't do it to be a mother. I didn't change diapers. I didn't get up in the middle of the night, even when I was there, Michael did it all." On Rowe's account, Jackson did all the fatherly stuff, reading to his baby, feeding him, and, of course, singing to him.

In April 1998, after Rowe gave birth to a second child, a girl named Paris-Michael Katherine Jackson, Jackson took both children and sent Rowe to live in a Beverly Hills mansion. It was, by all accounts, a consensual arrangement. Calligeros quotes Rowe, "I was no good. I don't want these children in my life." The children were brought up by a dedicated team of nannies. When asked what would happen to the children if Jackson died, Rowe replied that she trusted him to pick an appropriate guardian. "I'm sure he has a wonderful person in mind to take care of them."

In 2009, former actor Mark Lester suggested he might be Paris's father. "In 1996 Michael asked me if I would give him my sperm . . . no money was paid; it was something I was honoured to do," he was quoted in *Marie Claire* (August 10).

*   *   *

After her second child, Rowe was unable to have more children. So the divorce in October 2000 came as no surprise. As part of the divorce arrangements, Rowe agreed to relinquish custody of her two children and, in another hearing the following year, she gave up her parental rights. "I did it for him [Jackson] to become a father, not for me to become a mother," Rowe told the court. "I have done absolutely nothing to earn that title." She walked with an $8 million settlement, plus the Beverly Hills home and a yearly payment of $900,000 on the condition she didn't give interviews on Jackson or the children. (Parental rights in California refer to a set of legal entitlements that are judged to be in the "best interests of the child" and are organized around parents' right to have a relationship with their children.)

Although her contact with the children was minimal after 2000, Rowe claims the facemasks were her idea. Both children were rarely seen in public without their faces partially covered, if not by the masks by scarves. Whether this was protection from (a) viruses or (b) the media, isn't certain. Either way, Jackson himself was typically credited with the idea, which was widely interpreted as yet another sign of his escalating weirdness.

But Rowe had a change of heart and, in 2004, tried to reverse her earlier decision to give up parental rights (in 2001, a year after the divorce). She called Jackson a "great father" and admitted she saw the children infrequently. Jackson had earlier been ordered to pay $60,000 in legal fees. Rowe also sought $195,000 but the judge declined in view of the $8 million she'd already received as part of the divorce settlement. Prince Michael was then nine and Paris eight. Blanket, who was born in 2002, was two.

After Jackson had been arrested in November 2003 following the Martin Bashir documentary covered in Chapter 6, Rowe argued that she should take temporary custody of the children, pending the outcome of the case—Jackson was cleared, as we know. Rowe also proposed that Jackson's involvement with the Nation of Islam organization could be detrimental to the children's welfare. Rowe was Jewish. (The Nation of Islam was an exclusively black Muslim movement, which, it was reported in December 2003, was playing a role in running Jackson's affairs.)

What appeared to be turning into a bitter dispute took a U-turn when, at Jackson's trial, Rowe appeared as a witness. At first she was presented as a witness for the prosecution; it was thought her statements would buttress earlier testimony by the mother of Jackson's accuser, Gavin Arvizo. She was expected to confirm that Jackson was a danger to the children and that he consumed too much alcohol as well as drugs. Only when she was on the stand, did the content of her testimony become known; then she was declared hostile by the prosecution. "He's still my friend," Rowe said of Jackson, aligning herself squarely and unexpectedly with his defense team.

The surprisingly supportive testimony mystified many. The cornerstone of her claim for greater access to her children was Jackson's unsuitability. Perhaps she decided that her most effective strategy was to try to appeal to his better nature. Whatever her ploy, it didn't work resoundingly well. Within two months of the trial's end, Rowe met with her children but was prevented from referring to herself as their mother. This was never a problem. As she said, "My kids don't call me mom, because I don't want them to." Remember, she had not lived with the children, nor behaved in a way that would suggest anything else to Prince Michael or Paris. Jackson himself had little more to do with Rowe. When he left for Bahrain in 2005, the children joined him. In the same year, Rowe had her rights reinstated; the case was settled the following year, though the terms were not disclosed. Jackson retained primary custody.

After Jackson's death Rowe expressed an interest in raising not only her own children but Blanket too. Jackson's mother Katherine, then seventy-nine, was named by a court as the children's temporary guardian. Rowe had no claim to be Blanket's legal mother; she didn't give birth to him and wasn't married to Jackson at the time he was born. Of course, many courts favor keeping siblings together and the unexpected death of the father changed the parenting landscape. The *New York Post* (July 31, 2009) ran a story that claimed Rowe, a "human incubator," had accepted a $4 million payout from the Jackson family to drop her custody pursuit. Rowe's attorney denied this, but a custody battle was averted and Katherine remained guardian of the three children, who lived with her in Encino, California. Rowe was able to "exercise" visitation rights in regard to her biological children.

Next to the sheeny, showbiz Jacksons, Rowe was a plain Everywoman, albeit one with a Beverly Hills home and 8 million in the bank. After the visitation rights issue was settled, Rowe practically disappeared from public view, but in 2014 announced her engagement to Jackson's onetime videographer Marc Schaffel. During 2016 and 2017 she underwent chemotherapy to fight breast cancer.

Were different people involved in this tug-of-love, it wouldn't have been very interesting, but there were questions that had been left unanswered after Rowe and Jackson married. One was: Was Jackson the biological father of either or both of Rowe's children? And, if not, who was?

Exploring famous people's complexity is usually futile and always foolish: to conceive of Jackson as some deep, conflicted thinker eternally tormented in introspection is not my task. He spent forty-five of his fifty years singing and dancing, leaving him probably with insufficient time to ponder anything other than his performance. Yet the question posed by Richard Gerdau and Lee Hoffman and repeated at the start of this chapter requires us to scrutinize the period in Jackson's life when he got married and started a family, and at least to allow ourselves to speculate on what was going on in his mind, or in his soul.

Joining up the dots, we get the portrait of a man approaching forty who wanted his own children, but didn't mind if they weren't his own children in a biological sense. Perhaps he saw it as his fate to be a father and, when nature didn't oblige he took a more pragmatic route to destiny. But why pick—and we must presume he had a choice in the matter—a woman with whom he had no intention of allowing to get close, either figuratively or literally, to the children? Perhaps that was the master stroke: Rowe had no interest in raising them, nor protested at being utterly excluded, and Jackson knew he was in no danger of losing the children. Then there is the question we should raise gently, but needs to be asked: Why did he want a surrogate who was conspicuously not African American? This has a guessable answer, though not one that will please everyone. Perhaps he didn't want his children to be black. Rowe's admission that she was artificially inseminated allows us to guess more confidently.

Jackson's third child, Blanket, who was born in 2002, has the most puzzling origins; little is known of his ancestry or background. Prince Michael Jackson II, to use his full name, was born on February 21, 2002, to an unnamed surrogate. In Chapter 7, I referenced the unverified claim of a woman who said she was the mother, but even if she was telling the truth, what kind of mother was she? A surrogate presumably. But what kind of surrogate? For many, Jackson's three children resembled each other only superficially. Whether they resemble Jackson himself is hard to know: his appearance changed dramatically over the years. It would require software to create an impression of what he might look like at fifty (his age at death) without plastic surgery (interested readers can see a photoshopped version in *India Today*, May 5, 2016 at: http://tiny.cc/IndiaToday).

Jackson's eldest child, Prince, graduated from Loyola Marymount University with a business degree, while Paris worked as a model for IMG Models. Blanket asked in 2015 to be known as Bigi.

* * *

In April 1990, the playwright-turned-president Václav Havel addressed a gigantic, reverential audience in Czech Republic capital Prague. Hundreds of thousands were gathered to celebrate the country's peaceful revolution. "I am not sure that I know what a miracle is," he confessed. "In spite of this, I dare say that I am participating in a miracle: in a country devastated by the ideology of hatred, the messenger of love has arrived."

The messenger in question was Pope John Paul II, making his first visit to Eastern Europe since the fall of communism in the region. Six years later, Michael Jackson arrived to kick off a concert tour. How he would have loved an introduction like that. "The messenger of love has arrived."

In the place where the Pope's altar stood, Jackson's crew erected a stage; in the six years that had elapsed, the city, and indeed the country, had undergone a second revolution, this time replacing the Soviet pantheon with the A-list: on a pedestal that once held one of the world's largest statues of Josef Stalin, concert organizers hoisted a 33-foot, water-filled fiberglass likeness of Jackson. The Stalin statue was taken down after the death of the Soviet statesman in 1953. Jackson's edifice was part of a cargo that needed a chartered Boeing 707, two Antonov An-124 transport aircrafts, a 250-strong crew to move it and about 2,000 local workers to help the crew.

Jackson was in town for the week, visiting Havel's castle and a children's home. The media chronicled his every movement. About 100,000 fans were at Letna Plain for the concert, which lasted two-and-a-half hours. Jackson concluded with "Heal the World," with children between three and thirteen accompanying him on stage.

The Prague concert was in September—that was around the time Rowe submitted herself to stud—and it started a tour of 82 concerts. It was quite a modest number of dates compared to the likes of Ed Sheeran's 257-gig tour, 2017–19, or Elton John's *Farewell Yellow Brick Road* tour, which was due to conclude in 2021 and scheduled 300 concerts before the coronavirus pandemic intervened. Jackson's was the second most-attended concert in Prague's history, the Rolling Stones' holding prime spot with 127,000 in 1995. Jackson drew 125,000. Sheeran pulled in 80,000 in 2019.

The East European leg of the *HIStory* tour, as it was known, took in Hungary, Romania, Russia, and Poland before switching to Western Europe, then Tunisia, Asia, the Antipodes, Philippines, the United States, and back to Western Europe. As September 1997 approached, about three-quarters of the concerts were complete and ticket sales were healthy (about 98 percent of all available sold). The whole tour looked set to gross nearly $200 million (it actually came in at just under).

For the concert at Ostend, a port on the North Sea coast of Belgium, a town with a total population of about 70,000, 58,000 tickets had been sold. But at 4:00 p.m. on August 31, just as the doors to the Hippodrome Wellington horseracing track, which served as the concert venue, were about to open, the promoters announced that the concert was canceled. "He [Jackson] was deeply shocked and collapsed when he heard the news," explained Sony Music Belgium's marketing director for Epic. The same news overshadowed several concerts scheduled for around that time. Scottish band Wet Wet Wet postponed concerts, while Primal Scream canceled all shows for the week, reported *Billboard* (September 13, 1997). Record stores closed and radio stations dedicated whole days to the tragic event. Diana, Princess of Wales, had died.

* * *

As Jackson became, Diana was: remote and isolated, yet loved by many. Like Jackson too, Diana was made to seem a little unbalanced, in her case merely by the refined and snobbish inertia surrounding and probably suffocating her. They were both pursued by paparazzi and, while neither would concede it, both were proficient at handling and manipulating paps to their own ends. The irony was, of course, that, despite her adeptness, "the People's Princess" died while hastening from the media one night in Paris in 1997. Sony Music and Jackson's Paris-based producers of the *HIStory* tour, Quinto Communications, denied reports that Jackson was dining with the Princess on the Saturday before her death.

Jackson first met Diana in 1988: she was with her then husband Prince Charles in the audience for the *Bad* concert in London. Before the performance Jackson made a £300,000 ($500,000) donation to the Prince of Wales' charity, the Prince's Trust. He also gave Diana two jackets bearing the "Bad" logo for her two sons, William and Harry. Over the next few years, Diana and Jackson chatted over the phone and, while we should allow for embellishment, a former bodyguard of Jackson's told British newspaper the *Daily Star*, "he was in love with her, and he wanted to marry her." Matt Fiddes detected, "He felt she was the only person in the world who could understand his life in terms not being able to go anywhere, and the media stories that got out of hand" (September 3, 2017).

She probably did understand. And more than Fiddes realized. Writing for *Harper's* in the months following the death of Diana, Lewis H. Lapham detected an Arabian Nights-style bargain between the media that confers "temporary divinity" on individuals and all but guarantee "the gifts of wealth and applause" but in return for "remnants of his or her humanity" that are made available to "the ritual of the public feast." Diana always gave the appearance of "having been granted every wish in Aladdin's cave— youth, beauty, pretty dresses, a prince for a husband, and Elton John for a pet." Her fans, who came from all quarters, cherished her for her neediness, which was, on Lapham's account, "as desperate and as formless as their own." (Lapham appears to have conflated two myths because Aladdin wasn't offered a diabolical deal but was tricked by a magician into retrieving the lamp, complete with genie, from the cave.)

Did Jackson give the impression of neediness? He had everything. Apart perhaps from one of life's necessities: a childhood. This apparent paradox has mesmerized Jackson analysts for years: a man who wanted for nothing since he was old enough to hold a mic craved something he couldn't have. The Lost Childhood thesis is easy to understand and explains everything. Or nothing. Similarly, Diana was the woman with all the gifts, including the adulation of the world; but, on Lapham's account, she surrendered her "humanity" in exchange. I presume Lapham means that she gave up, or had torn away, the quality that the rest of us take for granted— freedom to move without warning, to talk without script, and emote without Palace approval. For all we know, Diana would have loved to have walked barefoot on the lawns of Kensington Palace at midnight and talk idly with security men about nothing-in-particular. Perhaps she did exactly this and we never learned of it. More likely, the temporary divinity Lapham believes we—and it wasn't only the media—conferred meant she had to act as a goddess at all times. That's one theory of why Diana's life unraveled so spectacularly.

Diana was three years younger than Jackson. Born in 1961, the third child of Edward John Spencer, Diana had sound aristocratic credentials and became Lady Diana Spencer in 1975 when her father became an Earl. Returning to England after finishing school (a private college where young women are prepared for entry into fashionable society) in Switzerland, Diana taught pre-school in London. She met and grew close to Prince Charles. They announced their engagement in February 1981 and married later that year.

The wedding ceremony was televised globally. Their first child, William, was born in 1982 and their second, Henry or Harry as he was to become known, in 1984. Even the most level-headed narration of her life seems like a fairytale: as raggedy servants are transformed into glass-slippered belles of the ball, and sleeping beauties are awakened by the kiss of handsome princes, Diana was changed from ingénue teacher to a twentieth-century deity. She was one of those "individuals who are defined in the first place as possessing some kind of ineffable 'essence'—an aura that sets them apart from ordinary mortals," as Giselle Bastin captures it.

As early as the mid-1980s, Diana was the most admired and, perhaps, widely accepted member of the royal family, somehow contriving to remain imperious while developing a common touch. Time and again, people would testify that "she touched me" even though they might never have met her, or even seen her in the flesh. There was a tangible quality not so much in her presence but in even her sheer image. And this was made possible by exhaustive media coverage that occasionally, in fact once too often, became dangerously invasive.

Interest in the British royal family had traditionally been reverential. Onlookers were exactly that: detached observers, watching as respectful subjects rather than participants. Only Queen Elizabeth's sister Princess Margaret induced a more involved curiosity, her trysting occupying the paparazzi, though without sending them into frenzy. But Diana was compelling: her love—"whatever that means," as Prince Charles fatuously and fatally remarked during a pre-marriage interview—was tainted. Scandal-tainted.

In1985 when visiting a hospice in London, Diana let slip what many took to be a surprisingly revealing comment. "The biggest disease this world suffers from," she murmured, "[is] people feeling *unloved*." What could she mean? Diana later revealed that she had attempted suicide over her suspicions about Charles's relationship with Camilla Parker Bowles. As worst kept secrets go, this was one of the worst: by the early 1990s, Diana and Charles were leading separate lives. When their separation was formally announced in 1992, both Diana and Charles continued to carry out their royal duties. They jointly participated in raising their two children. Many people knew and many regarded Charles's behavior as shameful. Diana, on the other hand, was widely seen as the victim.

Her image was that of a beautiful, yet lonely princess imprisoned in a loveless marriage with a prince, whose suspected infidelity with an older and less attractive woman was the talk of the court. Trapped and with no apparent escape route, she seemed defenseless against a powerful and uncaring royal family. Diana made an enchanting victim, a vision of self-sacrificial femininity. She kept her mask of motherly serenity, smiling beatifically to her millions of followers. And, as Scott Wilson wrote, "Diana's beauty remained indestructible and even blossomed when she became not only the most celebrated 'female victim of a brutal world,' but the patron of victims everywhere."

While Charles's infidelity was widely known, Diana's confession that she too had been unfaithful pushed the British monarchy toward its most serious crisis since 1936, when King Edward VIII left the throne to marry Wallis Simpson, a divorced American socialite (and subject of Madonna's 2012 movie W.E.). On November 20, 1995, Diana gave her first solo media interview. She was able to do so only by keeping her arrangement with Martin Bashir discreet and not asking for Palace approval. She opened up to Bashir about her postpartum (or postnatal, as British call it) depression and eating disorders, and her knowledge of Charles's adultery ("cheating" sounds too ignoble for royals). Rumors of Diana's own five-year affair with cavalry officer James Hewitt, whom she'd employed as a riding instructor, had circulated for a while.

There's no doubt that the fourteen words that became the most memorable of the interview, or perhaps of any other interview in modern times, were: "There were three of us in this marriage, so it was a bit crowded." If a single sentence can make and break lives, this was it. It helped turn Diana from an object of sympathy to a symbol of persecuted womanhood; it elevated Bashir to prominence as a journalist of rare mastery and finesse and gave him the leverage to secure an interview with Jackson, which effectively started the entertainer's annihilation.

As I mentioned earlier, twenty-five years after the Diana interview, Bashir was discovered to have used faked documents suggesting Diana's head of security had been paid by newspapers to convince her to grant him his exclusive. And independent inquiry concluded that Bashir had deployed deceitful methods to secure the interview, in breach of BBC editorial rules. In 2021, Bashir stepped down from his position at the BBC on grounds of ill health.

I risk hyperbolizing, but as celebrities go, Diana was *ne plus ultra*: the highest form of such a being. No woman or man has ever commanded such collective love from such a wide constituency, in her case, the world. Her popularity, as I wrote earlier, appeared to grow in inverse proportion to that of her husband. Diana threw herself into charitable work and aligned herself with great causes, visiting people living with Aids, children in hospitals, and other groups, all of whom responded empathically, as Jane Caputi reflected: "Those who participated in this flow of identification included people with AIDS, the young urban homeless, the injured, the socially marginalised, the poor, the imprisoned, the depressed, and the unloved." The "flow of identification" became tidal as people, especially women, from everywhere were drawn to someone, who, in her silence seemed to speak for everyone.

*   *   *

Diana carried on with her charitable endeavors, attracted battalions of journalists wherever she went. On one particularly photo-friendly occasion in January 1997, Diana, in her capacity as an International Red Cross VIP volunteer, visited Angola, on the west coast of southern Africa, to talk to landmine survivors of the years-long civil war (which eventually ceased in 2002). Front page-ready images of Diana in helmet and flak jacket were among the most memorable of the late twentieth century. She followed up this visit by traveling to another war-torn environment in Bosnia where again to talk to survivors of landmine explosions. And, from there, she went to see her companion Dodi Al-Fayed in France.

The tragedy unfolded late on August 30, 1997. Diana and Al-Fayed left the Ritz hotel in Place Vendôme, Paris, and were driven along the north bank of the Seine. Such were the dynamics of Diana's life that no move she made went unnoticed and, soon, journalists were in tandem. As Diana's Mercedes pulled away, a convoy of journalists sped after her. Remember, by 1997, interest in Diana was truly global and her every movement was monitored by the media. Being famous in the 1990s didn't mean only being known, recognized, or well regarded: it meant you were open to inspection. Diana never really had to do anything: the news came to her and appetite for it had, it seemed, no limits. "Diana," remarked Lapham, "was a celebrity of the most vulnerable and therefore the most nourishing type, a victim for all seasons."

At twenty-five minutes past midnight, nine vehicles carrying paparazzi and a single motorcycle followed Diana and Al-Fayed into an underpass below the Pont de l'Alma. As her Mercedes raced away from the pursuant pack, it clipped a wall and veered to the left, colliding with a pillar, then coming to a halt. There then followed a few tense, fraught moments in which the chasing photographers considered their options. Inside the wrecked car were four motionless bodies, including that of the world's most famous, most treasured, most idolized woman. Photographs of her would probably be worth a fortune. To delay aiding her and her fellow passengers for even seconds might jeopardize their chances of survival. How long should they allow themselves before giving assistance?

*   *   *

Still alive when they freed her, Diana was rushed to hospital by ambulance though attempts to save her proved futile. At 4:00 a.m., doctors pronounced her dead. Al-Fayed's bodyguard Trevor Rees-Jones was the only surviving passenger; none of the others was wearing seatbelts. Later, it became known that the chauffeur had been drinking prior to the journey. The media were cleared of blame, at least officially: Diana's brother, the Earl of Spencer, echoed the opinion of many when he declared, "I always believed the press would kill her in the end." Spencer, who was quoted by Jacqueline Sharkey in her 1997 article "The Diana Aftermath," pushed the argument further. "Every proprietor and editor of every publication that has paid for intrusive and exploitative photographs of her, encouraging greedy and ruthless individuals to risk everything in pursuit of Diana's image, has blood on his hands."

Sharkey reflected on how "the public and some members of the press denounced the photographers—and journalists in general—as 'barracuda,' 'jackals,' piranha' and 'vultures' feeding off celebrities." But few wanted to extend that same argument further. If they had, they would have been drawn to the uncomfortable conclusion that the paparazzi were motivated by money offered by media corporations that could sell publications in their millions to consumers whose thirst for pictures and stories of Diana seemed unquenchable. In the event, the photographers were cleared of any wrongdoing by a French court in 1999. The fact remains: all parties, from the paparazzi to the fans, were connected as if by invisible thread.

No one was quite prepared for what happened after Diana's death: there was the most extraordinary expression of public grief ever. The scope, scale, and intensity of the global response distinguished it from any comparable manifestation of sorrow. There had been moments of transferred emotion in the days following the deaths of John F. Kennedy in 1963, Winston Churchill in 1965, and Elvis Presley in 1977, but nothing quite like this: in the days leading to her funeral on September 6, over a million people went to pay their last respects, casting flowers along the length of her cortège.

A global television audience of 26 million watched the day's events. Elton John, who was a friend of Diana, released a new version of his Marilyn Monroe tribute, "Candle in the Wind," in allusion to Diana's Aeolian frailties and, while the venture was not for financial gain, there were plenty more that were. A foretaste of Diana's celebrity value, especially in death, arrived when the first issue of *Time* magazine following the tragedy sold 750,000 more copies than usual. Sales of a commemorative issue exceed 1.2 million. Merchandise proliferated: statuettes, decorative plates, and dolls appeared on shelves. Inevitably, conspiracy theories surrounding the death circulated, but this was 1997, before the internet had become the rumor-propagating phenomenon it became.

And then something happened that was to change the way we engaged with people we knew, or thought we knew, or at least *imagined* we thought we knew more than we actually did. "We became voyeurs to our own displays of 'suffering', playing 'Diana' to ourselves through blinking television monitors." This is how Donna Cox expressed it in her "*Diana: Her True Story*: Post-modern Transgressions in Identity."

I presume Cox meant that audiences not only watched the Diana fairytale reach its denouement but began to see themselves as bit part players in that same fairytale. This transformation was both revealing and concealing. The media's part in the death of Diana might have been laid bare, but consumers' complicity, though recognized, was left unexamined. While audiences might have agreed with the Earl of Spencer and condemned the media, they rewarded them with high sales and record viewing figures.

Anyone who was aware of Diana—and it's difficult to imagine anyone who wasn't—was made to inspect the way in which news values had been subverted by entertainment values. After all, Diana's greatest triumph was not so much in ushering in world peace, or saving the planet, but in offering pleasure to so many people. *She*, not what she did, was the attraction; and she was the reward. But it was an addictive reward: following figures who, like Diana, offered pleasure while presenting absolutely nothing that would materially enhance or alter in any way their lives or the lives of any other living thing. A reasonable expectation might be that an apparently irrational interest such as this would be either halted or massively interrupted by Diana's death. It was interrupted, but not massively: after a short spell of earnest introspection and critical evaluation of the media, the interest came back to life.

Although she didn't know it at the time, Diana surrendered her life in exchange for another in summer 1980 when it became known she was seeing Charles. She was nineteen. If she had met Jackson at the time he would have probably told her about the benefits of fame: respect, admiration, privilege, entitlement, and access to all areas, wherever you go. Even he wouldn't have known much about the other side of the bargain. Both truly understood only when the media refused to stop at the red disk with the white stripe. A few posed shots at arranged venues did not buy off the media. Diana discovered there was no escape. Mostly the media acted as if they had indisputable control of her life; a few paparazzi even went rogue and pulled off devil-may-care stunts to secure what they called the "money shots," crucial or climactic images they could sell to the highest bidder. Diana didn't own her own life. At least, that's how it must have felt.

She and Jackson coexisted in the same celebrity ecosystem. They came from totally different backgrounds and arrived by different routes, but they were in the same environment, both of them prey. That didn't mean they were helpless: in their own different ways, Diana and Jackson learned how to exploit their statuses. They were also opportunistic enough to use the media to their own ends. And probably vain enough to enjoy the machinations. Though ultimately, both were disempowered by the media.

* * *

The world would have been different without Diana: she was a new kind of being we now know as celebrities. One of life's wonders. In the 1980s and 1990s, it was legitimate to ask about a famous figure, "What are they famous for?" Now it seems gratuitous. "For? You mean you think celebrities have to do something apart from being celebs?" Diana had no talent comparable with Jackson's, or any other professional entertainer's: she grew organically from a story. It might, as I suggested earlier, have been a fairytale, but she was real enough: hers was a story of betrayal, neglect, perhaps catharsis, and definitely tragedy. She may not have sung or danced, but she aligned herself with humanitarian causes and that, when combined with her own lifestory, allowed audiences to endow her with whatever they pleased.

Without knowing it, Diana broke the boundaries of protocol. No one could answer exactly why they admired, respected, or loved her; but plenty did and they followed her like no one else in history. No Hollywood star, politician, or artist of international renown could rival her for global appeal. She demanded nothing of her followers: they didn't buy her cds, or go to her movies, or wear her own designer label clothes. The most valuable thing about Diana was her presence. Did the world need her? Not everyone in the world. Even after Diana's death, Queen Elizabeth did little to disguise her distaste for Diana's extraordinary populism. But everyone else, it seemed, mourned her passing; not because she humanized the royal family (though she certainly did that) but because she offered a unique figure, who offered the glamor and enchantment of a Hollywood star and the ordinariness and vulnerability of an abuse victim.

The media had changed appreciably in the 1980s, switching from its traditional reliance on facts to an approach that drew on conjecture and informed speculation. The collapse of the old private vs. public lives binary was hastened by Madonna and, to a more limited extent, Jackson, both of whom seemed to have studied Elizabeth Taylor's prescriptions for how to entice the media by offering glimpses into hitherto concealed areas of their lives. Coaxed by the media, especially the paparazzi (a word taken from the name of a fictional photo-journalist in Federico Fellini's1960 film *La Dolce Vita*), audiences grew to interact at distance with people who captivated them. They found the experience of involving themselves vicariously in others' lives surreally satisfying. How else do we explain the fascination with Diana? So again, did we need her? We did, if only because we wanted a human being as unpredictable and fallible as ourselves, but with the grace and majesty of a celestial being.

Today the intensive, invasive manner in which the media habitually ambush people, then make any crumb of information about them public, hardly merits critical comment. We take intel, especially insider intel, for granted. As Diana, Jackson, and many others who followed discovered, there were no secrets. Even though both played the media, they could never be sure, information they preferred to remain backstage would not be brought out front.

There's a line in Martin Scorsese's *The Irishman*, "Three people can keep a secret only when two of them are dead." After Diana, anyone who aspired to be a celebrity in any sphere, whether entertainment, politics, or anywhere else, would have had to pay heed to this, or some similar apothegm. Madonna voluntarily turned her confessions into hard currency; others had no choice. Jackson himself became party to what Lapham considered a bargain and learned the terms by heart. But even his on the fly education didn't equip him to deal with the stalking cameras and the gossip-sensitive ears that surrounded him.

Perhaps this is what James Hunter, of *Rolling Stone*, had in mind when he wrote, "He's angry, miserable, tortured, inflammatory, furious about what he calls, in 'Stranger in Moscow,' a 'swift and sudden fall from grace'." Hunter was interpreting Jackson's mood in 1995. He was basing his inference on the limited evidence of one track in particular on what was then Jackson's new album. "*HIStory* unfolds in Jackson's outraged response to everything he has encountered in the last year or so."

From Jackson's perspective, a most unhelpful contribution, unsolicited and without warning, came from sister LaToya Jackson. "I love Michael very dearly," she said, "but I feel even more sorry for these children because they don't have a life anymore."

10

Whatever Reality They Want

In Orson Welles's 1958 film *Touch of Evil* the protagonist's' body floats face-up in a dirty river as the gypsy Tanya, played by Marlene Dietrich, reflects, "he was some kind of a man," then asks, "what does it matter what you say about people?" Jackson, in 1993, was about to discover the answer.

As an entertainer commanding popular and critical regard, Jackson, by 1993, was probably the most successful in history, relegating Sinatra, Presley, and even his contemporary Madonna to also-rans. Who compared to a performer who had been around for three decades and had spent the last of these at the top of the business? Sinatra and the others profited from what people said about them. He was rumored to have had ties to organized crime, Presley was reported to have been enlisted by the FBI as an undercover agent. And Madonna had so many stories circulating that she probably forgot which ones she invented herself. In all cases, what people said mattered less than the fact that they were saying *something*. The worst possible stage of a celebrity career is when the talking stops. That's presumably what Jackson thought, at least until August 1993.

Jackson spent his thirty-fifth birthday (August 29, 1993) with Elizabeth Taylor and his sister, Janet Jackson. They were not celebrating. Instead, they were closeted away from the media in a Singapore hotel. Days before, Jackson had performed to 50,000 fans in Bangkok, Thailand. But any jubilation was tempered with concern.

Two days before, on August 27, 1993, the *Los Angeles Times* had run a story by Jim Newton and Sonia Nazario. Its headline was: POLICE SAY SEIZED TAPES DO NOT INCRIMINATE JACKSON. This was one of the first media reports to suggest, even hint, at a connection between Jackson and child abuse. It reported that police had executed a search warrant and taken videotapes from Jackson's home in Los Angeles. The article, in a serious newspaper, was written earnestly and circumspectly, quite unlike the media reports of the next several years. It described how a criminal investigation of Jackson had grown out of the custody battle between two estranged parents.

Jackson had been accused by Evan Chandler of sexually molesting his son Jordan. Police interviewed the son and two other boys, one of whom was Macaulay Caulkin, then twelve. The *National Enquirer*, sensing a story, but unable to contact Jackson, handed out business cards at the LA offices of the Department of Children's Services (the county's department that promotes child safety and wellbeing). But there was little to report. As the *Los Angeles Times* story emphasized in its headline, there was no evidence of any kind to implicate less still incriminate Jackson.

According to *GQ* writer Mary A Fischer's account, Jackson met twelve-year-old Jordan Chandler in May 1992 after the owner of a car rental business offered him a free rental on the condition Jackson agreed to call his stepson, who was a fan of Jackson's music. The owner's stepson got to talk to his idol and Jackson got a rental car (the *National Enquirer* story suggested Jackson regularly used rental cars to make himself less conspicuous). In February 1993, Jordan, along with his sister and his mother June, went to Neverland for the first of several visits. In late March, the family began traveling with Jackson to Las Vegas and abroad to places such as Morocco and Paris. Years later, in 2005, June Chandler revealed how she was initially comfortable with her son's growing friendship with Jackson but became concerned in March 1993, when Jackson took him to Las Vegas for a Cirque du Soleil show. Neither her son nor Jackson appeared at the show as planned. After confronting Jackson about their absence, she said Jackson became tearful and offended by her lack of trust in him. From then, Jordan would often stay and sleep in Jackson's room.

With Jackson still out of the United States, his head of security Anthony Pellicano arranged a news conference at which he introduced Wade Robson, who was ten, and Brett Barnes, who was eleven, both frequent guests of Jackson's at Neverland. Robson, who was later to feature in the *Leaving Neverland* documentary, said that he had shared a bed with Jackson "on dozens of occasions." Barnes advised reporters that Jackson caressed him lightly. "He kissed you like you kissed your mother," Barnes was quoted by Natalie Finn, of *E! News*. "It's not unusual for him to hug, kiss and nuzzle up to you." Barnes consistently defended Jackson and appeared in his support at the 2005 trial; for reasons that are not completely clear, he didn't appear in *Leaving Neverland,* and seems to have relocated to Australia. The documentary's director Dan Reed told Jason Guerrasio, of the *Business Advisor,* "I think we make it very clear in the film that they [Barnes and Culkin] deny to this day that anything sexual happened and I'm not about to try to change their minds about that."

The Chandlers were separated and Jordan's spells with Jackson upset the family's visitation schedule. Father Evan, a dentist, apparently became upset when the *National Enquirer* published a story headlined MICHAEL

JACKSON'S SECRET FAMILY—A MILLIONAIRE'S WIFE AND HER TWO KIDS, which depicted Jackson as a kind of paterfamilias (May 25, 1993). *Enquirer* writers Barbara Sternig and David Duffy quoted an "insider," who believed, "Michael 'adopted' June and her two children soon after he first met them."

June was seemingly relaxed about the situation. Evan Chandler was co-credited with writing the screenplay for Mel Brooks's 1993 film, *Robin Hood: Men in Tights*. It appears that during negotiations for a rescheduling of visitation, Jordan let slip to his father that Jackson had touched him on more than one occasion. (Evan Chandler closed his dental practice in 1994 and committed suicide in 2009, five months after Jackson's death.)

Pellicano speculated that the Chandler claim was part of a plot to extort $20 million from Jackson. About thirty attempts to blackmail Jackson were made every year, according to Pellicano. And he might not have been far off the mark. Mary A. Fischer asked the question, "Was Michael Jackson framed?" this being the title of her story for GQ in October 1994. The question raised the possibility that Jackson was being made to appear guilty.

The *Los Angeles Times* story raised the unconfirmed possibility suggested by "sources" that "the boy's father tried to cut a $20-million deal with Jackson." Hence the suggestion of extortion. In separate papers filed for the custody case, Jordan made no mention of Jackson. But, later, when in the presence of a psychiatrist, gave accounts of kissing, masturbating, and oral sex with Jackson. A similar account was provided by Newton and Nazario, the *Los Angeles Times* journalists.

Years later, in 2004, Josh Mankiewicz, of Dateline NBC, reported on an interview with a private investigator, who had worked on the case. "Back in 1993, Jackson's legal team, his representatives, were repeatedly saying that there was nothing to the charges because this was just a shake down for money, but in fact those two things aren't mutually exclusive," wrote Mankiewicz, who also reported that there was a payout to a twelve-year-old son of one of Jackson's employees at Neverland. "Dateline has learned that Michael Jackson paid that boy more than $2 million and the money came with a now familiar agreement: The terms of the settlement could never be discussed publicly."

Police certainly interviewed the thirteen-year-old son of Jackson's former maid, Blanca Francia and, while he initially denied being abused, he later told police that Jackson had touched his genitals, an account he later repeated on the witness stand at Jackson's 2005 trial. Bianca Francia also claimed she'd witnessed "improprieties between Jackson and several young boys, but didn't come forward until after she heard about the Chandler allegations," according to *Rolling Stone*'s Amelia McDonell-Parry.

* * *

From Jackson's perspective, a most unhelpful contribution, unsolicited, and without warning, came from sister LaToya Jackson, who called a media conference at short notice at a hotel in Tel Aviv, on the Mediterranean coast of Israel. Her damning news was that Michael had molested children for years and threatened to kill her if she spoke of it. "I love Michael very dearly, but I feel even more sorry for these children because they don't have a life anymore," she announced on December 8. "I hope he gets help." She maintained that their mother, Katherine Jackson, had shown her checks apparently made out to the families of young boys for substantial sums, though she didn't specify amounts.

It was an astounding submission. Perhaps less astounding once LaToya's relationship with the rest of the family is understood: she had maintained for years that her father had sexually and physically abused her as a child. The charge was disputed by the family and led to a severe estrangement. But she reaffirmed her earlier assertion in Tel Aviv when she declared, "My father molested me sexually and I don't like it. . . . That's what I don't want to see happen to these little kids." (The text of her announcement was covered widely, for example, by the *Washington Post*, December 9, 1993; viewable at: http://tiny.cc/bm2nuz under LA TOYA: CHARGES ARE TRUE.)

LaToya's claim started a bidding war between tabloids over what she claimed to be proof of her brother's activities. She set a reserve price of $500,000, but the proof never materialized. Another one of her ventures involved a phone hotline: for $2.99 callers could hear the "Jackson family secrets." Thirteen years later in 2006, LaToya, then forty-eight, recanted, informing ABC News that her comments "were orchestrated" by her husband at the time, Jack Gordon, "who forced her to read from a script, threatening harm if she didn't." In the years following her recantation, accusers came forward with allegations that appeared to bolster LaToya's original claim. Gordon, who died in 2005, aged sixty-five, had married LaToya in Reno in 1989; they divorced in Las Vegas in 1997. LaToya accused Gordon of abuse in their marriage and of violating her civil rights under the 1994 Violence Against Women Act. Gordon denied the allegations.

LaToya, like the other family members, was in showbusiness but lacked the cachet of Michael or the other brothers, or sister Janet, who had made her stamp on the entertainment world. LaToya had made records but became famous—or perhaps notorious—for appearing naked in a best-selling edition of *Playboy*. She also wrote a book with lurid details of what she portrayed as a deeply dysfunctional family. So, it seems fair to conclude that she most assuredly had an ax to grind and took the opportunity to sharpen and smooth its edge.

The Jackson family issued an immediate rebuttal. Jermaine Jackson raised the possibility that his sister was trying to revive interest in her by then weakening career. If so, he was probably right because she did manage to secure appearances on assorted reality tv shows and she had authored or co-authored three books by 2020.

Were they allowed, Chandler and his son would have probably offered an image of Jackson that would have been beyond the imagination of most at the time. But they had neither tangible evidence nor witnesses who would corroborate their story. Without either, no one would believe what must have sounded like an outlandish fairystory, would they? Jackson in 1993 was seen as childish in his predilections perhaps, and eccentric in his tastes for sure, but with no dark corners in his psyche. The story was implausible: the most celebrated singer on earth and sometime squire of Tatum O'Neal and Brooke Shields, Jackson was callow, but eligible. Why would anyone doubt his heterosexuality? There was nothing in his reported past—and pretty much everything he had done had been reported—to suggest he had any sexual tendencies that could be construed as deviant.

Surely, this was a hysterical shriek from some kid who had mistaken the soft-spoken Jackson's kindness for something more sinister. Jackson was reclusive and had some unusual practices; but global icons are allowed eccentricities. In any case, Elizabeth Taylor had been on Oprah a matter of months before and called Jackson "the least weird man" she had ever known. Actually, from Taylor that was an ambiguous commendation. At the time, Taylor had completed two spells at the Betty Ford Center and the benefits of them were not immediately apparent. She was drinking again and mixing tranquilizers with painkillers.

Meanwhile Jackson was complaining of migraine headaches and dehydration caused by tropical heat of Southeast Asia. He canceled two shows in Thailand in as many days. After becoming aware of the allegations, he issued a short statement through his lawyer: "I am confident the police department will conduct a fair and thorough investigation and that the result will demonstrate that there was no wrong doing on my part."

* * *

People waited the best part of three decades for an appalling if improbable revelation, then three came out of nowhere and stunned audiences like a Taser. Three months after the Chandler accusations surfaced, Jackson announced he was canceling his world tour to seek treatment for his addiction to painkillers. He attributed his dependence to the extreme distress and exhaustion, physical and mental, occasioned by what he continued to maintain were "false accusations." The tour had been beset by cancelations of concerts in Asia, Russia, Israel, and South America. Jackson had blamed health problems. But this was the first admission that he had acquired a dependency.

The *New York Times* (November 14, 1993) repeated Jackson's explanation that painkilling drugs had been prescribed after recent reconstructive surgery on his scalp, presumably part of the ongoing treatment for the injuries incurred while making a Pepsi video nine years before. Pepsi had remained sponsors of Jackson but canceled the contract immediately after Jackson's drugs acknowledgment. Years later, Dr. Stuart Finkelstein, who treated Jackson on the 1993 tour, reflected that Jackson appeared to have a high tolerance for morphine and had on a Duragesic patch, this being typically used to treat chronic pain in patients (pain severe enough to require daily, around-the-clock, longterm opioid treatment).

The decision to abort the tour—which cost Jackson about $10 million— was apparently Elizabeth Taylor's: she interrupted the tour after a concert in Mexico City and insisted Jackson checked into rehab. "Elizabeth takes us aside and says to us, 'We're going to get him out of the country after the show. He's going to go to London,'" recalled Jackson's personal assistant Frank Cascio, who was also a longtime friend, when talking to Alice Gomstyn and Chris Connelly in 2011. Exactly where in London was open to doubt: the media heard the Charter Nightingale Hospital in west London, which was something of a haven for damaged celebrities. The hospital refused to confirm or deny Jackson's presence.

The dependency revelation was a lot less stunning than the Chandler accusations, which still seemed impossible and unbelievable. They were connected of course and signaled that Jackson was being forced out into the open and made both to defend and protect himself, whether he liked it or, much more likely, not. In the process, the qualities that had once been integral to his appeal were turned into instruments of torture. Of course, Michael Jackson was infantile; geniuses often betray unusual traits. But Jackson was no longer just unusual: he was properly odd and not necessarily in a likeable way. He was also a habitual drug user, even if the drugs on which he was hooked were not the illegal variety usually associated with rockstars.

Drugs stories are a dime a dozen and, while Jackson's indisposition was news, it was yet another case in the unending saga of rich people succumbing to chemical mollification. America's broadcast media gave extensive coverage to the alleged abuse story, though the slightly more cautious press, presumably staying mindful that Jackson had not been charged with any offense, paid modest attention. If this was truly a kiss-and-tell story, it was arguably the greatest of its kind in history or an outright falsehood. It seemed the public wasn't in the mood for a morality drama, even one concerning the world's premier entertainer. The goodwill Jackson had earned over the decades seemed to stand him in good stead and, amazing as it may sound today, Jackson emerged, if anything, a victim.

On his return to the United States, Jackson, on December 22, released a video in which he implored, "Don't treat me like a criminal because I am innocent." He disclosed how he'd been "forced" to submit to what he called a dehumanizing and humiliating examination by the Santa Barbara County

Sheriff's department and the LAPD. This, he said, involved inspecting his genitals. The presumption was that the accuser had described an unusual physical characteristic. The inspection was inconclusive. A month later in January 1994, lawyers for Jackson and for Chandler announced that they'd settled a civil lawsuit and paid an undisclosed sum, later thought to be nearly $25 million—close to $45 million today if indexed to inflation. The deal was negotiated on Jackson's behalf by his lawyer, Johnnie Cochrane Jr., later to represent O. J. Simpson and Larry Feldman, who was retained by Chandler's parents. Part of the agreement reached was that the payment did not mean the case was settled. In the absence of any other witnesses, law enforcement officials dropped the prosecution. No criminal charges were ever filed. There were thirteen months between the first news report and the settlement.

Yet questions lingered. Did 35-year-old Jackson have the kind of sexual feelings typically associated with a man of his age? If so, how did he express them? With whom? Jackson was probably the most media-covered person in the world in the early 1990s. Despite his periods of solitude, he engaged with the media all the time through various channels; yet fans had learned nothing of his deeper motivations. He'd for long been an enigma; now he was an enigma of diverse sexual propensity.

Or was he? On May 26, 1994 (nine months after the *Los Angeles Times* story), Jackson married Lisa Marie Presley, the daughter of Elvis. She was then twenty-six and the tabloids leaked details of what was intended to be a secret ceremony in the Dominican Republic. This was the third taser-like stunning revelation after the Jordans' claim and the dependency confession. Jackson, at this stage, was hard-pressed to keep any kind of secret from the media. Eleven weeks after the wedding, in a prepared statement, Presley declared her love for Jackson. "I understand and support him, we both look forward to raising a family and living a happy, healthy life together," she announced. Then, in the most preposterous utterance of wishful thinking imaginable, she added, "We hope friends and fans will understand and respect our privacy."

The timing of the wedding announcement deserves a countback. In April 1994, Presley stated that she intended to divorce her musician husband Danny Keough after six years of marriage, having separated in 1993. They had two children, aged five and one. That suggested her courtship with Jackson was condensed into a matter of a few weeks. Jackson was, by this stage, something of a withdrawn character. Probably the most public recluse in history, thanks to a media willing to convey any particle of information on a figure whose appeal had grown in direct proportion to his unusualness. He'd certainly been seen with women, especially Taylor, who was twenty-six years his senior. But he didn't seem her type: she usually went for older, white men.

The year after he married Lisa Marie, Jackson completed a deal with Martin Bandier, who was then head of EMI Music Publishing, for the right to administer his ATV Music catalog. The advance paid to Jackson was $70 million and the arrangement meant that Jackson and Sony would form a joint venture to manage song rights. As part of the deal, Bandier agreed to sell three Elvis Presley songs to Jackson. Jackson became half-owner of Sony/ATV and, as such, held sway over about half-a-million songs, including more than 200 Beatles tunes. In 2016, Sony paid Jackson's estate $750 million for its 50 percent interest in Sony/ATV, gaining complete control of a company in which Jackson had held an interest since 1985, as we'll discover in Chapter 18.

*   *   *

When her father died of a heart attack on August 16, 1977, Lisa Marie Presley inherited a weighty legacy. Not only did she become the heir to a formidable estate that turned over nearly $40 million per year, but she inherited the reflected international fame of a man whose spirit would eventually entice over 500,000 pilgrims every year to his Graceland home. He couldn't bequeath his daughter his voice or his hips but he left her enough distinguishing looks to make sure, when people looked at her, they knew they were looking at Elvis's daughter. She had no known aspirations to be a singer.

Now pause: as childhoods go, Lisa Marie's must rank high on the extraordinary scale. Born into an ill-starred marriage (Elvis and her mother Priscilla separated in 1972 and were divorced in 1973), she survived her parent's breakup when she was four, went through her own marital breakdown and spells of depression and drug abuse, and lived her life, basically, as two people: secondarily, herself, but primarily as Elvis Presley's daughter. The latter was an inescapable designation that followed her, evoking gasps and gawps wherever she went. She could have made and sold more records than Jackson, won more Oscars than Katherine Hepburn (who snagged four), and ran for president more times than Hillary Clinton (twice), but, to hundreds of millions of people, she could never be anyone but Elvis Presley's daughter. This sounds unkind, but while the moniker might sound like more of a curse than a benediction, the benefits were substantial. Being the offspring—the sole offspring—of a legendary entertainer, no one expects you to surpass your dad's achievement, nor even get close; and your genes alone guarantee you the affection of every one of his fans. Plus, you never have to worry about working for a living. And, when it's time to trade in the private helicopter for a new model, you're never short of the cash difference.

After her parents divorced, Lisa Marie split her time between her mother's home in Los Angeles and Graceland, in Memphis, Tennessee, about 1,800 miles away. Her mother Priscilla joined the Church of Scientology after Elvis's death in 1977. She raised Lisa Marie as a Scientologist. The Church has several showbusiness believers, including Tom Cruise, Kirstie Alley, and John Travolta. Lisa Marie spent a while as a teenager at the Church's Celebrity Centre International, in Hollywood.

Actually, I told a white lie three paragraphs ago: Lisa Marie didn't become heir to her father's estate, at least not immediately after his death. In fact, three days after Elvis died, his ex-wife Priscilla was informed by the family accountant, Joseph Hanks, that the annual expense of running the Graceland estate was rising from $480,000, and the income was suddenly in steep decline. While Priscilla had not involved herself in budgets during her six-year marriage, she knew her husband was imprudent when it came to money: what he didn't spend on himself or his family, he gave away in gifts— like limousines. The 1968 Comeback Special discussed in Chapter 7 was motivated more by financial necessity than artistic endeavor. After he died, there were no more concerts, nor new films or records for that matter. Royalties from his back catalog went not to his estate but to RCA, which had bought rights to them for $5.4 million in 1973. Elvis was a calamitous mismanager of his own money: not only did he sell the rights to his 700+ recordings cheaply, he also, thanks to a prior deal with his manager Colonel Tom Parker, received only $2.7 million and, after tax, ended up with a paltry $1.35 million for what is comparable in value to the Beatles' catalog—bought by Jackson in 1984 for $47.5 million. Robert Hilburn wrote an account of the financial predicament faced by Priscilla in the Los Angeles Times, on June 11, 1989.

Lisa Marie was heir to the Presley estate, but she was not to take control until she turned twenty-five. In the meantime, Priscilla together with the family lawyer and the National Bank of Commerce had to keep the family financially sound. Her primary concern was, presumably, the financial wellbeing of Lisa Marie. In 1981, she decided to turn Graceland into a tourist attraction, replete with a Jungle Room (in homage to a Hawaii hotel where Elvis stayed), statues of monkeys, the King's bedroom with its round bed and inset mirrors, and a racquetball court ornamented with Elvis's gold records. So, by the time Lisa Marie was old enough to oversee the estate, the financial structure had been stabilized and Priscilla, Hanks and the bank had collectively established the late King as one of the world's highest earning dead celebrities, with a posthumous income of around $39 million (in 2019; Jackson made $60 million).

On February 1, 1993, Lisa Marie became sole inheritor of the by-then cash-generating Memphis mansion, which is still a rock 'n' roll equivalent of Mecca. By then, Lisa Marie was married to Danny Keough, a musician she met when at the Church of Scientology. Their affiliations prompted almost automatic speculation that a portion of the Elvis fortune would end up with the Church. Like many children with parents who have created rather than just existed in modern times (Nancy Sinatra, Julian Lennon, Michael Wilding Jr., son of Elizabeth Taylor) Lisa Marie made a spirited but brief attempt to get into showbusiness, but, unlike say Liza Minnelli or Michael Douglas, failed to make an impression. Mostly, she was just Elvis's daughter.

Jackson's interest in Lisa Marie, on her account, started when he heard a demo she'd made and asked to meet up. They met at a friend's house and became friends themselves. They'd met briefly years before in 1975, when a seven-year-old Presley went to a Jackson 5 concert and took advantage of her family connections to go backstage. By the time she and Jackson next met in 1992, she was married to Keough and had two children. But Presley told *Rolling Stone* magazine in April 2003, this time, she got "sucked into" Jackson's narrative, which was basically that of a "misunderstood person," what she described as a "Howard Hughes thing" (Howard Hughes was an American industrialist and film producer who spent twenty-five years of his final life as an obsessive-compulsive recluse. He died in 1976). "I think it worked for him [Jackson] to manipulate that image for a little while," mused Lisa Marie (April 20, 2003). "It made him mysterious."

Certainly, the pairing of Presley and Jackson was mysterious. And there was little clarification until they agreed to a television interview on ABC News' *Primetime Live*, in June 1995. Anticipating what she must have realized was the question everyone wanted answered, Lisa Marie affirmed that she and Jackson slept together. "Do we have sex?" she asked herself aloud. "Yes, yes, yes." Considering there were only twenty days between her divorce with Keough and her marriage to Jackson, "who popped the question?" seemed relevant. Unsurprisingly, it was Jackson: during a phone conversation. Presley agreed without hesitation. The 1995 *Primetime* can be viewed at: https://www.youtube.com/watch?v=H5xxK7ad-zg.

Six months after the tv interview, Lisa Marie allegedly asked for a separation. "Irreconcilable differences" were cited. Jackson was in New York's Beth Israel North Medical Center after collapsing with suspected low blood pressure. The marriage lasted twenty-one months (the divorce was finalized in August 1996). Lisa Marie spoke of it as a "delusional" episode in her life. She spoke of the similarities in their backgrounds and the distinction of being married to someone "more famous than me." Being Elvis's daughter, Lisa Marie presumably felt an obligation to marry someone of her own or even her father's standing. "They had the luxury of creating whatever reality around them they wanted to create," she compared Jackson with her father, years later in a 2010 interview. Keough was a jobbing musician, whose claim to fame was always destined to be: the first husband of Elvis's daughter. Jackson, on the other hand, was the man who aspired to be as big as Elvis. Not just as big either: as legendary. And indulgent. And epicurean. "Both Elvis and Michael Jackson could be described as secretive legends prone to fantasy, self-indulgence, excess and surrounding themselves with sycophantic employees," wrote Jessica Seigel of the *Chicago Tribune* (August 2, 1994).

Extravagance could also have been a key. The gifts her father lavished on Lisa Marie are now part of the Elvis mythology. One standout story involves her innocently mentioning she'd never seen snow: her dad summoned his jet to take his daughter to Idaho where she played in the snow for twenty minutes then returned home. He gave her a pony before she could walk and a diamond brooch for her sixth birthday. Hers was a childhood of excess. What husband could match her dad's generosity?

Maybe that was all she wanted from a marriage: a man to match her dad.

* * *

Jackson's enthusiasm for marriage is a different matter. Obvious or inscrutable? Think of him as the driver of a speeding car heading for a railway crossing as a train approaches: the brakes fail and he swerves, avoiding the locomotive but caroming into a parked car; his car is damaged, but not the total write-off it might have been otherwise—and he's alive. The Chandler embarrassment behind him, he must have been aware that he'd escaped not exactly intact, but with his reputation only compromised rather than wrecked. That's the obvious interpretation: he married Lisa Marie because it would bolster his heterosexual, heteronormative credentials and serve to strengthen the view that the Chandler allegations were what many already suspected they were: extortion. Who knows? Lisa Marie might even been a willing accomplice and threw herself into a sham marriage that served Jackson's purpose and, in a different way, her own: if she was planning a showbusiness career, what better pr than to get hitched to Michael Jackson? Her debut album, *To Whom It May Concern*, wasn't released until 2003 and entered the *Billboard* chart at number five. It was a long time after her much-publicized marriage finished (1996) but the fated liaison lingered in the memory. Presley married actor Nicolas Cage in 2002. The marriage lasted 108 days. She then married music producer Michael Lockwood, with whom she had twin daughters. That marriage lasted ten years and concluded amid a custody battle.

Jackson's motivations were explored, though not in depth in the *Primetime* interview in mid-1995, when host Diane Sawyer broached the subject by echoing the thoughts of others. "It was somehow too convenient," said Sawyer. "Lisa, did you ask Michael about the charges?" Presley advised that she didn't discuss the impact the marriage would have on the effects of the Chandler case. "I was actually part of the whole thing with him," she revealed, explaining how they were in contact by phone throughout the whole affair. She confirmed that she didn't need to ask Jackson whether the charges were false: it was implicit. The question that was probably on many people's minds was probably too awkward to ask and likely to get only one answer. But let me ask it here, as if Jackson was in the room and we were in 1995:

Michael, you'll probably be aware that, in the past, many showbusiness marriages were based less on love, more on the practical need to perpetuate a myth. I'm thinking of, for example, Barbara Stanwyck's marriage to Robert Taylor in 1939, which is now thought to have been arranged by her studio MGM to conceal her sexual orientation. Or, more famously, Rock Hudson's marriage to his agent's secretary Phyllis Gates, which was hastily arranged when a story about his proclivities surfaced and threatened to undermine his ladies' man persona. In both these and numerous other cases, marriage was repurposed as a safeguard for reputations. Now, you'll forgive me, I hope, for raising this possibility, but it is, I believe, on many people's minds: the allegations, which you vehemently deny, were made in July 1993 and you were married in May 1994. That's ten months. You see where I'm going with this? People are wondering if your marriage was designed, not necessarily to conceal anything; I accept that you reject the Chandler's account entirely. But perhaps to return to a certain kind of image of you, the kind of image that held sway before August 1993.

Once more, we're relying on informed guesswork, but Jackson might have replied:

You think we're faking this? It's the dumbest thing I ever heard. Lisa Marie is sweet and loving. We were dating for four months and never tried to hide it before we got married. There's really only one reason I asked her to marry me.

Are you in love?

Lisa Marie: *Of course.*
Michael: *Whatever in love means.*

Some readers will notice that I've used the words Jackson and Presley used in the *Primetime* interview, but perhaps unfairly, added Prince Charles's infamous proviso to the same question, "Are you in love?" when interviewed with Diana after they announced their engagement in 1981. It's doubtful whether Jackson would have added a phrase that sounded so uncaring. But, during the real interview, he didn't appear as a man bent on persuading skeptics or anyone else of his sincerity. If anything, he confirmed suspicions that this was a show marriage. And, even those who were prepared to accept the couple's genuineness might have been turned by the brevity of the conjugal relationship. The marriage lasted only twenty-one months, remember.

* * *

Jackson was rehearsing for the sixth *Billboard* Music Awards in New York when he collapsed on stage, apparently suffering from dehydration. He was taken to the Beth Israel Medical Center North to undergo tests. His sister Janet rushed to his bedside and left the hospital a few hours later without speaking to reporters. Jackson had been scheduled to appear at the Billboard ceremony, but Tina Turner accepted a career achievement awards on his behalf. Journalists tried to contact Lisa Marie through her agent Lee Solters, who also represented Jackson, but to no avail. Later accounts suggest that she went to the hospital and was allowed to see her husband but only for a limited period.

Jackson had accumulated something of a medical history over the previous decade or so. In 1984, he had been hospitalized with second-degree burns to the scalp after an accident while shooting a Pepsi Cola advertisement. He went to hospital in 1990 after complaining of chest pains and was released after a series of tests. As we noted earlier in this chapter, he canceled concerts in Singapore after citing the tropical heat as the cause of dehydration. Shortly after, he abandoned the whole concert tour and disclosed his dependence on prescription painkillers.

During his stay in the hospital, Jackson received a get-well wish from LaToya, who had earlier expressed the suspicion that the collapse was "a little scheme" to get attention. This was not the case: doctors described his ailment as a "life-threatening illness" that required him to stay in an intensive care unit before being transferred to a private room. His gastroenteritis was probably caused by a virus that affected liver and kidney functions. Jackson entered the hospital a married man and left still married but separated. His wife filed for divorce the next month.

Jackson might have thought the ripples caused by the Chandlers had disappeared and the once-roiling water was once again calm. If so, he was disillusioned: in 1996, a self-published book bearing the title *Michael Jackson Was My Lover: The Secret Diary of Jordy Chandler*, which purported to be a portrayal of Jackson's relationship with Jordan Chandler was published by its author Victor Gutierrez, a writer from Chile. Jordan is often abbreviated to Jordie, though "Jordy" in the book's subtitle. *Vanity Fair* writer Maureen Orth pointed out that Gutierrez had spent four years researching his "minutely detailed book," which had "utterly scatological details about Michael Jackson." Scatological refers to an interest in excretion and excrement. The book was not published in the United States, but Gutierrez published it privately in Chile.

Gutierrez presented a picture of Chandler's family as uncaring opportunists who accepted gifts from Jackson, including a $12,000 Cartier bracelet for the mother. Gutierrez claimed Evan Chandler negotiated with Jackson: he wanted houses, cars, and money in exchange for his silence. While it isn't directly pertinent to Gutierrez's book, I might point out that Jordan Chandler went on to attain legal emancipation from both of his parents when he was fourteen. (In the United States, a person is considered a child under the legal custody of a parent or guardian until he or she turns eighteen, in most cases; after that they're granted adults status. But, if child believes he or she would thrive alone and can support themselves and courts agree, then they can apply for legal emancipation. Statutes vary from state to state.)

In April 1998, a Superior Court in California, ordered Gutierrez to pay Jackson $2.7 million. The case centered on Gutierrez's claim on ABC television's show *Hard Copy* that he'd seen a 27-minute video of Jackson having sex with a minor. Jackson denied this ever took place and sued for slander. The court asked Gutierrez to produce evidence. He failed to do so. Gutierrez had filed for bankruptcy before the trial was scheduled to begin.

In the 1990s, the norm was that the person claiming to have had their reputation damaged by someone's false statement should demonstrate that the media or outlet for the slander either knew of the falsity of the statement or were either reckless or even malicious when the report was released. Without evidence of this, a favorable verdict was unlikely. Earlier, a Los Angeles Superior Court judge had dismissed Jackson's $100 million lawsuit against *Hard Copy*'s reporter Diane Dimond, the show's parent Paramount Pictures and KABC Radio. Dimond had appeared on a KABC show to discuss Gutierrez's claim.

Jackson's attorney told the *Los Angeles Times*, "I talked to the jurors [after the verdict], and they said they wanted to send a message to the tabloids to stop writing malicious stories about celebrities" (April 10, 1998). Gutierrez's attorney, Robert Goldman, agreed "some of the jurors wanted to send a message to tabloids." This was the late 1990s; the tabloids clearly didn't get the message.

After the court case, Gutierrez told Orth that he first learned about the videotape he claimed to have seen (but never produced in court, remember) from members of Jackson's extended family (that is, relatives beyond the nuclear Joe-Kathleen family).

* * *

The case must have given Jackson pause for thought on the striking number of stories about him and how these had multiplied in a relatively short period of time. Some of them were no doubt flights of fancy, but even they provided evidence that Michael Jackson had become a subject worthy of even the most untenable fabrication.

"What does it matter what you say about people?" For much of his life Jackson had a ready answer: not much, just as long as you're saying *something*. For much of his life, Jackson would have been right—almost. Rumors, half-truths, and even downright lies usually do no lasting harm and, indeed, can boost a celebrity's standing. But, in the early days of Hollywood, they could be fatal. The cautionary case of Roscoe "Fatty" Arbuckle functioned as a reminder of the cost of scandal.

Arbuckle died in 1933 but his specter roamed the backlots of Hollywood for decades. He was a silent screen actor, writer, and director who, in 1921, when thirty-four and at the top of his career, became involved in the twentieth century's first major scandal. Falsely accused of rape and manslaughter, Arbuckle went to trial three times before he was cleared. But, by the time he was acquitted, the talking was all done and his showbusiness career was finished. He died a penniless smackhead, aged forty-six. Arbuckle's quietus was effectively a warning to other entertainers and their employers. After his case, they avoided scandal for fear of the consequences. And the studios were skilled in cover-ups.

The likes of Stanwyck and Hudson were easy. Concealing the arrest of a promising young actor for marijuana possession in 1948 was a trickier assignment for RKO studio chief Howard Hughes. But he managed it and Robert Mitchum went on to an epic career. Joan Crawford denied she ever played in a porn movie, but the buzz continued throughout her career, yet without really jeopardizing it. Scandal sheets, in particular *Confidential*, flourished by recording scurrilous tales and inviting readers to step down from their high chairs to pronounce judgment. A little scandal-tinged hearsay did no one's career any harm. All the same, it was wise to steer clear.

The scandal, or rather the response to it that signaled changing standards was the near-infamous sex video featuring Rob Lowe in 1988. Today, as we know, sex tapes act as career propellants; the likes of Paris Hilton and Kim Kardashian have benefited in a most direct way. Lowe faced humiliation and possible pariah status. This was the late 1980s, remember; after Madonna had demonstrated how, with a little armtwisting, the public could be induced to enjoy being enraged or outraged. It was a dangerous art. Lowe's offense didn't go unpunished, but it wasn't till 1999 that he returned fully restored in the NBC's *The West Wing*.

Robert Downey Jr.'s career seemed in terminal decline after he was sentenced to three years in prison in 1999 for repeatedly violating his probation on drugs and weapons charges. He served less than a year. His first acting job after being released from a California state prison was for *Ally McBeal*. He was arrested again in 2001. Downey was officially pardoned in 2015 by which time he had risen like a Mavic drone. In 2013 he was named Hollywood's highest earning actor by *Forbes*, making an estimated $75 million.

Both transgressions seem tame today. Sex videos and drugs are hardly likely to horrify audiences. But they would almost certainly have assured both offenders tickets to oblivion earlier in the twentieth century. In the event, both artists managed to navigate safe passages back to the top. Jackson, having lived through the 1980s and 1990s, was no doubt aware of the value of a distracting irrelevance; a story doesn't have to have any merit nor even be genuinely worthy of anyone's attention: as long as it kept people talking about him, he stayed in the popular imagination. The problems for any artist typically start when audiences stop talking about them. The trick—and Jackson seemed to have mastered it—was to engage audiences without ever satisfying them. Always leave them wanting more, as adage goes. In Jackson's era, there was a seemingly unlimited curiosity among the public. He probably understood this as well as anybody and managed it better than most.

The gap in his knowledge seems to have been a lack of familiarity with the concept of taboo. All cultures have prohibited practices or pursuits restricted by customs. These include intimate adult associations with children, which are forbidden in a great many cultures, historical and contemporary. There is anthropological and historical evidence that pederasty (i.e., sexual activity involving adult men and boys) was acknowledged or condoned in Ancient Greece, feudal Japan, and the pre-Christian Roman Empire. But, in most known cultures it is strictly taboo (as are sexual relations between closely related people; this is known as the incest taboo).

Jackson was unpredictable, reliably unpredictable, and his audience expected to be surprised. Yet, the revelation that he slept with young boys was a surprise too far. Should he, a grown man, have known it would end in tears? Of course. Even a cursory reflection on the consequences of a trespass such as this would have alerted him. Perhaps he naively thought he was doing no harm (which was his interpretation of his behavior), or would never get found out (very unlikely he would assume this). Or maybe he felt the cultural protocols that govern the conduct of others didn't apply to the world's premier entertainer. If he had been entertaining eighteen-year-old men or women, his practice wouldn't have stirred controversy at all. If anything, it would have normalized him somewhat (eighteen is the age of consent in California). But Jackson was confident, supercilious, and heedless of the proprieties that affect *everyone*. The term "taboo" is from the Tongan *tabu*, meaning prohibited.

It *does* matter what you say about people. It's easy to imagine why Jackson thought it didn't. Jackson lived day to day in his own myth. Lots of great entertainers aspire to create myths about themselves; only a few of them assimilate the myths. Lisa Marie was probably right when she told *Primetime Live*, "it worked for him to manipulate that image," meaning that he yielded much of himself to the media in exchange for continual publicity. He led the media down blind alleys and disused mineshafts, of course; but that was all part of the project. "It made him mysterious," as she put it. "Then it backfired."

Perhaps so, but, at the end of the Chandler affair, the drugs confession and the perplexing marriage, Jackson was still as much a fascinating enigma as he was at its outset. A more disturbing one.

The scene from *Touch of Evil* is viewable at: https://bit.ly/2WKtuXd

The television show Good Times *was a perfect learning environment for the young Janet, who played "Penny Gordon" for two seasons. By the age of sixteen, she had made her first album.*

11

Shifting the Needle

Your name is Jackson and your brother is the most popular entertainer in the world. You were born in 1966. That makes you eight years younger than he is and the youngest member of your family. You can't remember much about the place where you were born because the family moved out of Gary, Indiana, when you were just two. The relocation was part of a career move. Not your career, of course; but your brothers'. Michael, Jermaine, Marlon, Jackie, and Tito were known collectively as the Jackson 5. They were beginning to make an impact as a band. Los Angeles was the logical place for any entertainer who intended to make progress. You had no aspirations to be a performer when you were a child. In fact, for a while, you looked destined for an altogether different life. You were home tutored rather than sent to a school and started horse riding at five. There was something of the tomboy about you: you played baseball, basketball, and habitually climbed trees. There was little to distinguish from other well-to-do children at this point.

When you were seven, your father asked you a question that no other father has ever asked his seven-year-old daughter. It was whether you'd like to sing in a Las Vegas show. Your reply was equally unique: "OK." Actually, it was probably, "OK, Joseph." You never called him dad, always Joseph. For most children of seven, this would be like being dropped into a whirlpool without a safety vest or a lifebuoy. But what did you do? Sang "Love Is Strange" with Jermaine, a couple of Sonny and Cher tunes and dropped in an impromptu Mae West impersonation. You did this twice a day for two weeks. You were too young to start a career on stage. But so was your brother. What is too young? Anyway, you are a Jackson and that means you are part of a family that lives life as a hard day's journey into showbusiness. Any dysfunctional stops en route are unwelcome but necessary breaks in the journey. So when Norman Lear took an interest in you, your father had no hesitation in encouraging the approach.

Lear (b. 1922) was the writer and producer of many tv comedies, including *All in the Family* and *Sanford and Son*. In 1974 he had spun off *Good Times* from an earlier show, *Maude*. He was looking for someone to play the role of an abused child. You auditioned and Lear was sold: he cast you in the role of Penny Gordon for two seasons and the studio proved a perfect learning environment. Later roles in *Diff'rent Strokes*, *Fame* and *A New Kind of Family* convinced you that acting is your forte. But Joseph was familiar with the music industry and saw the tv parts only as a prelude to a recording career. He negotiated you a deal with A&M records and your first album was released in 1982, when you were sixteen. Your brothers were, by this stage, well established and Michael was emerging as one of the top entertainers in the world, having three years before released his exalted *Off the Wall* album. Perhaps this is what motivated you: to match your brother's global appeal. Frankly, your first album wasn't likely to do it.

Then you met a guy who inspired you. His name was James DeBarge and he was part of the band DeBarge that was making its mark in the early 1980s. The band's most successful song was "Rhythm of the Night" and in 1984, the year of its release, you ran off with James to his hometown, Grand Rapids, Michigan, and got married. Your family knew nothing of this and, by all accounts, learned about the marriage only through the media. Other Jackson family members married young: Rebbie (the eldest), Tito, and Marlon were eighteen; Jermaine nineteen. Were they trying to break free of the family? Were you? Your marriage was annulled within a year, due largely to pressure from the Jackson family. Your father was still your manager. Another album in 1984 failed to impress and, in an incredible display of either impetuosity or independence, you relieved your father of his managerial duties and put yourselves in the hands of John McClain, an executive for A&M.

Your next album for A&M had a simple but colossal remit. "We were going for *the* black album of all time. Gritty, raw," pronounced the co-producer Jimmy Jam. The other co-producer was Terry Lewis and between the three of you, you came up with one of the albums of the 1980s. *Control* was released on February 4, 1986. You were twenty and already had three albums to your name.

The album went to the top of the *Billboard* charts and produced six top twenty singles (from nine tracks on the album), including the title track "Control." The norm back then was to release an album, usually on tape and cd, then select the strongest tracks to sell independently, often remixed, as singles over a period of time. The singles were accompanied by tailored videos that were featured by MTV and other music channels as well as in music shows on tv. Your dancing is still memorable. Paula Abdul, who was a cheerleader for the Los Angeles Lakers basketball team, choreographed the dance routines. She'd already worked with the Jackson 5 on a video.

Reviewing the album, Eric Henderson of *Slant* magazine, called *Control* "a quintessential statement on personal and artistic self-actualization."

Your two previous albums were relegated to a "prehistory." Many people interpreted *Control* as a kind of "coming-of-age." You had been largely under the influence of your family, in particular your father at that stage. The album sold 10 million copies and was later released on vinyl.

Most young women would have been pleased to have tv acting parts and three albums under their belts (not to mention an annulled marriage) by the age of twenty. But *Control* suggested you were a new artist, detached from your "old" self: the title described something you'd wanted but which eluded you under the family's influence. The word crops up in the lyrics and whenever journalists talk to you about your life. Your father never emerges from discussions as an angel. McClain, on the other hand, loomed ever larger and ever more influential as you matured. I wonder if you ever wondered if you'd replaced one Svengali figure with another.

But there were snippy whispers. Robert Hilburn, of the *Los Angeles Times*, summarized them in 1990 when he wrote, "She was a girl who got where she was because she was a Jackson and that she had enough money to bring in all these hired guns to shape her music and image for her. I'd probably think, 'I could be doing the same thing if I had her money'."

* * *

As Lisa Marie Presley had to come to terms with being "Elvis's daughter," so the youngest of the family was made to get used to "Janet Jackson, sister of Michael." The production team of Jam and Lewis were credited as the creators of *Control*, and Abdul, who went on to pursue her own singing career, often took the plaudits for the inventive dance routines in the videos. And, as Hilburn pointed out, "From certain angles on stage, Jackson looks remarkably like her famous brother." Janet had severed professional ties to the rest of the family.

The next album, *Rhythm Nation 1814*, arrived in 1989 and was a second resounding success. It had twenty tracks, eight of them spoken interludes. Janet played up the social consciousness aspect of this album, citing Tracy Chapman as an influence. It prompted some writers, like Joseph Vogel, to wonder if Jackson was "The most culturally significant female artist of the 1980s?" Vogel was mindful that Madonna, Whitney Houston, Annie Lennox, Tina Turner, and Cyndi Lauper had legitimate claims to the designation, and that Jackson had only two significant albums in the decade. "But none of these artists achieved the cross-racial impact (particularly on youth culture) of Janet," wrote Vogel for *The Atlantic*. "And none of them had an album like *Rhythm Nation 1814*."

Vogel offered the thought that, as a black artist, Jackson was recording "in the face of great pressure to conform to corporate formulas." The album's themes are unmistakably relevant and included poverty, racism, drugs, and war. Vogel compared the album with Marvin Gaye's *What's*

Going On, which was, in 1971, something of a cultural landmark. *Rhythm Nation 1814* is never mentioned in the same breath as Gaye's classic and Vogel reckons it was quickly forgotten. Unjustifiably in his opinion.

Not all commentators were won over. "Over the last three years, Ms. Jackson may have begun worrying about social problems, and perhaps she decided to use her popularity as a pulpit," wrote Jon Pareles for the *New York Times*. "Her motives may be sincere; the results are unconvincing" (September 17, 1989).

Rhythm Nation 1814 described a utopian society in which there were "no geographic boundaries, bound together through our beliefs. We are like-minded individuals, sharing a common vision, pushing toward a world rid of color lines." That's how Janet introduced it in her spoken "Interlude: Pledge." It sounds naïve, almost childlike, especially when compared to the sophisticated critiques of Stevie Wonder or the muscular invectives of Public Enemy and Grandmaster Flash in the same period. *Rhythm Nation*'s impact owed much to its accessibility and its capacity to self-replicate. At least according to *Entertainment*'s Kyle Anderson, who maintained the album, "provided the DNA for everything from Lady Gaga's 'Paparazzi' to the bulk of Beyoncé's *4*."

Timing is everything, of course: 1989 was the year of the Central Park Jogger; the case, as we learned in Chapter 8, combined sex, race, and violence, recalling centuries-old panics over black rapists. Myths about blacks' sexual propensities lay not too far beneath the surface of what became an episode in a great American racial psychodrama. More episodes were to follow. Three years after the album's release, boxer Mike Tyson stood trial for rape in Indianapolis. He was found guilty and sentenced to six years imprisonment. As the jury deliberated for ten hours, thoughts must have turned to an earlier case involving a celebrity and a little-known accuser.

In December 1991, William Kennedy Smith, the nephew of Senator Edward Kennedy and member of the illustrious extended family, was acquitted of rape in Palm Beach, Florida. He faced up to four-and-a-half years imprisonment if convicted of sexual battery and assault. After seventy-seven minutes of deliberation, six jurors found him innocent. The thrust of his defense was that accuser wasn't credible, having had abortions and been abused as a child. There was also the matter of the skimpy black underwear she favored: this was used by the defense to signify intention. While some felt that the ruling in favor of the accused boded well for Tyson, there were several significant differences, the obvious one being that Kennedy Smith was white.

Released in 1995 on four years' probation, Tyson continued to insist he was innocent. At the time, it's difficult to imagine anyone who provided so much scandalous copy as Tyson. The subject of this book maybe. (Research conducted by Indiana University Public Opinion Laboratory for the *Indianapolis Star*/WRTV surveyed 800 blacks and 407 white respondents: 28 of whites believed Tyson received a fair trial; 67 percent of blacks thought he had been wronged.)

Further enhancing the significance of the *Rhythm Nation 1814* album was the *cultural turn* of the late 1980s and early 1990s: this referred to an emphasis on the importance of ideas, arts, and intellectual achievements in affecting society. It signaled a shift away from politics and economics as the decisive forces in life and toward literature, film, and music as influences that shaped the way we live. Some would bracket Janet Jackson with the likes of Alice Walker, Toni Morrison, bell hooks, Michele Wallace, and Patricia Hill Collins in repositioning black women in the popular consciousness and advancing the distinct intellectual and artistic movement called black feminism.

There was also a driving force of historical change at work. When Janet talked and sang idealistically about a new world, a new one appeared to be emerging. Maybe Janet had listened to President Ronald Reagan who, at the height of the Cold War, speculated that rivalries between nations would vanish in the event of an invasion by aliens. In the absence of aliens, the Cold War ended just the same, the people of Germany taking down the Berlin Wall in November 1989 to symbolize the dismantlement of a 25-year-old division. It was Reagan's final year in office. His fellow negotiators in ending the Cold War lasted a little longer: Mikhail Gorbachev, the Soviet president, and Margaret Thatcher, Britain's prime minister, left over the next two years. In 1990, Nelson Mandela was released from a South African prison, the apartheid system collapsing the following year. Mandela became the country's first democratically elected president in 1994. So, in a sense, *Rhythm Nation*'s quixotic sensibilities were very much in sync with the mood of the time.

The album sold 8 million copies worldwide.

*   *   *

Rhythm Nation 1814 established Janet as a fully formed artist in her own right, rather than another member of the Jackson family. After the success of the album, she arguably approached Madonna as the world's premier female artist. Yet Madonna was—and is—interpreted, understood, and acknowledged differently: cleverer, more dangerous, and possessed of an antic spirit of mischief. Even in her sixties, Madonna is recognized as a genuine cultural icon. Janet might have shrugged the "sister of . . ." sobriquet, but her stature was never elevated to that of Madonna.

By the time of Janet's emergence, Michael had begun to manifest the kind of unusual habits that were to become integral to his persona: sequestering himself at Neverland and wearing surgical masks on his occasional forays in public space (pre-2020's Covid-19 pandemic, of course). Reports of his sleeping in an oxygen tent also contributed to a growing perception that he had grown eccentric. Michael wasn't the only member attracting attention: LaToya's book *LaToya: Growing Up in the Jackson Family* issued a broadside in 1991. LaToya's central argument was that the children of Joseph and Katherine Jackson paid for their success by enduring emotional, physical, and sexual abuse.

In 1991, Janet, still only twenty-four, agreed with Virgin Records to a deal for three to five albums; the estimated yield was between $40 million and $50 million. In the same year, she married for the second time, this time to songwriter/director René Elizondo, with whom she'd worked for many years; he wrote several of her songs and directed some of her videos. They separated in January 1999 and the petition for divorce the following year cited "irreconcilable differences."

Janet was noticeably secretive about her marriage and, indeed, other aspects of her life she regarded as private. Presumably mindful of the way her brother had engaged with the media and paid for it, she tended to limit interviews and confine her topics to music and professional activities. In a sense, this was bucking a trend: in the early 1990s, everyone with aspirations of a showbusiness career was compelled to strike a bargain in which they surrendered all semblance of a personal life in exchange for a media presence and the commercial success that typically followed.

Sister LaToya had signed the contract in 1989 when she posed nude for *Playboy*. Janet did not follow her example. Well not exactly. In September 1993 she appeared on the cover of *Rolling Stone*: she was topless, the hands of Elizondo covering her breasts; her jeans were partially unbuttoned. The image was part of a photoshoot by Patrick Demarchelier, whose work supplied part of the artwork for the cover of her fourth album *janet*. Note the lower case "j." That's how she wished to be credited; no reference to "Janet Jackson" on the record, though that's how she was billed in John Singleton's 1993 film *Poetic Justice*. (Singleton, who died in 2019, was both the first African American and the youngest ever filmmaker to be nominated for the best director Oscar. He was, with Spike Lee, Darnell Martin, Mario van Peebles, and others, part of a new generation of black filmmakers in the 1990s. Singleton's 1991 film *Boyz n the Hood* is still regarded reverentially.)

But, if Janet had anticipated shockwaves after the topless cover picture, there were only ripples. A month before the magazine's publication, the LAPD's Sexually Exploited Child Unit started its investigation into allegations against Michael. Two days before the *Rolling Stone* issue was published, Jordan Chandler's parents filed a civil suit against Michael. The Chandler case dominated the media's coverage of Jackson family affairs, at least until the settlement in January 1994. Even though Michael was the accused, the Jackson family was involved, if only by implication. Unlike LaToya, who believed the allegations (at the time, at least) and actually added to them, Janet was a stalwart defender of her brother. Her video with Michael, "Scream," was intended as an attack on the media, especially the tabloids that had, in Janet's view, vilified him unfairly. "The lies are disgusting," they sang. "You're selling souls." The video won three MTV Video Music Awards in 1995. It was on Michael's *HIStory* album.

Janet must have flinched when she watched her brother with his wife Lisa Marie on television in June 1995. What was he trying to do? Make himself appear a victim? If so, a victim of what, or who? The media? If so, isn't that like complaining to a playground bully that another playground bully is picking on you? Even after the interview, answers were not apparent. The media had been an ally of Michael's and, indeed, the whole Jackson family for two decades. Even while the Chandler case was developing, the media had been more reserved than might be expected, considering child molestation charges had been leveled at one of the world's eminent entertainers. Jackson surfaced miraculously unscathed (miraculously, that is, by today's standards: in the third decade of the twenty-first century, it is unimaginable that even an unproven assertion like Chandler's would not have caused the downfall of an entertainer).

Janet had studiously tiptoed around the media, perhaps mindful of their power, but even more mindful that she preferred a quiet life and wanted the media to observe purdah. Michael's flight into his version of seclusion was more of an invitation for the media to become more creative in their storytelling. Michael's interview wasn't the calamity Janet might have anticipated. His trouble was that, for all his skill in surviving rumors that could have been terminal and navigating his way through crises, he couldn't help letting the truth interfere with good judgment. Honesty is not always an attribute.

Asked whether there were photographs of young boys found in his room, Jackson jumped in, "Not of young boys; these were children. All kind of girls, everything." Then, when presented with the possibility that the subjects of the photographs or books were undressed, he qualified, "Not that I know of. Unless people send me things that I have not opened." He stated that he loved children and that people send him material on children. It may have been truth, but it opened the door a little wider for his doubters. Why would an adult such as Michael Jackson want young boys to share his bed unless he were up to no good? "I have never invited anyone into my bed," Michael told interviewer Diane Sawyer. "Children love me. They follow me. They want to be with me." Janet must have watched through parted fingers.

*   *   *

There had never been a comparably famous brother and sister in entertainment. Karen and Richard Carpenter were renowned as the Carpenters and had great success until Karen's untimely death in 1983, aged thirty-three. In acting there had been Julia and Eric Roberts and then Maggie and Jake Gyllenhaal. But, there were no brother-sister sibs in showbusiness close to Janet and Michael Jackson. Some measure of how commercially successful they were can be taken from the second deal Janet struck with Virgin Records in 1996: this put her in the same financial ballpark as Madonna and brother Michael. Four albums for an estimated $80 million (Madonna's and Michael's contracts at the time were thought be worth $60 million each). This included a $35 million advance on royalties and $5 million for each album, plus a 24 percent royalty on sales. The masters would go to her after seven years. The agreement also required Virgin to allocate about $25 million in video production, marketing, and promotion costs; this is a much larger amount than in most deals and is presumably why many believe this is the shrewdest deal in music industry history.

The Velvet Rope was released in October 1997; it was her sixth and the first album under the new contact and was, for many, the last contribution of artistic note from Janet. This was the last collaboration with the production team of Jam and Lewis until 2015 and *Unbreakable*. The rope of the title was generally understood as a metaphor for the cord she believed had strangled her for years. *The Velvet Rope* was credited simply to Janet, but Janet Jackson was listed as co-producer and songwriter. She told David Ritz around the time of its release, "My last name represents a part of my past that I've been working through. I've always wanted to be just Janet. I've always wanted to simplify and feel like I'm standing on my own." She was thirty-two at the time.

This was the album that turned her into a LGBTQ+ poster girl. The track "Free Xone" dealt with homophobia and same-sex relationships and "Tonight's the Night" was a lesbian reinterpretation of the Rod Stewart tune. The single "Together Again" was spun off the album and she donated a portion of its sales receipts to the American Foundation for AIDs Research (amfAR), the organization co-founded in 1985 by Elizabeth Taylor. "Janet Jackson was one of the first black artists to talk about issues of sexuality within a pop/R&B context," said Craig Seymour, of "Craig's Pop Life" podcast about entertainment from black and gay perspectives, to *Variety* writer Jeremy Helligar.

Shortly after the release of *The Velvet Rope*, René Elizondo filed for divorce. With the announcement came the revelation that they had been married since 1991. Elizondo then filed suit against his ex for $10 million, claiming uncompensated work on her albums from *Rhythm Nation 1814* onward. Janet then became involved with producer Jermaine Dupri. Their relationship was, as she described it, "drama-free." But the Jackson family was never far from drama.

In December 2003, Michael Jackson was charged with seven counts of child molestation. Janet was still an ardent defender and stuck close to his side during pretrial hearings; though she didn't appear at the trial until the final stages. She'd dismissed the Chandler accusations ten years before as a "money grab." Her collaboration with her brother on "Scream" suggested she was vigilantly aware of the potency of the media in making or breaking artists. Perhaps this is why she was judiciously absent during most of the trial. Perhaps she was plotting something that would outdo even her brother's conquest of the media.

* * *

Mention "Janet Jackson" to anyone today and they will respond with a phrase: wardrobe malfunction. Unfair? Definitely. But, for all her record-breaking, zeitgeisty albums, and her blood ties, Janet will be remembered for her rendezvous with Justin Timberlake during the 2004 Super Bowl halftime show. How it must madden her. Or maybe not. For someone who had closely observed her brother's ascent and must have understood the potency of the media, Janet avoided the kind of controversies that had tormented him in the early 1990s and beyond. In fact, had she retired in 1999, she would have looked back on a stupendous career, replete with three stunning albums, a few tv and film parts, and forward to a long luxurious retirement living on royalties undisturbed by the prying journalists; and she would have been thirty-three. Instead, she remained productive without ever approaching the peak of 1989–97.

But, despite the profundity of her contribution, she would never completely shrug the "sister of Michael" clause at the end of her name. She probably didn't mind, either, though she never acknowledged this. The independence she craved and got was from her family and, in particular, the head of the family. So the wardrobe malfunction came as a surprise. It happened in Houston on February 1, 2004. Janet was booked to perform at the Super Bowl halftime show. At the time, this was quite an honor: the television viewing audience was usually huge, and, in preceding years, the likes of U2, Shania Twain, and Sting had appeared. The plan was for Janet to duet with Justin Timberlake, their song being "Rock Your Body." As Timberlake sang the line, "I bet I'll have you naked by the end of this song," he tugged at Janet's clothes, briefly exposing her right breast in front of about 114 million tv viewers. She was ornamented with what's called a nipple shield, this being a silver bar that fits through a nipple pierce, in this case in the design of a sunburst. The very fact that she was wearing such an item of jewelry suggested to most people that the incident was less a spontaneous gesture, more a carefully rehearsed stunt designed to provoke outrage. It did.

Michael Powell, the chair of the Federal Communications Commission (FCC), which regulates television, radio, and other media, received 540,000 complaints persuading the agency's chair Michael Powell to order an investigation. CBS got landed with a $550,000 fine, later overturned by courts, though not until 2008 when the decision effectively rebuffed the regulator, which had, under the administration of George W. Bush, taken a hardline against tv indecency, issuing record fines against broadcasters.

Viacom, owner of CBS, MTV, VH1, and several other media outlets show apologized. "The tearing of Janet Jackson's costume was unrehearsed, unplanned, completely unintentional and was inconsistent with assurances we had about the content of the performance," it explained. Later in the year Viacom was fined $3.5 million for comments by shock jock Howard Stern and other transmissions. Broadcasters began to air live events on a delay. Powell resigned in 2005. The following year, Super Bowl organizers opted to play safe and booked Sir Paul McCartney.

Timberlake blamed the incident on a "wardrobe malfunction" and, while the phrase became an addition to pop music's lexicon, it was surely intended as a wisecrack. "It was fun," he told the media. Jackson though was more contrite. She confessed she and Timberlake had planned the disrobing, but not to the point where her breast would be revealed, prompting the thought, "why did she have her nipple covered by the jewelry then?" Jackson publicly distanced herself from MTV, CBS, and the National Football League, accepting full responsibility. "I am really sorry if I offended anyone, that was truly not my intention," she claimed.

Apparently, she had offended a great many Americans, many of whom presumably had few qualms with watching violent news events on their tvs; in 2003, networks showed live the first bombing of Baghdad, which kicked off round-the-clock media coverage of the Iraq War (the conflict in which a US coalition overthrew the government of Saddam Hussein). We should stay mindful that America was colonized by religious puritans, the republic created out of fighting and the constitution predicated on the right to bear arms.

Skeptics discerned a spectacular pr event; particularly as Janet's eighth studio album *Damita Jo* was due for release on March 22. The infamous incident was covered lavishly all over. But there was unexpected pushback: Janet's videos were dropped by Viacom, owner of MTV, VH1, and several radio stations. Clear Channel Communications followed suit. So her album was largely ignored and sold poorly. (Janet Damita Jo Jackson was Janet's full name.) Timberlake suffered no comparable reprisals.

Janet certainly did not want this event to define her, but it probably did. It had the effect of, as *Rolling Stone* described it, "killing off her previously indestructible career overnight." At thirty-eight, she was unlikely to rebound, especially with debut albums from Taylor Swift, in 2006, Katy Perry and Lady Gaga (just ahead) in 2008. The next generation was taking over. So why? Even if her interpretation of events was accepted, why even venture close to a maneuver that was going to create controversy, even if it had gone according to plan?

Margo Jefferson hinted at a possibility when she wrote of Janet, "She had watched Michael find his own producers; she did the same. She had seen him enhance and revise his looks; she did that, too, dieting, fiercely working out, and using surgery to reduce and enlarge various features and body parts. Onstage and in videos, she was choreographed to within an inch of her life. She was the original . . . hardest-working sex toy in show business."

Jackson may have thought she had the talent to emulate her brother but had avoided the very thing that was beginning to torment him: infamy. Artistically, she may have been his equal. But maybe she lacked a dash of that *je ne sais quo* Madonna had traded on for a couple of decades.

Janet appeared in the film *Why Did I Get Married?* in 2007 and its 2010 sequel *Why Did I Get Married Too?*—both Tyler Perry movies. Two more albums in 2006 and 2008 and then nothing till 2015 and the reunion with Jam and Lewis for *Unbreakable*. Nothing, that is, in terms of records. In 2010, Janet, met Wissam Al Mana, a Qatari billionaire, whom she married two years later. He was Muslim with no connections with the music business. So the marriage was a surprise, though not such a surprise as her pregnancy at fifty. And the surprises kept coming. Within months of the birth of her son Eissa in January 2017, Janet announced her separation from Al Mana. It was her third failed marriage, and she had also had a seven-year relationship with producer Jermaine Dupri (2002–9).

Janet's initial meeting with Al Mana was in the year following her brother Michael's death and it's at least possible that the harrowing experience sent her reeling; she had no obvious presence in showbusiness for many years. The 2015 tour to promote *Unbreakable* was met with an appreciative rather than rapturous response. She gave a studied fifty-minute performance at the Glastonbury Festival in 2019, gliding through her back catalog without missing a note, or a step in a perfectly choreographed show. *Guardian* writer Michael Cragg grouped her with Madonna, Prince, and Michael Jackson as singers "who have properly shifted the needle when it comes to pop." It's not clear whether she would have been pleased by the same writer's description of her as "pop's elder stateswoman." She was fifty-three.

* * *

"Mamet—yes. Madonna—no." That was how the *Los Angeles Times* summarized the critical reaction to Madonna's acting debut as an office temp in a Broadway production of David Mamet's *Speed-the-Plow* in 1988 (May 7, 1988). Other reviewers derided her performance more cruelly. "Being vacant on the stage requires more effort than it does in real life," mocked Howard Kissell in the *Daily News*. So what did Madonna do? Retreat shamefaced and learn her lesson? Fly at your own level and no higher—remember Icarus! Not likely. Two years later, she was playing opposite Warren Beatty in the film *Dick Tracy*. In 1996, she was Eva Perón in the movie of *Evita*. And in 2011 she directed and co-wrote the screenplay for the film *W.E.*, about Wallis Simpson, the American divorcee who married King Edward VIII, of England.

You might think this is an unfair question, Janet. But had it been Madonna who had inadvertently—or intentionally—malfunctioned in 2004, would history have been different? Somehow, you can't imagine she would have lost a minute of sleep or let the hysterical reaction faze her in the slightest. In view of her personal history of improprieties and potentially reputation-wrecking scandals, she would have probably popped the corks of a few bottles of Dom Pérignon Rose Gold to celebrate her latest *succès de scandale*. If the television networks pulled her albums, she would have probably laughed and pointed out that fans would download her new album from one of the pirate digital music services that grew after the shutdown of Napster in 2001.

Misadventures were as alien to you as cricket. Every move you'd made since you were seven was not exactly scripted, but conceived of with a purpose in mind. Your father determined the purpose for your formative life. Even when you decided on your own course, you stuck to his methods, which rested on certainty rather than spontaneity. By contrast Madonna's sometimes maladroit actions and unfathomable persona changes seemed about as methodical as a roll of the dice. That's not to say, your art wasn't on par; just that your progress seemed plotted and—dare I say—safe. So, an artist more accustomed to condemnation from all manner of authority, including the church, television networks, and global corporations, might have adapted to the adverse circumstances. It seems you were stung, perhaps worse. You're recording career suffered. It wasn't the first time the media had bruised a showbusiness career.

A wider nightmare was looming. The year after the wardrobe malfunction, Hurricane Katrina contributed to the deaths of almost 2,000 people and displaced tens of thousands of African American residents of New Orleans. In the aftermath of the hurricane, police officers shot and killed two brothers, Ronald and Lance Madison. The officers were charged with first-degree murder and three others were charged with attempted murder. The case dragged on for eleven years and, in 2016, the five officers were sentenced to between three and twelve years in prison, reduced from their original sentences of six to sixty-five years. The Madisons were just two victims of the epic trail of encounters between police and blacks, climaxing in 2020 with the death of George Floyd. Events like this encourage us to ponder. That was just a couple of months after the coronavirus pandemic forced you to call off your world tour. This was a personal misfortune, but nothing compared to the tragedies of others.

All the same, the malfunction precipitated a downturn in fortunes after two high-flying decades. You split with Jermaine Dupri, with whom you'd been involved since the breakup of your second marriage. As usual, you camouflaged your private life and your marriage to Wissan Al Mana became a source of curiosity to the media. It was not an exemplar of married bliss. In fact, if brother Randy is to be believed, it was "quite an abusive situation." He didn't mean physically abusive. The marriage ended in 2019. The deaths of Michael in 2009 and father Joe in 2018 must have come as severe losses. You were never as strident as Michael in criticizing Joe, though your most creative period came once you'd struck out on your own.

Just in case you were thinking the wardrobe malfunction was wholly bad, you should know that the national outrage (nations other than the United States were amused but not outraged) occasioned by the event changed the world, according to some. About a year after the event, three employees of PayPal were talking about it and expressing regret that no footage of the shameful episode was readily available online. Super Bowl viewers taking a halftime break missed it. As did everyone else not watching carefully. This was 2005. The three tech-savvy guys, all in their twenties, were Chad Hurley, Steven, Cehn and Jawed Karim. You can guess what's coming next. A year later everyone was viewing and talking about a new online repository for videos called YouTube. Your incident may have brought temporary dishonor and a reversal of fortunes, but it helped start a revolution of sorts—and your malfunction is memorialized. Check it out: https://bit.ly/2MR2aRk.

In the late 1980s, Madonna vied with Jackson as the world's preeminent entertainer. They both sold prodigious numbers of records and had lucrative contracts with Pepsi. Both held the media spellbound.

12

From His Sexuality to His Face

Those whom the gods wish to destroy, they first make rich.

Sometimes you'd swear celebrities with great wealth and an abundance of everything are chosen by mischievous gods to connive in their own doom. They have a habit of succeeding, then succeeding more, then, Midas-like, discovering the magic touch is conditional. They can use it only for so long, before the celestial beings demand payback, usually in the form of self-sacrifice.

Michael Jackson's *Thriller* and *Bad* were the two highest selling albums of the 1980s and his world concert tour, 1987–9, was seen by more than 4.4 million people, grossing over $125 million, the most commercially successful concert tour of the decade. At the time, *Forbes* rated Jackson as the second highest paid entertainer in the world, earning a total of $100 million in 1989 and 1990 behind top-placed Bill Cosby, then fifty-three, who made $115 million. In 2018, Cosby was sentenced to a three- to ten-year sentence in prison for drugging and sexually assaulting a woman, which we will cover in Chapter 15. Whitney Houston earned $33 million from the soundtrack of *The Bodyguard* alone in 1992; she was the third highest earning female, behind Oprah Winfrey and Barbra Streisand at the time. As we learned earlier, she died in 2012.

* * *

Jackson was less than two years away from being investigated by the LAPD when, in October 1991, he invited Elizabeth Taylor to marry her sixth husband Larry Fortensky at his Neverland ranch. Jackson footed the bill—estimated at over $1.5 million—for the wedding. Taylor wore a $25,000 Valentino gown, this probably a gift from her designer friend. In addition to the 160 invited guests, there were, 500 feet or so above the ceremony, 15 helicopters carrying airborne paparazzi, all desperate to capture pictures. One daredevil photographer leapt from his aircraft armed with only a parachute and a helmet camera and landed within 100 feet of Taylor and Fortensky as they prepared to take their conjugal vows. He was quickly handcuffed by Jackson's security guards, who whisked him away, thus depriving him of what would probably have been one of the most celebrated pap photographs in history. The incident illustrates the lengths to which photojournalists were prepared to go in order to secure an image.

Aerial maneuvers like this were dangerous, but rewarding at a time in history when public fascination in the private lives of celebrities was soaring. "I want to make one thing clear—I am not a fruitcake," the intrepid pap emphasized to Greg Braxton, of the *Los Angeles Times*, in 1991. "I'm a commercial photographer. I'm not a particularly big fan of Liz Taylor's . . . I was just amazed at how much money was being offered by the tabloids for a shot. They were offering in excess of six figures." A million. For a single shot. In 1991 too. This offers some measure of the appetite for any story or picture of the rich and famous. The harder they tried to secrete themselves away, the more valuable the pictures became. "For that kind of money, I'll do anything, as long as it's reasonably safe and reasonably legal," parachutist-cum-paparazzo Harris acknowledged.

Safety and legality were not always observed when paparazzi went in pursuit of Princess Diana, who, by the early 1990s, was unquestionably the most sought-after woman in history. Every endeavor to shield herself from the media was met with another, usually more adventurous endeavor to snatch an image of her. Days before her death in 1997, she spent a while with her friend Dodi Fayed aboard a $20 million yacht moored off Portofino, Italy. Jason Fraser, who captured the couple kissing, was later fined by a French court for breaking Fayed's privacy. He earned about $1.6 million for his photographs. Neverland's interloper was not, on his own account, a fruitcake but a risk-taking, money-motivated journo in search of a payday. He was also a precursor: in the years that followed, every celebrity wedding would have uninvited guests, if not as daring as Harris, as ingenious in their efforts to grab the money shots.

Jackson didn't respond to the intrusion, though the sight of an earthbound parachute descending into his very private 2,700 acre, $22 million domain must have weighed heavily on his mind. He was no brooding recluse; but he cherished his privacy. He'd created what he assumed was a secure, enclosed environment far from journalists and, indeed, everyone else apart from his immediate family, staff and a coterie of young friends. But he hadn't anticipated entry from above. It didn't happen again, but how that incident must have given Jackson bad memories and plagued him for the rest of his life. It must have been like looking up and seeing a California raven falling from the sky, a bird of ill omen.

*   *   *

"He is a symbol of purity who does not drink, smoke, swear or eat junk food. He fasted weekly to purge impurities in his body." That's how Utah saw Jackson in 1990. Or at least, how the state's oldest newspaper the *Deseret News* saw him. At the time, Jackson, while not exactly a paragon of virtue, was the alkaline to the acid usually associated with rock and pop stars.

So when, in June, he was hospitalized in Santa Monica, California (about 5 miles from his Los Angeles home), after complaining of chest pains, there was panic. Jackson had no history of heart problems, nor, as far as anyone knew, any other malady. At thirty-one, he seemed hale: if his energetic dancing was any measure (and it probably was), he was full of vim. Jackson was taken to Saint John's Hospital and Health Center, where Elizabeth Taylor was, at the time, undergoing treatment for pneumonia. Taylor had spent three months hovering between life and death with a pulmonary virus before she was discharged in June. Jackson's illness turned out to be a cartilage inflammation of the front part of the ribs, called costochondritis— athletes sometimes suffer with it (LA Clippers' Chris Paul had it in 2015, as did Portland Trail Blazers' Damian Lillard in 2019). Sister Janet broke off from her *Rhythm Nation* tour to visit him.

Asked about the cause of the ailment, Jackson's publicist Bob Jones answered, "Stress is a very important factor . . . I would certainly like to see him rest more" (quoted in *Washington Post*, June 7, 1990).

It didn't seem a wholly satisfactory explanation: stress was, in 1990, not the catch-all infirmity it is today (stress-related illness is the leading cause of sickness absence from work), but it was more popularly understood as a type of strain that led to other, more serious conditions in 1990. Hence Jones's wish that he wanted Jackson to "rest more," the implication being that Jackson's tireless striving for perfection in his performances, whether on stage, record, or film, was a factor in his rib inflammation. He'd been working exhaustively on a new album, which would, he believed, be his magnum opus.

Jackson wasn't back at work in a hurry. Well, not unless you count earning $20 million as work. In August, Jackson walked, danced, and mimed in a pair of "MJ" branded shoes made by LA Gear. Actually, Jackson had signed to make the short commercial film months before, but LA Gear planned to start screening it in August 1990. Jackson scooped the first installment of the lucre: a $7.5 million upfront payment, with a percentage of sales royalties to follow. The popular story is that Jackson asked LA Gear to estimate the value at $20 million to surpass the $18 million basketball star Michael Jordan had received from Nike.

LA Gear launched as a public company in 1986 and, for a while, looked a worthwhile contender for the sports apparel and shoes market leadership held by Nike, with adidas usually not far behind. But in 1989, its stock started to drop like a stone and the deal with Jackson seemed, to many, fanciful. The reason: sports corporations typically contracted athletes to endorse their goods, as Nike did with Jordan in the 1980s, and adidas did with tennis' Stan Smith, among others, in the1970s. Unlike actors, singers, or models, athletes were usually more dependable, wholesome, and unlikely to taint the sports brand. Jackson's reputation as a duteous, drugs-free, teetotal, non-womanizing straight arrow raised a Jehovah's Witness and possessed of a healthy work ethic, if a few puzzling idiosyncrasies, must have made LA Gear assume he was a trustworthy emblem for its products. The commercial video cost $700,000 to produce, a formidable amount at the time.

It was a gamble for a company trying to stop a commercial slide: its stock had fallen from a peak of over $50 to around $20 when the Jackson video was announced. It didn't air for several months. The company later claimed Jackson delayed the release of the video. Sales were disastrously weak, and by 1992 the company had become so disenchanted with Jackson that it sued him for more than $10 million in damages, claiming violations of the contract, including fraud, negligent misrepresentation, and breach of good faith. Jackson, alleged LA Gear, missed deadlines to deliver the contracted videos. Jackson filed a $44 million countersuit against LA Gear. The suit was settled in 1994, though details were not disclosed. The company filed for bankruptcy protection in 1998.

It seemed to typify the often-acrimonious relationship Jackson had with corporations that wished to exploit his global popularity and, at that stage, glamorous public image. Jackson knew his own worth and presumably instructed his representatives to negotiate prodigiously lucrative agreements—which often went toxic. Other companies followed LA Gear's logic. But market forces abhor an ill-fitting symbol. And Jackson's hit-to-miss ratio was not inspiring. Would Jackson swap his beloved soft leather Italian loafers for unwieldy-looking boots, ornamented with buckles? (LA Gear specialized in sturdy ankle-high footwear.) If he did, would anyone believe he did so for anything other than money?

Jackson's love affair with his audience seemed to be of the pure kind: his followers didn't want it polluted with branded goods that reeked of crass commercialism. He wasn't a vehicle to sell products; at least not to them. As far as he was concerned, he chose freely to accept millions in exchange for the use of his name and image. But that's all.

*   *   *

Sony inherited Jackson. Sort of: in 1988, the company bought CBS Records and, with it, appropriated all its contracted artists, including Jackson. In March 1991, Jackson signed a new longterm contract with Sony Music's US subsidiary, which was estimated to be worth more than $65 million. It eclipsed sister Janet's recording contract with Virgin, signed only weeks before and valued at $40–50 million. At the time the deal was concluded Sony asserted that it expected to realize $1 billion in revenue from the partnerships. Would Sony have agreed to the contract if its executives had been forewarned of what was to come eighteen months later? Jackson, at the time of the contract, was an unusually androgynous character. Curiously childlike, mysteriously reclusive, he was a bit of an oddity, who spurned sex, drugs, and other dissipating pursuits. But he appeared harmless, was blessed with rare talent and could move records like no one else in history. At that stage, over 40 million copies of *Thriller* had been sold. People appreciated that Jackson was no longer just a singer who entertained audiences; now he was a mercurial, shapeshifting magician, who enchanted them.

The unprecedentedly generous deal entitled Jackson to start his own record label, known as Nation Records, and he could sign established and new artists. There was also provision for Jackson to make films for Sony's Columbia Pictures. At thirty-three, Jackson was intent, it seems, on exploring his creativity in new areas. Jackson's perfectionism meant he was far from prolific; in fact he had released only three solo albums since 1979. With this kind of production rate, he would be sixty by the time of his final album under the terms of this contract. Either Sony believed he would speed up, or it had faith in the Jackson's eternal spell.

Sony and LA Gear were not the only global corporations to buy the magician story. PepsiCo Inc. too dropped its millions into the maestro's hat. A masterstroke or an expensive disaster? The softdrinks company had both kinds of deals on its track record. So, on February 5, 1992, when it announced that Jackson would appear in a series of tv commercials, no one was congratulating the dealmakers. What looked like tumbler of icecold Pepsi with a slice of lemon could have been a goblet full of wormwood—a poisoned chalice, in other words. Pepsi also confirmed that it would underwrite a four-continent tour by Jackson beginning in June.

How much was the deal worth to Jackson? "A lot," replied PepsiCo, claiming it was the largest sponsorship deal ever between a corporation and a musical entertainer. The same corporation had done two sponsorship deals with Michael Jordan in the 1980s and, together, these totaled $20 million. In 1989, Madonna earned a mere $5 million for one advertisement featuring "Like A Prayer" and, such was the controversy about the video, Pepsi decided to spike the ad anyway. In 2012 PepsiCo signed Beyoncé to a similar deal to Jackson's, believed to have been worth $50 million. So twenty years before, Jackson's contract was no doubt worth less than this, but probably more than Jordan made.

Pepsi must have known Jackson was capable of miracles, at least marketing miracles. If the new decade followed the same trajectory as the last one, Jackson would consummate his status as the greatest entertainer of the twentieth century. The tour PepsiCo was sponsoring was called *Dangerous* after the title of his album, which was already on sale (it was released in November 1991). The second single from the album, "Remember the Time," was out; the accompanying video was directed by John Singleton and featured Eddie Murphy, supermodel Iman and basketball player Magic Johnson. The tour was scheduled for Europe, Asia, Australia, and Latin America, though the United States was missing from the itinerary; the tour was destined never to reach North America, anyway. And Jackson was aiming high with the tour too. "My goal is to gross $100 million by Christmas 1993," Jackson told the media at the signing ceremony in New York City. The rationale of the tour was simple: to raise money for Heal the World, a charity he had founded to benefit children and the environment.

This, remember, was February 1992. Less than nineteen months later and LAPD officers were searching Jackson's property while he was on tour. By then, PepsiCo execs must have felt like they had drawn the pin on a grenade and then decided to halt their attack: What could they do? Scramble about trying to find the pin and then replace it? Or just let the thing explode? They threw themselves on bomb, hoping to suppress its impact, at least on their company. In November 1993, PepsiCo terminated the record-breaking contract. Jackson had canceled his tour shortly before, complaining of various maladies including a dependence on painkillers. The allegations of sexual wrongdoing presumably alerted Pepsi that its commitment to Jackson was misplaced.

Well-paid endorsers who are suspected of, rumored to be, or reported as transgressors are guilty until proven innocent. But, in early 1992, there were not even murmurs. The famously scoop-hungry *National Enquirer*, with its extensive celeb intel network and its extra-sensory gift for detecting scandal, did not report on Jackson's "bizarre obsession with a woman and her two children" until May 1993.

* * *

"Jackson wants to be a classic star," declared *Rolling Stone's* Michael Goldberg, citing his paragons, Elizabeth Taylor, and Katharine Hepburn. He was commenting on Jackson's historic contract with Sony, which provided for him to diversify into all areas of showbusiness. But Goldberg was aware that Jackson either was or should be prepared to allow the media into all aspects of his experience. "Times have changed since his cinematic role models achieved fame. Today's stars are public figures whose private lives are open for discussion. And as [*Thriller* director, John] Landis noted, Jackson, knowing or unknowingly, has provided the public with a series of personal topics to discuss and debate, ranging from his sexuality to his face." Knowingly or unknowingly?

In November 1991, Jackson released the first single from his new *Dangerous* album. The album had been expected on the market during the summer, but Jackson had spent much of the previous four years in various studios, so another few months was neither here nor there. Under the terms of his extraordinary Sony contract, Jackson had unheard-of autonomy for a recording artist and this meant no deadlines. Sony was content to wait for what Jackson hoped to be his best album to date. Such was his striving, he wanted every recording to be better—and, presumably sell more copies—than the last. To this end, he'd abandoned the previously productive collaboration he had with producer Quincy Jones, with whom he'd worked on three albums. Jackson replaced Jones with Teddy Riley, known as the "Godfather of New Jack Swing," a hybrid r'n'b subgenre that combined hip-hop with soul. Earlier, in 1989, Jackson had also dispensed with the services of Frank Dileo whom he had appointed as his manager in 1984. (Dileo died after experiencing complications following heart surgery in 2011.) His attorney John Branco acted as his de facto manager for a while, but Jackson dismissed him in 1990.

Sony, far from complaining at Jackson's painstaking refusal to accept anything short of his exalted standards, allowed him full reign. The corporation indulged Jackson, but he was extravagant: during periods, up to four studios were engaged in production, each costing about $30,000 per day. Jackson compiled fifty tracks, then pared them down to just fourteen songs for the final cut. The final production costs of the album were estimated between $8 million and 10 million. (For comparison, Guns N' Roses' *Chinese Democracy* is popularly thought to be the most expensively produced non-Jackson album, costing $13 million; it was released in 2008. Jackson's own *Invincible*, from 2001, is in a class of its own: $30 million.)

"Jackson wants to have it every possible way," proposed Chris Willman, reviewing the album for the *Los Angeles Times* and detecting a dismaying triteness compared to previous material. "Jackson covers most of the conceivable bases—coming off in these 14 tracks and 77 minutes as a little bit sexy, a little shy, a little spiritual, a little lusty, sort of sensitive, intensely paranoid, sweet, demanding, put-upon, misogynist, hugely humanitarian and, of course, just a wee bit dangerous."

In other words, all things to all people. Or, in still other words, generic. That's probably not an adjective Jackson would have liked, if only because of its associations with lacking imagination, originality, and individuality. But the record company would have. And given the remit, at least the remit implied by the dollar value of the contract, a crowd-pleasing effort was just what Tommy Mottola ordered (probably—Mottola was then ceo of the Sony Music; Jackson later had a serious falling-out, as we learned in Chapter 7).

Although he didn't put it this way, Willman's conclusion was that *Dangerous* was what Brits call a curate's egg: partly good and partly bad. Most of the other reviewers found it splendid and unsatisfactory, in roughly equal parts. Willman sensed the presence of too many yes-men advising Jackson on the final cut.

"Black or White" was an immediate success, reaching the top of the *Billboard* Top 100 in its first week of release and remaining at the top for six weeks, making it Jackson's most commercially successful single in nine years. Sales were assisted by a video, or "short film," as Sony insisted on calling it, which was viewed by a television audience of 500 million when it premiered simultaneously in 27 countries on November 11. It was shown in sixty-nine countries over the course of the day. This was 1991, before YouTube, remember. Macaulay Culkin featured in the film.

The tune, written by Jackson himself, echoed sister Janet's *Rhythm Nation* ideal, with lyrics like, "It's not about the races . . . if you're thinking of being my brother it don't matter if you're black or white." The images of the video conveyed the sentiment, featuring Jackson, in black-and-white apparel, dancing around the world alongside Africans, American Indians, Russians, Thais, and Indians. There was also a sequence in which images of the faces of men and women of different ethnic backgrounds morphed smoothly from one to another, as if to suggest the visible differences are merely superficial and that all humans are really part of a single population.

Like Janet's album of the previous year, the motif was congruent with the times, but starry-eyed. Eight months before the album reached the stores, Rodney King, an African American, was stopped by LAPD officers, ordered out of his car and kicked and beaten with batons for fifteen minutes. The officers were acquitted the following April. Fury over the acquittal exacerbated by decades of racism and inequality erupted in rioting all over America, as chronicled in Chapter 8. Even today, the cultural diversity both albums lauded seems vital and necessary; the racism both opposed remains obdurate.

Whether Jackson had the King beating in mind when he made the "Black or White" video isn't known. There is certainly a controversial late passage that appears to represent an anger not typically associated with Jackson. The voice of director John Landis is heard and he walks on set, "Cut! That was perfect." The music stops and the camera pans across the studio to a black panther, which it follows down a flight of stairs where it shapeshifts into Jackson himself. (The Black Panther Party was the name of a militant organization set up in California in 1966 to fight for black rights.) There's still no music, just the sound of Jackson's feet, gusting winds, and shrieks as Jackson dances as if enraged. He grabs his crotch, rubs, adjusts his zipper, and then goes on a kind of rampage, smashing cars and storefront windows.

Even for Jackson, it was an extraordinary video: technically adventurous and appended with a perplexing postscript that seemed intended either to puzzle or provoke outrage. MTV and Fox tv both considered pulling it, but eventually excised the four-minute segment and screened an expurgated version, stirring conjecture—would an outright ban have hurt or helped Jackson? (Stylistically the coda has a similarity to the LA Gear video. Readers can compare them: LA Gear video https://bit.ly/2Z9minu; "Black or White" https://bit.ly/3ew7Bl3.)

Shortly before, in 1989, Madonna had shown scant respect for sensibilities with her "Like a Prayer" video, which got jettisoned from a Pepsi advertising campaign and must have tested to resolve of MTV execs. Madonna had plenty of resolve: the next year, she got her "Justify My Love" banned by MTV. It became the first video single (as they were in the 1990s) to sell over 250,000 copies and the audio record spent two weeks as the *Billboard* charts bestseller. No one should ever underestimate the value of a ban. It transforms not only the meaning but the worth of something. Ban a book and it instantly becomes sought-after. Pull a film and everyone wants to see it. Take a video off the tv and the same rationality applies: public fascination blasts off.

Entertainment Weekly's cover story on its November 29 issue was headlined MICHAEL JACKSON'S VIDEO NIGHTMARE: WAS IT A MISTAKE? OR ALL PART OF THE MASTER PLAN? At the time, *Rolling Stone*'s Michael Goldberg suspected that Jackson, with twenty years experience in showbusiness, had accrued enough wisdom to know that the reasonless, destructive and sexual finale was bound to shock. "If he didn't plan to create controversy, it simply means that, yes, Jackson really is quite detached from reality, as many believe," thought Goldberg. Jackson couldn't have known that four months later, in May 1992, his fateful meeting with twelve-year-old Jordan Chandler would steer him toward far greater controversy.

Turning an album into a *cause célèbre* was a feat in itself and no amount of hype generated by Sony or Jackson's management could have surpassed the exposure granted by a possible ban. Which is not to say that promotion was lacking: in fact the burlesque title King of Pop was a product of such promotion, according to Goldberg. A memo dated November 11, 1991, on MTV letterhead notepaper was circulated to MTV personnel to refer to Jackson as the "King of Pop" at least twice a week. Fox and BET were already using the cognomen. It seemed archly unconvincing but, somehow, it worked: people still call Jackson by this name, even though, in time, his domain stretched beyond pop music.

The British media had their own less reverential appellation, "Wacko Jacko." Jackson's biggest audience outside the United States was in the United Kingdom and Japan, so the name didn't reflect a lack of affection. But the British media's portrayal of Jackson highlighted the weirdness that would become central to his character. They call some celebrities "scandal-proof."

Not Jackson: such was his sense of self-worth that he seemed to believe he could fabricate scandal and emerge more admired, more captivating and more marketable as a result. In this instance, he was right.

Sales of *Dangerous* would have made most artists deliriously happy: Mottola revealed at the Pepsi media conference that *Dangerous* had sold 10 million copies in its first two months of release. That was a faster sales pace than any previous album by Jackson or the Jackson 5. The sales figure soon doubled. But moving 20 million units off the shelves was comparative failure to Jackson. He was, after all, the biggest star in the world.

That may have been the problem. In order to consolidate that illustrious position, Jackson wanted to turn himself into an icon, a symbol worthy of veneration. This is one way to understand his bid to transcend age, sex, ethnicity, and all other relevant demographics. Not even Elvis, Sinatra, or the Beatles, for all their worldwide popularity, could appeal to every person alive. Jackson probably thought he could. And, given the scale of his contract with Sony, his record company thought he could give it a good shot. And this Promethean aspiration was the problem, if indeed a 20-million-selling album can be considered problematic.

*   *   *

Nowadays concert tours are huge moneymaking ventures: gross receipts of $250–300 million are not uncommon. Ed Sheeran's 2017–20 tour grossed $776.2 million. In the early 1990s, concert tours were more like showcases or promotional presentations, the saleable products being the records. As pirate streaming became more prevalent, record labels lost out on sales revenues and the industry sought new ways to capitalize on the continuing popularity of entertainers. The era of the 360-degree contracts arrived in the early twenty-first century and these involved artists agreeing, for a sum, to offer albums, tours, and merchandising, as well as film projects and other ventures to a single corporation, such as Live Nation, for a finite period of time. Madonna's deal in 2007 was worth an estimated $120 million to her.

At the time of the tour to promote *Dangerous*, such arrangements weren't established. Instead, Jackson struck deals with the likes of PepsiCo and HBO. The pay-tv network's initiative was to screen one whole concert from the tour live from Bucharest, Romania. It was the final concert of the European leg of the tour and was scheduled for October 10, 1992. The whole two-and-a-half hours of the concert would be shown on HBO. The cost to HBO was thought to be about $20 million. Jackson pledged some of the fee to Romanian children. The show became HBO's highest-rated special ever, scoring a 21.4 rating, 34 share in HBO's 17.5 million American homes. That meant approximately 3.7 million households tuned in (HBO had separate deals for international distribution). It was the first time Jackson has allowed one of his concerts to be screened on tv. To continue the inescapable comparison with Madonna: her 1990 *Blonde Ambition* tour concert on HBO scored a 21.5 rating and a 31 share. In other words, a tie.

The concert itself is less interesting than a non-disparagement clause included in the contract between Jackson and HBO. As the name suggests, this meant that neither party to the agreement would disparage the other. To disparage is to represent someone or something as of little value, though, of course, this is wide open to interpretation.

Should we blame Jackson for turning what started as amicable and, certainly for him, profitable arrangements unfriendly and costly? Well, in the case of LA Gear and Pepsi, maybe. But by the time the HBO deal went sour, he'd been ten years dead. This doesn't mean he was exactly blameless. The 2019 two-part documentary *Leaving Neverland* was screened by HBO. Jackson's family, which had been understandably critical of a program that centered on James Safechuck's and Wade Robson's posthumous allegations, realized the network was in a relatively strong position: it isn't possible to libel or defame dead individuals. But the Jackson estate instead filed a $100 million lawsuit, claiming the documentary violated the non-disparagement clause in the 1992 contract. HBO accused the estate of seeking to silence victims of sexual abuse. I referred to this in Chapter 3.

"HBO profited off the *Dangerous* World Tour by airing a concert from the tour," argued Jackson's estate in the 2020 legal dispute. Were HBO, Sony, and all the other corporations who rushed to throw money at Jackson motivated by acquisitiveness and self-interest? Of course: corporations are not charitable organizations; they exist to maximize profits. So, when they climb aboard a spacecraft seemingly headed for the stars and find themselves on planet hubris, no one should sympathize. In fact, "serves them right" might be an apposite response. Sponsors, advertisers, and other media were not interested in Jackson as human being: he was a living, breathing marketing instrument. Where audiences saw a thrilling virtuoso, corporations saw a ready-made advertisement for their subscriptions, footwear, or sugary drinks. They were not patrons of the arts: they wanted to sell products. So when the deals didn't live up to expectations, a few million went on the righthand side of the balance sheet and the corporation moved on. In HBO's case, the deal didn't go sour for twenty-seven years, anyway.

Those who believed in Jackson's supernatural powers would swear his habit of jinxing corporations continued beyond the grave. AEG, the promoters of his doomed O2 Arena concerts in London, had sold—and would have to refund—more than $85 million worth of tickets and spent $30 million on the production-that-never-was. Reports from David Teather in the *Guardian* at the time of Jackson's death in 2009 suggested that the company was insured only for the first ten nights of Jackson's residence. Insurers were wary of Jackson's ability to complete fifty concerts, leaving AEG with a potential liability of up to $500 million.

*   *   *

Jackson didn't publicize his habit of inviting his young friends to Neverland. He didn't make a secret of it either. Possibly because he was so naïve that he couldn't see the wrongdoing. Or possibly because he'd calculated that his openness would disarm the media, encouraging them to reason, "How can he be up to no-good, when he's so transparent?" As everyone later discovered, Jackson may not have been as transparent as many supposed.

In January 1992, *Rolling Stone*'s Michael Goldberg coolly observed, "Jackson frequently has children over to play." These included his personal friends but also, according to aides, "busloads" of underprivileged and terminally ill children. There was no attempt to disguise the visits of children, nor of Jackson's close associations with them. "Jackson is extremely fond of children. Those who know him believe that one reason he can relax with kids is that he truly believes they like him for himself, not because he's a big star." Goldberg detected no improprieties, at least none that he wrote of.

Jackson would be only an intermittent visitor himself at Neverland. He'd spent much of the previous few years in recording studios, working on *Dangerous*. And the world tour to accompany the album was due to start and run for seventeen months till November 1993. A private visit to Africa should have provided a refreshing change of scenery. In the event, Jackson would probably have preferred to stay in Los Olivos: he aborted the tour after he angered his hosts in Côte d'Ivoire, West Africa, by constantly holding his nose. Most of us know what this gesture means. Ivorians certainly did and, despite, Bob Jones's insistence that it was not intended as an insult, the media interpreted it differently. Jackson, sensing a pr debacle, hastily rearranged his schedule and returned in February.

It was an unfortunate end to what started as a dream visit. His arrival in Gabon, West Africa, was greeted by adulatory school students carrying a banner that read, "Welcome Home Michael," he'd been crowned honorary "King of the Sanwis" and seated on a golden throne in a Côte d'Ivoire village where he'd received a medal of honor. He'd also met with Tanzania's foreign minister. But as with many Jackson ventures, what started propitiously, ended in calamity.

*   *   *

"Those whom the gods wish to destroy, they first make *mad*" was how the ancient Greek playwright Euripides understood the preferred route to destruction as chosen by the deities in the fourth century BC. He might not have agreed with my amendment. And he would be right: becoming rich does not always lead to destruction. Whether it was God, fate, destiny, karma, or some other unknown force, we'll never know. But consider: in 1990, Jackson was worth $175 million, according to *Forbes*. In 1991 (the year of his Sony deal), he earned $55 million, taking his net worth to $230 million. Bill Cosby had amassed a fortune of $290 million by then. Now one man is dead, both have been destroyed.

In November 1993, Jackson canceled the eight remaining concerts of his *Dangerous* world tour, citing an addiction to painkillers.

The eighteen-minute video for "Bad" was directed by Martin Scorsese, with a script by Richard Price, and a co-starring role for Wesley Snipes. The video was shot in Brooklyn's Hoyt-Schermerhorn subway station in November/December, 1986. Here Jackson takes a break from filming.

13

True or Not, It Didn't Matter

"There are, by latest count, six people in the world who cause a fuss simply by moving around. They are the Pope, President Reagan, Michael Jackson, Jacqueline Onassis, Frank Sinatra and Elizabeth Taylor." That was the verdict of John Anderson, of the *Chicago Tribune*, in 1987 (September 27).

Five were regular visitors, often reluctant visitors, to the parallel cosmos originated by the *National Enquirer*, a weekly publication that challenged commonsense assumptions with claims such as "Frank Sinatra Murdered Monroe!" (September 3, 2018) or announcements like "Plan to Assassinate Jackie and Onassis" (February 9, 1969). Pope Francis would become a kind of *ex gratia* member of this not-so-exclusive group, featuring in a Vatican-related story about "shocking secrets" on September 18, 2015.

Every week, *Enquirer* journalists would discover scarcely believable "facts" about celebrities, including politicians, and spin them into stories that would astound and sometimes horrify readers. Occasionally, the magazine would run into legal trouble, but, by and large, it was a tabloid with enough reverb to make it one of the essential publications of the late twentieth century. There was never a more remarkable literary conduit between the consumer and the celebrity.

On September 16, 1986, the *Enquirer* published a picture of Jackson in what seemed like one of those transparent pods you see in films about missions to distant planets and in which crewmembers go into hypersleep for years. The photograph seemed genuine enough and Jackson issued no legal challenge. It was enough to make readers look and say, "never," then read and keep repeating "never," until they reached the end of the article, when they'd say, Amazing! And that was job of an *Enquirer* story.

Around this time, Jackson was becoming a kind of Ross store for journalists: always worth a visit because you never knew what you'd find and, every so often, you'd come up with a genuine bargain. The *National Enquirer*'s story was a masterpiece of tabloid journalism. Beneath the picture of Jackson at repose in the pod was the heading "Michael Jackson's Secret Plan to Live to 150," followed by details of the sleeping vessel, which was not part of an alien spacecraft at all but a common-or-garden oxygen chamber. Perhaps not common-or-garden, then or even now; but a hyperbaric chamber that athletes have been known to use in attempts to accelerate healing (the chamber is pressurized with oxygen).

Was Jackson serious? Did he genuinely think he could, or even want to live for 150 years? The oldest person in history only made it to her 122nd birthday, plus 164 days (her name was Jeanne Louise Calment and she died in 1997). These questions are irrelevant: the reason the story was so outstanding in its artistry was its preposterousness. It was so contrary to reason or what most people would regard as good sense that it provoked readers into reading more.

Now, the bigger question: Why would anyone buy a magazine to read a story they knew before they opened the page was unbelievable? The answer: same reason people read horoscopes; not because they believe the movements of celestial bodies have a bearing on everyday human affairs, but because they have curiosity and want to learn what the future holds for them. They know they won't learn about that future from some charlatan's forecast, but the joy is in suspending disbelief temporarily and imagining what if the predicted seismic shift in lovelife and the unexpected moneymaking opportunity come together? The reward in learning about Jackson was not in deciding whether or not to believe it, but in imagining how someone's life could be so gaga.

The *Enquirer* knew this a long time before this author and should take credit for amalgamating the sublime and the ridiculous and delivering the endproduct to shoppers as they waited at the supermarket checkout. The hugely influential publication was the conception of Generoso Pope who, in 1954, bought a horseracing guide called the *New York Evening Enquirer* and changed it into a weekly catalog of incredible and gruesome stories, with irresistible headlines like I CUT OUT HER HEART AND STOMPED ON IT and I ATE MY BABY! These shared space with reports on the adventures of Hollywood stars, but the main stories concerned accidents, illnesses, and deaths, usually accompanied by stomach-turning photographs. Who would have thought gore could persuade grocery customers to part with their money?

In 1968, Pope (Generoso, not Francis) moved the editorial offices from New York to Lantana, Florida. Pictures of carcrash victims and other sickening images remained its focus. The only news items consisted of stories about the excesses of Hollywood stars. Judy Garland (1922–

69), in particular, was a generous source of news: her drunken binges, overdoses, and serial marriages were staples. When she died in 1969, the *National Enquirer* might have faced a crisis. But it adapted quite efficiently, specializing in stories about the Hollywood set's miscreant behavior. In the 1960s and 1970s, stars, unlike those of today, were bashful when it came to sharing secrets; journalists became adept at digging for stories.

They hit paydirt with married couple Sonny and Cher, who were a bit too good to be true when they emerged as recording artists and tv show hosts in the 1960s. The *National Enquirer* was not easily put off the scent. Every marital indiscretion was faithfully recorded so that their marital collapse happened in full view of the world. This was a kind of portent that private lives were becoming obsolete. The more stars urged, "Leave us alone," the more the *Enquirer* defied them. By the mid-1970s, the magazine was selling 5 million copies per week and was skimmed-through by probably five times that many supermarket customers. Another masterstroke of Pope's was to do a deal with the stores rather than newsstands: consumers were tempted to pick up a copy of the publication as they waited to pay, then become so engrossed that they couldn't put it down—well only briefly, to drop the magazine on the conveyor belt.

The publication's success encouraged other similar magazines to launch in the 1970s. These included *People* and *US Weekly*, both appearing in 1974 and both sticking with the celebrity scandals boilerplate. The approach of all the magazines was the same: catch hold of the merest hint of a story concerning a well-known figure, then, as Billy Ingram put it in his *Short History of the Tabloids*, "Just throw in a few other bizarre details, true or not, it didn't matter—because it's perfectly legal to print just about anything you like about a celebrity."

Pictures of celebrities became the currency of choice and the pushy approach pioneered by Italian paparazzi came to the fore. When Elvis Presley died in 1977, the *National Enquirer* featured a picture of him lying embalmed in his coffin and was rewarded with sales of 7 million (the *Enquirer* reportedly paid one of Presley's cousins $18,000 to get the photo of the corpse). Celebrity deaths proved to be dependable boosts to circulation, as strong sales following the deaths of Bing Crosby and John Lennon indicated. Images of dead celebrities had a democratizing effect: death couldn't be dodged; in one way or another it would get to everyone, regardless of wealth, glamor, or anything else. Perhaps Elvis was the exception: sightings of him in the most unlikely places kept *National Enquirer* readers wondering (and actually keeps them wondering).

The magazine didn't just capture the spirit of the 1970s and 1980s: it bottled it and put it on sale. But, as those times changed the *National Enquirer* wasn't so quick to adjust as some of its competitors and the sightings, the accounts of alien abductions and the gory reports seemed dated alongside the celebrity muckraking of its rivals like the *Globe* and the *Star*, both cheap newsprint tabloids that also sold off the stands near the supermarket checkouts. *People*'s recipe was the most congruent with the times. Its "focus was entirely on the active personalities of our time," wrote Jill Neimark, in *Psychology Today*, in 1995.

In the 1990s, Bill Clinton's affair with Monica Lewinsky and Jesse Jackson's "love child" were the kind of stories that sold magazines more effectively than "Loch Ness Monster Ate My Husband." The O.J. Simpson trial in 1994 was a major event for the media: its focus was a celebrated ex-athlete and popular entertainer who was arrested and accused of murdering his wife and her male companion, but acquitted after probably the highest profile trial in history. Princess Diana too became a mainstay, though the *National Enquirer* showed taste when it refused to publish photographs of her after her fatal accident in 1997. Copies of the previous week's edition, which bore the headline "Di Goes Sex Mad," were pulled from circulation.

*   *   *

The genius of the "Secret Plan to Live to 150" story was that it seemed at first glance laughable, but, by the fifth paragraph, had readers wondering if there was such an invention that could delay the aging process. Because if there were, Jackson would be first in line for one, no matter how much it cost. Ergo: it *could* be true.

So how did the magazine get the story? It had an extensive web of contacts stretched all over America and beyond and paid handsomely for reliable information, while mainstream media considered payment off-limits. So the *Enquirer*'s intel was second to none: no national newspaper received insider information more reliably. It also had surreptitious arrangements. Publications specializing in lurid and sensationalistic subject matter—"yellow journalism"—had, for years before the *Enquirer*, operated with their equivalents of stool pigeons, who were often eminent celebrities themselves.

For example, Bob Hope was the target for investigations that revealed his serial philandering, but the *Enquirer* agreed to bury the story in exchange for access. Hope became an unlikely and presumably unwitting accomplice, aware that the magazine could at any time run a story that would ruin his unblemished reputation and jeopardize his career. Yellow publications had operated with this kind of arrangement since the days of *Confidential* magazine, which began publishing in 1952. In the 1940s and 1950s, influential gossip columnists Hedda Hopper and Louella Parsons could exact compliance from many actors simply because everyone knew a well-placed sentence could make or break Hollywood stars. So the *Enquirer* continued in this tradition.

Jackson was, by 1986, well versed in the dark art of manipulating the media and though he was no stoolie for the *Enquirer*, he knew there was a symbiosis between media and stars: the two existed in separate spheres but in close physical association. Gone were the days when studios, agents, or managers sought to secrete stars away and ration the media to anodyne pictures and insipid stories. The media wanted excitement and Jackson seems to have had an intuitive grasp of what, years later, Gwen Stefani was to call "the game."

In 2005, Stefani admitted, "You never quite get used to being public property" to the *Independent Magazine's* Nick Duerden, then shrugged, "I understand how the game works." She seemed to mean that success in showbiz, as we understand it today, is less a state, more an activity in which one party engages and occasionally competes with another. Individuals are obliged to surrender some portion of their private lives to a media that liberates it through their channels and, in the process, fabricates fame. There are no explicit regulations or principles, just unwritten codes and, on Stefani's account, these are just understood to govern practice.

Jackson, in 1986, wouldn't have been old enough to remember when gossip mavens like Hopper and Parsons wielded influence, but worked hand-in-glove with the big studios, if only because they knew their professional existence depended on it. The media in the 1980s had grown from a domestic pet into a big beast and, as such, could, if it wished, rule the jungle. Even global stars like Madonna, Whitney Houston, Prince, Julia Roberts, and Tom Cruise depended on the good grace of the media. The *National Enquirer* is rarely bracketed with MTV, HBO, *Vanity Fair*, *Cosmopolitan*, Sirius XM, and other corporate media. But, in the 1970s and 1980s, a circulation consistently over 5 million suggested its force. (*People* now has a circulation of 3 million, *US Weekly* slightly less than 2 million).

The *Enquirer* could legitimately be said to have changed politics. In the late 1980s, Gary Hart was an aspiring Democrat, whom many thought was a future president. The magazine exposed his affair with Donna Rice, featuring a picture of them together in the Bahamas on the cover of a 1987 issue (June 2). Maybe it wouldn't destroy a political career today; but it did then. Hart was history—and Michael Dukakis, the Democratic candidate, was crushed by George H. W. Bush in the 1988 Presidential Election.

Jackson probably knew a big beast needed to be fed, or else, it would come hunting. A tasty morsel every so often might keep it friendly. Sometimes, the *Enquirer's* journalists didn't need to go looking for stories.

Jackson never acknowledged that the long life story was his own invention, nor did he reveal whether or not he'd ever spent a full night in the oxygen chamber. But he knew how to present and promote himself. The story was perfect for the *National Enquirer* and perfect for Jackson. Perfect, that is, for someone trying to affirm his place as the most publicized star in the world, but who had grown comfortable with seclusion.

"Jackson sightings have been rare over the past year," reported William Scobie, of the *Chicago Tribune* in June 1986. Jackson had made guest appearances at charity dinners at the request of Elizabeth Taylor and posed with his likeness at Madame Tussauds in London. "But for the most part the enigmatic Michael stays closeted behind the high walls of his Encino castle with pets that include a boa constrictor named Tinkerbell." (Encino was the neighborhood of LA where Jackson's mother lived in a 22-room Tudor mansion in an acre of grounds.)

Jackson had been missing. But he'd been busy, making a film with Francis Ford Coppola and George Lucas, a new album with Quincy Jones, and some new commercials. He'd also been closing several merchandising deals and was considering a new tour, this time encompassing Japan and Australia. The prospects were exciting, not only for Jackson but for his record label Epic and its parent company CBS (soon to be Sony), PepsiCo for whom he made commercials and Disney. Yes, even Disney came knocking at Jackson's door.

The purveyor of high quality family entertainment and guardian of true American values had secured the acting and singing services of Jackson for a seventeen-minute feature film shot in 3-D. Production started in June, 1985. Jackson wrote and two sang the songs. Coppola directed and Lucas produced. Special effects were done at Lucas's Industrial Light and Magic studios and Disney handled the animated sequences. The production costs—at $20 million, the most expensive per minute film in history—were met by Eastman Kodak Co. and Disney, which screened the film exclusively at its own resorts in Orlando and Los Angeles. There was no theatrical release beyond. Disney went to the lengths of building new movie theaters specifically for the film called *Captain EO*.

The trail from the *National Enquirer* story to Disney now becomes visible. Other entertainers might have been concerned at the preponderance of adjectives like weird or freaky, but Jackson, in the mid-1980s, seemed to welcome his growing reputation as a gifted-but-odd Howard Hughes-type. It excused him the customary celebrity duty of being seen, or speaking to the media, or even doing anything at all in public. At twenty-eight, Jackson seems to have become resigned to being known for distinguishing qualities that had no bearing on his creative work. He discovered that he could use his reputed oddness.

When the prominent early-twentieth-century newspaper editor Arthur Brisbane said, "a picture is worth a thousands words," he couldn't have had Jackson in mind—or he would have made it "millions," if not "billions" of words. The oxygen pod image was a marvel. It set pulses racing and tongues wagging almost synchronously with the release of *Captain EO*. The only way people could view the film was to go to Disney resorts. It opened in September 1986 and played at the World Epcot Center, in Orlando, until 1994 and Disneyland until 1997. The film was also shown at Euro Disney (now Disneyland Paris) from 1986, and Tokyo Disneyland from 1987. It was brought back in February 2010, shortly after Jackson's death, closing (presumably for good) in December 2015. By then, few people remembered the oxygen chamber. But it was recovered in 2019, gathering dust in a California warehouse.

(The benefits of hyperbaric chambers for athletes are probably exaggerated, but the medical uses are reasonably well documented: they're used to treat gas gangrene, carbon monoxide poisoning, and decompression sickness; oxygen can be used to accelerate healing and reduce the risk of infection. They're not known to prolong otherwise healthy lives.)

*   *   *

"Since he first came to public attention as the cute little lead singer of the Jackson Five in the late '60s, any change Jackson has made in the way he looks, the way he sings, the way he thinks, has taken place under the spotlight," Bridget Byrne was writing for the *Los Angeles Times*, in 1987. That was nineteen years after the group's first hit and twenty-two years before Jackson's death. In some respects, he conformed to typical images of blacks; in others, he was an exception. In mainstream print and broadcasting, blacks were represented as entertainment and sports figures, victims of discrimination and criminals; they appeared as experts on news programs, but usually on black issues.

These were the findings of research by communications professors Robert M. Entman and Andrew Rojecki, in 2000. Completely absent from their analysis were portrayals of blacks as misfits, free spirits, unorthodox characters, or, as Jackson could fairly be described at this stage, an extreme individualist. Also conspicuous by their absence were black politicians. In 1987, Barack Obama made a visit to Kenya, as a private citizen. He was elected to the Illinois Senate in 1996.

Jackson's relationship with the media was changing. He'd stopped giving interviews around 1983 and controlled his public appearances closely. Limiting exposure made commercial sense because he had an authorized biography in the works. Incidentally, the book was going to be edited by Jacqueline Onassis, at the publishers Doubleday. So the title could boast two of the six people in the world who could create a commotion by just moving. The book was published as *Moonwalk* in 1988. Onassis herself commissioned the project and, eventually, wrote a foreword. But Jackson was apparently guarded and shared few details. "Had it been written by anyone else *Moonwalk* . . . could be dismissed as an assiduously unrevealing, frequently tedious document," wrote Greg Lawrence in his *Jackie as Editor: The Literary Life of Jacqueline Kennedy Onassis*. "Ultimately, however, these are precisely the qualities that make it fascinating."

Jackson seems to have regarded his publishers in the same way as he did other media: with mistrust. So, while the publishers might have been expecting insights into Jackson's predilection for exotic pets, his family life and perhaps even his sexual proclivities, what they got was "more about damage control than revelation," according to Lawrence. In other words, the narrative gave nothing away. That was, in short, Jackson's aim: to give the media nothing—apart from fabrications. If this was his idea of feeding the beast, Jackson had grievously underestimated its appetite.

Jackson, for all his practical experience with print and broadcasting journalists, didn't appear to grasp that the media itself was changing: though not yet the dominant global behemoth it was later to become, its influence was growing. (The World Wide Web was made available to the public in 1991; Facebook and Twitter launched between 2004 and 2006.) Television channels were multiplying and a syndicated tv series called *Lifestyles of the Rich and Famous*, which had started in 1984, reflected the near-voyeuristic fascination in, as the title suggested, the way moneyed celebs lived (the series lasted until 1995). A crucial development came about ten years before this when the media granted itself license to become conjectural. From the mid-1970s, the media, perhaps in an effort to satisfy audiences' interests, allowed themselves to be speculative rather than straightforwardly factual.

The media also evolved what Macarena Gómez-Barris and Herman Gray called a "preoccupation with race" manifested particularly in its endless coverage of Jackson, "The figure moves from 'cute, young, Black singer' . . . to 'weird, unfixed racial identity' in his [Jackson's] adult years," wrote Gómez-Barris and Gray, the "figure" being the popular media portrayal of Jackson. If this thesis is accepted, Jackson's transition in the mid-1980s was perplexing and challenging to a media habituated to stock stereotypes of black people. Jackson initiated an "unresolved social tension" in the ways America imagined black people. The tension slackened when Jackson's insalubrious practices were revealed and the media gave shape and identity to the figure. It wasn't cute.

Starved of tangible evidence or observations, the media's treatment of Jackson became a manipulation of increasingly implausible scenarios that, after a kind of inflection point, became less implausible as they accumulated. Audiences were like *Enquirer* readers writ large: "Never . . . never . . . Amazing!"

Jackson showed up in Disneyland where *Captain EO* opened in 1987, wearing a surgical mask, an accessory that looked a lot stranger then than it does in the post-Covid era (one of his bodyguards later claimed, "He knew that a natural disaster was always there," according to the British newspaper, *The Sun*, May 25, 2020). He'd worn the protective mask briefly when he visited London. It became a feature of his everyday outdoor ensembles from that point, most people presuming it was another sign of his uncommon habits, others wondering whether he was covering telltale stitches from cosmetic surgery—his visage was visibly changing in the mid-1980s. Either way, it was evidence he was behaving unusually, perhaps obsessively, as Hughes did in his later years when he became mysophobic—fearful of germs and contamination. It was a good story and kept journalists too preoccupied to notice the young boy that accompanied Jackson.

Jackson retained ownership of nearly every photographic image of himself. Musicians with whom he collaborated were obliged to sign an airtight nondisclosure agreement, or NDA as they're often abbreviated nowadays. Yet paradoxically, the more he controlled the availability and distribution of information about himself, the more curiosity ratcheted. A Greta Garbo-like mystique came into being. Garbo, 1905–90, was the Swedish actor, who retired in 1941, insisting, "I want to be alone." Her withdrawal from public life piqued public fascination in her even more.

Jackson was twenty-nine, lived with his mother and had friends, not paramours, and friendships rather than *affaires de coeur*. Those friends weren't always human either: Louie was a llama, Crusher was a 300-pound python, and Bubbles was a chimpanzee whom Jackson used to dress like himself and take to various events. The media would have probably scrutinized Jackson's relationship with Bubbles more deeply had they not found it so hilarious. The chimp was a constant companion, as Cheetah was to Tarzan and Scooby Doo to Shaggy. But these were fictitious partnerships. Jackson and Bubbles was the real thing. Jackson anthropomorphized the chimp—attributed to him human qualities; for example, he let him eat at the dinner table and sleep in a crib in Jackson's bedroom. Cynics might argue that, as Jackson matured, so he grew more cunning and to prevent the media noticing his singularly close friendships with children, deliberately held out distractions like shiny jewels that would dazzle and occupy everyone's attention, while he held other things behind his back. But that's a cynic's interpretation: another is that he just had a new chum.

*   *   *

Spike Lee's 2012 documentary *Bad 25* includes a scene in which Jackson's collaborators remember his writing "100 million" on a note stuck on a bathroom mirror. He might have been adopting a similar tactic to athletes who are advised by sport psychologists continually to remind themselves of their goals with pictures or Post-Its. Of course, athletes train, diet, and abstain from unfavorable practices in pursuit of their goals. Jackson channeled his efforts into his albums. For his forthcoming album *Bad* 100 million was the target sales figure. That would have made it the best-selling album in history and by some way. Sister Janet's album *Control*, released in 1986, had sold 4.5 million, and would go on to pass 6 million copies. It was considered a tremendous success. So neither Jackson's label, his manager, his sponsors, his father, nor anyone else invested in him would, even in a tyrannically aberrant moment, put pressure on Jackson to sell 100 million. The pressure came from Jackson himself: not just a perfectionist, but an evermore perfectible perfectionist, he wanted each successive album to be more exquisite, more faultless, and more possessed than the last.

Jackson wrote sixty-two songs, and recording started in Los Angeles in Fall, 1986. Quincy Jones was a veteran of three decades, having produced the likes of Ray Charles, Ella Fitzgerald, and Frank Sinatra; he and Jackson had become a fructuous combination. Jackson took breaks from recording, but only to shoot videos for singles. Martin Scorsese directed the title track's video, which was actually a short film, complete with narrative structure, a script by Richard Price (who had written the screenplay for Scorsese's *The Color of Money* among many other features) and a role for Wesley Snipes (these extended videos were popular in the 1980s). There was also a series of themed Pepsi ads featuring the song. The deal with Pepsi (which would be followed by the huge 1992 contract) was worth $15 million to Jackson. He would not be obliged to appear holding, less still drinking from, a can of Pepsi: he drank only fruit juice and Evian water. Even this dietary stipulation added, however, tinily, to Jackson's growing reputation as a fastidious misfit. As well as the oxygen chamber and Bubbles, there were rumors that he wished to acquire the skeleton of the Elephant Man and that he frequently availed himself of the services of cosmetic surgeons.

Jackson's slight but multiplying peculiarities were, by about 1986, apparent. This didn't make him any less of an artist, or even less of a marketing phenomenon, though it did mean advertisers needed to exercise discretion. While Pepsi proceeded to invest incautiously in Jackson, other companies were chastened. Max Factor, for instance, paid a reputed $18 million for the rights to use Jackson's image and signature to promote its Magic Beat fragrances range, which was aimed at the teenage market. The cosmetic giant's marketing was geared to the release of *Bad* and the products were in stores by November 1986. Sales were uninspiring and Max Factor dropped the range in early 1987, months before the eventual release of the album—August 31, 1987.

Consumers were entertained and enthralled by Jackson; and clearly they found his music irresistible. But perhaps they didn't think his whiff was especially desirable. (LaToya had more success with cosmetics: in 2010, she launched Dream Cream for German company Alessandro International.) Jackson's overall marketability was not in doubt. But, as I wrote in Chapter 12, market forces abhor an ill-fitting symbol. He fitted inside some products as snugly as a smartphone and charger; with others, he was like a vinyl LP and a cd player.

Weeks before the release of *Bad*, *People* magazine ran a front cover story headlined MICHAEL JACKSON: HE'S BACK. HE'S BAD. IS THIS GUY WEIRD OR WHAT? The magazine, remember, took over from the *National Enquirer* as the premier celebrity-oriented publication. It wasn't so much a damning assessment of Jackson, as an expression of what many were thinking and wondering. "There's more to Jackson than meets the tabloid reader's eye," pronounced the story mystifyingly; after all, the tabloids had delighted in revealing his quirks. What more could there be? (For perspective: on the same front cover of *People* was a picture of Princess Diana holding her youngest son and the line, "Di's darling, Prince Harry, turns 3.")

Jackson had been silent since his interview for *Ebony* three years before, though he spoke at the 1986 Pepsi press conference to announce his new endorsement contract. His words were simple and uninformative. "This is a great honor. Thank you, Mr. Enrico [Roger Enrico, ceo of PepsiCo] and Pepsi Associates. Ladies and gentlemen, thank you." Jackson had a voice that could move the world; but, he chose to remain almost voiceless when it came to communicating information about himself. He preferred to do this through images and deeds, and these can be variously interpreted.

"There is, clearly, a childlike aspect to the Jackson persona," wrote *People*'s Cutler Durkee, noting that playing with pets is not the preferred pastime of most 29-year-old rockstars. Jackson's manager, Frank Dileo, subscribed to the Lost Fun Theory, which hypothesizes that Jackson, who was performing as a five-year old, was "doing things now that he couldn't do then," and sounds like a variant of what I called in Chapter 9 the Lost Childhood thesis. It's equally valueless. Those who, at this time and right up till today, propose that Jackson's lack of a structured childhood with supportive parents, schooling, peer groups, mischievous practices, and so on accounts for his apparently stilted or unnatural psychological development tend to neglect that Jackson was mature, sensible, and totally level-headed when it came to negotiating fabulously lucrative, often record-breaking deals. He also had a shrewd, discriminating sense when it came to appointing the very best producers, musicians, and choreographers to work with. And, when, in January 2004, he pled not guilty to child abuse charges, he did so in the secure knowledge that he had assembled the finest legal team money could buy and shielded himself with the sturdiest defense possible. There was nothing kid-like about any of these actions; they were those of a studious, self-willed adult.

Jackson also had a circle of adult celebrity friends. Elizabeth Taylor was the preeminent one. But, as Durkee pointed out, he was longtime friend of Gregory Peck and knew Sophia Loren, Marlon Brando, and Liza Minnelli. The *People* writer gathered quotes from many of his friends, none of whom recorded anything vaguely unusual in Jackson's speech or behavior. "Nice" is the adjective practically everyone who spent time with Jackson used to describe him. "I didn't see anything freaky," said Helene Phillips, who was an assistant choreographer on *Captain EO* and who also worked with Madonna, Miley Cyrus, John Travolta, and others.

* * *

With 2.25 million copies pre-ordered, *Bad* broke a record before it was even released: CBS had never taken so many orders before a record went on sale. *Bad* was released on August 31, 1987. It spent six consecutive weeks at the top of the *Billboard* charts and spun off five singles, all of which went to number one; the norm was to release singles, sometimes remixed, from the album. Whitney Houston's *Whitney* (1987), George Michael's *Faith* (1987), Paula Abdul's *Forever Your Girl* (1988), and Janet's *Rhythm Nation 1814* (1989) each released four singles. Jackson's feat of five number ones wasn't matched until 2011 when Katy Perry's *Teenage Dreams* repeated it. To date, *Bad* is estimated to have sold nearly 35 million copies. This was a long way shy of Jackson's goal, but, in commercial terms, *Bad* was a staggering success and, if the analysis of the *New Yorker*'s Bill Wyman, is to be accepted, the eleventh highest selling album in history. Jackson's *Dangerous* sold just over 30 million units, according to Wyman's calculations, making it the twenty-third best-selling album.

The concert tour associated with *Bad* comprised 123 concerts over 16 months and spanned 15 countries. It was Jackson's first major tour without his brothers and was a commercial triumph, grossing $125 million. Tour organizers claimed 4.4 million fans had attended concerts, 2.5 million on the continental Europe leg of the tour alone. In England 40 fans were hospitalized after a 125,000-strong crowd at Aintree racecourse surged forward. The 7 sold-out shows at London's Wembley Stadium drew 504,000 people.

A review of the Kansas City concert included the comment, "If its goal is to give Jackson, 29, a new boost, the media are more than willing to cooperate. Something like 300 media representatives descended on this Heartland capital." When the tour concluded in Los Angeles on January 24, 1989, Jackson could afford to comport himself with the swaggering self-entitlement of someone who thought of himself as the world's premier entertainer and could produce record sales and concert receipts as evidence. And, while money is not necessarily a reliable indicator, *Forbes* determined that he was the top earning entertainer of 1989 with $65 million.

* * *

A couple of months after the tour had ended, a thin man wearing a red baseball cap and RayBans was spotted in Zales, the diamond store, in Sycamore Plaza, Simi Valley. He seemed suspicious, glancing around furtively as he surveyed the rings. Ironically, his attempt to evade attention made him stand out: his mustache was clearly fake, and ill-fitting dentures were part of a disguise, surely. He had a young male companion. They left the store for a while, then returned to resume shopping. Fearing a hold-up, a sales employee called a store security guard. The guard carefully approached the man and asked him to step outside the store, where he asked him about the manifestly false appendage above his lip. Why was he concealing himself? "I have to. I'm in disguise," the man replied softly. "I'm Michael Jackson."

He explained that, unless he camouflaged himself in public, he risked being mobbed. He'd just finished his spectacularly successful world tour and had a best-selling album. The guard asked him to remove the disguise. The man complied and, sure enough, he was Michael Jackson and, just as surely, he was mobbed; crowds gathered almost immediately, clamoring for autographs—it was before we knew about smartphones or selfies. "Jackson and a boy he was with visited a gift store and bought several toy figurines and a pair of heart-shaped sunglasses. . . . Then they drove away in a brown Mercedes-Benz," wrote Philip Gollner of the *Los Angeles Times*, on May 3, 1989.

Years later, TMZ obtained Zales' store security video, as they used in the pre-digital 1980s. "Michael Jackson put on a cheap disguise to go shopping for jewelry with a young boy back in 1989," the online publication reported. "The child was James Safechuck."

Jackson was in a kind of semi-retirement. He'd announced that, at thirty, his touring days were over. "He'll do a live show every so often," confirmed Frank Dileo. "But he's not going to tour again." Jackson had recently bought a ranch that he would rename Neverland, and intended to spend much of his time there. Jackson's brother Marlon was skeptical. "I can't understand why Michael's decided not to tour anymore," he told *People*'s Steve Dougherty and Todd Gold in 1989. "I think he's going to tour again. I mean, you say something like that and then there or four years pass and you get the urge again."

*   *   *

"We can actually *control* the press." Not many people can get away with saying this without being laughed-at. W. Randolph Hearst (1863–1951) in the early twentieth century maybe. Possibly Rupert Murdoch (1931–) later in the century. Disney's ceo, Bob Chapek (1960–), perhaps. But Jackson said it. Michael Goldberg and David Handelman believed Jackson had a "control mania" and this was especially evident in the way he addressed the media.

In the month when Jackson opened the *Bad* tour with the first of fourteen concerts in Yokohama, in September 1987, Goldberg and Handelman wrote an article for *Rolling Stone*, with a question in its title, "Is Michael Jackson for Real?" Their answer was broadly compatible with Cutler Durkee's: Jackson was certainly a "flighty-genius star-child, a celebrity virtually all his life, who dwells in a fairy-tale kingdom of fellow celebrities, animals, mannequins and cartoons." But he was also a calculating exploiter of his own eccentricities and that "helped him remain in the news without any new product."

After the oxygen chamber story had circumnavigated the world's newspapers, magazines, and broadcast media, Jackson concluded, "It's like I can tell the press anything about me and they'll buy it," according to biographer J. Randy Taraborrelli. The control Jackson believed he had in his grasp wasn't the kind of megalomaniacal obsession for power often attributed to media tycoons. But the capability to create and distribute narratives about himself in the confidence that they would not be challenged. "I think this is an important breakthrough," said Jackson. It would have been too. If he'd been right.

Then again, who could blame Jackson for assuming he had the media eating out of his hand? He'd fed them the kind of story that most editors would have dismissed as an April Fools prank five months too late. People still talk about it today. But there is a thin membrane separating a belief in one's own ability and an idiosyncratic impression sustained by friends and close colleagues, but contradicted by rational argument. Self-assurance is one thing. Delusions of grandeur are another.

In ancient Rome, victorious generals would return after battle and be drawn through the streets of the imperial capital by a chariot while Romans acclaimed them and drank wine. The generals would bask in glory acknowledging their worshipful acolytes. A slave would be assigned the task of standing close behind the general, holding a gold crown inches above his head, whispering in his ear, "*Remember, you are mortal.*" How Jackson could have used someone like this.

In November 1983, the boxing promoter Don King, shown here in the foreground, announced himself as the man who would be promoting the next Jacksons' tour. He had a tetchy relationship with Jackson, here holding child star Emmanuel Lewis, and flanked by brothers Marlon (right of picture) and Randy.

14

Wearing Different Masks

"In this country, for a dangerously long time, there have been two levels of experience," wrote James Baldwin (1924–87) in his 1964 essay, "The White Problem." He personified one of the two levels in Doris Day, one of "the most grotesque appeals to innocence the world has ever seen." Day (1924–2019) was the wholesomely freckled blonde singer with the sunny smile who emerged from the 1940s big band era to become one of Hollywood's top boxoffice stars, specializing in what we'd now call romcoms. The other level was, as Baldwin put it, "subterranean, indispensable, and denied" and was encapsulated "in the tone and in the face of Ray Charles." Charles (1930–2004) was the gospel, blues, and soul singer, whose musical influence is still pervasive, and whose personal life was marred by the familiar problems of drugs, paternity suits, and conflicts with other musicians.

As Michael Jackson transitioned from a cheerfully handsome, outgoing entertainer to a self-absorbed, unworldly recluse with multiplying eccentricities, he seemed restless to evacuate his old identity and discover someone new. Someone who transcended the sexual binary, the ethnic divide, and even the age barrier. Someone whom it was impossible not to love. Someone who was the biggest, most renowned, most illustrious star in the world. Someone like Doris Day. He almost got away with it too. Only almost: audiences would never let go of the idea that he was a lot more like Ray Charles.

Jackson had been told as much, though in blunter terms when, in the 1980s, the impresario Don King issued a reminder. "What Michael's got to realize is that Michael's a nigga. It doesn't matter how great he can sing and dance," King contended. "He's one of the megastars of the world, but he's still going to be a nigga megastar." Years later, in 2016, King remembered the conversation when on the campaign trail with Donald Trump. "You're going to be a negro til you die," King recalled telling Jackson, adding that he didn't actually use the word "negro." While King's advice has been documented (by Rachael Revesz, of the *Independent*, among others), Jackson's response has not. But, in a sense, he seems to have spent the rest of his life contriving one.

*   *   *

On January 28, 1984, United Press International (UPI) released a story by Jeff Hasen concerning Jackson. He had, according to the report been hospitalized after being burnt during the filming of an advertisement for Pepsi. Sparks from fireworks used in the studio ignited his hair. Jackson's personal doctor, Steve Hoefflin, believed it was best for Jackson to stay at Brotman Hospital, in Culver City, California, "for several days." Jackson ignored his advice and discharged himself. Then twenty-five, Jackson had worked closely with director Bob Giraldi to produce the commercial. There was apparently little or no artistic input from Pepsi, nor its advertising agency, and, while Michael's four brothers were on set, they had no control over the production.

After five takes, Giraldi called for a sixth: the brothers appeared and pyrotechnics illuminated a stairway on which Jackson stood. A fiery particle from the special effects smokebomb made contact with his hair and set it alight. Jackson's hair had very probably been treated with a flammable product. Astonishingly, Jackson didn't realize straightaway that his hair was actually ablaze and continued his routine unperturbed. Then, realizing the danger, he cried out "Tito!" to his brother.

A studio audience of 3,000 at LA's Shrine Auditorium witnessed the barely believable accident. "Some studio audience members said he [Jackson] was so calm, they thought the incident was part of the act," reported BBC Home.

Jackson sustained second-degree burns (i.e., that cause blistering but no permanent scars) and a third-degree burn on the back of his neck (i.e., affecting the tissue beneath the skin's surface). He requested through a representative that a tape of the accident be made public as soon as the film could be processed. An edited video of the event, about a minute long, surfaced. It didn't include Jackson leaving the auditorium via the front entrance—where a crowd was assembled—on a stretcher, but some reports indicate that Jackson, swathed in bandages, instructed paramedics carrying him not to remove his famous jewel-encrusted accessory, "Leave the glove on . . . the media is here." (The incident still viewable here: https://bit.ly/3pKxIMW.)

Was this early evidence of Jackson's desire to master the media? He obviously wanted audiences and, by implication, the media to witness the full visual extravaganza of him, his hair alight, being swamped and doused by studio staff. Viewers could watch as Jackson combusted in mid-song and was then drenched. "Michael wants to make certain that his fans know exactly what happened," spokesperson Larry Larson told reporters. Exactly why wasn't clear. Few artists would have been in a hurry to disclose what could have been, in slightly different circumstances, a fatal accident. Jackson wasn't like other artists. His appeal was not based on straightforward admiration; no one knew this better than him. (Strands of Jackson's burnt hair salvaged from the accident went up for auction in London 2009, after Jackson's death. The twelve strands of hair were valued collectively at $1,600.)

Some might argue that Jackson was oblivious to or willfully heedless of warnings. King's scalding reminder may not have been welcome, but had a little too much wisdom secreted in it to be dismissed. The Pepsi accident may have been less direct, but it was a reminder that no matter how much status, influence, money, and control Jackson possessed, he was still mortal and, as such, susceptible to the same kinds of misfortunes as other humans. The sixth-century fabulist Aesop could have created a story about the lion that ruled the jungle, but forgot that, when wounded, he was no more a ruler than an ant. Jackson could have learned from both King and his mishap: he would live and die a black man and, when wounded, his reputation would be no protection: he would be helpless.

*   *   *

Jackson, blistered but, it seemed, not charred, appeared in public within a month of the accident: on February 28, he returned to the Shrine Auditorium for the Annual Grammy Awards Ceremony. He won eight awards. Jackson was accompanied by Brooke Shields, then eighteen, and already a valuable Hollywood star with movies such as *The Blue Lagoon* and *Endless Love*. Shields, like Jackson, had also known success—and, in her case, controversy—at a young age: in 1978 when only eleven, she played a child living with her prostitute mother in a New Orleans brothel for the film *Pretty Baby*. Jackson had another companion whom he held in his arms at times during the ceremony. No, not Bubbles. Emmanuel Lewis was the third child star in the trio; he was playing in the ABC tv sitcom *Webster*, which ran 1983-7. He was then thirteen. He'd met Jackson the year before and had since been a friend. Many people must have found Jackson's trilateral party puzzling.

At this point, Jackson was rarely out of the news: he was on the front cover of the March 19 edition of *Time*, his visage given the Andy Warhol screenprint treatment. The headline was: MICHAEL JACKSON: WHY HE'S A THRILLER. Among the many other magazines to carry approving stories about him was *Jet*'s cover story, March 26: THE JACKSON FAMILY TALK ABOUT MICHAEL. The most unusual headline of the period was above a *Rolling Stone* cover story, March 15: TROUBLE IN PARADISE? MICHAEL JACKSON.

The article by Michael Goldberg and Christopher Connelly established Jackson's status in the 1984 in the opening paragraph. "Michael is now, quite simply, the biggest star in the pop-cultural universe—if not bigger than Jesus, as John Lennon once boasted of the Beatles, then certainly bigger than that group, or any other past pop icons." Then it suggested "a struggle for power" threatened to disturb the familial harmony typically associated with the Jackson family at the time.

Michael realized that he was to the Jacksons what Buddy Holly was to the Crickets. This is not meant to diminish the value of the Crickets, one of whom, Jerry Allison, co-wrote "Peggy Sue" and "That'll Be the Day," but Holly was the main attraction. As was Jackson. So, when it became known that the brothers would be touring as a group, everyone tacitly understood Michael was being unselfish. He was striving to interrupt the group's slide toward oblivion. Without him, the Jacksons would struggle to sell tickets. With him, they would sell out any venue. Joe Jackson, though not involved in Michael's career in any hands-on way, seems to have made a fatherly request and Michael agreed. So, it wasn't one of life's capricious breezes that blew Michael and Don King together: it was Joe Jackson.

It's not hard to understand why Joe Jackson and Don King were able to work together. Jackson was born in Fountain Hill, Arkansas, in 1928, moved to Oakland, California, when he was twelve and then east to Chicago when, at eighteen, he began to show promise as a boxer. When his first child Rebbie was born in 1950, he abandoned sports and moved 30 miles south to Gary, Indiana, to work fulltime at US Steel. The family lived in an all-black neighborhood.

King was born in 1931 also in the Midwest, in Cleveland, Ohio, and, like Jackson went to school at a time when America was split into haves and have-nots. The former were white and, while there were many poor whites, all blacks were poor; society had a way of ensuring it stayed that way. Segregation enforced the separation of blacks and whites in schools, housing, work, and most other areas. Both Jackson and King were born into this divided world and, like most blacks, would have wondered at some time: How does a black person get on? In the 1940s, the racial divide seemed as permanent as ever. The 1950s promised little more. The name Emmett Till meant something to both men. As did the phrase "money whitens." It wasn't a key to a magic kingdom where race was irrelevant and fairness prevailed; but legal tender made an individual's life more bearable. Jackson and King both arrived at the same conclusion.

They were both young men in 1955 when Rosa Parks was arrested for refusing a driver's order to give up her seat to a white passenger on a bus in Montgomery, Alabama. They lived through the civil rights struggle and were in their thirties when the 1964 Civil Rights Act ended segregation. They would have both been, of necessity, familiar with America's racism of the mid-twentieth century. Joe's Protestant work was the stuff of legend: it informed the way he lived and the way he expected his children to live. Neither he nor King felt conflicted by their enthusiastic pursuit of money.

King was released from Marion Correctional Institution, Ohio, in 1971. He was forty. Meeting him as he emerged from prison was his friend Lloyd Price, a rock 'n' roll singer who wrote and recorded "Lawdy Miss Clawdy" in 1952. Elvis's version four years later was a big hit. Price knew Muhammad Ali. King persuaded Price to ask Ali to box an exhibition at a Cleveland hospital that was in danger of closing. Price used his influence to bring Marvin Gaye, Wilson Pickett, and other black singers to the show and they performed a concert before the main attraction. Eight and half thousand paying customers turned up to watch Ali spar, and the spoils were shared between the hospital, Price, Ali, and King. The show marked the start of King's promoting career. Previously, he'd lived off his wits running a numbers racket in Cleveland before he beat a debtor to death and got sent to prison. Four years later, he resurfaced and resolved to earn an honest living. Boxing offered something resembling that.

King pursued his own American dream in a New World liberated from the old restrictive bonds that had held back black people. Like so many other ambitious African Americans, he yearned to become a black bourgeoisie, a member of that small, but elite group that had transcended race, or, more accurately, had enough money to make it largely irrelevant to them personally. Like King, Joe Jackson saw his blackness as an obstacle to progress, though not an insurmountable one.

"Blacks enter the mainstream wearing different masks," detected the writer Shelby Steele in a 2008 interview with Ibram Rogers for *Diverse Issues in Higher Education*. One of those masks is that of the "bargainer," whose sales pitch is, said Steele, "I will not rub the history of racism in your face if you will not hold my race against me." Both King and Jackson were bargainers.

*   *   *

King's spot on the space-time curve couldn't have been better. The rebellious mood that had fired rioting in Los Angeles in 1965 and spread over the following two years was reflected in sport when Tommie Smith and John Carlos lowered their heads and raised gloved fists of defiance at the 1968 Olympics in Mexico City. Muhammad Ali, who had been stripped of his heavyweight title for his refusal to go to Vietnam a year earlier, converted to the Nation of Islam, a black separatist movement that strove for economic independence for African Americans. This boded well for King, who reminded Ali that, if he didn't let him promote his fights, he would be making money for white capitalists rather than a brother.

When Ali was persuaded, King promised him big money, even though he didn't have it. What he had was the gift of the gab and, with it, he created the illusion that he was a bigtime promoter. His braggadocio was rewarded with one of the most momentous fights in history—Ali regained the world heavyweight title at the age of thirty-two, knocking out George Foreman in Zaire in 1974. The fight was memorialized as The Rumble in the Jungle.

Jack Newfield's 1995 book *Only in America: The life and crimes of Don King* chronicles the rise and rise of King up a greasy pole that was left even greasier after King had climbed it. Newfield charts how King's boxing related disputes, usually revolving around money, became a feature of his progress. But they didn't stop him becoming one of the major sports figures of the twentieth century. Allegations of kickbacks, fixing and mob connections followed King, but he became adept at dismissing them, often arguing that every successful black person is instantly suspected of misdeeds of one kind or another.

Those who saw in King a progressive, could see a black man who dragged himself out of the underground economy after a rehabilitative spell behind bars and forced himself into a sport dominated by white businessmen but populated by black fighters. Those who saw him as regressive could see someone who looked and talked like a black man but whose ruthless pursuit of money made him indifferent to the people he exploited, black and white. Among the African American boxers King had managed or promoted, but who turned against him were Larry Holmes, Mike Dokes, and Tim Witherspoon. All complained that King had wronged them in some way. "Don's specialty is black-on-black crime," said Witherspoon. "I'm black and he robbed me" (quoted by Newfield).

King dismissed this and the other claims. "Are they *all* lying?" asked *Esquire* writer Mike Lupica in a 1991 article "The Sporting Life." "Or is King a hypocrite, screaming about racism on one hand and preying on black fighters himself?" Former heavyweight Mitch Green had an answer. As he told writer Jim Brady, "King gives you this bro' stuff and tells you that the white man did this and we should stick together." Adding the unnerving afterthought, "You put your head in a noose when you sign with Don King."

Carping comments like these were commonplace and King was never unsettled by them. "Machiavelli taught me it was better to be feared than loved, because if you are loved they sense you might be weak." Whether or not King actually uttered these words is not certain, though they are often attributed to him and they seem consistent with his demeanor: he never acted as if he wanted to be loved. Joe Jackson was similarly unapologetic when answering critics.

In her 1991 book *Growing Up in the Jackson Family*, LaToya revealed that her father had abused his children. Jermaine, Tito, Marlon, and Jackie denied this. In 2003, Joe told BBC's Louis Theroux that he hit Michael as a child. "I whipped him with a switch and a belt," he revealed (a switch is a flexible shoot cut from a tree). Yet, in his mind this was different from "beating" him. "I never beat him," he said. "You beat someone with a stick." It seemed a fine distinction. Years later in 2010, he was unrepentant and told Oprah Winfrey, "I don't regret it" (The *Guardian*'s Adam Sweeting recounted his comments in his obituary in 2018).

In many ways a shameless acknowledgment, Joe's approach was characteristic of many African Americans' tough love (research from the Pew Research Center in 2015 reported that black parents are more than twice as likely as white and Latino parents to use corporal punishment on a regular basis). The philosophy was that making others take responsibility for their actions is beneficial for them in the longterm. Self-reliance is the priority in life: pinning one's faith on others, whether a family, a welfare system, or a protest movement, encourages dependency. Oprah herself might not have expressed approval for his methods, but she surely shared an allegiance to the underlying principle, as did Barack Obama, who once proudly declared, "That mother of mine gave me love; she pushed me, and cared about my education. . . . She took no lip and taught me right from wrong" (reported by Steve Holland, of Reuters, in 2009).

Both King and Jackson were individualists. Blaming racism, whites, or more abstract forces for the persistent inequalities in American society was not the favored option. Individuals were better off pursuing their own course of action, striving to improve themselves rather than surrounding themselves with other well-meaning, but not necessarily effective compatriots. This sometimes, perhaps often, meant upsetting others, and among those others were black people. Oprah didn't endorse hurting or ripping off others; but she promoted a worldview in which individuals are independent agents capable of changing themselves—and that was entirely consistent with the philosophies of King and Jackson. I'll return to Oprah in Chapter 17.

Michael was cut from a different cloth. He was only eight going-on nine when the Jackson family relocated from the industrial Midwest to California. In Los Angeles, he mixed with the likes of Motown boss Berry Gordy, Diana Ross, and Smokey Robinson, all African Americans but prosperous, high-achieving African Americans. In December 1969, Jackson had, with the band, a number one single on the *Billboard* charts. It was the first of many hugely successful records. By his teens, Jackson had a solo career, his single *Ben* making it to the top of the charts. A regular on television, Jackson was an internationally acknowledged pop star at an age when many boys are earning a little money from babysitting, delivering newspapers, or serving for a few hours in their parents' store. Jackson never knew what it was like to have to save money, less still to have to wait for a bicycle, a videogame, or anything at all. The concept of deferred gratification was meaningless: he had any material thing a child or young adult could have wanted.

Joe and Kathleen Jackson and their brood may once have scraped a living from industrial work in the steel mills of Gary, but, once in California, they found respite from the grind. The Jacksons discovered a life that must have seemed distant from the one described by Martin Luther King, or Malcolm X (who had been assassinated in 1965), or the Black Panthers, a militant black movement that challenged police brutality and was based less than 400-miles away in Oakland. Joe and Kathleen would have been familiar with this life. It informed and encouraged their desire to leave it in the past, and, for Joe, justified his unforgiving attitude toward his children.

Michael knew nothing of his father's world: his reality was a dizzying mix of showbiz celebrities, tv appearances, and hit records. Money was never a problem. He never even had to contend with the irksome chores that occupy most of us as we mature: saving for the downpayment on the first car, negotiating a mortgage, and pulling allnighters before an important examination. Jackson didn't even have classmates with whom he could learn about these bothersome ordeals. His was a proper SoCal life.

It's not hard to understand why Michael found King's acquisitiveness repugnant. His relationship to money was totally different: while King scrapped, squeezed, and, if some are to be believed, chiseled for every buck, Michael probably never even saw a greenback. If he wanted something, he just told someone and, as if by magic, it arrived. He probably thought King was an avaricious, coarse, grasping, tasteless philistine, whose one-dimensional pursuit of money clashed violently with his own altogether more spiritual scope on life. Jackson was a man who, in the course of his lifetime, earned an estimated $1.1 billion and died between $400 and 500 million in debt. This gives some measure of his recklessness; he spent with the profligacy of Nero. King's prudence was hewn out of his experiences on the unfriendly streets of Cleveland. Jackson's extravagance from the palm gardens of West Hollywood.

*   *   *

Place: Tavern on the Green, Central Park, New York City. Date: November 30, 1983. Present: Dustin Hoffman, Andy Warhol, Roberta Flack, Ossie Davis, Ruby Dee, several prominent boxers, and representatives of many media organizations. Plus: Michael Jackson, his brothers, and their dad. And Don King. "Be not afraid of greatness. Some men are born great. Some achieve greatness and others have greatness thrust upon them." King very nearly quoted the famous extract from Shakespeare's *Twelfth Night*; there was no "others" in Malvolio's speech. But everyone knew what he meant. Or did they? King had a tendency to extreme loquacity—he talked a lot, often in a way that didn't make much sense. "It was a cross between a press conference for a heavyweight title fight and a revival meeting," wrote *Vanity Fair's* Lisa Robinson.

King was in his usual form: bombastic, word-mangling, and full of his own self-importance. In fact, if he was familiar with Shakespeare, he might have taken tips from Dogberry, the constable in *Much Ado About Nothing*, who is never wracked by doubt. "I am a wise fellow" is the nearest he gets to self-criticism. King introduced himself to the gathered media as the man who would be promoting the next Jacksons tour. The immediate question that everyone must have asked themselves was: What does a boxing promoter know about pop music? It didn't matter: King was a promoter; whether a heavyweight title fight or a world tour by popular entertainers, the essence was the same for King—sell tickets and make money. King used his well-tested formula of barnstorming the media.

At the New York conference to announce his new venture, King gave a long speech, showed a video about himself, and kept himself at the center of attention. Joe Jackson probably smiled gnomically. This was King doing what King did best: brag about himself. Michael would have hated the swagger, the bluster, and the conceit. He remained virtually silent throughout the media conference. When King eventually paused for breath and passed him the microphone, Jackson answered in a soft voice, "I really don't have anything to say." It was the kind of response Jackson would use time and again, giving nothing away but somehow granting the media license to use their imaginations.

Jackson had cultivated a style of communicating with the media; it was a style, or method, that he would refine over the years; it was a style completely different from King's PT Barnum-meets-Shakespeare technique. Jackson could probably sense dangers. According to *People*'s Peter Carlson and Roger Wolmuth, "Michael reportedly sent King a letter stating in no uncertain terms that King could not speak or deal for Michael." It was the kind of response King expected. "With Michael . . . you always on trial," he said. His lack of faith and reluctance to trust an African American entrepreneur was presumably a factor in the crucial, if indelicate piece of advice King later submitted. And, in a sense, King was well versed in dealing with all kinds of people who wanted to keep him at arm's length. Part of his overall strategy seems to have been gaining the confidence of just one key figure. In this case, it was Joe Jackson. This is where their common interest in money came in handy.

Contractually, King was employed by the Jacksons. Joe and his sons had met six entrepreneurs and prospective promoters of their next tour. King was the one they chose. Whether he considered himself their employee is doubtful. King acted as if he were in charge of the whole shebang, as he usually was when he promoted a fight night. His success in sports promotion is derived from his ability to squeeze money out of the most unpromising situations. The Jacksons, on the other hand, offered him a promising situation; all he had to do was maximize the revenue.

To this end, he introduced a complex voucher system for ticket applications: applicants would have to order in blocks of four tickets at a cost of $120 (in money orders, which, unlike checks, are pre-paid) and then wait until days before the concert before learning whether they'd been allocated tickets.

This made it a very expensive concert by 1984 standards, but lucrative for the organizers. "Assuming some twelve million fans shelled out for the forty-plus concert dates," wrote biographer Christopher Andersen, "that meant $1.5 *billion* in sales." About 1.2 million tickets were expected to be available, meaning a gross of $24–30 million. The rest of the money—over $1.3 billion—would be returned to the unsuccessful applicants. This made little sense—until the logic is revealed. Andersen pointed out that the time between sending the money and having it returned was about two months, "a period during which the Jacksons stood to collect well over $100 million in interest on that money."

The band took the lion's share of the receipts after expenses, leaving the rest to be divided between Joe, Katherine, and King, who would, according to Oldberg and Connelly, walk away with about $1.8 million for their labors. Remember: most pop concert tours in the mid-1980s were not designed to make money, but to showcase a new album, in this case the Jackson 5's *Victory*. Boxing promotions were and are a different kind of event. Gate receipts are still a source of revenue, but for boxing shows, television typically provides the core money.

Andersen reckons the tour's overheads were so enormous—a million dollars a week to move the equipment alone—that the *Victory* tour actually lost money. This is unlikely: King had negotiated a remunerative sponsorship. PepsiCo had shown interest in sponsoring a Jacksons project for some time before King became involved. Once King took the helm, Pepsi was obliged to sweeten the pot. The benchmark rock tour sponsorships at the time were the perfumier Jovan's deal with the Rolling Stones for the band's US tour in 1981, and the brewer Schlitz's sponsorship of The Who's 1982 tour, both of which were worth $2–4 million. Oldberg and Connelly suggest the Pepsi deal was "far in excess" of these. The Pepsi deal was exclusive, so it effectively torpedoed any other tentative offers of sponsorship. It also initiated a long and fruitful, if at times fraught commercial relationship between Pepsi and Michael.

The tour was a rich pie and, as such, had a lot of fingers stuck in it. By its conclusion on December 9, 1984, 2.3 million paying customers had seen the show and more than a few of them had bought commemorative tee-shirts and other sorts of merchandise. Whether everybody got paid as much as they expected is open to doubt. Several legal actions sprung from the tour and there were times when the tour looked like it could come to a halt. "As recently as a few days ago, tales and rumors of dissension among the Jacksons and their platoon of advisers had some observers wondering whether there was going to be a tour," wrote Robert Palmer of the *New York Times*, on July 7, 1984, suggesting how deep some of the disputes had become. Money caused an awful amount of friction. Perhaps it was King's presence that set the mood.

Los Angeles Times' Dennis McDougal's headline described it as "the biggest, splashiest and most troubled rock concert tour in history." Jackson himself tried to fly serenely above all the disputes. "While the others fought and clamored over money, Michael came to dance and sing," reported McDougal. He claimed that he gave any money due to him for the tour to charities. He called the *Victory* tour his "Last Hurrah" and "the Final Curtain," an allusion to his intention to sever links with the band. As if to underline his individuality, he traveled separately. It's not known whether he actually talked with King during the tour. Probably not.

* * *

Physical copies of the album *Victory* arrived in stores to coincide with the start of the tour. Commercially, it was already successful, 2 million advance orders guaranteeing that. "Michael Jackson fans may feel a little short-changed; there's less of their idol on the record than they may have hoped for," wrote Palmer. Jackson, by then an artist in his own right, probably wanted to limit his exposure. His solo albums were still selling strongly and in a competitive market populated by the likes of Prince and Bruce Springsteen, Jackson must have wondered whether the soul sound of the brothers was challenging enough for the mid-1980s. Palmer wondered how many of the concertgoers bought tickets primarily to see the band. At that point, *Thriller* had sold 35 million copies. Jackson was prominent on only two or three of *Victory's* eight tracks. Jermaine also had ambitions as an individual artist and was working on his own album at the time of the tour.

The first concert was at Kansas City's Arrowhead Stadium. The *Newsweek* reviewer compared Jackson to old-style entertainers Frank Sinatra, Fred Astaire, and Judy Garland as well as contemporaries James Brown and Diana Ross and a white singer who shot to fame with vapid versions of black artists' songs such as "Tutti Frutti" and "Ain't That a Shame." "Like Pat Boone, the prototype of rock teen idols, he's cute, wholesome and pious." The comparisons probably pleased Jackson himself as much as they tickled Don King. Everyone in the world, it seemed, either adored Jackson or held him in high esteem at this point in history. He must have felt close to Doris Day.

* * *

Was there more than one Michael Jackson at this point? According to Robert E. Johnson, in a story in the December 1984 issue of *Ebony*, "The White media's Michael Jackson, portrayed mostly through gossip, rumors, hype" was one such being. Another, the one "nobody knows," was "warm, sensitive, vibrant, keenly aware of the mysteries of life and the wonder and magic of children" (p. 156). The magazine's cover featured a picture of Jackson alongside the headline THE MICHAEL JACKSON NOBODY KNOWS.

Jackson, then twenty-six, had just returned from the Victory tour and Johnson was writing from notes he took at an interview a few months earlier. "He told me that he was tired of the wave of lies in the White press," wrote Johnson, who quoted further from a Jackson statement delivered via Frank Dileo: "No! I've never taken hormones to maintain my high voice. No! I've never had my cheekbones altered in any way. No! I've never had cosmetic surgery on my eyes. YES!! One day in the future I plan to get married and have a family."

Much of the interview was about Jackson's habit of praying every night and often several times in the day, his platonic relationships, and his future acting projects. "Whatever role you play, people link it with your personality," said Jackson. "But it's acting . . . if you're acting, you're imitating realism. You should create realism." When *Ebony* asked what kind of questions Jackson wished he was asked, but never was, he responded, perhaps surprisingly, "Probably about children or writing." He then went on to praise Marvin Gaye's classic 1971 album *What's Going On*, which he believed "educated" people. "Mainly Blacks were educated. 'Wake up. What's going on? Wake up.' I mean the ones that don't watch the news, don't read the papers to really dig in the depths of humanism."

The interview included a question on Jackson's travels and whether they influenced "the way you think about races of people?" Jackson replied, "The main thing that I hate most is ignorance, like the prejudice problems of America." He drew short of linking this with his comments, or, more specifically, Johnson's comments, about the "lies in the White press" but there was at least room to infer an association.

The story concluded, "Those are the thoughts of the Michael Jackson nobody knows." No doubt there were many more nobody knew about. Some they would discover over the coming years. Others they would never know. The importance of the article though lay less in its claim to have disclosed hitherto unknown thoughts, more in its recognition that Jackson was due a chance to present himself as he really wanted. *Ebony* was a publication launched in 1945 by John H. Johnson with a specific remit: to focus on African American figures, issues, and concerns, not in a critical but in an affirmative way. In other words, it was designed to mirror the black experience in America, though it probably more accurately mirrored the upwardly mobile black experience. This was a full two decades before civil rights. Segregation was an institutional and personal reality in the United States. The magazine became more political as the African American population became politically engaged in the 1950s and 1960s.

The Jackson story wasn't political, at least not in an obvious way; though the reference to the "White media" and its alleged "lies" was presumably intended to invite readers to compare the substance of the *Ebony* article with the stories that were by 1984 circulating in the mainstream media. I too stand accused: in this chapter I have referred to Jackson's "eccentricities," my purpose being to draw readers' attention to the unconventional or slightly strange nature of his reported behavior in the early 1980s and beyond. *Ebony* writer Johnson believed the mainstream—that is, "White media"—peddled "gossip, rumors, hype, and sometimes slander." Instead, he opted to understand Jackson, an artist "motivated by a deep concern for all of humankind and an unyielding love for his profession."

*   *   *

In April 1983, about a year before the *Victory* tour launched, Jackson went to see someone who was to have an important and usually underestimated influence on his life and, for that matter, Elizabeth Taylor's. "It was Taylor who endorsed Arnold Klein, the cosmetic dermatologist to Hollywood's A-list, to Jackson," according to Gerald Posner, of the *Daily Beast*. Taylor certainly appreciated Dr. Klein's work and praised him wholeheartedly; so it's conceivable that she recommended Klein to Jackson when he was concerned about a rash that had appeared on his face and scalp. Klein diagnosed lupus (which refers to a group of diseases marked from inflammation of the skin) and, more controversially, vitiligo. Klein's diagnosis in itself was not controversial, but vitiligo is a condition in which pigment is lost from the skin, leaving whitish patches and was often cited as the reason Jackson grew paler as he matured. Some suspected he deliberately used skin-whitening agents and yearned to be white. I'll return to this.

But Klein's influence went deeper. Posner advanced the now widely accepted theory that the habits that ultimately killed Jackson had their origins in the aftermath of Pepsi shoot incident: "This was around the time Jackson first began using some of the same pain and sleeping pills as Taylor." Klein visited Jackson when he was in the hospital being treated for the burns sustained during the fateful video shoot.

It is worth bearing in mind the context of Taylor's friendship with Jackson: he first met her shortly after she'd emerged from her first visit to the Betty Ford Center. Taylor would return in 1988, again undergoing treatment for alcohol and painkiller dependencies. She was unembarrassed about this and spoke openly about her habits. Within eighteen months of her leaving the center, the California state attorney general's office with the assistance of the Los Angeles County district attorney investigated several physicians and eventually in 1994 reprimanded three doctors for prescribing Taylor "more than 1,000 prescriptions during a five-year period dating back to 1983 for 28 controlled substances, including sleeping pills, painkillers and tranquilizers," according to Claire Spiegel and Virginia Ellis of the *Los Angeles Times*.

In the mid-1980s, Jackson's butter-wouldn't-melt image was a far cry from the creepy child abuser he would become in the eyes of many. It wasn't until 1993 that Jackson publicly acknowledged his "addiction" to pharmaceuticals. Jackson, by then thirty-five, said the drugs had been prescribed after reconstructive surgery on his scalp, presumably part of the ongoing treatment for the burn injuries. *Vanity Fair*'s Mark Seal called Klein Jackson's "Demerol dermatologist," this being a reference to the trade name of the synthetic opioid pethidine, often used as a painkiller by women in labor. Taylor was known to favor this narcotic.

After Jackson's death, Klein was subpoenaed by the California Medical Board and investigated by the Drug Enforcement Administration for allegedly overprescribing Demerol to Jackson. It was suggested by Conrad Murray's defense team that Klein provided Jackson with vast amounts of Demerol "for no valid medical purpose," thus inducing an enfeebling dependency. The judge said it was "not relevant" and Klein was spared an appearance. Murray was convicted, of course. No Demerol was found in Jackson's body after his death. But the adverse publicity ruined Klein's business and he declared bankruptcy.

Klein's other area of influence in Jackson's life was in providing him with a wife and perhaps more. Debbie Rowe worked for Klein and grew to know Jackson, as we learned in Chapter 9. She would marry and bear two children, Prince and Paris. Klein "entertained speculation that he was the biological father of Jackson's eldest children," wrote Julie Miller in her obituary. She says he told television host Larry King, "Once [I donated] to a sperm bank." When asked directly whether he had fathered any of Jackson's children, Klein's answer was lukewarm, "Not to the best of my knowledge."

Klein was noncommittal but, in a culture steeped in celebrity gossip and innuendo, his declaration was emphatic enough to set tongues wagging. It also raised the suspicion that Klein had decided to become mischievous. In 2010, Klein told the online celebrity gossip publication TMZ.com that Jackson was gay and that his own office manager Jason Pfeiffer had been "the love of [Jackson's] life." The syndicated tv magazine *Extra* aired an interview with Pfeiffer, who declared, "I just assumed he [Jackson] was probably bisexual," and the story circulated around the world.

The *Sydney Morning Herald*, for example, carried an article under the headline "Jackson was my lover, says gay man" on May 1, 2010 (which is still available at: https://bit.ly/39Kh9Y2). "I know we loved each other, I know he told me that all the time," said Pfeiffer. As everyone knows, rumors and telltale stories multiplied after Jackson's death when it was impossible to libel him. Klein explained, again to TMZ, that his declaration was meant "to shoot down rumors that Jackson was a pedophile" (TMZ staff, May 3, 2010: http://bit.ly/1suHElk). Interesting choice of ammunition.

Althea Manasan, of the *National Post*, reported the same story. "Even death can't help Michael Jackson escape rumours about his sexuality," she wrote, presumably not realizing what a laughable understatement she was making. The *Los Angeles Times'* Harriet Ryan, in January 2012, wrote:

"Jackson's family blasted the report, which Pfeiffer later conceded was 'embellished,'" and Taylor castigated her longtime friend publicly. "I thought doctors, like priests, took an oath of confidentiality. May God have mercy on his soul," Taylor tweeted. Considering Taylor's famous friendships with gay men and her heroic work with Aids charities, especially the American Foundation for AIDS Research (amfAR), which she helped found, and The Elizabeth Taylor AIDS Foundation (ETAF), an attribution of homosexuality, however spurious it may have been, would surely not have been the cause of her upset.

Then, out of nowhere, Klein issued a message on his Facebook page (no longer available), in which he denied Jackson had been involved in a relationship with Pfeiffer. TMZ.com once more reported this, as did *Vanity Fair*'s Mark Seal: "Klein took back his statement about the purported affair, posting on Facebook, 'Allegations about . . . Jason being Michael Jackson's lover are ridiculous. That story was made up.'"

If the origins of Jackson's dependence on narcotics, especially anesthetics, lay in his efforts to find relief from pain following his Pepsi misfortune, then it's possible to trace the links all the way back to his first pivotal meeting with Klein in 1983. But it's a leap of faith: even if Jackson did seek relief from the pain occasioned by his burns, there's no evidence that this caused a dependency.

* * *

King and Klein make an odd couple. There's no evidence they ever met. But Jackson is the nexus. He probably had a love-hate relationship with both of them. At first, he must have hated King's overbearing manner and his fixation with money, though, in 2002, as we learned in Chapter 7, he accused his record company of conspiring to disempower black artists and advanced an argument that might have been ripped straight out of the Don King playbook. Klein hove into view as a kindly soul, willing to dispense favors in exchange for bragging rights; he sought an A-list client list and, in the mid-1980s, Jackson was in the A+ class. But the longer-term effects of the habits acquired in this period were baneful and there is a suspicion that Klein could have initiated Jackson into those habits.

In common with every other human on the planet, Jackson was, to some extent, shaped by other people. Parents, teachers, and peers exert influences on early life, and, as people mature, they come into contact with countless ciphers, most of whom are instantly forgotten. But, at intervals, everyone engages with figures who leave footprints; not like footprints in the sand that are quickly washed away by the ocean, but like those at Hollywood's Chinese Theatre. The impression they leave is permanent. Every reader can reflect on one or perhaps several influential people who have changed them, not necessarily in a way they desired, or even in a way that benefited them.

The people in question may have no intentions, virtuous or corrupt; that doesn't diminish their impact.

Jackson probably thought he learned nothing from King. The loudmouth must have annoyed Jackson from the outset: having struck out on his own after years under the unamicable tutelage of his dad, he found himself forced into the company of another bargainer, to use Steele's term again. Jackson could never bond with King, but a spoilt millionaire with money to burn the world at his feet must have found the experience educative. Uncomfortably educative. Granted, there was no damascene conversion, but the hard-nosed way Jackson conducted his later business deals, squeezing potential sponsors and record labels for every last cent, suggests the lessons he picked up from King were not merely cosmetic.

If we flash-forward twenty years from Jackson's first encounter with Klein—which, in a sense, is how this book approaches Jackson's life— it should be possible to gauge the weight and depth of Klein's legacy. But, is it as simple as that? Had Jackson refused what seems to have been Liz Taylor's advice and visited, for example, an acupuncturist or a homeopathist, would his life have rattled along differently? Would he have managed his pain with fewer or no opioids or anti-inflammatories? Would he have reduced or dispensed of his use of analgesics? Setting aside the conspiracy theories of Jackson's death, the coroner concluded there were at least six different drugs in his body at the time of his fatal cardiac arrest. According to the 2009 autopsy report, "the cause of death is acute propofol intoxication," propofol being the hypnotic drug generally used for anesthesia.

As with much of Jackson's life, not knowing is more interesting than knowing. Everybody thinks they know a lot about Jackson. Everybody thinks they know about love and death. None of us know very much about any of these things. They are often best approached as a mosaic—combined of small diverse elements that fit together in a more-or-less coherent but everchanging whole. The more elements we can gather, the more sense our composition makes. Klein, like Jackson, is dead (he died in 2015, age seventy), so we can only infer from the aftermath of their meetings what actually transpired. It's believable that Klein diagnosed Jackson's skin condition, without treating it, if indeed it required treatment. It's equally believable that he supplied him with prescription drugs so that Jackson could better manage the pain resulting from his burns. I write "better manage" because the hospital where he was taken would probably have prescribed medication. Jackson, being the perfectionist he was, might have thought he could improve on the prescription.

There's more to Klein's footprint, of course. His cupid-like role in introducing Jackson to the mother of two of his children outlasts his influence, however large or small, in Jackson's drugs habits. Again, neither I, nor anyone else, know the detail of this bafflingly unconventional arrangement. Debbie Rowe knows her side of the story and, if it's to be believed, she was a passive partner. In her words, "I offered him my womb." Most people can figure out for themselves what inspired her to do so. That she commanded the friendship and generosity of Jackson is apparent from the way he treated her. His kindness and warmth are more debatable. But undeniably, this was a match made not in heaven but in Klein's surgery and, for this reason alone, the cosmetic surgeon's influence on Jackson's life was far-reaching. Jackson's two children by Rowe will almost certainly make their presence felt in entertainment or some analogous industry in years to come.

We can scroll through Jackson's story, as we can anyone's life, and discover a cast of hundreds, maybe thousands, all denting him in some way that made him different. Most of the dents will be unnoticeably minor and he just moved on and forgot them. The same goes for every one of us. But every so often, someone emerges with the charisma and authority to influence not just us but everybody around us. I'm not thinking of religious or political leaders, who consciously aspire to influence as many people as possible. I mean someone who strikes whole populations as an authentic human, but with the unworldly grace of a paragon. Sometimes they are lovable, sometimes venerable, sometimes abominable. Occasionally, all three—at once. Jackson, like every black person alive in the United States in the 1980s, was affected in some measure by Bill Cosby.

The Atlantic's *Adam Serwer called Bill Cosby the Prophet of Black Conservatism, and Cosby's commitment to traditional values and opposition to drastic changes made him a perfect proponent of conservatism. His image of a free-willed individual making his or her own way through the world chimed with the kind of philosophy advanced by Oprah Winfrey.*

15

Prophets of Black Conservatism

Some people will never forgive Bill Cosby. Others will never stop praising him.

On May 9, 1985, John J. O'Connor, of the *New York Times*, wrote a story under the headline BILL COSBY'S TRIUMPH. It was the kind of accolade Cosby had become used to. "You look at 'The Cosby Show' and you feel, most of the time, just plain good. Television life on Thursdays at 8 P.M. on NBC suddenly displays signs of intelligence, insight and a clever sense of humor," thought O'Connor. "At a time when blacks were once again being considered ratings liabilities by benighted television executives, the middle-class Huxtables have become the most popular family in the United States."

The Huxtables were a fictional family at the center of a tv sitcom that dominated audience ratings in the 1980s. The show was credited to its creator, executive producer, and lead character Bill Cosby, then forty-eight, and approaching the peak of his immense popularity—for which he was richly rewarded. In 1987, Cosby was the world's top earning entertainer with $57 million, edged into second place by Jackson ($60 million) the following year. The two vied for top spot for the rest of the decade, according to *Forbes'* calculations.

Cosby spent his eighty-third birthday behind bars in a state prison in Collegeville, Pennsylvania, having been convicted of three counts of aggravated indecent assault and sentenced to three to ten years for drugging and sexually assaulting a woman in 2004. Falls from grace are always dramatic and the abrupt descents of O. J. Simpson, Tiger Woods, Lance Armstrong, and Jackson himself were among the most spectacular in recent history. But none more so than Cosby's. He wasn't so much a popular entertainer as a redeemer. Martin Luther King's widow, Coretta Scott King, called *The Cosby Show* "the most positive portrayal of black family life that has ever been broadcast." And the show could legitimately be said to have changed all subsequent shows featuring black characters. *Ebony* magazine in October 2007 rated the best "Black TV Shows of All-Time" and *The Cosby Show* came number one.

Cosby's cultural impact in the late twentieth century can scarcely be exaggerated and, while it wasn't limited to the television show, *The Cosby Show* was a genuine gamechanger. Before 1967, when Cosby was cast opposite white actor Robert Culp in the secret agent drama *I Spy*, blacks were not allowed on network television in straight roles, only comedies; and, even then, as clowns or dullards, who invited audiences to laugh at rather than with them. *Amos 'n' Andy*, a popular tv show derived from an equally popular radio series, was taken off-air in 1966 after protests from the National Association for the Advancement of Colored People (NAACP) and other civil rights groups. But, even then, sitcoms featuring blacks didn't depart significantly from the distorted image of the self-deluded fools depicted in the *Amos 'n' Andy* show (which had been around since 1928, when the radio program started).

When *I Spy* finished in 1968, Cosby, having appeared in all eighty-two episodes, maintained his public profile with roles in tv shows and movies, before moving to his magnum opus in 1984. Essentially, *The Cosby Show* format stuck with the conventions of nuclear family-based sitcoms with the father played by Cosby, an obstetrician; his wife, played by Phylicia Rashad, a lawyer; and their five children, including one son, all well-educated. They lived in a brownstone in the affluent residential area Brooklyn Heights, New York. They were a "normal," well-to-do family who just happened to be black. And that was the subversive element of Cosby's project. The Huxtables were described by *Ebony* as "a Black family that TV hadn't seen before," meaning they weren't super-dysfunctional or cartoon-like.

Popular images of blacks on television rarely strayed from a well-tested historical matrix. Even when a black artist featured prominently, as for example, in the *Nat King Cole Show*, a musical variety series in the 1950s. Cole was the star, but his guests were usually white and his band leader, Nelson Riddle, was white. Even in the more enlightened 1980s, a modish drama such as *Miami Vice* featured a black central character, Rico Tubbs (played by Philip Michael Thomas) but alongside a white detective, Sonny Crockett (Don Johnson). So, Cosby's project was a major departure for NBC, the network that featured the series, and must have been considered a gamble. In fact, it started with shorter odds: Cosby's original plan was to make his character a limousine driver, which would have been safer, but wouldn't have been praised to the heavens. Nor would it have been hit by brickbats, such as that from Sut Jhally and Justin Lewis, two communications professors who complained that, with his show, Cosby introduced a "new and insidious form of racism."

It was a stinging criticism of someone who had garnered the support from far and wide for his services. But no challenging cultural item ever gets a unanimous thumbs-up. Jhally and Lewis argued that whites saw *The*

Cosby Show as a slice of life, a comic but faithful depiction of America in the 1980s, meritocratic, and open enough for anyone, black or white, to advance as far as their talent and hard work would take them. But viewers also recognized that the well-heeled Huxtables were far from typical of African Americans. Conclusion: blacks who have not managed to clamber as far as Cosby's make-believe characters have probably come up short because they are too lazy or feckless. At a time when the desirability of affirmative action was being questioned, Cosby's upwardly mobile family offered its critics weapons. "The Huxtables proved that black people can succeed; yet in so doing they also prove the inferiority of black people in general (who have, in comparison with whites, failed)," wrote Jhally and Lewis in their 1992 book.

There's an ironic backstory to the research on which Jhally and Lewis based their critique. The *New York Times* in November 2008 reported the classic case of biting-the-hand-that-feeds-you. "In 1994 Sut Jhally, a professor of communications at the University of Massachusetts, Mr. Cosby's alma mater, persuaded Mr. Cosby to donate $16,000 for research on why the show was so popular among white as well as black audiences," wrote Tim Arango.

Cosby had no influence on how the research was conducted, nor any editorial rights. The researchers used focus groups and in-depth discussions with a culturally and economically diverse sample. The two main questions they used as a starting point for discussion were: how much the image of the Huxtable family reflected viewers' conceptions of black people, and how "real" were the characters and events in the show.

Leslie B. Inniss and Joe R. Feagin also studied viewers' responses to Cosby's show. "The overall impression is that the American dream is real for anyone who is willing to play by the rules," Innis and Feagin concluded, and, while they didn't explicate what those "rules" were, let's guess they involved not carping about racism or getting mixed up in radical politics. Inniss and Feagin were writing in 1995, before Black Lives Matter effected a modification of these rules, making certain types of protests against racism compliant.

It seemed some people recognized the world Cosby portrayed. Others recognized it, but felt alienated from it. Still others probably thought it was just make-believe. Whatever viewers thought, they watched it conscientiously: between 1985 and 1990, *The Cosby Show* was the most-watched show in America. That in itself was achievement enough to establish Cosby in the cultural pantheon of African Americans of the twentieth century. But he also left a durable legacy—and I mean something more long-lasting and far-reaching than an influence.

* * *

O'Connor, in another *New York Times* story, this time in 1986, reported that, after NBC's unexpected success, several other television networks rushed onto television schedules programs featuring black actors and nearly all of them flopped. Reason? "The bulk of them are trapped in demographic gyrations that manage to distort the everyday lives of both whites and blacks in this country."

In other words, Cosby's unexpected success might have induced other networks to try to replicate the combination of unfamiliar black folk in familiar sitcom settings, but the mere presence of black actors was not sufficient to engage audiences: Cosby's innovation was to show them in a way that wasn't redolent of history and tradition, but of the 1980s. Audience ratings suggested that tv audiences were either exhausted by or just plain bored with stereotype portrayals of black people and craved something more daring and congruent with the reality that saw all around them. "Despite the civil-rights struggles of the 1960's and the unprecedented emergence of black 'crossover' superstars, especially in sports and popular music, the battles to increase and improve images of black people on television can claim only sporadic victories," wrote O'Connor, blaming media organizations that persisted in "homogenizing its products so as not to upset significant portions of their audiences." Jackson was one such crossover superstar, of course.

Cosby's show had an alertness lacking in many other shows with black cast members. Each character was given his or her own signature, so there was no trace of caricature. They were funny, but in a way that never permitted audiences to mock or laugh contemptuously at black people. The Huxtables were a "normal" family, at least as television visualized familial normality in the 1980s. In this sense, the show became educational. Entertainment is never just amusement, distraction, or enjoyment: there's always intellectual or moral instruction involved. *The Cosby Show* never lectured audiences, but it did offer a form of enlightenment, however deeply buried under the laughs. The meaning of television goes far beyond that piece of technology that's kept us entranced since the 1950s: it's become a life force affecting every aspect of culture, including the way in which we see, understand, address, and engage with others.

For example, Cosby "inspired thousands of young adults to achieve their dream of a college education," pronounced Pamela Browner White, chair of the Marian Anderson Award committee, when awarding him Philadelphia's prestigious honor for "individuals who have helped change society through their art and the courage of their convictions," in 2009. Past recipients included Harry Belafonte, Maya Angelou, Elizabeth Taylor, and Gregory Peck. It was one of many acclamations collected by Cosby, who used his enormous popularity to admonish absentee black fathers and encourage strengthening families and communities. Shelby Steele, who coined the phrase "bargainers" (as mentioned in Chapter 14) argued, immoderately, in his 1990s book *The Content of Our Character* that racism had diminished. It might not have gone completely, but, as long as African Americans continued to labor in the role of perennial victims and squander their energies fighting it, they would not progress as individuals, Steele insisted. This is much the same argument Cosby advanced (and which would no doubt get the endorsement of Joe Jackson and Don King, among others).

It was an argument that earned Cosby a large, respectful, and perhaps even worshipful following; it also earned him the nickname "America's dad." In addition to his television show, he did philanthropic work, appeared in ads for Jell-O pudding and other products, wrote books, made an album, and addressed live audiences on issues of the day, always berating "ignorant, gun-toting, babymaking and jail-deserving young blacks," as Earl Ofari Hutchinson put it in the *Chicago Tribune*. "Why waste collective energies fighting a beast that had long since been tamed?" Cosby seemed to be asking rhetorically. To climb out of the depths of poverty and shrug off the effects of racism, backs needed to study more and make their stamps as individuals. In the eyes of many blacks and whites alike, this made Cosby a kind of moral exemplar, a funny man, who told clean jokes, respected family values, and was unafraid to tell black Americans what they were doing wrong. Not what society was doing wrong: what *they* were doing.

The Atlantic's Adam Serwer called him the Prophet of Black Conservatism and the description makes sense: Cosby's commitment to traditional values and his opposition to drastic changes made him a perfect proponent of conservatism, particularly as he had been an advocate of civil rights. His image of a free-willed individual making his or her own way through the world was doctrinally spot-on. But perhaps this is where his status as a popular entertainer actually worked against him.

It's a hypothetical question, but a relevant one: Would Cosby have been emboldened to make some of his more extreme proclamations had he been as popular as, say, Redd Foxx, LaWanda Page, both of *Sandford and Son*, or Jimmie Walker, of *Good Times*? These were all successful contemporaries, who became famous largely because of their presence in sitcoms. It's at least possible that, had Cosby plateaued early and enjoyed a loyal and appreciative following he might have been more restrained in his social commentary. But he had disciples. Or at least he behaved as if he had. Either that or he just couldn't "resist hectoring others on how to behave," as Serwer put it.

He scolded black Americans who disagreed with him or pursued lifestyles he found disagreeable. He even upbraided fellow entertainer Eddie Murphy for his flagrant use of expletives. There's little doubt that Cosby spoke sincerely and with good intentions, but once rolling, he had no brake. He somehow left his Cliff Huxtable character behind after 1992, when *The Cosby Show* ended. It was as if Cosby had unfinished business and was prepared to use his popularity to finish it, perhaps not realizing that he was effectively sawing off the branch of a tree that was supporting his ladder.

"In our cities and public schools, we have 50 percent drop out . . . we have men in prison. No longer is a person embarrassed because they're pregnant without a husband. No longer is a boy considered an embarrassment if he tries to run away from being the father of the unmarried child," declaimed Cosby in his 2004 address to the NAACP. Individuality and self-determination were his motifs. This was not the nice avuncular character with the almost childlike sense of humor and an uncanny ability to enchant almost anybody. It was a curmudgeonly old reactionary who had done well out of society and thought, if he could do it, anyone else with enough resolution, sense of purpose, and moral fortitude can. "To no surprise, the cheers for Cosby from the racism deniers were wilder and louder than ever," wrote Ofari Hutchinson.

Cosby had been "America's dad" in the 1980s and the Prophet of Black Conservatism in the 2000s. There was a third identity too.

*   *   *

For all his academic critics in the late 1980s Cosby's worst (known) offense was his too-good-to-be-trueness. He had been nominated fifteen times for Grammys, winning nine, and over the course of his life won seventy-four awards for his various contributions. His was a laurel-strewn career. By the time *The Cosby Show* finished its first runs in April 1992 (re-runs played long after), it still had its critics, but, as the *Los Angeles Times* put it on the eve of the final show, "there has never been a more universally beloved series." It seems safe to say that most people were thankful, if not for Cosby himself, for the body of work he left behind. And by "body of work," I include the countless tv programs featuring black people in roles that wouldn't have existed in the early 1980s and the corresponding disfigurement of racist stereotypes in the media, as well as the jobs in production that Cosby opened up for black people on his show.

Martin Luther King, Presidents Lyndon B. Johnson, and John F. Kennedy were all subjects of scurrilous talk, much of it empty, about their sexual conduct. So, allegations of sexual impropriety went with the territory, especially if the territory was the domain of clean-living family men with impeccable reputations. Cosby had previously dismissed or ignored them, though, in one case, in 1997 it was discovered that he'd paid $100,000 over twenty-two years to a woman with whom he had a sexual relationship in 1975. The woman claimed she'd had his daughter named Autumn Jackson. When Jackson was twenty-two, she threatened to sell her story to a tabloid unless Cosby paid her $40 million. She was convicted of extortion and sentenced to twenty-six years in prison. Jackson spent fourteen months in prison, with two associates, before the decision was reversed and all three were released.

Cosby had been married since 1964. Would it have damaged his reputation were it known that Cosby had a brief extramarital relationship with a woman in the 1970s? Probably not much at the time: *The Cosby Show* didn't air until 1984. Cosby disputed his paternity. But he may have thought it politic to support the child financially rather than risk any kind of publicity. A more charitable interpretation would be that he gladly funded the education of the daughter of a woman with whom had a relationship even if the daughter was not his own. Over the years, he was similarly benevolent to several hundred other young people. In 1997, the case had a different complexion: Cosby's straight-living family man image took a hit, but he was probably due some forgiveness.

Had that been the only blemish on Cosby's otherwise unspoiled reputation, he would have probably receded gradually in the popular imagination and been left to a peaceful retirement: a once popular and, in many ways, iconic entertainer who held strong views on how black people should progress and used his fame as leverage to promote them. Those views were out-of-sync with approaches of most blacks and he might have been quietly ignored—had it not been for two people. The first is Andrea Constand, whom Cosby met in 2002, at Temple University, where she managed the women's basketball team. He was sixty-four, she was twenty-eight.

Two years later, on Constand's account, Cosby drugged and sexually assaulted her at his home in Philadelphia. She reported this to the police. Cosby maintained the sex was consensual and the police decided not to press charges. Constand then sued for sexual battery and defamation, prompting Cosby to settle for $3.4 million after four days of deposition in 2006. Some other women went public with descriptions of their own experiences of drug-induced sex with Cosby, but, like Constand's claims, they were treated, at least initially, much like other accusations against highprofile celebrities. Cosby's reputation was left intact and he repeatedly denied any wrongdoing. And, were it not for an unexpected denunciation from a second key person, the mellow years of Cosby's life would have been very different.

Cosby's persistent reprimanding of black people for avoiding what he considered their responsibilities earned him detractors, especially among African Americans, who followed his career with more than the customary scrutiny. Hannibal Buress was one such detractor: a standup comic who was not enamored by what he called Cosby's "old black man public persona," he decided in October 2014 to use his spot in a Philadelphia club to call out Cosby. This, remember, was twenty-two years after the finale of *The Cosby Show* and ten years after Cosby's NAACP address. Buress was thirty-one. Philadelphia was Cosby's hometown.

Buress was upset by what he saw as Cosby's hypocrisy. He wasn't the first to infer condescension in much of what Cosby had been preaching. But he was the first to spell out the apparent paradox. "He [Cosby] gets on TV, 'Pull your pants up black people, I was on tv in the '80s! I can talk down to you because I had a successful sitcom!' Yeah, but you rape women, Bill Cosby, so turn the crazy down a couple notches." He urged his audience to Google "Bill Cosby rape" and cautioned, "It's not funny." A clip of Buress's set was posted on the website of *Philadelphia* magazine, on October 17, 2014 (it's since been taken down, but the copy is still at: https://bit.ly/3aHc9nt) and went viral.

American history is full of false rape accusations against African American men: from slave days onwards, there are cases of wrongful arrests and convictions, many motivated by racism. Emmett Till, as we learned in Chapter 8, was the fourteen-year old mutilated and murdered for flirting with a white woman in 1955. Over sixty years later, the woman retracted parts of her story. The Central Park Five case of 1998, covered in the same chapter, is another notable of instance of false rape allegations involving black men. "One of the greatest myths about rape is that it is primarily a crime committed by Black men against white women," concluded Tracey Owens Patton and Julie Snyder-Yuly in their scholarly analysis in 2007 for the *Journal of Black Studies*. A case involving an Iowa State University student's accusation against four black males was the focus of the study.

Perhaps this weighed on the mind on many, especially African Americans, when the occasional imputations against Cosby had surfaced over the years. Perhaps it was still on their minds when, in the aftermath of Buress's damnation, several women stepped forward, all claiming they had been assaulted by Cosby over the previous four decades. But when the several became dozens and many of their stories bore similarities, the unthinkable became thinkable. America's dad, a man who glorified family values and chastised absentee fathers, might actually have been too good to be true after all. Cosby's lawyer issued a statement confirming he wouldn't "dignify these allegations with any response." It did no good: the waves of accusations kept coming, the earliest incident related being from 1965. The total soon reached sixty. The similarities were compelling: Cosby had, according to many of the accusers, plied them with drink and drugs before assaulting them.

NBC and Netflix clearly thought there was too much collateral damage to continue with two Cosby projects they had planned and pulled them in November 2014. Viacom Inc.'s TV Land announced that it would stop broadcasting re-runs of Cosby's show. The *New York Times* described Cosby as "radioactive," meaning he was a man to be avoided.

In July 2015 court documents related to the 2005 civil suit against Cosby were unsealed at the behest of Associated Press. They revealed a crucial piece of information: Cosby admitted at the time to having obtained Quaaludes, the prescription sedative, with the intention of giving them to young women with whom he wanted sex. Bear in mind the allegations surfaced before the Harvey Weinstein scandal started to unwind in October 2017, giving rise to the MeToo movement. So, when Cosby was charged in December 2015, a gambler would probably have bet on him: despite being cut loose by some media and alienated from sections of the black populations, he had a following accrued over several decades. He also had what Roman Catholics call supererogation—a special reserve fund of credit for doing more than duty requires and which can be drawn on by sinners (Cosby was raised by Methodist and Baptist parents).

Most of the claims fell outside the statute of limitations, so Cosby faced just three counts of aggravated sexual assault on Constand arising from one incident in 2004. There was no rape kit, nor DNA evidence, nor toxicology tests and no witnesses. The result of the trial was a deadlock, or a hung jury, in which jurors could not agree on a verdict after six days of deliberation. Cosby was then seventy-nine and escaped a possible lengthy prison sentence. Whether this was in the minds of jurors, we don't know; but incarcerating a near-octogenarian with more than his fair share of goodwill would have been a big decision to make in the circumstances.

MeToo was like an eclipse: a celestial body, it passed across another celestial body, blotting out its light so that observers were plunged into a temporary darkness before it moved away. But when it continued its path, everything was illuminated differently. People saw the world in a different light. Cosby's retrial was conducted after the Weinstein revelations. So, the circumstances were radically different from those that surrounded the first trial. Everything changed once MeToo was in the popular consciousness. Its arrival was a tumultuous moment in culture and Cosby's two trials reflected its impact. His retrial began in April 2018 and Cosby had a different legal team that included Thomas Mesereau, who had defended Jackson in 2005, as I recorded in Chapter 5. This time, the defense foundered. Cosby was found guilty and became the first celebrity in the MeToo era to be imprisoned for his crimes: his sentence was three to ten years. "The higher the ascent the sharper the fall. I recognize that impact upon Mr. Cosby, and I am sorry for that," Judge Steven O'Neill told Cosby almost apologetically, when handing down his sentence.

Gloria Allred, attorney for several of Cosby's accusers—and longtime critic of Jackson—concluded: "This has been a long journey to justice for all of the accusers . . . we're glad that judgment day has finally come." Cosby publicist Andrew Wyatt waxed ecclesiastic when he spoke for Cosby, "They persecuted Jesus and look what happened. I'm not saying Mr. Cosby is Jesus, but we know what this country has done to black men for centuries."

It sounded like a requiem, but Cosby was far from dead. In June 2021, the Pennsylvania Supreme Court overturned his conviction after discovering a violation of a prior agreement Cosby had made with a previous prosecutor. At eighty-three, he was released from prison after serving two years. The ruling meant Cosby could not be retried for Constand's assault. He continued to deny any wrongdoing.

* * *

For many, the true menace of Cosby was never Cosby, the sex offender: like other abominable men, who have serially abused women, he was, once exposed, at least visible. In view, threats are a lot less potent than they are when concealed. And Cosby wasn't just concealed: he operated behind the mask of an easy-going, companiable kind of guy, humorous and neighborly, always kind and hospitable, and disposed to help like a good neighbor. You'd gladly let him take the kids to the movies and buy them popcorn. You might even go with them. In times of strife, you might turn to him. The real nightmare was Bill Cosby, the nice guy. Unforgivable. But should he be?

In the 1980s, his service to African Americans was substantial. As such, he was a redoubtable figure, comparable with other luminaries, such as Oprah Winfrey. Novelist Toni Morrison, whose 1987 book *Beloved* told the story of a runaway female slave, and who won the Nobel Prize for Literature in 1993, was another leading light who enriched cultural life for African Americans. Sports icon Michael Jordan was in their company. As was Whitney Houston. Robert L. Johnson, who founded Black Entertainment Television (BET) featured, as did fellow entrepreneurs Reginald Lewis, Bertram Lee, and Peter Bynoe. David Dinkins, in 1990, was elected the first black mayor of New York. Michael Jackson was also in this pantheon, though with the same kind of provisos as Cosby.

Cosby was part of a generation of African American dignitaries and, while attitudes toward him changed in the wake of revelations that appeared to strip away his more humanitarian layers, his overall contribution remains: no one can unchange change and Cosby helped reorder popular culture. For that reason, his legacy has to be acknowledged. It is a durable legacy too; but one full of paradoxes, uncertainties, and double-edges. Cosby's heritage remains. His reputation was crushed and his image was remade. His brand, if we can call it that, was shattered and his persona as an easy-to-love friend was replaced by that of a deceitful predator. But Cosby's presence left its mark permanently. This may seem implausible in view of Cosby's now-discovered transgressions, but let me add historical context, then the reader can decide.

In 1986, Alphine W. Jefferson, a professor of Black Studies and History, wrote an essay, "Black America in the 1980s: Rhetoric vs. Reality" in which he assessed the progress of blacks since the crucial civil rights legislation. Unemployment for black American was "frozen at 20 percent." In Jefferson's view, "The failure to find employment is not in the individual workers themselves, but in a racially discriminatory and class-based system." Two decades after the official end of segregation, housing and schooling remained rigidly divided, according to Jefferson. "Segregation cuts off untold numbers of blacks from recreation facilities, swimming pools, libraries and the chance for part-time jobs."

In measured terms, Jefferson addressed key areas of social life before arriving at his conclusion, "In 1986, Black America as an aggregate is not better off than it was in 1963. [Martin Luther] King's dream has not become a reality . . . Blacks are told to 'pull themselves up by their bootstraps,' and when they do, they are denied access to equal education, housing and public services." In the mid-1980s, there was what Jefferson described as a dichotomy between the rhetoric of black progress and the reality, which, for most meant "lost hope."

Clarence Page, of the *Chicago Tribune,* offered his appraisal a little later in 1989. While not as disheartening as Jefferson's evaluation, it was "a mixed bag," with reports of gains made by an emergent black middle class and losses. "More prosperity at the top, more misery at the bottom" is how Page summed up, picturing America's black population as an hourglass. A roundbottomed chemistry flask might be a more accurate image—those vessels with a long, narrow neck and a balloon-shaped container for holding liquids; the neck represents the small number of affluent and middle-income blacks, while the bulb is the poor. The 1980s, he judged, was "A great decade for individuals, perhaps, but not so great for groups."

Both accounts agree that black Americans, endured a tough period in the late 1970s, hit disproportionately hard by back-to-back economic recessions. The initial promise implicit in civil rights had given way to a more hard-nosed acceptance that the racism practiced for centuries before would not just vanish. The economic recovery of the 1980s lifted the boats of the black upper class, as Page puts it. But 31 percent of black Americans consistently lived in poverty and seemed stuck there.

Page's analysis was slightly more uplifting than Jefferson's, but had a supplement: even those blacks that had bootstrapped their ways to affluence were bracketed into a "separate society." Affluent blacks might have had more in common economically with affluent whites, but socially they still belonged to the black underclass. While no one realized it at the time, America, at the dawn of civil rights, was in "normalcy," by which I mean the state of being usual. There may not have been another incident quite as harrowing as the Till murder, but racist thoughts and practices were part of a condition that had been largely undisturbed for over 400 years. During that time America had risen to the world's premier superpower, the epicenter of consumption and prosperity and, of course, the exemplar of meritocracy, by which I mean a society in which rewards are distributed according to merit alone.

The Cosby Show started on September 20, 1984, four months before Ronald Reagan started his second term of office as president. He left in 1989, his near-decade becoming known as the era of Reaganomics, in which taxes were kept low, public spending limited, and unrestricted or deregulated free market activity fulsomely encouraged. It was a conservative set of policies consistent with supply-side economic theory. The premise was that, if the affluent elite at the top of the economic pyramid had less tax to pay, they'd have more disposable income, which they'd invest in a way that created more jobs. Hence the money would "trickle down" the pyramid.

Twenty years after "discrimination based on race, color, religion, sex or national origin" had been outlawed, inequalities of the past remained and were beginning to look unmovable. Yet the policies associated with Reagan offered a prescription for black America, as indeed they did for the whole nation. Essentially, they complemented Cosby's advocacy of initiative and self-help. Reagan's dislike of affirmative action also found favor with Cosby, who had no truck with race-specific remedies to what were, to him, individuals' problems.

Cosby never claimed his character Cliff Huxtable or the other family members were representative of anyone or any group; though, had he done so, he could have marshaled evidence to support a decent argument. The Huxtables could have represented the small but growing elite, what the sociologist E. Franklin Frazier (1894–1962) called the *black bourgeoisie*. In the mid-1980s, Cosby, in many ways, epitomized the smart, successful, refined sophisticates. So did Jackson, Oprah, and the other upwardly mobile African Americans, whose good fortune was based not on social policies but on their own initiative.

Cosby, Jackson, Oprah, Jordan, and the several other African American VIPs who grew to prominence in the 1980s were exploited, not in the sense of being victimized or treated unfairly, but utilized, or used to good advantage. The "good advantage" in this instance was to present an image of America as a country where cultural diversity flourished and the only obstacles to progress were ones of individuals' own making.

* * *

History will no doubt be kind to Oprah Winfrey, an entertainer, inspirational businesswoman, and guiding light for all women and many black Americans. From 1986, when *The Oprah Winfrey Show* went national, Oprah was a kind of pole star, attracting and leading all manner of people to better lives. It became internationally popular and established Oprah as one of the most well-known and respected women in the world. By the time of the last show in 2011, Oprah's personal wealth was estimated at $2.7 billion. She was, by then, in the process of starting her own venture, the Oprah Winfrey Network (OWN). Her cultural authority was renowned. A couple of well-chosen sentences could send shudders along Wall Street. A reminder such as "We need Barack Obama" (in her speech at Des Moines, Iowa, on December 8, 2007) could change political landscapes. As influential people go, she was without equal.

In 1989, when Oprah was approaching the peak of her global popularity, Barbara Grizzuti Harrison, writing for the *New York Times Magazine*, wrote, "Winfrey embodies the entrepreneurial spirit; she is an Horatio Alger for our times," a reference to the nineteenth-century novelist, whose stories were themed with the message that anyone, no matter how poor, can succeed with honest hard work. Like Cosby and the other black dignitaries that emerged in the period, Winfrey attributed her success largely to her own labors; as she put it, "I've been blessed—but I create the blessings."

"She is as likely to rest her beliefs on Ayn Rand as on Baba Ram Dass," suggested Grizzuti Harrison (Rand was the author of *Atlas Shrugged*, which argues for "rational self-interest," endorses the value of earning as much money as possible and is thought to legitimize the worst effects of capitalism; Ram Dass was a New Age spiritual leader and founder of the Seva Foundation charity). Oprah had, like Cosby, bootstrapped her way through America's free market, defying all her putative impediments. I'll return to Oprah in the next chapter.

Whether from business, the arts, or showbusiness, the demonstrably successful African Americans of the 1980s shared a commitment to the value of individual advancement, though not without regard for the wellbeing of others. This is not a criticism: simply an acknowledgment that, for the Cosby, Oprah, and co, the blame for the continued predicament of blacks lay not in corporate America and the capitalist system that it sustained, nor with successive government policies that failed to open up opportunities, nor even with the discriminatory practices of employers or the police. The responsibility lay with people; to be effective, blacks had to seize the initiative and break the cycle of self-abasement and negativity that had maintained an almost permanent underclass. Most black celebrities of the time were silent on issues like the crack epidemic, apartheid in South Africa, the racial tensions exposed by the O. J. Simpson trial, and the police brutality that was to set off the Rodney King riots in 1992.

Black celebrities of the 1980s were perfect emblems of the Reagan era: they were enchanting, irresistible, and mighty reminders not of the success of black Americans but of their failure. As Grizzuti captured the effect of witnessing the rise of breathtaking success, "A black person has to ask herself, 'If Oprah Winfrey can make it, what does it say about me?' They no longer have any excuse. If you don't believe that I should make it, you absolutely don't believe you should, either.'" *What does that say about me?* The message couldn't be clearer, or more in line with the injunctions of Republican politicians; people are as responsible for their failures as they are for their successes. Resplendent black celebrities were human reminders. The argument echoed Jhally and Lewis's exposition of *The Cosby Show*'s effect.

Was there a design behind this? No. While it makes a sinister image, there was no cabal of politicians and heads of industry conspiring to keep the black population docile after years of protest, riot, and unrest and devising a plan to pacify them. "Let's get a few black entertainers, turn them into household names, make them mega-famous and mega-rich and provide them with rags-to-riches backstories. Everyone will lap it up and we can use them as examples of how America genuinely is the land of opportunity—for everyone, regardless of ethnic origin." Of course, there was no conspiracy and no gullible public ready to lap up the story. But the scenario is only lightly fictionalized: the effect of prominent African Americans who were idolized by audiences and critics was to drain off some of the anger, opposition, and defiance that had characterized the previous two decades. So, how did it happen?

When Grizzuti Harrison wrote of Oprah, "Her audiences are co-creators of the self and the persona she crafts," she seemed to be posing a puzzle disguised as a statement. How can audiences originate, develop, and complete a persona, by which I presume she means an image, or a public face? Surely Oprah and possibly some of her colleagues did that. Or media organizations with the know-how, resources, and influence could project a certain kind of vision or portrayal of someone even if it bore little resemblance to the actual person. Some might see it that way, but I suspect Grizzuti Harrison has a more complex relationship in mind: audiences collaborate in the fabrication of personas. Stars and other famous figures offer raw material and invite audiences to define their meaning and give them relevance. Oprah's persona became a touchstone of the times, not because of anything she did or said or the way she looked, but because audiences made her tangibly personal, a reflection of their own thoughts or even struggles. Her public image might have been a product of others' simplified compositions, but that didn't make them any less powerful. Similarly, audiences were, to use Grizzuti's term once more, *co-creators* of the famous African Americans who appeared in the 1980s and perhaps helped deflect what might otherwise have been apocalyptic conflict. I'll return to this when I probe how Jackson was co-created.

The rise of black stars in the 1980s may not have been the result of a diabolical connivance, but it wasn't the product of fate's machinery either. There was a willingness to leave racism behind, but no motive power to advance social change. People like Cosby, Oprah, and Jackson were alternatives to tangible change: they provided the illusion of progress, while leaving social arrangements fundamentally in place. Fundamentally: all effected changes in their spheres of influence and, in Cosby's case in particular, beyond. His oeuvre, like Jackson's, was muddied after years of brilliance. Even those for whom Cosby's humor, personality, or presence fails to impress would acknowledge he contributed toward changing the character of popular entertainment and, in the process, affected perceptions. As did all of the figures mentioned in this chapter.

*   *   *

In the final accounts, vices outweighed the virtues of Cosby and Jackson. This doesn't lessen their impact; though, if the view I've described here is accepted, that impact is open to debate. Some might say they retarded radical change by providing concessions to appease a section of the population whose main concerns and demands were never properly addressed. Others might reply they prised open gaps in the entertainment industry and the gaps continue to proliferate to the present day. The damage they did to historical stereotypes was irreparable.

In trying to be a socially responsible, mold-breaking, progressive entertainer, Cosby managed to become the villain who perpetrated a new kind of racism, one disguised as "enlightenment." Actually, if he'd have stuck with the limousine driver, he wouldn't have been damned. But he wouldn't have left much of a legacy either. And he might not even have ended up in prison. But Cosby clearly saw himself as much more than a popular entertainer. Earlier I called him a redeemer. The trouble is: he did things in reverse, making amends for his sins before they became publicly known. Obviously, the problem with that order is that no one, or at least not many people, remembers the redemption-in-advance. Jackson's life followed a similar redemption-and-fall arc, in his case the fall arriving postmortem after a few stumbles.

It seems a bold claim, but any examination of racism in the popular arts will reveal the effects of Cosby's show. It did change history in much the same way, perhaps ironically, that MeToo changed it. Nothing was quite the same after each made their ways into the popular imagination.

The grim revelations about Cosby's double-life were not only shocking but iconoclastic: they invalidated cherished beliefs. No doubt Cosby's many fans would look back to the 1980s and complain their childhoods were tainted retrospectively by the fall of someone they looked up to. His victims' responses would be more rancorous. But there is no denying Cosby's cultural impact and, for this reason alone, the way we process or interpret him, especially in the 1980s, is worth trying to understand.

Anyone born after, say, 1985 will be familiar with Cosby through re-runs of his programs, but much more aware of his analysis and judgment of America's black population. Whether or not they agreed with his conservatism they would probably be rendered irrelevant once he was convicted and imprisoned. Those born earlier would probably have grown up with Cosby, whether as a serial endorser of puddings, candy, soft drinks, among other consumables, or a character in one of his shows; he voiced-over in an animated series *Fat Albert and the Cosby Kids* which ran until 1985; or as the author of children's books. It seems fair to suppose Cosby in some form has been part of most Americans' formative years. Like Jackson, Cosby forced audiences to ask themselves a question: Can we love their work and hate the men themselves? I have an answer and I will furnish it over the next several chapters.

Eddie Van Halen could hardly believe it when he got a call from someone describing himself as Quincy Jones, asking him to play on a Michael Jackson recording. But it started a fruitful creative collaboration and may even have been a masterstroke.

16

Nothing Was the Same After

"By the mid-eighties, Jackson had become the biggest black star ever, in part by shedding conventional images of blackness," wrote Bill Wyman of the *New Yorker* in 2012. Others believed he was not just the biggest black star ever. "Michael Jackson was the most luminous, powerful, influential star in the music business, and no one else was even close," according to the *Guardian*'s Joe Queenan. The "Michael Jackson" era started in 1983 and lasted roughly till the end of the decade, in Queenan's view. It would be naïve to assume the two writers' observations are unrelated: Jackson became the primo star and instituted his own era because he discarded something approximating "conventional images of blackness."

* * *

At the start of the Jackson era, music could still be understood as a distinct self-contained entity: artists recorded an album, singles were spun off it and they were all for sale, whether on audio tape, vinyl, or cds which became popular after 1985 (the year of release of Dire Strait's *Brothers in Arms*, which is regarded as the kind of watershed album). But, the arrival of MTV ended this: audios became visual and videos became integral to the music industry. Listening no longer happened in isolation; a video could make a tune or even an album successful. And MTV was responsible. It was also responsible in no small part for the transformation of Jackson from the enchanting, handsome, and unthreatening frontboy for an above average band to what he became.

Like Jackson, MTV had its own era. It may now seem an anachronism but it was once the prime mover of a revolution in popular music; the changes it started were far-reaching and are still felt today. Music videos are very much a part of today's landscape and, every so often, one goes viral. Childish Gambino's "This is America" racked up 180 million views on

YouTube in the first month after being uploaded in May 2020. And that's a measure of success nowadays: views. The method by which audiences view have changed since the early days of MTV, shifting from traditional media, like television, to all manner of digital online platforms; the devices on which we watch have also changed. But the action of watching a screen while listening to music is essentially the same. And MTV started this.

How did it start? Let's imagine. In 1977, two television executives go to see the John Badham movie *Saturday Night Fever*, the film that effectively launched disco. The plot, such as it was, visited a few social issues, such as abortion, teenage pregnancy, gang rape, and death by misadventure, but the film was essentially 118 minutes of flashing lights and mostly Bee Gees music. One exec turns to the other and says, "Nearly two hours of throbbing music and John Travolta's moves . . . and I still wanted more. I reckon we could start a tv channel and just run stuff like this." The other exec scoffs, "A movie is one thing. A tv channel is another. How could you just play music all day and night without stretching viewers' patience?" The first exec is not easily put off. "Many viewers would get impatient and probably bored too. For sure. But I'd be interested in targeting only one slice of the demographic: young people. Maybe just young white people."

Four years later, MTV launched as a 24-hour cable tv station, playing nothing but music videos (the actual launch date was August 1, 1981). Following the format of a top forty radio show, it rotated the best-selling records of the day, splicing in a few intros and comments from veejays. The content was repetitious, necessarily so: the channel was at the mercy of record labels, which were understandably wary of the new and unprecedented innovation. They became convinced only when sales of the records featured on MTV started to rise. If the channel featured a record, it sold. Heavy rotation of tracks yielded higher sales. Soon the record companies were falling over themselves to get exposure on MTV. The *Saturday Night Fever* scenario may not be too far wide of the mark. MTV was started by John Lack, who worked for Warner Cable, Robert Pittman, a radio programmer for NBC, and Les Garland, all of whom had taken note of a small tv station in New Zealand, which just aired pop videos and, by implication, promoted record sales. The distinction between promotional material and entertainment is, today, indistinct; in the 1980s it was clearer, but getting smudged. Was MTV entertaining audiences or promoting sales? The answer is, of course, both.

Reliant as it was on record companies, MTV's real strength lay in its viewership. The demographic was perfect for advertisers: eighteen to twenty-five, white, with disposable income and no dependents. The cable outlet was effectively providing free, targeted advertising for record companies. The channel's income came from advertising revenue, which went up in proportion to viewing figures and its share of the cable subscriptions. So, all parties benefited. Not every commercial record was accompanied by a video, but the record industry recognized MTV's potential and it soon became inconceivable to release a record without a video. All this seems obvious—now. In the late 1970s, it must have seemed preposterous. It probably seemed preposterous after its first year of operation too. Fewer than 1 million subscribers augured badly. But key artists appeared and, as they rose, so did the station. Madonna, Peter Gabriel, ZZ Top, Duran Duran, and the Police all had strong presences in MTV's formative period. These artists owed their success to MTV as much as MTV owed its success to them. Van Halen also featured regularly on MTV's playlist in the early days. But not Michael Jackson.

* * *

In 1982, Eddie Van Halen got a phonecall from Quincy Jones. Now, what would a well-respected producer known for his work with jazz artists and, more recently, Michael Jackson, want with the lead guitarist of a hard rock band? In his thirty years in the music business, Jones had never gone anywhere near rock, let alone metal. It must have been a hoax, thought Van Halen, who swore at his caller and cut him short. Jones persisted. When he convinced Van Halen it was really him, he explained he was working with Jackson on song that needed a guitar solo. Not just any guitar solo, either: one of those blisteringly fast sequence of notes for which Van Halen was known—his technique was known as shredding. The next day Van Halen drove to Westlake Recording Studios, in West Hollywood, to discover there was a recording in progress. It was an a capella version of what became "Beat It." Van Halen listened to what was recognizably rock music, quite different from anything else in Jackson's oeuvre at that stage. He agreed to do the solo.

On the eventual recording, Van Halen's contribution occupied thirty-two seconds of a four-minute track: it was classic Van Halen shredding. The distinct riff that repeats throughout the tune was played by another guitarist, Steve Lukather, of the band Toto, who was perfectly capable of playing solos. So why was Jones so insistent that Van Halen played? Jones was producing an album for Jackson and he was aware of MTV's growing influence. He was probably also aware that Van Halen got regular plays on the new channel. Jackson was completely absent. As were all black artists.

Rick James, who died in 2004, was enraged by MTV after it refused to play his track "Superfreak," which was a big seller in 1981 (and later sampled on MC Hammer's 1990 "U Can't Touch This"). James, an African American, used the phrase "blatant racism" to describe MTV's policy, though, in truth, it wasn't that blatant. The channel featured a few black artists, including Tina Turner, though many of the artists featured were from England, where videos were made for practically every single. Black English artists such as Joan Armatrading and Eddy Grant appeared on MTV, though it was a white English artist who embarrassed MTV.

David Bowie gave an interview on MTV in 1983 in which he raised an uncomfortable question. "I'm just floored by the fact that there are so few artists featured on it [MTV]. Why is that?" He pointed out that black artists were making good videos that didn't appear on the channel. "A frightening predicament" is how Bowie described MTV's exclusion of black artists. The interview—on MTV, remember—was inconclusive. But Bowie, whose work was included on MTV, had shared his observation and it was much the same as James'.

Jackson's popularity at this point had risen after he appeared on an NBC special to commemorate the twenty-fifth anniversary of Motown. *Motown 25: Yesterday, Today, Forever* featured the label's artists, past and present, including Jackson who displayed his version of what became known as the Moonwalk. Jeffrey Daniel, of the band Shalamar, had been performing a similar move for years before and called his routine "backsliding."

"The point I always made was that MTV was originally designed to be a rock music channel," said Buzz Brindle, the channel's director of music programming in the early 1980s. "It was difficult for MTV to find African-American artists whose music fit [*sic*] the channel's format that leaned toward rock at the outset." Maybe MTV had an agenda for its music. But it also had an agenda for its customers and by "customers," I don't mean viewers who watched their tvs for pleasure, but the advertisers who paid MTV to show advertisements and so provided it with its raison d'être.

"In the 1980s and 1990s, advertisers could reach desired consumers instead of addressing a mass market," Jennifer Fuller pointed out in her 2010 article "Branding Blackness on US Cable Television." Media markets segmented, enabling a specialist TV channel like MTV to offer its advertisers a direct route to the youth market at a time in history when young people were becoming the most sought-after consumers (sought-after, that is, by ad agencies and their clients). Fuller again: "The most coveted demographic was young urban whites."

Epic released "Billie Jean" as a single on January 2, 1983; the concurrent video featuring Jackson with Jheri curls and co-respondent shoes helped propel it to the top of the charts. MTV did not play it. In March, when Les Garland eventually decided to allow "Billie Jean" onto the MTV playlist, he didn't explain his unexpected change of heart, though it was thought to have been influenced by the prospect of CBS, the owner of Jackson's label, murmuring that it could withdraw its full roster of music. "CBS Records Group President Walter Yetnikoff had to threaten to remove all other CBS videos from MTV before the network agreed to air the video for 'Billie Jean'," Nadra Kareen Nittle summarized the circulating story in her 2020 story "How MTV Handled Accusations of Racism and Became More Inclusive."

Garland dismissed this as myth: "There was never any hesitation," he was quoted by *Jet* magazine in an article titled "Why It Took MTV So Long To Play Black Music Videos" (October 9, 2006). Garland claimed, "I called Bob (Pittman, MTV co-founder) to tell him, 'I just saw the greatest video I've ever seen in my life. It is off the dial it's so good'." Yetnikoff has been silent on the issue. But, if he—or perhaps his vice-president David Benjamin—did make the threat to Garland, real or imagined, it was one of the most influential statements of intent in cultural history. As *Rolling Stone*'s Christopher Connelly put it, in his "The Year in Music: 1983," "The door that blocked black artists from getting exposure on rock & roll TV and radio stations had been kicked down by the industry's most talented foot. Nothing was the same after that."

James's broadside and the disapproving comments of Bowie were probably awkward for MTV, but containable. Yet they ensured that there was at least awareness that MTV did not feature black artists, certainly not in proportion to their presence in popular music. MTV would certainly have become sensitive to criticism, especially at a time when the African American population was evolving into an exploitable market for consumer goods. To snub a conspicuous and, by common consent, talented performer such as Jackson could have been fatal. "Fortunately, Michael Jackson helped us to redefine the musical parameters of MTV," reflected Brindle. Whether his use of "fortunately" suggests MTV made an auspicious decision, or was just lucky, we can't know.

"Billie Jean" was duly added to the MTV playlist. Connelly believed this was a turning point. "It exposed black music to a white rock & roll audience for the first time in the post-disco era . . . it signified the utter primacy of MTV." The music tv station became the preeminent channel for popular music, certainly in America and, later, in the world. Perhaps propelled by a decision it was probably forced to take. Almost immediately, Jackson's second solo album for CBS became the biggest-selling LP in the record label's history (it started in 1962).

"Beat It," released on Valentine's Day, quickly followed "Billie Jean." The video for this had a *West Side Story*-style narrative, with Jackson breaking up a gang fight. Van Halen's record company refused to let him appear, though the guitarist guested on stage during the Victory tour. It might not have been a cause-and-effect relationship, but a number of black artists had major successes soon after the MTV door had been opened. Eddy Grant scored with his "Electric Avenue." Donna Summer's ode to either a sex worker or a bathroom attendant, "She Works Hard for the Money," was also a major triumph.

Van Halen's presence on "Beat It" was doubtless a factor in its appearance on the playlists of album-oriented rock radio stations, or AOR, as they were known. They catered largely to young white listeners and played hardly any music by black artists. So, when, in early 1984, the *New York Times*' Jon

Pareles wrote, "Mr. Jackson had broken through the color line," he wasn't referring to the segregation that forcibly prevented blacks and whites mixing in the early twentieth century but to the cultural partition that divided black-and-white genres in music. Radio stations specializing in r'n'b, soul, or the then incipient hip-hop were known as urban, or dance stations. But Pareles wasn't exaggerating: Jackson's feat in breaking through would, as he put it, have "a profound effect on mass entertainment."

*   *   *

MTV may have had to "redefine its parameters" to accommodate Jackson, but it was to have them stretched further and in different directions. No one at the tv station, or beyond, had any idea just how powerful music videos were about to become. Not only did they change the way people consumed music; they left their impression on movies, television, fashion, advertising, and televised news. The visual potential of pop music had been realized since the dawn of rock 'n' roll. *Rock Around the Clock* was a full-length feature released in 1956; while it had a plot, it was really a sequence of what were later to become videos (the actual track "Rock Around the Clock" had been used to good effect in a 1955 film *The Blackboard Jungle*, about what was then called juvenile delinquency). Films like *Jailhouse Rock* (1957) and *Hard Day's Night* (1964) had narrative scaffolds to support music, while concert movies like *Monterey Pop* (1968) and *Wattstax* (1973) were more documentary accounts.

Television orthodoxy dictated that channels should offer a kind of menu of programs rather than just one type of fare. That was challenged when cable stations ESPN and CNN focused solely on sports and news respectively. The former launched in 1979, the latter in 1980. So, MTV was part of the same trend. It's no exaggeration to suggest the music industry transformed in response to the tv station's success: by about 1984, it wasn't possible for a record to succeed independently of a video. The short film may have started as a vehicle to promote music sales, but quickly became an artform in its own right. As the format gained respectability, so directors specializing in video, such as David Fincher, Antoine Fuqua, and Zack Snyder, transferred to movies. Established film directors like John Sayles, Brian De Palma, and Martin Scorsese moved in the other direction.

John Landis had acquired his reputation as a filmmaker with *The Blues Brothers* (1980) and *An American Werewolf in London*, the latter catching the eye of Jackson when it was released in 1981. Landis was asleep in London the first time Jackson called him in 1983. The time difference (London is eight hours in front of LA) didn't seem to bother Jackson, who asked Landis if he'd direct a music video in which he—Jackson—would "turn into a monster." Jackson had been impressed by the transformation of humans into four-legged beasts—in Landis's werewolf film, that is. Videos were still a novelty and film directors were probably hesitant about risking their reputation on three or four-minute clips. The story goes that Landis persuaded Jackson to depart from the typical video format, in which the visuals followed the music, and opt for a two-reeler, this being a reference to a short film, about twenty minutes long. The music would function effectively as the film score. But there was a problem.

The track for which Jackson wanted the video lasted only five minutes fifty-seven seconds. So, Landis proposed a new narrative structure, in which the song occupied only a segment; the film could be marketed as a legitimate motion picture that could play in cinemas. His budget reflected his ambition: in addition to filming and special effects costs, there were ten days of dance rehearsals, taking the estimate north of half-a-million. The video for "Beat It" had cost $150,000 and Jackson had paid for it. The values might not seem much today, but consider: the highest grossing film up till then was 1982's E. T.: The Extra-Terrestrial and this cost about $10.5 million to make; much more than Landis's project, but this was full-length Steven Spielberg blockbuster, not an experiment.

MTV never paid for the production of videos. But Showtime, then a new subscription cable channel, agreed to pay half the budget, and MTV changed its mind and stumped up an estimated $250,000–300,000 (in 1985, Viacom International initiated a complex series of deals that gave it ownership of both MTV and Showtime). Epic contributed only $100,000. Landis's producer George Folsey is credited with the idea of making a parallel video, a 45-minute "making-of" documentary that tracked the entire production of the first; this could be marketed independently of the main video. Walter Yetnikoff was not enthusiastic about either project: the album from which the track was taken had been at the top of the album best-seller charts for almost a year, sold 16 million copies globally, and was unlikely to sell more on the back of a new video, no matter how original. And this was certainly original. Daringly original.

Readers will already know the video was Thriller. Landis shot it in October 1983 mostly at the Palace Theater, Los Angeles. There was an invitation-only screening on November 14 and a week later an official premiere. This was unheard-of: music videos were just cycled into schedules, not afforded the importance of a major film or theatrical work and granted the status of a first performance—and in a cinema where it was shown with Disney's Fantasia. The reason for this is that Landis wanted his film to be eligible for Oscars and, for this, it needed to have at least one week's theatrical release. The real premiere—the one that revealed Landis's masterpiece to the world—came on December 2. At the witching hour. And, of course, on MTV.

Remember: MTV, on its own account, was a rock station, modeled, presumably, on AOR. In a few months it had become a different kind of entity and its growth reflected this. By 1992—only nine years after Thriller's premiere—MTV was reaching 112 million homes worldwide and taking more than $400 million in revenue; its dominance was fleeting, however: by 2000, music videos were deader than disco. But in the early 1980s, there was no mistaking its impact: twelve months after its release, the *Thriller* album had sold 20 million, a surge in sales coming toward the end of 1983, when the Landis video received rotation.

At the time, Jon Pareles, of the *New York Times*, wrote: "He [MJ] is one of the few musicians at ease in rock video clips, song-length films that simultaneously promote and reshape a hit single and that have had a profound effect on mass entertainment." He might have added that Jackson's videos gave his music an imperishable quality, as evidenced, for example, in trailer for Netflix's second season of *Stranger Things*, in which a mix of the track "Thriller" was used to effect. It's here: https://bit.ly/36KzIKT.

*   *   *

The *Michael Jackson's Thriller* (to use its full name) video was breathtaking: what many assumed was going to be no more than Jackson's vanity project were stunned by a film-within-a-film-within-a-dream plot, adventurous cinematography, choreographed zombies, and metamorphoses that not only looked but sounded terrifying. A voiceover by horror film staple Vincent Price was an inspired detail. "Grisly ghouls from every tomb are closing in to seal your doom," intoned Price, as if divining Jackson's fate. "No mere mortal can resist the evil of the Thriller."

The changes from human to werewolf, then to one of the undead were visually spectacular and kept audiences rapt. But those metamorphoses also provided what the *Los Angeles Times* called "trace evidence of the obsessions that would sink the greatest pop star of his generation into Hollywood Babylon" (February 11, 2008). In particular, the "racial ambivalence he'd encode on his body." It's quite a phrase and implies Jackson had mixed feelings or contradictory ideas about his own ethnicity and used his body to convert this into coded form. In the video, Jackson's eerie changes from human to wolfman were products of cinematic special effects. They were astonishing. Perhaps something even more astonishing was going on.

David Brackett, a professor of music history, noticed that at this stage, "A general aura of freakishness grew to surround Jackson such that many assumed the worst motives for his changed appearance." He means that Jackson's physical transformation—not the special effects—began to become discernible. More difficult to discern was which changes "were voluntary and which were not." For many this was the great and abiding mystery in Jackson's life. Was he trying to lose his blackness?

Recall Wyman's argument: Jackson shed conventional images of blackness. His success depended on it. It's a powerful point, though one that leaves questions unanswered. What were the conventional images of blackness Jackson discarded, for example? In 1973, ten years before the start of the Jackson era, the cultural historian Donald Bogle offered a serviceable answer based on his examination of film and, by implication, entertainment in general. The premise of Bogle's analysis was that African Americans appeared in film, but only in a narrow range of types. These were often clichéd, predictable, and caricatured in a way that would be offensive today. But they served a film's purpose, which was to provide entertainment, mostly to comfort and reassure, not provoke and challenge. Notable exceptions were Daniel Petrie's 1961 film of Lorraine Hansberry's book *A Raisin in the Sun*, featuring Sidney Poitier, Martin Ritt's 1972 *Sounder*, about black sharecroppers in the Great Depression, and Eric Monte's highschool drama *Cooley High*, in 1975. Mainstream films were less likely to portray black subjects with comparable nuance and subtlety or in diverse roles.

Black men were typically represented as Uncle Toms, jokesters, or predators. The first is a black man who is excessively obedient or servile to whites, the name derived from the hero of Harriet Beecher Stowe's anti-slavery novel *Uncle Tom's Cabin*, first published in 1852. The jokester was the equivalent of the clown, fool, or, in medieval times, the court jester; someone whose principal task is to make others laugh, usually at rather than with him. By predators, Bogle meant sexually dangerous males with a taste for white women. These weren't intricately historied characters, remember: Bogle was interested in stock types denoting conventional characters that recurred in film, literature, and theater. But they weren't greeted with cynicism: audiences largely accepted them as plausible.

Women were often cast as what Bogle called Mammies, these being nursemaids, cooks, or some other sort of domestic servant, who were dutiful and always willing to serve or please others. Hattie McDaniel's character in the 1939 film *Gone With the Wind* was the definitive portrayal. The "tragic mulatto" was Bogle's most ambiguous character: someone who, because of a mixed heritage (Bogle used "race"), struggles to find acceptance as either black or white—hence she is sad, or even suicidal. Bogle's classification is deliberately crude simply because he was trying to convey how popular images of black people were exactly that: crude. When Bogle first published his scheme in 1973, it seemed a viable way of interpreting how African Americans had been depicted and understood in film. While Bogle didn't argue there was a porousness between make-believe and real-life, the force of his argument was that popular perceptions of black people were affected by their portrayals in film. But his argument was shaken by several real-life black people who subverted the types.

Five years before, Shirley Chisholm had become the first African American woman elected to the United States Congress. Andrew Young was elected as a member of the House of Representatives in 1973 (and later became the US ambassador to the United Nations). In the 1940s and 1950s, when the idea of an African American performer in anything but a subservient role in a movie with an otherwise all-white cast was unthinkable, Lena Horne consistently appeared against type. The abovementioned Sidney Poitier, the first black man to receive an Academy Award for Best Actor in 1964, played suave and intelligent characters who defied categorization. Even at the time of Bogle's delineation, there were enough contradictions to make a skeptic wonder whether the conventional images of blackness Jackson was supposed to have cast off were widely shared. Jackson was certainly an original, but he was far from the only black entertainer of his time to escape the racist cookie-cutter of the Bogle thesis.

It wasn't sheer serendipity that carried Jackson through the 1980s: it was his desire and willingness to dramatize personal changes, though in a way that inclined audiences to ponder. He was a human conundrum who reflected or resembled vexed questions, one of which was "what does it mean to be black in the 1980s?" If Bogle's types offer a picture of conventional images of blackness in the 1970s, they were already consigned to history by the 1980s. So, what did Bill Wyman have in mind? Jackson wasn't shedding conventional images of blackness; these had already disappeared, leaving a less indistinct and complicated landscape. Black people were not characters in search of types. Where whites—or, at least, many whites—once thought there was a comfortably secure and unchanging set of types, there were now living, breathing people, with the same kinds of expectations, motivations, and ambitions as their own.

Jackson was obviously aware of his blackness, but didn't accept that this implicated him in meditations of African culture and history. He wasn't prepared to preach about empire, and he definitely wasn't interested in disclosing the myriad ways American society had failed black people. Jackson's blackness was not a blackness that had been disparaged. He didn't seem to belong to a people that had been suppressed and exploited by whites and he didn't carry his blackness as a visible marker of people who had been regarded as disposable. He was a symbol of unmistakable affluence, flamboyant prosperity, and conspicuous consumption. The album cover of *Thriller* featured him reclining in a white suit, black shirt, his hair coiffured—an image of social ascendancy. Jackson might have avoided discussion of blackness, but he depicted it majestically. Perhaps that was his genius. And ruination.

*   *   *

"I'll never do a video like that again," Jackson promised. "I don't want to do anything on 'Thriller.' No more 'Thriller.'" Jackson was quoted in the May 1984 edition of *Awake!* an illustrated magazine distributed by the Jehovah's Witnesses. Jackson's statement sounded like an abandonment of his masterwork, though it was not. He didn't refuse the royalties he earned from the album or video, for example. But he did insist on prefacing the video with a disclaimer consistent with the Jehovah's Witnesses' position against demons, devils, magic, and other elements of diabolism. "Due to my strong personal convictions, I wish to stress that this film in no way endorses a belief in the occult," it reminded viewers.

It might have seemed an incongruous way to introduce a spirited trek into the heart of darkness, but there was a reason for its inclusion. Jackson had been threatened with disfellowship, that is exclusion from the Jehovah's Witnesses, which is a movement (the Watch Tower Bible and Tract Society) founded in 1872 in Pittsburgh. Although it's basically a Christian movement, Jehovah's Witnesses deny many traditional Christian doctrines, refuse to allow members to serve in the military, and will not allow them to have blood transfusions. It prohibits allegiances to countries or governments. It also issues periodic prophecies about the end of the world. Prince was a follower, as is Serena Williams. The movement claims 8.6 million Witnesses.

Jackson was raised in the faith and, according to his mother Katherine, would proselytize on the street, circulating copies of *Awake!* and its companion publication *Watchtower*. Jackson's renowned abstinence from sex, liquor, and drugs was exemplary from the church's point of view, though, shortly after *Thriller*, there were rumblings. A *New York Times* article by Ari L. Goldman in April 1984 reported that members of the church's hierarchy were concerned that Jackson himself had become the focal point of what was described as a "cult." According to the report, Jackson was the Archangel Michael referenced in the Bible's book of Daniel 12:1: "And at that time shall Michael stand up, the great prince which standeth for the children of thy people." Jehovah's Witnesses oppose cults of personality. I should point out that "cult," while a legitimate word to describe a group of people sharing patterns of worship and practices that deviate from denominational religion, is often regarded in the United States as something sinister.

Goldman cited the October 15, 1983, edition of *Watchtower* in which there was a barely disguised slur: Witnesses were encouraged to "destroy albums and videos with verbal or visual references to witches, demons or devils," and discouraged from imitating "worldly musicians" in "dress, grooming and speech." Years later, a form letter from the Jehovah's Witnesses' headquarters in New York, dated May 18, 1987, stated that the movement "no longer considers Michael Jackson to be one of Jehovah's Witnesses." Jackson did not disclose any details, leaving Frank Dileo to confirm that there would be no comment from Jackson himself. One of the consequences of a dissociation is that ex-followers are shunned, meaning they get cold-shouldered by existing Witnesses. Jackson's mother remained a devotee, though she didn't shun her son, as Witness prescripts would command. Family ties were stronger than church ties, in her case. Katherine had been baptized a Witness in 1963, when Michael was five.

An event that seemed to convey Jackson's drift from Jehovah's Witnesses came on Katherine's fifty-fourth birthday on May 4, 1984. Katherine remembered her present "was a Rolls Royce with a big ribbon on top of it." She recalled the event when talking to Josh Mankiewicz, of the *NBC News* website on June 26, 2010.Jehovah's Witnesses condemn as creature worship the celebration of birthdays and denounce those who give gifts on such occasions.

It was never confirmed by either Jackson or the Jehovah's Witnesses that *Michael Jackson's Thriller* precipitated his departure. He left a long time after the video's first transmission. No doubt the church's hierarchy, like everyone else in the world, was taken aback by the success of what became a global phenomenon. In 1987, sales the *Thriller* album had reached 20 million in the United States and 38.5 million worldwide. Clearly, Jackson's denial at the start of the video had done nothing to harm album sales and, while he clarified his position on the occult, he did nothing more. What did the Witnesses expect him to do?

"He [MJ] also promised to block further distribution of the film over which he had control, according to a Witness official," wrote John Dart for the *Los Angeles Times*. A quotation in the May 1984 edition of *Watchtower* confirmed this, though Jackson's press agent Norman Winter later declined to discuss the authenticity of this quotation (in the *New York Times*, May 22, 1984, pages 19–20). It's possible that Jackson could have emulated Stanley Kubrick, who, in 1973, requested distributors to withdraw his own film *A Clockwork Orange* from release. Kubrick became convinced that the violence in the film provoked real fighting. Brian Wilson, of the Beach Boys, scrapped almost all of the early runs of *Smile*, the follow-up to 1966's *Pet Sounds*. A version of the album, without the original recordings, was eventually released but not until 2004. The reasons are thought to derive from Wilson's perfectionism. A 2001 album *The Smile Sessions* featured some of the original material. In 1992, Peter Gabriel withdrew copies of his album *Us* from the Japan market because of a complaint about a bonus track. There are not many cases of artists pulling their own work from public consumption, but Jackson had precedents if he had felt strongly about *Michael Jackson's Thriller*. There would have been consequences, though we can only speculate on how history might have been different had the video disappeared long before it had chance to resonate across the decades.

(Presumably, CBS Records would have opposed any attempt to withdraw the video or its own album. But the label objected to the release of MCA Records' *E.T.: The Extra-Terrestrial*, which featured an extract of Jackson reading and performing the original song, *Someone in the Dark*. This was available a few weeks before November 30, 1982, when *Thriller* was released.)

Over the next few decades, Jackson's religious convictions vacillated: for a while he befriended and, it appears, respected Rabbi Shmuley; he also reportedly converted to the Islam and changed his name to Mikaeel in

2008. Before that, Jackson wrote for *Beliefnet*, the religion and spirituality website, "When I became a father [Prince, Jackson's eldest child, was born in 1997], my whole sense of God and the Sabbath was redefined." This was in December 2000. "Every single day becomes the Sabbath" (https://bit.ly /2NJNPda).

Michael Jordan, like Jackson—and every other African American celebrity who lived the dream in the 1980s—was compelling because he delegitimized a critical evaluation of American society, or at least made it a lot less plausible.

17

Phantasmagorical Bubble Machine

There's a scene in Spike Lee's 1989 film *Do the Right Thing* in which Pino, an Italian-American (played by John Turturro), utters under his breath, "How come niggas are so stupid?" Mookie, a black pizza deliveryman (played by Lee), asks his fellow worker, "Who's your favorite basketball player?" "Magic Johnson," is the reply. "Movie star?" "Eddie Murphy." "Who's your favorite rock star?" Mookie anticipates his answer this time and jumps in with "Prince." But Pino corrects him: "Bruce." Mookie then invites him to unlock the logic of liking prominent black artists and entertainers, while despising blacks and calling them niggas. Pino insists the likes of Johnson and Prince (whom he actually does rate, though not as much as Springsteen) "are not really black, they're *more than black*." There's no resolution and Mookie eventually retaliates, "Fuck Frank Sinatra," to which Pino replies, "Well fuck you too, and *fuck Michael Jackson*!" Mookie and Pino are both low-paid workers at a pizzeria in the Bedford-Stuyvesant section of Brooklyn. They both wear Nike, as do most of the other characters in the film.

There is a logical answer to Mookie's question, though not one that springs readily to the mind of Pino. He reveres Magic Johnson and admires Murphy and Prince, but brackets these figures in a way that separates them from the African Americans he mingles with in Bed-Stuy, which has one of the largest black populations in the United States. He hasn't concerned himself with the exact reason his heroes are different: they just are. They might have more talent, or are prepared to work harder, or maybe think differently from others. All Pino knows is that they're "more than black." Perhaps he means they are a new type of black person, freshly sanitized so they carry none of the unacceptable traces of civil rights. They aren't deliberately combative or uncooperative, or continually expressing feelings of ill will for injustices, past or present. They never try to leverage their fame in a way that offends anyone. Even if they harbor potentially challenging thoughts, they either keep them to themselves or share them in a way that kept audiences in stitches—as Eddie Murphy does.

Whites, Italians, and, indeed, anybody could enjoy and respect the black entertainers, who emerged in the mid-1980s and whose arrival seemed to herald a new epoch. They set the tone. The media contributed to the emollient effects of these figures, maintaining their profile and, without consciously trying, advancing the conception of the good life they personified. It was an intoxicating conception and one that remained forceful through the following decades.

*   *   *

On Wednesday, September 12, 1984, destiny was changed. Michael Jordan signed to play professional basketball for Chicago Bulls. The Bulls, an, at-best, ordinary team went on to win six championships. Jordan became an uncategorizable entity with the kind of following usually reserved for messiahs and a gift for selling anything, literally anything. But in 1984, Jordan wasn't even considered the top draft NBA pick: two other players were rated above him. Jordan's agent, David Falk, somehow secured him a $6 million contract with the Bulls and an unusual deal with Nike, the sportswear company, that would earn Jordan several million more over the next four or so decades. "I'm going to offer you someone who will become the most famous basketball player in history and, in the process, will put Nike in same league as McDonald's and Coca-Cola," Falk might have opened his pitch. "Same league as McDonald's," Nike chief Phil Knight may have thought he heard him say before digesting what must have been the most counter-intuitive idea he'd ever heard.

Nike took a gamble: its competitors adidas, Puma, and Reebok were taking advantage of the new enthusiasm for aerobics, which Nike had neglected. Nike's market position was faltering. It was planning to launch an adventurous and risky concept—what it called a signature shoe, designed and marketed to reflect a person. The basketball merchandise market was dominated by Converse at the time. There was an additional risk: Jordan was, like the majority of other National Basketball Association (NBA) players, black. The NBA itself had an image problem: it was widely regarded as, to quote the *Los Angeles Times Magazine* writer Edward Kiersh, "a drug-infested, too-black league." Its players were seen, to use Tyrone R. Simpson's memorably vivid phrase, "excessively libidinal, terminally criminal, and socially infernal."

This had commercial implications summed up by Kiersh: "Sponsors felt the NBA and its black stars had little value in pitching colas and cornflakes to Middle America." The assumption was that a prominent black player could be a valuable pitchman, but for a black market. In the 1970s New York Knicks' Walt Frazier, better known as "Clyde" (as in *Bonnie and Clyde*) advertised wares, usually pimped-up with fedora and fur coat. But Nike envisaged Jordan differently: his role was to move branded footwear and apparel in the mainstream market. The company sensed an occasion and an opportunity, presenting Jordan as an "atypical Black figure," as David L. Andrews and Michael L. Silk called him, with none of the "irresponsibility, hypersexuality, deviance, unruliness, and brutish physicality routinely associated with African American males in general, and NBA players in particular."

Question: Were those truly characteristics routinely associated with black men? They might have been at one time in history. But in 1984? Eddie Murphy's movie *Beverly Hills Cop* was released in this year, as was Prince's record "When Doves Cry." *The Cosby Show* started in the same year. The year before, Oprah Winfrey arrived in Chicago to host *A.M. Chicago,* a half-hour morning show on WLS-TV. *The Oprah Winfrey Show* launched in September 1986 (much more of which later in this chapter). White America's reliance on racist stereotypes might have once seemed inexhaustible, but, two decades after civil rights, it was gone. There were too many resplendent and accomplished black celebrities ready to defy them. In Jordan, there was another.

Jordan's greatness lay not so much in what he did as what he didn't do. He barely raised an eyebrow, let alone his voice. Unlike many prominent black athletes who had spoken out or gestured in favor of just causes, at least as they saw them, Jordan did just two things: played ball and sold products. His character became iconic by doing no more. Audiences had complete freedom to think what they wanted about him or what they thought he stood for. This was the case right from the start. When he first stepped on court in October 1984 for the Bulls, he was wearing Nike's specially designed shoes. They were red and black, with some white, but not enough to satisfy the league. NBA's dress code stipulated white footwear and Jordan's Nikes were promptly banned. Nothing enhances attractiveness like a ban: prohibiting, forbidding, or outlawing something instantly makes it fascinating.

Without actually doing anything (apart from wearing the shoes), Jordan had sprung a coup. Nike ran a series of ads featuring censor bars across the footwear. Demand for the shoes spiked. Jordan was a 21-year-old rookie, barely known outside the amateur game and completely unproven as a pro. The ban arrived like a gift. But Nike knew how to exploit it. Jordan wore the shoes again. The NBA fined him $5,000. He wore them again. The league fined him again. At least that was the popular story. That's all that mattered. The infamous shoes, known as Air Jordan, were the must-have items of the day. They remain historical artifacts, housed mostly in the glass cases of collectors. It's easy to forget that sports shoes had less cultural significance at the time than a Swatch wristwatch or a Zippo lighter, both still circulating but neither of much consequence now. In 1984, sneakers, or what Brits call trainers, were sportswear. As such, they weren't cool—by which I mean fashionably attractive rather than chilly.

Unlike any other athlete in history, Jordan was delivered to his audience like a product. "It was Nike's commercials that made Jordan a global superstar," Naomi Klein suspected. There had been other virtuoso athletes before Jordan, though none reached what Klein called "Jordan's other-worldly level of fame." She wasn't questioning Jordan's prowess. But, pre-Jordan, sports stars, no matter how proficient, were athletes who happened to advertise products when they were asked. They weren't synonymous with a brand, as Jordan was. Nike changed all that: the company embarked on what Klein called "mythmaking," creating an aura around Jordan. "Who said man wasn't meant to fly?" asked one of Nike's early ads. The series of ads Nike commissioned from aforementioned director Spike Lee helped power Jordan and the Air Jordan shoes into the popular consciousness. It seems obvious today, but using an individual, known but not yet globally recognized, to front a marketing campaign was an inspired decision, but one laden with risk. Jordan's blackness was probably one of the least risky elements. At least in 1984 when it was almost as if a different age had begun: people, or perhaps more precisely consumers were responding to the appearance of black men and women in positions of authority, influence, and stature, as well as having—at least in Jordan's case—street cred.

In the years that followed Jordan became a cultural artifact for the age; and I choose the word "artifact" with care—Jordan, like Jackson, was flesh-and-blood, but he was also like a work of art—created. By whom? In Jordan's case by a combination of Nike, its advertising agency Wieden and Kennedy, and, of course, the people who attributed him with qualities, features, and characteristics usually associated with superheroes. Or saints. (Mental note to self: write to Marvel to suggest Saint Jordanaire, a virtuous mutant who carries an enchanted ball that only a worthy elite can throw.)

Everyone had been aware of the power of advertising, at least since 1957, when Vance Packard's book *The Hidden Persuaders* exposed the techniques used by advertisers to discover or develop consumers' motivations, then exploit them. Advertising is colossally powerful in shaping our tastes and buying habits. But Nike couldn't have just foisted Jordan onto gullible consumers. An untested pro at an unfashionable, underachieving ball club in a league that was floundering, at least until David Stern took over as NBA commissioner in 1984. It could be argued that Jordan was a demigod waiting to happen. Black people who were greatly admired, respected, or glorified like a minor deity were in short supply. Jordan was raised by the same cultural swell that carried Jackson and other notable black artists to preeminence. Flamboyantly successful black people were in the zeitgeist for the first time in history.

Jordan was another success story in an unfolding triumph: America, so it seemed, had emerged from the national unrest that followed the killing of Martin Luther King in 1968 and was now parading imperishable illustrations of its success. There was no triumphalism, just a steady rise of prominent black people recognized for their achievements and judged, as MLK would have put it, on the content of their character. Of course, fulfillment today can frequently lead to disquiet tomorrow. The wave of riots that followed the Rodney King case started in 1992. By then, Jordan had galvanized the Chicago Bulls and was leading the United States' national basketball team to victory in the Barcelona Olympics. The shirt he wore in the games sold for $216,000 (£174,053) at auction. The "jumpman" graphic plastered across Nike products was a silhouette of Jordan and, in a sense, Jordan himself eventually morphed into a kind of human brand. He appeared in advertising campaigns, not only for Nike but for McDonald's, Coca-Cola, Hanes Underwear, Wheaties breakfast cereal, and several other commercial products, including Gatorade, the sports drink that used "Be Like Mike" in its ads.

* * *

Jordan's presence threw up all sorts of questions that have never been adequately answered. His athleticism, affability, and reluctance to say anything remotely controversial about social or cultural affairs were qualities valued by advertisers, but hardly enough to propel him to the unique position he occupied in the 1980s. Bill Cosby was a credible and appealing endorser too, at least until his disgrace. Klein's argument that Nike lifted Jordan is believable. Coca-Cola and McDonald's lifted him even higher. Similarly, Cosby's status was undeniably changed by his associations with Coca-Cola and Jell-O pudding, among others.

Neither mixed with gangsta friends, or, to anyone's knowledge, used illicit drugs. Unlike Cosby, Jordan never preached. Cosby's moral advice was typically consistent with mainstream conservative cultural norms. Jordan's only indiscretion was his gambling habit; it was an unsavory but perhaps not totally unwholesome pursuit, discordant with popular perceptions of him, but by no means as transgressive as Cosby's or, for that matter, Tiger Woods's misdeeds.

Jordan was proud of his virtuousness: in the documentary *The Last Dance*, he recounted how, shortly after being drafted, he walked into a hotel room to witness a bacchanalian gathering of his teammates, indulging in cocaine, weed, and other indiscretions. He declined to join the unchaste assembly and returned to his room. "From that point on, I was more or less on my own," said Jordan.

"Michael Jordan is both Muhammad Ali and Mister Clean, Willie Mays and the Marlboro Man," wrote Henry Louis Gates Jr. in 1998, in allusion to a pair of great African American athletes and a pair of make-believe characters used to advertise household cleaners and cigarettes, respectively. Jordan both amalgamated these figures and surpassed them. He "has become one of those things that constitute our identity as Americans, as citizens of the winner-take-all society." One of those *things*. Did Gates really mean to dehumanize Jordan? Was he an object, an article, a contrivance designed simultaneously to pimp commodities and appease consciences—perhaps making one contingent on the other? If Jordan was a product, maybe there were laws of supply and demand in operation. This was surely not Gates's point, but it's a compelling one even so.

If Jordan was fabricated, it was probably to meet a demand for a new type of black person, a living advertisement for a society that had not yet eliminated racism, but was well on its way to doing so. Who or what was involved in the production process? Nike, obviously. Wieden and Kennedy, Nike's ad agency. The NBA too. And NBC, the tv network that, in 1991, paid a then-staggering $600 million to broadcast NBA games. McDonald's and all the other corporations that hitched their wagons to Jordan's star by featuring him in their advertising campaigns. The demand side is, at once, simpler yet more complex. Simpler because Jordan's demographic was young and culturally diverse. His devotees were prepared to pay a premium over alternatives because they wanted commodities that carried the big man's imprimatur.

The complicated part is trying to fathom why America needed to demonstrate that the rights of all of its citizens to political and social freedom and equality were now respected. Wasn't it a bit like taking an AK-47 to a fist fight? Yes, but only if you have no ammunition for the assault rifle. Jordan, like the gun, was for show. He was a human exhibit, demonstrating how it was possible for anyone to rise to the top, no matter what their ethnic or class background. Just as long as they had talent, perseverance, and an appetite for hard work. Skin color, "race," or bloodline were spurious impediments. They were the past, anyway. Jordan was the present and future. He was a new, spectacular representative of the American dream, a symbol of the triumph of striving over privilege. This is precisely why he was so beguiling.

Jordan heralded the arrival of what some called the "colorblind society." Ethnic studies professor David J. Leonard, in a 2004 article, argued that Jordan and other black athletes "not only elucidate the fulfillment of the American Dream but also America's imagined racial progress." Note Leonard's term "imagined" racial progress. The colorblind society was where America was imagined to be, at least by those dazzled by Jordan. Leonard didn't suggest it had actually materialized. He meant whites' enthusiastic admiration for, if not idolization of, the likes of Jordan and— to use Leonard's example—Denzel Washington permitted and justified the image of American society as a place where race or ethnicity were no longer relevant. People were evaluated solely on ability, or merit.

Leonard's approach is provocative, though, to this writer, unconvincing. The glamorous high achievement of Jordan was more than an "elucidation," as Leonard suggests. It was more of a parody: an imitation or version of something that falls far short of the real thing; a travesty. Jordan and the apparatus that buttressed him promoted a particular kind of vision in which the good life was one that could be bought for the price of a pair of sneakers. This treated decent people contemptuously.

Jordan didn't just advertise products: he was himself a living advertisement for a way of life in which everything could be bought and sold as if they were commodities. Ideals, commitments, allegiances, and any other abstraction could be reduced or replaced by buyable things. Where previous generations had hungered for freedom, equality, and an end to discrimination, Jordan's cohort craved Nike footwear. The appeal of sneakers lay not in their utility, use, or purpose but in their possession. Jordan's acolytes celebrated merchandise. Unlike many other famous black figures, he didn't ask much of his followers. Not like Martin Luther King, who mobilized hundreds of thousands to march and protest, nor Muhammad Ali who urged all blacks to pursue a form of separatism MLK would have found abhorrent.

All Jordan asked of his acolytes was to marvel at him and buy Air Jordans. Some would argue Jordan was not a leader, not in the sense of MLK or Ali, and certainly not in the mold of Malcolm X or Jesse Jackson. But he was a different kind of leader, someone who could command, guide, or direct others, though not in a collective way. What he wanted them to do was behave like individuals. Specifically, individuals who were also avid consumers. Of all Jordan's abundant skills, his greatest was his ability to persuade people they should buy products they never knew they needed. And perhaps that he distracted young minds from issues that materially affected black lives, banished what might have been healthy skepticism, and stimulated appetites that would eventually turn cannibalistic.

* * *

Jordan's exemplary rise to wealth and fame probably occupied a lot of attention during a period when the dream he epitomized was disappearing for many American blacks. Ronald Reagan was elected president in 1984 and almost immediately began his assault on affirmative action, the main policy instrument introduced in the 1960s to promote equal opportunity across minorities. Reagan's attitudes toward black people were made known through his language. When making his case for reduced federal social service spending, Reagan described young black men as "strapping bucks" and black women "welfare queens." He had also used demeaning language in a 1971 conversation with then president Richard M. Nixon. Governor Reagan, as he was, referred to "those monkeys from those African countries—damn them, they're still uncomfortable wearing shoes!" Earlier, he'd opposed the 1964 Civil Rights legislation. So, it was no surprise when Reagan tried to veto the Civil Rights Restoration Act of 1988, which required publicly funded institutions to comply with civil rights laws in all areas of their organization. (Both Reagan quotes are reproduced in John Baldoni's 2019 article for *Forbes*.)

Reagan's conservative golden age of self-reliance, libertarianism, and supply-side economics (in which regulation and taxation are minimized) was the perfect time for a unique presence like Jordan. But it also encouraged the kind of avarice and materialism that released a different kind of aggressive consumerism. People started killing each other for their Air Jordans. Desperate to get the coveted sneakers, young people began attacking and, often, killing each other for their shoes. The marketing was aimed at the demographic that could least afford the $150+ price tags at a time when the average salary in the United States was about $20,000 (or $385 a week) before tax.

Neither Nike nor Jordan had intended their project to promote internecine street wars, but, even when it became clear this development was a consequence of their strategies, neither did much. In fact, Nike continued to assign value to specific lines or models of footwear by making limited editions. The operation resembled the diamond market in which scarcity equates to value and desirability. Nike was careful to make sure supply never met demand. Jordan's silence on the issue was deafening. Even after Jordan's unexpected departure from basketball for a spell in minor-league baseball and then a return to Chicago in 1995, street assaults and robberies of his branded footwear continued. Like other cultural trends, they persisted and mutated: in 2020, journalist Gene Collier reported on a killing in Miami for a pair of adidas Yeezys, a much-desired product endorsed by Ye, formerly known as Kanye West.

Jordan retired for good in 2003. His cultural reign had been both splendid and dire. He'd been rewarded for staying tabloid-proof. In May 2020, *Forbes* estimated Nike had paid him $1.3 billion since the first contract in 1984. It described this as "the biggest endorsement bargain in sports," emphasizing Jordan's role in establishing Nike's "virtual monopoly" in the once-competitive sportswear market (Nike, in 2021, led the market with a 27 percent share).

True, there were intrinsic satisfactions in watching Jordan play ball and perhaps even in watching his sometimes sublime Nike ads. But imagine if Jordan had brought his considerable influence to bear on issues that really mattered. Dare to think what could have happened if he had turned his attention to victims of racism, oppression, or neglect: to people instead of products. What if Jordan had spoken out about the skewed distribution of income and wealth that created and kept a struggling black underclass? How did he resist the temptation to say something, anything at all about the underlying causes of racial inequality? His glib responses to every attempt to tease from him a statement on something outside his own narrow scope suggests a man intent on not making trouble. The world waited till 2020, when Black Lives Matter had changed the entire cultural landscape of the world and the NBA star's light had faded to the point where no one really cared what he thought, before it heard him espouse. "We have been beaten down (as African Americans) for so many years," he told Rick Bonnell, of the *Charlotte Observer* (June 5). "You can't accept it anymore."

If only Jordan had used language like this before he retired from competitive sport seventeen years before. "This is a tipping point," he said of the George Floyd killing in 2020. "We need to make a stand. We've got to be better as a society regarding race."

Jordan could have made much the same point about the Amadou Diallou killing in 1999, or even the Rodney King beating in 1991. Then, it would have sounded as loud as a thunderclap. As it was, it sounded and felt like a hushed ritual, using tropes that had become familiar to everyone. Even the donation of $100 million to causes "attacking ingrained racism [and] supporting educational opportunity" lacked the impact it would have had two or three decades before when he never strayed from a script Nike seemed to have written for him. After the Floyd case, everyone became subversive overnight, giving rise to a global protest that turned facile, predictable, and ultimately self-congratulatory. Jordan's decision to join the protest at a late stage almost invited questions about his reasons. His calculating indifference to anything outside sports and commodities was famously captured when he declined to make a political endorsement because "Republicans buy sneakers, too."

Had Jordan spoken out against racism and embraced causes he considered capable of bringing about a just, egalitarian world, would he have still been the consumer-friendly icon he was? Put another way, would Pino have idolized him as "more than black"? Or would he have just been dismissed as another black athlete with a chip on his shoulder?

* * *

On Monday, January 2, 1984, eight months before Jordan signed for the Bulls, a lowly tv show in Chicago changed its anchor. It was "lowly" in the sense that WLS-TV's *A.M. Chicago* was consistently bottom of the viewer ratings. There was an immediate bounce and, within a month, the morning talk show's viewing audience rose steeply. The show's success continued, so that by September 1985, the station decided to change its name to reflect the anchor; it became *The Oprah Winfrey Show*. In 1986, it was syndicated nationally. The program moved to the epicenter of popular entertainment and remained there for 25 years—and 4,000 shows. Oprah was a member of the clique of black artists who grew to prominence in the mid-1980s. But, unlike many, she had no interest in maintaining the status quo; her disposition wasn't to accept existing arrangements, but to challenge them.

For example, within months of going national with her show, Oprah ventured into dangerous territory by featuring residents of Forsyth County, Georgia, where there had been no black residents since 1912, when three black men, all of whom were hanged, allegedly raped a white teenager, prompting whites to burn down black churches and schools. She, a black woman, asked questions of white people who openly refused to welcome black people and defended their right to do so. "We have a right to have a white community," said one woman. Unflinchingly, Oprah persisted with her investigation, perhaps knowing the show would attract the kind of publicity that would push viewing figures higher. The show was screened during one of four annual sweeps months during which viewer ratings are recorded and used to determine advertising rates. Oprah's idealism often had a pragmatic part, but viewers rarely noticed.

Oprah stopped at nothing: if sponsors or advertisers, or even government agencies told her not to do something, she'd probably do it. She thought nothing of embarrassing the high-and-mighty, of confronting power-brokers, or taking issue with presidents. With the possible exception of documentarist Michael Moore, Oprah had few equals when it came to mischief and provocation. No social or personal issue was off-limits: as well as racism, she tackled homophobia, addiction, infidelity, and child abuse—sometimes drawing on her own experience as a victim. It was a new type of show. She took aim at figures from entertainment, but from politics too, and from big business; in fact, no one was spared. Her approach made her show the highest-rated talk show in American history.

Oprah's gift was that she was neither a firebrand nor a demagogue, she insinuated herself into people's lives by speaking to audiences plainly. Before her arrival, television talk shows were little different from radio interviews, hosts asking prepared questions and guests answering them. Oprah, whether by design or chance, changed this format: her interviews were chats, relaxed conversations between two friends, often about matters that would, at the time, qualify as personal, if not intimate. It was as if Oprah was inviting viewers to become guiltless eavesdroppers. When she talked to the camera, it was not as a host, but as a confidante, someone with whom audiences could share a secret and trust them not to repeat it. These stylistic features are commonplace today, but in the 1980s they were innovations that were perfectly in sync with wider cultural shifts.

Many public figures appeared less exceptional, more ordinary. Oprah herself lacked the other-worldliness of Jordan and, for that matter, Jackson. In fact, there were few other entertainers who could match her for ordinariness. Viewers didn't so much watch and admire her as relate to her. The word might not have been in use during the 1980s, but Oprah was *relatable*: she enabled audiences to feel that they could identify or somehow connect with her. So, when she opened up about her troubled childhood and her determination not to let putative impediments like poverty, racism, or misogyny stop her, audiences felt a rapport.

No one becomes as popular as Oprah did in the 1980s without the occasional critic. As we know from the previous chapter Barbara Grizzuti Harrison was one of Oprah's. In her sarcastically titled *New York Times* article, "The Importance of Being Oprah," Grizzuti Harrison appointed a "born-again capitalist" response to bellyaching African Americans: "A black person has to ask herself, 'If Oprah Winfrey can make it, what does it say about me?' They no longer have any excuse. If you don't believe that I should make it, you absolutely don't believe you should, either."

It was a typically down-to-earth pronouncement: don't blame other people or abstract forces beyond your control, just follow my example. Not everyone would regard this as a criticism, but Grizzuti Harrison saw it as a kind of exoneration—of whites (Grizzuti Harrison was a white New Yorker, whose grandparents were from Calabria, southwestern Italy). "We are encouraged to believe we are doing something, embroiled in something; whereas in fact we are coddled in our passivity," argued Grizzuti Harrison.

Oprah allowed "audiences to feel superior to blatant, uneducated racists, while cherishing their own insidious subtle racism." The logic behind this is deadly simple: by watching Oprah and sharing in her disgust, anger, or whatever emotion she expressed, whites could find comfort and assuage their guilt, while blacks could remind themselves that the racist barriers were largely illusory. From this perspective, Oprah expedited the "dissociation from past sins" that Shelby Steele believed was central to the post-civil rights experience. Oprah's greatest service was to penitential whites. (I touched on Steele's arguments in Chapters 14 and 15; his worldview seems to complement Oprah's.)

For Grizzuti Harrison, Oprah's sudden surge to prominence was based partly on her no-holds-barred interviewing, her unsparing choice of subjects and her persistent challenges. But she was also offering a "salve to white's burdened consciences" and a "quick fix" that provided a feeling of contentment, a feeling that became addictive in the years that followed. Oprah's seemingly limitless popularity, on this account, was predicated on her appeal to whites. She held a mirror to blacks and made them stare, forcing them to ask whether they were failing because of society or, more likely, because of themselves. The program was perfectly congruent with the spirit of the 1980s.

The *New York Times* article was published in 1989, the year Denzel Washington won an Oscar for his role as a runaway slave in the civil-war film *Glory. Driving Miss Daisy* won the best picture award. And *Do the Right Thing* heralded a series of cinematic portraits of the ghettos. The all-conquering *The Cosby Show* was in its fifth year and, of course, Michael Jordan was treading his immaculate path to sports consecration. Mike Tyson was still a few years away from damnation. Janet's *Miss You Much* had sold 4 million copies globally. Dazzling black stars were living proof of the power of individuality and self-determination. They also masked the racism Grizzuti Harrison and many others suggested was still circulating after two-and-a-half decades of civil rights.

Other critics, like Vicki Abt and Mel Sheesholtz, considered Oprah's style as a "vulgarized version of traditional psychotherapy ... where strangers get to watch and listen to hideous confession and confrontations." They were characterizing Oprah's uninhibited interviews which were closely observed by audiences. Abt and Sheesholtz were writing in 1994 when the voyeurism that is now commonplace on tv and elsewhere was just coming into existence and there was an understandable surprise at the relish audiences and participants seem to take from sharing what might in earlier times have been regarded as private, even intimate experiences.

The writers took issue with Oprah's focus on "the atomistic individual" and her "search for personal satisfaction, good feelings, freedom from blame, shame or social responsibility." By atomistic, Abt and Sheesholtz mean distinct and independent rather than parts of larger entities, like groups, societies, or cultures. They might have been right, but you can hardly imagine Oprah turning to her audiences and thundering, "You're not here for the contextual or any other kind of analysis 'cause there really isn't any. You're unrepentant, philistine voyeurs, who derive pleasure from others' misfortunes." She was more likely to point her finger and remind her audience, "Pay attention: this could be you."

In other words, Oprah offered a philosophy in which individuals were autonomous, self-reliant, and capable of changing themselves. That applied not just to people on the show but to everyone watching. Perhaps it simplified the power of other people, circumstances, and institutions to license or restrict individual freedoms; and it probably eliminated the role of history in influencing how freedom is distributed. For example, in discussing racism, Oprah took the individualist approach "by defining racism as a psychological 'illness' for which individuals, and, by extension, society need 'healing,'" wrote Janice Peck in her 1994 article "Talk about race." "Subjective rather than objective change" was the goal.

*   *   *

Any criticism of Oprah sounds curmudgeonly. She was one of the most successful tv personalities in history, commanding the kind of popular and critical regard enjoyed by the likes of Johnny Carson, Walter Kronkite, and Lucille Ball. She changed countless people's lives by urging anyone who would listen to remake themselves. "What is your inner voice telling you?" "What is your intention?" "What are you grateful for?" "What is your truth?" These are the kind of questions she told followers to ask themselves. "The whole point of being alive is to evolve into the complete person you were intended to be."

Oprah's signature was individual aspiration. It endeared her to vast audiences. It was as if she prodded black people and said: "Why wait for society to help you when you can help yourself?" Or: "Why waste effort trying to move mountains when you can move your own butt?" Oprah might not have used the exact words, but the inquiry was implicit. She didn't try to change society. She didn't even try to change human beings. She tried to make people change themselves.

Oprah probably knew what it was like to have the system rigged against her. More importantly, she knew what it took to succeed in that system. In 1988 she established her own production company, known as Harpo Studios (later, Harpo Inc.). In 2000, she launched *O: The Oprah Magazine*, a glossy lifestyle monthly that competed in the same market as *Martha Stewart Living*. A second magazine *O at Home* followed in 2004. She seemed unstoppably on her way to becoming not just one of the most commercially and influential black people but sovereign of her own empire.

She probably guessed her initiatives would upset some people, particularly people who wanted the system changed. But she didn't seem to struggle with any inner conflict about this. At least, not during her ascent. Once at the top, she broadened her focus and, at times, even tantalized audiences with hints that she might enter politics. In a way she did, but not how many might have imagined.

On December 8, 2007, she told a 10,000-strong crowd in Des Moines, Iowa, "I am not here to tell you how to think . . . I am here to tell you to think." She reminded the audience that she had voted Republican as many times as she had Democrat and that her conviction was personal. "I feel compelled to stand up and speak out for the man who I believe has a new vision for America." She was talking about Barack Obama. In endorsing the senator from Illinois, Oprah referred to Ernest J. Gainer's 1971 novel *The Autobiography of Miss Jane Pittman*, which tells the life story of a woman born in slavery at the end of the civil war. The book recounts how each time a new baby was born, its mother would take it to Jane Pittman who would hold the baby John the Baptist-like and wonder aloud whether the child would be the deliverer of black people. "Is you the one?" Oprah polished the grammar, changed the context, and answered affirmatively that Obama was indeed The One. Obama was elected president in November 2008.

In January 2018, Oprah, perhaps by accident, set off rumors that she would herself run for the presidency after delivering an impassioned speech at the Golden Globes awards ceremony. She quashed the rumors, but without completely ruling out a foray into politics. At that stage, Oprah had left her talk show to concentrate on her own television channel, the OWN, which she launched in 2011 as a joint venture with Discovery. It was a 50/50 partnership, each party investing $100 million. By 2018, the channel had two of the top five ad-supported cable dramas among the sought-after demographic of women aged twenty-five to fifty-four; the network consciously targeted black viewers.

Forbes valued the channel at $285 million in 2017, though this dropped over the next three years and Oprah cashed out some of her ownership in 2020 to focus on her work with Apple TV. She revived her popular book club and presented an interview series called *The Oprah Conversation*, that featured guests like Barack Obama and Dolly Parton. The Apple deal was valued in nine figures. *Forbes* estimated that Winfrey was worth $2.6 billion. This made her the richest black person in America, at least until 2020 when Robert F. Smith, the private equity investor, took over (he was worth $5 billion).

There's a scene in Regina King's film *One Night in Miami* (based on Kemp Powers' play) in which Sam Cooke explains why he's not content to be just a singer-songwriter and has ventured out with his own publishing, recording, and management firms. "I don't want a piece of the pie," he says. "I want the recipe." So did Oprah. Cooke, in 1959, started his own record label, SAR, which he co-owned with JW Alexander, with whom he also wrote. They also established Kags Music to take advantage of the burgeoning market in music publishing. Running parallel with these, Cooke pursued his solo career, signing a favorable deal with mainstream label RCA Victor that gave him ownership of his master recordings. Oprah seems to have reached a similar conclusion to Cooke: performing can be rewarding for the artist but is usually more rewarding for the industry supporting the artist. So, taking an executive role in their own performances was the recipe for achieving lasting success. (Cooke was killed in 1964, age thirty-three; in 2015, his estate was valued at $100 million.)

No other African American had ever ruled an empire like Oprah: over half a century, she created a sphere of activity that extended in time and space, and a commercial organization that ensured its growth and continuity. Idolized by audiences and praised (mostly) by critics, her popularity can barely be exaggerated: practically everything she did spread influence and spun out money. She rose "to the very top of the phantasmagorical bubble machine we call the entertainment industry," as Patricia Williams put it in her 2007 article, "The Audacity of Oprah" (a pun on Obama's book, *The Audacity of Hope*).

* * *

In every respect, Oprah became the personification of her own philosophy, which chimes with that of every other African American aboard the bubble machine, including BET founder Robert L. Johnson, to whom I referred in Chapter 15. Racism is like rain, he said. So, what do you do when it's raining? Stay indoors and grumble about the weather? Or grab and umbrella and get on with life? For some, this made Oprah as much a symbol of conservatism as Cosby or as apolitical as Jordan. "She can never admit the need for systematic structural change and collective political activity," complained Dana L. Cloud. Maybe Oprah wouldn't admit to it because, if she looked at a building, she saw bricks, not the structure; individuals were her concern. Does this make her a conservative? Possibly. In the sense that she accepted the status quo. But not inertia: she wanted people to recognize some of the more unpleasant and disagreeable aspects of American society and work toward changing them. It was how Oprah's philosophy translated into action that drew the ire of critics.

At a certain point in the middle of the 1980s—I've decided on 1984 as the crucial year—the American cultural climate changed, moving from We to I. In the 1960s, people like Martin Luther King, Malcolm X, John Lewis (who led the march from Selma to Montgomery in 1965), and Daisy Bates (president of the Arkansas chapter of the NAACP) put African Americans first and themselves second. But, against a background of rising individualism, the exemplary black figures were people who put themselves first and expressed no shame in urging others to do the same. Their circle of moral concern didn't exclude communities, groups, or even nations; they were as moral as their forerunners. The difference was in their prescription: "Don't blame others for everything that's gone wrong in your life—take responsibility for yourself."

Black celebrities who succeeded in entertainment and sport were not necessarily less altruistic than previous generations. Theirs wasn't a Devil Take Hindmost philosophy in which everyone should look after themselves without regard for the fate of others. It was more like the approach of Maimonides (1135–1204), the philosopher, who is often credited with the proverb about giving someone a fish and feeding them for a day, or teaching them to fish and giving them the ability to feed themselves for a lifetime. And when Oprah urged individuals to take control of their individual lives, or control their own destinies, she wasn't just issuing maxims: she backed up her claims with her own story, demonstrating that everything she preached, she had practiced. In this sense, she was proof that the racism remaining in America was annoying, but not necessarily destructive. This is precisely why Jackson, Jordan, Cosby, and every other African American celebrity who were living the dream in the 1980s were so compelling: they delegitimized critical evaluation of American society, or at least made it a lot less plausible. Everyone can dream, everyone can follow that dream, everyone can overcome what remnants of racism are left behind in the trail of civil rights.

Earlier, I proposed that black celebrities of the period embodied the good life: they seemed to lead exciting, rewarding lives and gave the impression that the kind of things that hindered many other blacks in education, employment, or the criminal justice system didn't frustrate them. In this sense, they helped create and perpetuate an impression of America as inclusive, embracing all ethnic groups, respecting difference, and favoring diversity over uniformity. Wittingly or not, conspicuously successful black entertainers and athletes advanced the intriguing prospect that the good life is available to all.

Black celebrities who emerged in the 1980s were ideal advertisements for the good life America offered to anyone with enough resolve and determination. Jordan, Oprah, and the others were evidence of what was possible, though Jackson was the ultimate exemplar: he was unique for sure, but he wasn't a one-off. A contradiction? No: he was an individual but shared the same assumptions of Jordan, Oprah, and the others. Sure, there were obstacles, but none of them were insurmountable, at least to those with enough resolve. There was a good life and it was every black person's responsibility to try to live it.

Paul McCartney enjoyed a productive collaboration and friendship—for a while. In 1983, they celebrated McCartney's success at the annual BRIT Awards. Also successful were Michael Grant and Junior Waite (right of picture) of Musical Youth, a five-piece band from Birmingham, England, that in many ways resembled the Jacksons: Michael Grant, wearing hat, was nine when the band was formed, eleven when the band's first single was a hit. But success was short-lived: the band soon went into decline and its members' lives unraveled tragically.

18

Without the Grit of Reality

By 1983, the world was dominated by three things. Aids was a virus that had emerged a couple of years before and which was cutting down swaths of mostly gay men and some women. Reaganomics were the policies associated with the eight-year presidency of Ronald Reagan and involved unrestricted free trade, low taxes, and a new respectability for acquisitiveness and opportunism. Michael Jackson was a puzzle.

For the first time in history, the world's most mesmerizing entertainer was black. Jackson's record sales set new historical precedents. In one remarkable decade, Jackson sold 110 million records, over 75 million as a solo artist; sales of the *Thriller* album surged after the video, and again in 2009 following his death. His videos proved he could hold the camera's gaze better than most film stars. Only Madonna would have dared suggest he was not the world's most popular artist. And Jackson hit the height of his popularity when American racism, though not as virulent as it was earlier in the twentieth century, was still pernicious.

Yet Jackson still puzzled people. Susan Fast thinks she knows why. "It was really his more substantive, underlying differences that were most troubling," she writes, listing Jackson's apparent refusal to stick to "normative social codes." Fast means Jackson didn't fit easily into racial or ethnic categories or into recognizable gender roles, for that matter. "Please be black, Michael, or white, or gay or straight," Fast imagines people pleading as if wanting him to slot into established categories. It's an interesting proposition, but there's no evidence to support it. Did people really want Jackson to conform to a recognizable status? And, if so, why?

It's at least possible that Jackson's ambiguities, far from being troubling, were the very source of his humongous global popularity. In other words, it was Jackson's refusal to comply to obvious types that made him so popular. Maybe he did excite troubling feelings but there was no handwringing.

In fact, his enigmatic qualities could have made him more appealing. In contrast to Fast's understanding, I'd argue that nobody wanted him to fit into established roles associated with black men. The dread that might have been engendered by a virile 25-year-old African American who commanded the fantasies of countless young women of every ethnic background didn't apply to Jackson. He was, to use Jan Nedeerven Pieterse's evocative term, a symbolic eunuch. Actually, Ellen T. Harris compares Jackson to an actual eunuch—Carol Broschi, aka Farinelli (1705–82), the eighteenth-century *castrato* singer, who was also "idolized."

We can't be sure which, if any, of these arguments adequately accounts for Jackson's staggering popularity in the early 1980s, or whether it needs explanation at all. Maybe he was just an entertainer par excellence and his work was simply enjoyed by an enormous amount of people. His racial and sexual propensities might have been irrelevant. Maybe. But unlikely. There had never been a black person so admired, venerated, perhaps even glorified. Even Muhammad Ali, a universally popular athlete, who transcended sports in the late twentieth century, was far, far less likeable in 1963–4, when he converted to the Nation of Islam, befriended Malcolm X, and preached racial separatism. Twenty years later, there was still enough racist sentiment around to ensure a black performer would *not* attract widespread acclaim and affection if he or she betrayed immodesty or self-importance, advocated radical social and political reform, or conducted their private lives in a way that upset whites.

Several black leaders grew to prominence only when they were candidates for symbolic neutering. Even Martin Luther King, perhaps the most lauded African American of the twentieth century, became more popular, immeasurably more popular, after his untimely death in 1968. There's a weird kind of potency in becoming more admired, appreciated, and respected as actual potency declines.

Jackson was, in no way, reflective of the mood of the 1980s when the then emergent hip-hop expressed an anger previously unheard from black musicians. There was more fury in 1984 when Bernard Goetz shot and seriously wounded four black teenagers on a New York City subway car, a case documented in Chapter 8. The attempts by the Reagan administration to rein back affirmative action and welfare programs, while not always successful, had the effect of polarizing black-and white America. A different entertainer might have used his or her status as a weapon in culture wars, issuing statements on racism, bigotry, and xenophobia. Jackson represented a detachment from the mood, a young black man who looked like he might hold political views but was, in reality, a complete innocent.

Even in his teens, it was easy to imagine he was a child, a gifted child, confirmation perhaps that blacks were naturally compensated for their lack of achievements in education, commerce, and politics. In manhood, Jackson was even more comforting: an African American who had risen to the top on merit. Not all blacks, he seemed to be saying, were preoccupied with racism and the obstacles it strewed in their paths. Some were interested only in progress as individual people, not as members of a group that claimed a special status.

The importance of this was clear: he was silently making a statement about America's ability to accommodate black progress; about the possibilities awaiting black people with talent and determination enough to make it to the top; about the disappearance of the age-old American Dilemma. He was a black man who could almost make you forget he was black. You could almost forget he was a man. From this different perspective, he validated whiteness by seeming to try to erase his own blackness.

Celebrity status can be a dangerous thing: it can flatter its bearer with delusions of infallibity. Had Jackson heeded Don King's warning (the one I wrote of in Chapter 14), he would have realized that his status was granted by a culture dominated by white people with white values. As such, his acceptance was destined to be conditional. Here was a boy, a cornucopia of natural talent, who developed and expanded that talent in manhood. His dancing could fascinate people, his singing could enchant them. He didn't talk politics and his comments about the condition of black people were so fluffy as to be meaningless. Christopher Andersen believes his fans—and, by implication, all of us—played their parts in "infantilizing" Jackson: "We were happy as long as he played Peter Pan and never grew up."

At a time when America was almost embarrassed by its seemingly neverending racial problems, it was comforting to know that blacks, however humble their origins, could soar to the top. Even more comforting to know that, however high they soared, they still wanted to be white, if indeed that's what Jackson wanted.

*   *   *

A review in the *New York Times*, of July 9, 1984, was headlined: PSYCHOLOGISTS EXAMINE APPEAL OF MICHAEL JACKSON. It wasn't the kind of analysis anyone would consider today: Would it require psychologists to figure out why the likes of Ariana Grande or Billie Eilish draw praise and sell out concerts? It wasn't as if Jackson had just sprung onto the scene: he'd released his first solo album twelve years before and was an established presence in pop music. "Admittedly, he's a talented performer, and his popularity undoubtedly stems from his abilities as a singer, songwriter, dancer and performer," the *Times* recognized. But there was more to the "adulation for Michael Jackson." There was something about the image he projected that was unclear; it was "highly unusual and goes against many earlier rock-star stereotypes," as journalist Daniel Goleman put it.

The premise of the examination was that it was the "very unconventionality" of Jackson's persona—his public image—that endeared him to contemporary audiences, especially the young. This was 1984, remember. Jackson was compared to David Bowie (1947–2016) and Boy George, both of whom wore clothes that, at the time, could be described as androgynous. Then again, so did many, many other artists. And makeup worn by men was by no means unusual. Jackson had, in Goleman's view, a "sexually ambiguous appearance and voice," but this was hardly sufficient reason for his global popularity. Perhaps, it was his lifestyle: then twenty-five, Jackson lived with his family "as a virtual recluse," never touched alcohol or drugs, avoided red meat, and "is a virgin." Red meat apart—both Grande and Eilish are vegans—this sounds about as un-rock 'n' roll as you can get. There was more: Jackson spent his spare time watching cartoons or having imagined conversations with mannequins. This last part would almost definitely be regarded as symptomatic of psychosis today.

"Michael Jackson embodies that innocent lost boy whose life is unfettered, full of style and beauty without the grit of reality," affirmed James Hillman, a psychologist of the Jungian persuasion. Although he didn't spell it out, Hillman presumably meant Jackson offered an archetype, which is a primitive mental image inherited from our earliest human ancestors and supposed to be present in a "collective unconscious" common to all humankind (if Carl Jung is to be believed).

Goleman collected the opinion of psychiatrist Robert Gould, who believed Jackson's shyness and inarticulacy brought out protective feelings in audience. "He's almost like a pet you want to adopt," Gould conjectured, citing his "sweet innocence." Again, I remind readers: this was 1984.

Another psychological wisdom was that Jackson's "ambiguous sexuality" was attractive to young girls (thirteen and under) who were threatened by the traditional macho rock star, and to young boys who found it hard to give up the possibility of being both sexes. This sexual ambivalence "goes underground" when the young person moves through puberty. By underground, I presume the clinical psychologist advancing this theory meant unconsciously diverting or modifying the impulse in a culturally acceptable form, what Freudians call sublimation. Once more, Jackson is thought to embody something, this time, "someone who seems to live out that ambisexual fantasy." Ambisexual is not a term we hear much today, but seems to be the synonymous with the more familiar bisexual, or maybe pansexual.

Another psychologist climbed aboard, carrying another fantasy Jackson supposedly—let me avoid embodied, this time—gave visible expression: perennial youthfulness. Jackson evaded adult responsibilities, according to David Guttman, a professor of psychiatry. This is not, as most would assume, a poser most of us face as we approach the annoying complications of life, like cooking, rent money, and ironing clothes.

Guttman argued that Jackson was someone who had resisted growing up and refused adult responsibilities. His ability to do this was, if not unique, specific to child stars who matured in the protective custody of their family and close confidantes. But that mattered less than his flamboyant everlasting youth. This was something young people in the 1980s desired; Jackson seemed to have it. In the years that followed, this became a clichéd explanation, or excuse—depending on perspective—for Jackson's fluctuating behavior.

There were more teenagers in the United States than ever and the pop music demographic was getting younger. Although the *New York Times* analysis didn't cover this, it might have pointed out that, in the space of thirty years, teenagers went from being a postwar generation of rebellious misfits to a valuable consumer segment: market neophytes, always ready to embrace new music, new fashions, and new technology (the Sony Walkman went on sale in 1979, for instance). It was a time when youth was not just lived through, but enjoyed, celebrated, and even glorified. Instead of the traditional right of passage on the way to responsible adulthood, youth was a state to relish. Jackson held out a kind of promise that, even five years off his thirtieth year, he could still act and perhaps think like a young person. As Jackson himself acknowledged, "I totally identify with Peter Pan, the lost boy of never-neverland."

Psychologists must sometimes shrink with embarrassment at what colleagues of an earlier vintage propounded. Suggesting, as Guttman did, that Jackson was an "antidote to excessive violence" seems implausible now. "With all the violence kids are subject to these days, Jackson's sweet and pure appeal speaks to an inner need." Our understanding of violence has expanded since the mid-1980s and we recognize it as any exercise of destructive or unpleasant force, not only physical force, as it would have once been understood.

In 1984, Jackson was not the threatening presence he became in the eyes of many. He did, however, pique curiosity. A different and, in many ways, challenging character, who projected an unusual persona, he had some journalists, psychologists, probably a few sociologists, and even semiologists (they study signs and symbols) scratching their heads. But should he have? After all, consider his companions in pop's A-list: George Michael, who was gay (he died in 2016), Elton John, also gay, and Prince, like the aforementioned Bowie, an androgynous character. Did Jackson deserve such a special analysis—and a psychologists' analysis too.

It's at least possible that the sources of Jackson's unrivaled popularity at that stage lay not in his invisible traits, predilections, or "embodiments" but in the more obvious fact that he was an accomplished artist who merged song and dance to create something wondrous and delivered records that are still woven into popular culture today. The point is this: even in the mid-1980s, Jackson was attracting the kind of attention that had never been afforded pop stars. No one would have considered pulling together experts to fathom out the appeal of Sting, Tina Turner, or Lionel Richie on a psychological level. It would be unthinkable. Jackson was a special case.

There is arguably a more final, yet obvious question: Were the conclusions of Goleman's analysis right? It was interesting when Jackson's friend Jane Fonda told the *New York Times'* writer, "Michael reminds me of the walking wounded. He's an extremely fragile person." Fragile? It doesn't chime with the professional toughness he showed when he upended Paul McCartney's chances of reclaiming the rights to his own music. If McCartney is to be believed, there was nothing delicate or vulnerable about him. Jackson was an ambitious and fundamentally decent artist who had to prove that he could be hard-nosed, perhaps even unfriendly, in order to get what he wanted. There was a cold, calculating quality about the way he pursued his business goals. You might say, "He was as Machiavellian as they come." Quincy Jones actually did say this in an interview for the New York magazine *Vulture*.

Talking to David Marchese, Jones, who collaborated with Jackson on three albums, offered an account that seemed to refer to a different person to the one who occupied the psychologists' (and Fonda's) analytical frames. "Michael stole a lot of stuff," claimed Jones. He meant songs written by others. For example, "State of Independence," a hit for Donna Summer in 1982, was written by Vangelis and Jon Anderson, and produced by Jones. Jackson worked on backing vocals. The song's central riff resembled the famous bass introduction of "Billie Jean," according to Jones.

Nor was this the only song from which Jackson had appropriated sections, said Jones, who concluded that Jackson was "greedy." His was an acerbic portrait of Jackson and one that revealed a bitterness that had roots in a dispute thirty years before, as we will discover in the next chapter. Even without testing Jones's impugnments, it seems obvious that there was probably enough "grit" in Jackson's reality to equip him for a lifetime in the rough-and-tumble of the entertainment industry. The psychologists' depiction of him as weak and ill-protected probably owed more to the public image he skillfully created and maintained.

*   *   *

Paul McCartney was discussing Michael Jackson with David Letterman on Letterman's CBS show in 1985. "He [MJ] was talking to me and asking my business advice and one of the things I said to him was, 'Think about getting into music publishing.' And he looked at me—and I thought he was joking—and he said, 'I'm gonna get yours' . . . and it turned out to be true." Later, McCartney and Jackson "drifted apart," as he put it, appearing to play down the stories of his displeasure that circulated after Jackson bought ATV Music in October 1985. It was thought McCartney, having given Jackson what he considered valuable advice and scoffed at Jackson's suggestion that he'd buy the rights to McCartney's own songs (and his collaborations with John Lennon), was furious when he learned Jackson had outbid him for the publishing company that held the rights to the Beatles' music.

Jackson and McCartney became friends in the early 1980s. After the killing of John Lennon in 1980, McCartney worked very briefly with George Harrison, but preferred to concentrate his energies on Wings, the band featuring him, his wife Linda and Denny Laine, before continuing as a solo artist (his first solo album was actually released in 1970, his second ten years later). Wings had recorded a track called "Girlfriend" for a 1978 album and Jackson made a cover for his *Off the Wall* album the following year. It was released as a single in the UK. So began a productive collaboration and what seemed a friendship. Between 1981 and 1983, Jackson and McCartney wrote songs, made videos, and recorded both singles and album tracks. McCartney had previously collaborated and made records with Stevie Wonder and Carl Perkins in separate projects in 1982.

"The Girl Is Mine" was McCartney's first joint-effort with Jackson. Written by Jackson and produced by Quincy Jones, the track appeared on *Thriller*, listed as "The Girl Is Mine (with Paul McCartney)." It was also spun off as a single, selling 1.3 million copies by the end of 1985. The second release was "Say, Say, Say," this time credited to Michael Joseph Jackson and Paul James McCartney. This was recorded at the Abbey Road studios in London in 1981. Remember: it was almost compulsory to provide an accompanying video and Jackson and McCartney brought in American director Bob Giraldi to make a narrative about a couple of snake oil salesmen, slightly reminiscent of the Bob Hope/Bing Crosby *Road to . . .* movies. At $500,000, it was a prodigiously expensive video for the early 1980s.

The video was released in October 1983. It was probably during the shoot for the video (in California) that McCartney imparted the crucial piece of advice on publishing, though McCartney had mentioned it earlier when in England, according to Ray Coleman, author of *McCartney: Yesterday and Today*. It seems McCartney thought nothing more of it. But Jackson took the advice to heart and became acquisitive, asking John Branca to secure the publishing rights to, for example, Sly and the Family Stone's backcatalog and several 1960s singles.

While McCartney must have assumed Jackson was unworldly when it came to business, Jackson had in fact started his own publishing outfit in 1980. Mijac Music was his personal company, largely to catalog his own material. But, with Branca's prospecting, it developed into a formidable collection. Among its titles were: "Ain't No Stoppin' Us Now," "If You Don't

Know Me by Now," and "Shake, Rattle and Roll." A year after Jackson's death, *Billboard* estimated the value of Mijac to be $150 million, a sharp uptick in sales doubling annual revenues to $50 million.

Here we need a digression. "Love Me Do," the first Beatles single, had been released in the UK in 1963 and the band enjoyed unbroken success thereafter. Lennon and McCartney's compositions sold well, whoever recorded them, whether the Berlin Philharmonic Orchestra or Alvin and the Chipmunks (and they both recorded Lennon and McCartney compositions). Northern Music was set up by the Beatles' manager Brian Epstein and Dick James (a music publisher and singer, famed for singing the theme to the *Robin Hood* tv series), Lennon, and McCartney. As with any publishing company, it was responsible for making sure composers were properly rewarded when their music was used commercially, that is, on radio, on tv, in films, and in advertisements (and, nowadays, on ringtones and over the internet).

Epstein died in 1967 and within eighteen months, James sold his interest in the company to ATV Music Publishing, which was a subsidiary of Britain's ATV (Associated Television—a tv network). He was able to do so, even in defiance of Lennon and McCartney, because he controlled 51 percent of the company. In the deal, ATV acquired over 200 Lennon and McCartney compositions, including all the big Beatles numbers. So, ATV basically could dictate where and Lennon and McCartney's songs were used and for how much. This would have been irksome for Lennon and McCartney, who after the release of *Sgt. Pepper's Lonely Hearts Club Band* in 1967 were arguably the preeminent and most prolific composers of the time. They sold their stock in 1969, apparently for tax purposes.

ATV was integrated into an entertainment conglomerate known as Associated Communications Corporation, or ACC, which, after running into financial problems, put the publishing division on the market. In 1982, the company was acquired by an Australian entrepreneur, Robert Holmes à Court, who had several other media interests and who became known as Australia's first billionaire. He had the knack of buying at the right price and turning a profit. Having no sentimental ties to the Lennon and McCartney portfolio he waited for a favorable economic climate then put the company back on the market.

McCartney had recommended music publishing to Jackson for several reasons, the main one of which was that it was lucrative and required little effort. He probably explained to Jackson that the role of a music publisher is to maximize the royalties music earns from, for example, being played under advertisements, in film soundtracks, on television, or practically any other medium that reproduces the song. Live performances too: every time a number is performed, the composers are due a small amount, which, of course, multiplies as the song becomes more popular. Today, we'd use the verb "monetize" to describe what music publishing companies do to artists' work: they enable composers to earn revenue for years after they've finished writing and recording a song and they take responsibility for collecting that revenue.

McCartney had become a major music publisher himself by buying the rights to hundreds of songs and, according to the *Los Angeles Times* (August 15, 1985) earned more than $50 million a year from record and song royalties. Hence McCartney's advice and his implicit caution. When Holmes à Court was prepared to sell, McCartney missed out. His version of events is that he felt uncomfortable becoming the sole custodian of work that he'd only part-composed. As Lennon was dead, he approached Yoko Ono to determine whether she was interested in a joint venture. The figure $20 million was discussed, but, for undisclosed reasons both McCartney and Ono declined. A story in *Jet* (May 7, 1990) reported that McCartney suggested to Lennon's widow that they each "put up $10 million each to get back rights he and Lennon had signed away." Ono's reply was, "I think that's too high a price, I think we can get 'em for five."

Branca, meanwhile, was continuing to acquire publishing rights for Jackson: acting on Jackson's counsel, he bid a reported $46 million for ATV. Even without McCartney, there were several other bidders, including one who was prepared to go over $50 million. Branca was obliged to up Jackson's bid to $47.5 million with a promise of a quick closure on the deal. In 1984 alone, Jackson earned $91 million, according to *Forbes*; the *Thriller* album had sold 39 million copies by the completion of the deal. So, there were few doubts about whether he could afford the best part of $50 million. Asked how Jackson would finance the ATV acquisition, one source quoted by William Knoedelseder Jr, of the *Los Angeles Times* answered, "Out of pocket. It was probably one of the simplest financing deals in history." (For comparison, in 2021, Bruce Springsteen sold the master recordings and publishing rights for his life's work to Sony for $500 million (£376m), according to the *New York Post*, December 16, 2021.)

"I think it's dodgy to do something like that," McCartney reacted to Jackson's acquisition, appearing to contradict his later statements. "To be someone's friend and then, buy the rug they're standing on" is how he described Jackson's move. In Jackson's defense, he didn't deceive or double-cross McCartney—at least, as far as anyone knows. And it's difficult to imagine McCartney was unaware that Branca was deeply involved in the due diligence and other protocols that would have been part of such a deal, which took almost a year to complete. In 2020, McCartney was estimated to be worth £800 million by the *Sunday Times* newspaper. In the mid-1980s, he was no doubt well-off, but perhaps not rich enough to spend nearly $50 million on a music publishing company.

"You know what doesn't feel very good . . . is going on tour and paying to sing all my songs," McCartney groaned years later, in 2006. ABC News' Dan Harris quoted him: "Every time I sing 'Hey Jude,' I've got to pay someone." He would have to pay the publishers, in fact. Theoretically, every time someone sings "Happy Birthday to You" in a public place, they should pay the publishers (at least that was the way it was until 2015, when courts declared the song was in the public domain and invalidated copyright claims).

Harris reckons McCartney was still furious after two decades. Should he have been? As a co-composer, McCartney would continue to earn money from his compositions. But he had no control over the various uses to which they were put. This became evident two years after Jackson's acquisition when "Revolution," a track from the Beatles' 1968 untitled "White Album," appeared on an ad for Nike. The three surviving Beatles objected and became embroiled in a legal case. As we learned in Chapter 4, Jackson, in 1995, merged the business with Sony's publishing arm to form Sony/ATV. Sony assumed full control in 2016 with a $750 million deal. This brought to an end Sony's partnership with the Jackson estate. The deal didn't include Jackson's master recordings or Mijac Music, which still owned Jackson's own compositions.

So, as it stood in Fall 1985, Jackson controlled the copyrights to 40,000 songs, including 251 Beatles compositions and valuable material written by Little Richard, Pat Benatar, the Pretenders, and the Pointer Sisters, among many others. McCartney put on a brave face and, as if to prove his indifference to the deal, posed with Jackson in 1990. Fellow Beatle George Harrison was less inclined to smother his thoughts and, in 1995, told Angella Johnson of the *Guardian*, "every Beatles song is going to end up advertising bras and pork pies" and McCartney chimed in with a claim that the compositions had been "cheapened."

"All You Need Is Love" has been used in an ad for BlackBerry phones. "When I'm Sixty-Four" for an Allstate insurance tv commercial. Apple's iTunes advertising has featured "Let It Be." "Come Together" can be heard in Vodafone ads. There are other commercial applications of Lennon and McCartney compositions, which may have upset McCartney. But how about if Jackson had pulled out of the deal? His bidding rivals included Virgin Music and the Entertainment Company (both since integrated into other corporations). Would Virgin have behaved differently, for example? Would the company have been more judicious in its choice of advertising partners? Women's lingerie and traditional English baked goods have not been advertised to the sound of "Help!" or "The Long and Winding Road" (at least not to the knowledge of this writer).

Why shouldn't any pop song, or any kind of music for that matter, be used to advertise wares? Songwriters may not have had this purpose in mind when they created the art, but advertising gives topicality to a tune that has often been forgotten. So, it creates a kind of afterlife for a song. A rewarding afterlife too. Presumably, that was on McCartney's mind when he recommended the business to Jackson in the first place. If it was such a pain for songwriters to hear their music used to shift phones or insurance policies, why would McCartney have advised Jackson to get into it?

Eleven years after Jackson's death, a feeding frenzy for music publishing rights broke out: funds, record labels, and private equity buyers scrambling to invest in lucrative back catalogs that appreciated in value as streaming became one of the main methods of accessing music. Fleetwood Mac's "Dreams" was streamed 3.2 billion times on TikTok after a video featuring it went viral. The song was written by Stevie Nicks who sold a majority share in her catalog to US fund Primary Wave for between $80 million and $100 million. Even Neil Young, who had in his 1988 song "This Note's For You," mocked the likes of Jackson ("Ain't singin' for Pepsi/Ain't singin' for Coke . . . Makes me look like a joke") sold 50 percent of his catalog to Hipgnosis Songs Fund Limited, a UK investment firm, for an estimated $150 million (£110 million).

*   *   *

In 1983, no one, it seems, knew very much about Jackson. He was as graspable as quicksilver. Yet he'd been on the scene since 1969, when "I Want You Back" was released, so he was hardly a newcomer. Audiences and the media should have become used to him; but, again like quicksilver, he moved quickly and changed shape so often that he was impossible to contain long enough to study. He was young, slightly weird, spoke with a shrill voice, but there was something singular about his singing. Something singular about him too. At twenty-five, he was at the top.

At his age, Elvis had sold more records than anyone in history: 18,000,000. He made *G.I. Blues*, his fifth film. His "It's Now or Never" reached number one in the charts and was the best-selling single of the year 1960. From then on, his career went into gradual decline, necessitating his Comeback Special in 1968 (covered in Chapter 10). Sinatra, at twenty-five, joined the Tommy Dorsey band (in 1940) and was two years away from striking out as a solo artist. Elvis died in 1977, age forty-two; Sinatra in 1998, age eighty-two. Unlike them, Jackson, at twenty-five, was a veteran. So, it's surprising, given all the seemingly inscrutable aspects of him that were emerging, no one asked how close he was to burnout. Fourteen years in the public gaze, touring, making records, appearing on talk shows, responding to interviewers' questions, and doing all the other chores the world's most popular entertainer is obliged to do would surely take their toll. It can't all have been showbiz heaven, floating on clouds with the likes of Madonna and Tina Turner.

He clearly wanted to earn as much money as he could, but perhaps money didn't excite him as it does many other artists. In any case, he had more than enough for this and probably two or three other lifetimes. The adulation of the world would have been comforting, but, even so, Jackson often appeared weary of attention and exhausted by the love he was getting from practically everywhere in the world. The best guess is that Jackson found satisfaction in excellence alone. The best, but perhaps not the most accurate. Maybe it was wrongdoing that thrilled him. He'd reached a position from where he probably thought he could do as he wished, bend, stretch, and break rules with impunity. Smash them to pieces if he wished; and not have to explain. Nor even offer enough raw material for anybody to explain. Some entertainers and athletes have seemed to behave in a way that announces, "Explain this if you can. Bring in psychologists, psychiatrists and any other psychs and let them try to fathom me out."

Michael Jordan did it in 1993 when he claimed to be "exhausted" by basketball and, at the peak of his powers, signed with the Chicago White Sox baseball club before being assigned to the franchise's minor-league system. Lance Armstrong retired at the age of thirty-three after winning a record seven Tours de France. If he'd stayed that way, we would still regard him as one of the greatest pound-for-pound athletes of all time. Instead, he came back in 2009 after a three-year hiatus, finished third in the tour, and became involved in the greatest doping scandal of all time. Actors also act without rhyme nor reason: Why did Rob Lowe allow himself to be videoed having sex with two females, one of whom was sixteen? That was in 1988 and Lowe was able to rehabilitate his reputation. Martha Stewart was, in 2004, convicted of several fraud violations and served a prison sentence. *Forbes* rated her personal value at $420 million on the morning of her trial; $85 million as she left the courtroom. Inexplicable behavior is literally that: unable to be explained or accounted for, at least in conventional terms. Maybe we should consider the rewards it offers.

We all know transgressive behavior is exhilarating: What person has never broken a rule, violated a norm, or misbehaved and not felt an enlivening tremor? Even the most respectable, high-minded, and law-abiding among us has trespassed at some time or other, and felt agreeably buzzed. This may sound a preposterous theory without foundation. It's also untidily constructed and lacks supporting evidence. But it's at least as plausible as the various, more thoughtful, perceptive, and ingenious accounts that purported to explain either Jackson, his remarkably large record-buying audience or both. At this stage in his life, he started to take on a life of his own. "Didn't he always have a life of his own?" you ask. Yes, but there were always others who owned stock in it. They remained stockholders, but Jackson himself was prepared to outlive them.

This was the stage at which psychologists and other-ologists started to crease their brows as they stared at the Manchild in the Promised Land (to borrow Claude Brown's autobiographical phrase). Jackson was a mature infant adrift in a world where he could have everything but valued nothing. As I stated at the start of this chapter, in 1983, Michael Jackson was a puzzle. He still is.

What would the world be like if John Lennon hadn't met Paul McCartney? Or if Anni-Frid Lyngstad hadn't met Benny Andersson? Or if Michael Jackson hadn't met Quincy Jones? "I'm getting ready to do my first solo album," Jackson told Jones about his plans on the Epic label. Jones agreed to produce it and the result was Off the Wall.

19

The Wand

"Mr. Jones and Mr. Jackson had worked together for years, forging one of the most productive and profitable relationships in pop music," the *New York Times'* Colin Moynihan reported, "the two worked together on albums . . . that sold tens of millions of copies and catapulted Jackson—already famous from his days in the Jackson 5—into superstardom." "Mr. Jones" was Quincy Jones, friend, colleague, and, judging from the fruits of their collaboration, artistic catalyst for Mr. Jackson. And yet, years after Jackson's death, Jones found himself in court, head to head with the Jackson family.

In 2013, Jones claimed Sony Music Entertainment and Jackson's estate owed him close to $30 million in royalties for edits and remixes of music he produced with Jackson. Four years later, in 2017, a jury in Los Angeles County Superior Court decided that Jones had not been sufficiently rewarded by the Jackson estate for the use of record Jones had produced and which were featured in the film *Michael Jackson's This Is It*, released in the year of Jackson's death, 2009. The court awarded him $9.4 million in 2017. Three years later, a California appellate court sliced this down to $2.5 million, this being the amount due to Jones for the use of his master recording and other fees. It seemed a bitter conclusion to a relationship that, in many ways, transformed Jackson and, while Jones maintained his dispute was not with Jackson himself, the attorney representing the Jackson estate was quoted by Martin Macias Jr., "Quincy Jones was the last person we thought would try to take advantage of Michael Jackson by filing a lawsuit three years after he died asking for tens of millions of dollars he wasn't entitled to."

Jones too seemed to turn vindictive. While he'd enjoyed an amicable relationship with Jackson over many years in the 1970s and 1980s, he later reflected, "He [Jackson] was as Machiavellian as they come." In a 2018 interview with David Marchese, for *Vulture* magazine, he declared, "Michael stole a lot of stuff," meaning his compositions incorporated passages from other people's music. The enmity—if that's what it was—and the legal case centered on two contracts Jackson and Jones signed in 1978 and 1985 and its origins go even further back to 1979.

* * *

Jones was a musician, producer, composer, and arranger whose work encompassed several genres of popular music, especially jazz. Born in Chicago in 1933, Jones was already hugely experienced in the music business when he first met Jackson. He had worked with the likes of Ray Charles, Count Basie, Dinah Washington—in fact, it was more meaningful to identify the artists he hadn't worked with in some capacity. For a while, he worked as an artists-and-repertoire (A&R) agent for Mercury Records and eventually became a vice-president of this label, one of the few African Americans to hold executive positions at major record companies.

Such was his reputation that he was often approached to write scores for feature films. These included *The Pawnbroker*, in 1964; *In The Heat of the Night*, in 1967; and *In Cold Blood*, also in 1967: all prestigious films. These were detours that gave him alternatives to the jazz he had pursued in early career. He wrote the theme music for the television series *Roots* in 1977. It was unusual for black composers to get commissioned to write scores. The actor Sidney Poitier (from *The Heat of the Night*) and director Sidney Lumet (*The Pawnbroker*) were instrumental. Jones once said of Poitier, a black actor, with firsthand experience of the film industry, "He handed me the wand for black composers." But it was Lumet who put him in touch with Michael Jackson.

Lumet was directing a film version of the Broadway musical *The Wiz*, based on the 1939 film *The Wizard of Oz*, with an all-black cast. Diana Ross played Dorothy, originally Judy Garland's role. Garland was seventeen when she played the girl whisked away by a tornado to the magical land of Oz. Ross was thirty-three. But she was buoyant after well-received acting parts in *Mahogany*, in 1975, and *Lady Sings the Blues* (1972) in which she played Billie Holiday, the ill-fated jazz singer, who succumbed to alcohol- and drug-related complications in 1959, age forty-four. Ross's transition from music to film was probably a natural kind of evolution for one of the world's best-known artists. She had been with the Motown label since 1960, and Motown owner Berry Gordy acquired the film rights to the stage show, his intention presumably being to showcase Ross.

Incidentally, *Lady Sings the Blues* was the film that inspired Lee Daniels to make *The United States vs. Billie Holiday* (2021), the director told Emanuel Levy, of the *Financial Times*. Daniel's experience of being rebuffed by several studios reminded him, "The studios are not interested in authentic black stories, they want tales that are easily palatable for white Americans." The observation obviously shaped his understanding of accomplishment in the entertainment industry. "It was white people who embraced her [Holiday] and pushed her into fame," observed Daniels.

From 1964, for about four years, Ross and her group the Supremes rivaled the Beatles for radio and chart ubiquity. Founder member Florence Ballard was fired in 1967 after substance abuse rendered her unreliable. The group's name was changed to Diana Ross and the Supremes. Ross started to record as a solo artist the following year. She made her exit after a stage-managed farewell show at Las Vegas' Frontier Hotel in January 1970. Her replacement, Jean Terrell (sister of heavyweight boxer Ernie Terrell, who fought Muhammad Ali in 1967), helped maintain the group's momentum for a few years, but there were many personnel changes and the band split for good in 1977, by which time Ross was building her reputation as an actor and preparing for *The Wiz*.

If the film looked like a vehicle for Ross, it was because that's effectively what it was. Motown was, with Universal Pictures, a co-producer of the movie and Ross was, with Stevie Wonder, the company's best-known artist. But John Badham, who was initially approached to direct the film, wasn't impressed and considered her too old for the role of Dorothy. Badham was coming off a spectacular success with *Saturday Night Fever* and could probably pick-and-choose his films. He decided to move on, leaving Lumet to take over. But he too must have wondered how much control he would have when Ross suggested to him that Jackson had expressed interest in the film. Ross had known Jackson for several years. Were Motown boss Berry Gordy a man who thrived on schadenfreude, he could have taken pleasure from intervening, rejecting Jackson and casting Jimmie Walker as the Scarecrow. Walker had become popular, appearing as "JJ" in the CBS tv series *Good Times*. Lumet was known to favor him as the Scarecrow.

In the late 1970s, Jackson was a known commodity, but far from being the world-renowned figure he became. He'd released four solo albums, none of which foreshadowed his later work. Unlike Walker, he had no acting experience. So, casting him in a key role made the film look even more of a vehicle than it already was. Lumet's arm was twisted by Universal Picture's executive producer Rob Cohen and Jackson got the part.

Meanwhile, the Jacksons were still an act based in California. The shooting for *The Wiz* was scheduled for the Astoria Studios in Queens, New York. So, Michael furloughed. He was approaching his twentieth birthday and still best known as the child prodigy who fronted the Jacksons. Asked later whether being separated from his brothers "hurt," he answered, "No . . . it's wonderful, I feel as if I'm accomplishing what I'm supposed to do." In a 1980 interview included in Spike Lee's documentary *Michael Jackson's Journey from Motown to Off the Wall*, he explained that his brothers understood why he was striking out as a solo artist. Joe Jackson was unnerved by the prospect of Michael's departure from the band—which would have left the Jacksons rather like the Supremes after Ross had gone. But he was mollified by a $100,000 fee.

In New York, Jackson became an enthusiastic visitor to Studio 54 and, perhaps surprisingly for a Jehovah's Witness, celebrated his twenty-first birthday at the Manhattan club. Between 1977 and 1980, the place was a hive for celebrities, cocaine, and disco music. Here, Jackson would have heard the likes of Chic, Sylvester, and Sister Sledge. The Jacksons' music was typically melodic and soul-influenced but lacked the throbbing bass beat characteristic of disco and, while often funky, the Jacksons' material wasn't intended primarily as dance music. Disco was. Whether it made much impact or not, we'll never know, but Jackson would probably have witnessed men dancing with each other at Studio 54; in New York, men weren't allowed to dance together till 1971. Like other disco clubs, Studio 54 offered a temporary escapism particularly for gay men, who felt excluded by mainstream entertainment.

Now comes the puzzling part of the tale. Jackson was, at the time, contemplating, a new solo album and his label Epic was part of the CBS organization. As was Philadelphia International Records (PIR), a label started in 1971 by Kenny Gamble and Leon Huff. CBS provided $75,000 startup for the label. Gamble and Huff wrote, played, and produced a series of records that were known collectively as the Sound of Philadelphia. It was crisp, cosmopolitan music for a new audience, and a new age when many black Americans no longer felt doomed and were looking forward rather than to the segregated past of their forebears. The O'Jays, Patti LaBelle, Teddy Pendergrass, and Harold Melvin & the Blue Notes were among the artists who benefited from Gamble and Huff; they were all suave, urbane, and slickly confident acts that thrummed bourgeois sophistication.

PIR was a notoriously tough environment: there was competition between artists, and, sometimes, whole albums were recorded in one exhausting sixteen-hour day. But the results were prodigious. Gamble and Huff built up Philadelphia International into one of the five biggest black-owned companies in America. So, if Jackson was looking for producers for the new album he was planning, he could have done a lot worse than approaching two people who had their fingers perfectly on the pulse of the time. And yet he turned to Jones, a man of distinguished credentials, but with no experience at all in pop music.

*   *   *

What would have happened if John Lennon hadn't met Paul McCartney at the Woolton Parish Church Garden Fete, Liverpool, in 1957, or if McCartney hadn't liked the sound of Lennon and his band the Quarrymen when they played? Or if Martin Scorsese hadn't been introduced by director Brian De Palma to his friend Robert De Niro in 1973? Or if Anni-Frid Lyngstad hadn't, in 1969, sang at Sweden's Melodifestival where she met Benny

Andersson and started a collaboration that would lead, within three years, to the formation of ABBA. No one can say, but there seemed a divine providence at play in all those rendezvous; as there was when Jackson met Jones.

Lumet was an old friend of Jones and wanted him to provide orchestral gravitas for *The Wiz*'s soundtrack. Jones wasn't impressed by the musical, but apparently felt he owed Lumet a favor or two. He and Jackson didn't know each other before the film, but struck up a serviceable working relationship. Jones later told *The Hollywood Reporter*'s Seth Abramovitch that he remembered Jackson approached him with a task. "I need you to help me find a producer. I'm getting ready to do my first solo album."

They discussed the possibility of renewing that relationship again on the projected solo album for which Jackson had already written three songs. Jones became curious about how Jackson was able to write songs without a musical instrument. According to Steve Knopper, of *Time*, the conversation went something like: "I hear something in my head. I make the sounds with my mouth." On hearing this Jones grew interested. "There's an instrument that can make the sounds you want. I can write anything down on paper," Jones replied. "If you can hear it, I can write it down." We'll never know whether Jackson's career would have soared and crackled like a rocket or merely hissed like a squib had Jones not been intrigued and agreed to work on the mooted album.

All the same, inviting Jones to take the weighty role of producer carried some risk. Like any other entertainer, Jackson must have been aware of audience expectations: they must have been sharpened to a point by the Philadelphia Sound and the *Saturday Night Fever*'d disco that captivated everyone in the mid-1970s. The sweet-sounding Jacksons were perfect for the late 1960s and early 1970s, but against a background of, say, Sylvester's thumping synth on "You Make Me Feel (Mighty Real)" or Chic's twanging bass lines on "Dance, Dance (Yowsah, Yowsah, Yowsah)," they might have sounded rinky-dink. The last thing Jackson wanted at this pivotal stage in his professional life was to sound old-fashioned. So, Jones, for all his mastery, wasn't an obvious choice. He was forty-five in 1978. Five years earlier, he had produced Aretha Franklin's "Hey Now Hey (The Other Side of the Sky)," which lacked Franklin's gutsy blues quality and hadn't overly impressed critics or consumers. His own double-album *I Heard That!* had been released in 1976 but without much impact.

Somehow, Jackson became convinced Jones could provide him with the kind of makeover he wanted. Perhaps it was a compelling incongruity: like casting Charlize Theron as prostitute-cum-serial killer Aileen Wuornos in Patty Jenkins's 2003 film *Monster*. It looked so odd, it might just work. Known for her glamor, Theron gained weight, wore false teeth, and transformed herself into a believable Wuornos. Jones seemed such an unusual producer for Jackson's project, it too might yield something surprising.

Once the two men had agreed in principle on the musical framework, there was the matter of contracts. In addition to the usual producers' fee, Jones was entitled to a share of net receipts from a "videoshow" of the songs. This was the 1970s, remember: when music videos were hitting their stride and practically every record had a short companion movie. A feature film, it was later argued, was not encompassed in the meaning of "videoshow." This became relevant years with the release of Kenny Ortega's film *Michael Jackson's This Is It*, a documentary feature based on rehearsal footage shot while Jackson was preparing for his proposed comeback in 2009. Songs originally produced by Jones were included in the film's soundtrack album. Jones filed suit against the Jackson estate, claiming, as *Rolling Stone's* Miriam Coleman summarized it, "under the contracts, he should have been given the first opportunity to re-edit or re-mix any of the master recordings and that he was entitled to producer credit for the master recordings, as well as additional compensation if the masters were remixed." Obviously, no one could have foreseen how such an opulently smooth album could lead to legal convulsions decades later.

The recording sessions for the album took place between December 1978 and June 1979 at Allen Zentz Recording, Westlake Recording Studios, and Cherokee Studios in Los Angeles. Neither Jackson nor Jones discussed the dynamics of what became a prolific partnership. But George Benson, once a guitar prodigy who grew to prominence with his distinctive style of soul-infused jazz, once reflected on his own particular relationship with Jones. Benson was for years discouraged from singing by his record company. Jones produced his breakthrough album *Give Me the Night* (1980) and issued contradictory advice. "Quincy Jones looked at me and said: 'I know you better than you know yourself.' This made me feel angry, though I didn't say anything. But he was pushing me to do things that didn't come naturally to me," Benson told the *Financial Times'* David Cheal. "He was always pushing me to do things. He persuaded me to sing in a way that didn't feel comfortable." Once outside his comfort zone, Benson sang in the unnatural way Jones suggested and the process yielded a record. "And it was a smash." The album won Benson three Grammys in 1981. Jackson never said Jones has pushed him in the way Benson described, though the product of the collaboration suggests Jackson might also have been displaced from his comfort zone—with similarly agreeable results.

Those results were well received. *Rolling Stone's* Stephen Holden called *Off the Wall*, "A slick, sophisticated R&B-pop showcase with a definite disco slant . . . A triumph for producer Quincy Jones as well as for Michael Jackson." There was disagreement over Jackson's voice. For example, Jim Miller, in *New Republic*, discerned that, "Jackson's voice has deepened without losing its boyish energy. He phrases with delicacy, sings ballads with a feather touch." But Dennis Hunt, of the *Los Angeles Times,* thought, "The adolescent frailties that linger in Jackson's voice are nagging enough to, if uncontrolled, undermine good material and production" (in his review of October 14). In the end though, "Thanks to producer Quincy Jones, that didn't happen here. The result is one of the year's best R&B albums." Presciently, Hunt wondered, "Is it possible that he's outgrown the Jacksons?"

"Jones . . . added a classy veneer of elegance to the singer's nervous new style," reported *Newsweek* staff in a review headlined "Michael Jackson: The Peter Pan of Pop," in the January 9, 1983, issue. Barney Hoskyns described the album glowingly, if indecorously, as "a triumph of studio-crafted miscegenation . . . the first real mass-audience black/white album." Miscegenation refers to the interbreeding of people considered to be of different racial types, so employing it in the 1980s was anachronistic and incongruous.

Between them Jackson and Jones captured the audacity of a notionally prosperous, upwardly mobile African American population. They were willing to take risks, avoiding a disco saturation, but absorbing enough of the euphoria that animated dancefloors around the world. They added lush arrangements that might, with another artist, have sounded too traditional, or, worse, clichéd. Here, they sounded clever and sophisticated. Even the cover art radiated impudence: 21-year-old Jackson was wearing black tie, tuxedo, and loafers. He seemed to be searching for something. His right to be free from his brothers? Or family, perhaps? Or more likely, self-validation: with Jones, he seemed to discover a license to be a full-fledged independent artist. Sure, he had released four solo albums before; but none came close to *Off the Wall* in terms of artistry and imagination—and maybe irony: the expression "off the wall" meant unusual, bizarre, oddball, or strange and the chorus of the title song was, "Life ain't so bad at all if you live it off the wall."

Reviews for *The Wiz* bore no resemblance to the warm approval *Off the Wall* had drawn. *Time* magazine expressed the film critics' consensus in its headline "Nowhere over the Rainbow" (October 30, 1978). "What we see is not a fairy tale but a wounded budget projection creeping off to die," wrote John Skow in his review of *The Wiz*, which, while scathing, was well-measured. To attract funding for films, producers have to offer stars, bankable stars at that: names that will draw customers to the box office (this was the 1970s). So, argued Skow, a beautiful, young black girl who can sing would be a logical choice for the lead role.

But film industry logic is different: Diana Ross, at thirty-four, was a known star, with a background in the Supremes, then as a garlanded career as solo artist, both in music and in a couple of movies. The problem, Skow pointed out, was that the film script called for shy 24-year-old schoolteacher from Harlem. Skow could also have added that, with an all-black cast, even one that included Eddie Murphy as a co-star, the film was still not assured an audience. True, there had been predominantly black films that had been successful. Gordon Parks's *Shaft*, for example, cost only a million dollars to make but recouped that ten times over after its release in 1971. Even so, *The Wiz*, with a budget of about $24 million had work to do. It earned only £21 million. It also effectively ended Ross's film career: she had a couple of television movie roles but focused on singing after the chastening experience.

Not that it was that chastening for Jackson. *Variety* concluded, "Michael Jackson, though vocally great, needs more acting exposure." He never got much (*Captain EO* in 1986 and brief appearances in Barry Sonnenfeld's *Men in Black II* in 2002, and a 2004 tv movie by Bryan Michael Stoller, *Miss Castaway and the Island Girls*). "Michael Jackson fills the [Scarecrow] role with humor and warmth," decreed the *Chicago Sun-Times*. The comments were lukewarm, but, in the context of a damned venture, they did Jackson no harm. From Jackson's perspective, the poor reviews for *The Wiz*, which was released in October 1978, were overwhelmed by the praise heaped on *Off the Wall*, released ten months later.

In the interim, the Jacksons released *Destiny*, a studio album they had jointly produced. They had also written all but one of the tracks, the exception being the best-known tune, "Blame It On the Boogie," which was written (slightly confusingly) by British composer Michael Jackson, who recorded his own version under the name Mick Jackson (not to be confused with the Brit film director of the same name, who made Whitney Houston's *The Bodyguard*). The single was released ahead of the *Destiny* album and its modest success provided a glimpse into the status of Jackson and his brothers at that stage. It reached fifty-four in the *Billboard* charts, meaning it was the band's first entry in the top 100 in 5 strikes.

A crisis? Perhaps not quite: its sales disguised its popularity in the discos, where it became something of a staple. As did another tune from the album, "Shake Your Body (Down to the Ground)," which, according to *Rolling Stone*, "presaged Michael Jackson's disco reinvention a year later on his *Off the Wall* solo album" (January 29, 2021). The album was remixed, augmented with bonus tracks, and re-released in 2021.

The band's tour to promote the album (this was when tours were not meant to be money-turners, but vehicles to stimulate album sales) was a year-long trek across Africa, North America, and Europe. There was a four-month intermission to allow Michael to complete *Off the Wall*. After the resumption, extra numbers from the album were added to the stage act. There is no doubt the purpose and rationale of the tour was to sell albums, but not just to African Americans. "It wouldn't be bad at all if The Jacksons are able to also come up with products that will achieve 'crossover' appeal to legions of White record buyers," wrote Charles L. Sanders, of *Ebony*, during the tour.

Sanders went on, "'Almost every day we're working on new things,' says Tito; Michael adds: 'All of us think we've got whatever's necessary to appeal to everybody'." It was an acknowledgment, though of what? "Whatever's necessary to appeal to everybody": clearly the music didn't need repurposing for new audiences. *Destiny* was selling respectably, and *Off the Wall* was set to become Jackson's most commercially successful record to date. So, what did Jackson mean?

* * *

Some entertainers don't care if audiences don't like them. In fact, some base their popularity on being disliked. That isn't an oxymoron. People can be popular because rather than in spite of not being liked. Are people fond of Gwyneth Paltrow? Justin Bieber? The Kardashians? Do they care? Jackson probably became more indifferent as he grew older, but, at twenty, he desperately wanted to be liked. In the late 1970s, he and his brothers were making a spirited attempt to crack the mainstream, white market. Their secret weapon was avoiding popular expectations: they were flashy dressers and could sing and dance with the best; but there was never going to be a hint of the kind of scandal that would invite audiences to scream, "There, I told you so! They're just like all those other blacks: take them out of the ghetto, but you can't take the ghetto out of them."

Black entertainers' reputation for notoriety was well established, demonstrated by the alcohol- or drug-induced deaths of Billie Holiday (in 1959), Dinah Washington (1963), Frankie Lymon (1968) and Jimi Hendrix (1970). Drink, drugs and miscellaneous debauchery were off-limits for the God-fearing Jehovah's Witnesses. "We may be blacks, but we're good blacks," the Jacksons seemed to be saying, as if inviting a stress test of received wisdom. As we now know, part of that received wisdom survived. No one contemplated it at the time, but could Jackson have arrived at the conclusion, perverse as it was, that acceptance by white audiences would be easier if he looked less black. Perhaps that's what he meant by "whatever's necessary."

Shortly after the release of *Off the Wall*, Jackson fell while dancing, hurting and possibly breaking his nose. It was "an accident that would change him forever," according to an ABC News team led by Jon Meyersohn. It's widely accepted he had a surgical procedure on his nose, though whether it was exclusively for medical purposes is not certain. Several years later in 2002, Jackson told Martin Bashir, "I've had no plastic surgery on my face . . . just my nose. It helped me breathe better so I can hit higher notes." This is plausible, though the shape of his nose changed quite significantly in the years following the accident, giving rise to suspicions that he was deliberately trying to alter his physical appearance.

Some speculated he was trying to resemble Diana Ross; others thought he might be trying to look like Elizabeth Taylor. There were other theories about Jackson's puzzling changes in appearance. Among them was that of Margot Jefferson, who told ABC News team, "he was obsessed with staying timeless . . . he wanted to look like some, you know, being who has gone into some eternal realm of fame . . . beyond life and death." Pamela Lipkin, a surgeon, offered the same team of journalists another possibility: Jackson developed an addiction. "It means that no matter how much surgery you have, you're still not happy with the way you look." Some pontificators believed he had a psychiatric condition; his was a "classic case of body dysmorphic disorder," according to Dr. Anthony Youn, speaking to CBS News in 2011. If it was, it went undiagnosed.

What's certain is that, after the reparative work on his nose, Jackson's visage underwent something of a transmogrification—in other words, an almost magical transformation. In fact, his physical appearance seemed to be in perpetual motion for the rest of his life. Joan Kron, of *Allure* the beauty magazine, analyzed the changes year by year, noticing how the size and shape of Jackson's nose changed. His nostrils narrowed noticeably, the ridge, protrusion, and tip changed so that it turned snubby. She also traced the blanching of Jackson's facial skin, which may have started in January 1984 when he was treated for burns following the accident when recording the Pepsi advertisement. Steve Hoefflin, a plastic surgeon whose clients included Joan Rivers and Ivana Trump, tended to Jackson on this occasion. Jackson returned to him over the years. Asked in 2001 about his work for Jackson, Hoefflin told Michael Shelden, of Britain's *The Telegraph*, "In the case of high-level entertainers, the result may not be what the average person would want. But remember, these are performers who want to create a certain image for a special reason."

With some artists, the phrase "whatever's necessary" might include cosmetic surgery to augment or reduce areas of the body and, historically, the likes of Marilyn Monroe and Elvis Presley were known to have undergone procedures before "work" became commonplace in the entertainment industry. Nips and tucks were and are still parts of many celebrities' maintenance checks. Yet Jackson's project, or challenge, seemed slightly different: he did seem to have "a special reason," as Hoefflin called it, without spelling it out. It appeared to go beyond vanity: Jackson was average height (5 foot 9 inches), slim, and handsome, with no obvious disfigurements. Unless, of course, he regarded the color of his skin an undesirable visible characteristic.

If so, the changes would be signs of an attempt to escape his blackness, or as philosophy professor Darryl Scriven described it, "Michael's flight into synthetic white-skinned privilege." Scriven doesn't necessarily believe this was Jackson's project; his preferred interpretation is that, "Michael used his body and personal life as canvases on which to paint a mural of inclusion that transcended race and gender while teaching his audience to embrace his behavior as a paradigm shift." A paradigm shift usually refers to a profound change in worldview, or fundamental assumptions about life.

If so, Jackson's efforts would be commendable and ambitious, outlandish even. What many interpreted as an escape attempt may have been a munificent, even selfless attempt to become more than a symbol: an embodiment of cultural inclusion. Scriven's faith in Jackson's liberal progressivism might be misplaced, however.

After all, in 1993, Jackson informed Oprah Winfrey and a television audience that the changes in his skin color were occasioned by a disease called vitiligo. "I have a skin disorder that destroys the pigmentation of the skin," said Jackson. After his death, an autopsy revealed that Jackson did have the skin disorder. This doesn't altogether negate the paradigm shift argument: Jackson could have had the skin condition and also used various products, like glutathione, to lighten the skin's appearance. Whether he did or not is less relevant than what people thought.

* * *

Recall from Chapter 14, Don King's prescription, "What Michael's got to realize is that Michael's a nigga." King uttered these scalding but not unfriendly remarks in the 1980s when it was apparent that Jackson was undergoing a physical transformation. By then Jackson's facial features were unmistakably altered. But in 1979, it was possible to accept that the rhinoplasty—if indeed it was plastic surgery on the nose—was occasioned by a genuine accident. Hoefflin himself never verified this, though he is known to have continued to treat Jackson and tended to him after the burns injury in January 1984. Readers will call to mind that Jackson's hair caught fire during the filming of a Pepsi advertisement—an episode described in Chapter 14.

Off the Wall, the album that announced the arrival of Jackson as a mature 21-year-old artist, was released in 1979. Oprah was hosting a local talk show in Baltimore, Bill Cosby was fronting a Saturday morning cartoon show, Barack Obama was graduating from high school, and Stevie Wonder was reaching the end of a creative period that had established him as arguably the world's preeminent popular musician. Jackson, as much as any other prominent figure of the time, symbolized not just evident affluence and conspicuous consumption, but an extravagant, flamboyant prosperity. His lavish eccentricities, though not yet the stuff of legend they became, were about to surface, particularly in his appearance. He'd shown not only a willingness, but enthusiasm to submit to and operate within white parameters. His music could be heard, but he was also silently making a statement about America's ability to accommodate black progress; about the possibilities awaiting black people with talent and determination enough to make it to the top; and, as I pointed out in the previous chapter, about the disappearance of the American Dilemma.

Over the next decade or so practically every feature of Jackson's face changed so that he became unrecognizable from the *Off the Wall* album cover. And, at an age when most young men with money, status, and the pick of desirable partners might be inclined to pursue an intemperate lifestyle, Jackson was remarkably chaste. Even at twenty-one, he was set apart, though the events that emphasized Jackson's apartness were to follow.

"They sang and I was blown away," said Suzanne de Passe after hearing the Jackson brothers perform for the first time. Next morning she called her boss Berry Gordy and suggested he sign the brothers for Motown. "I don't want any kids," replied Gordy with scarcely a moment's thought. He changed his mind and changed history.

20

Old Soul in a Young Body

The Jackson 5 arrived in Detroit to audition for Motown Records in 1969. They sang "Who's Lovin' You," a Smokey Robinson composition. Motown boss Berry Gordy later reflected, "Michael sang it better than Smokey. It was just amazing. A 10-year-old kid!" He was, Gordy recalled, "a sponge." He meant that Jackson was forever asking questions, trying to learn about the music industry, often spending hours in the control room with sound engineers, absorbing their wisdom. "Even when he was auditioning, he was looking at me all the time. I told somebody this kid is weird; every time I look at him, he's watching me. We started calling him an old soul in a young body."

The original recording "Who's Lovin' You" by the Miracles was released in 1960. The Jackson 5's cover is on the 1969 album *Diana Ross Presents the Jackson 5*.

* * *

Gordy was one of eight siblings, all of whom were inculcated with the value of a strong family, hard work, and mutual benefit (more of which in a moment). But it was a lesson he picked up himself that was to stand him good stead for the rest of his life. As a boy in the 1940s, Gordy supplemented his pocket money with the earnings from a job vending the *Michigan Chronicle*, a weekly newspaper, which he sold on the streets of Detroit's east side. Soon, his entrepreneurial ambitions took hold. If the newspaper sold quite well in a relatively poor, mainly black neighborhood, it would probably sell even better in a more affluent area of the city where mostly whites lived. His initiative was immediately rewarded with higher sales and, hence, more money. Encouraged by his success, Gordy enlisted the help of one of his brothers to carry the bundles of newspapers and help him sell. But the results were quite different: sales plunged. Gordy learned a valuable lesson: "One black kid was cute; two were a threat to the neighborhood." (The story is recounted by Lisa Capretto in the *Huffington Post*.)

Gordy's imprint on pop history is as recognizable and as indelible as Jackson's. His creation was Motown, a record label, a sound and a cultural precedent. It wasn't the first label owned by an African American, specializing in music by black artists, but it was the first to avoid being assigned to that pernicious bracket black music. Why pernicious? Because, the instant the adjective black preceded not just music but also film, theater or art generally, it became less valuable—if only because it invited unfavorable comparisons with its equivalents in the mainstream. Not "white equivalents": the mainstream *was* white. It may sound a slight exaggeration to claim Motown changed everything in popular music. It may also be true. Some will say, the social changes of the 1960s would have impacted popular music anyway, with or without Motown.

History and geography sometimes collide to bring about particular types of music. For instance, in early-twentieth-century New Orleans, black musicians were not allowed to play with whites, so stuck with each other, bringing influences from Baptist church choirs, African-style percussion, Caribbean rhythms, and the brass and woodwind-driven marching music popular after the civil war (1861–5) to produce a form of improvisation once called "jas." The Beatles came from Liverpool, a port in the English northwest, where American vessels docked and sailors sold early rhythm 'n' blues records to local stores, ensuring a steady supply of raw material for bands to source and draw on for inspiration. The Mersey Sound didn't pop out of a vacuum. Memphis sits on the Mississippi River in southwest Tennessee, where strains of gospel and blues music could be heard in churches and less spiritually uplifting establishments respectively, and which eventually fused to form rock 'n' roll. About 150 miles from Memphis, Muscle Shoals, Alabama, collected the influences of rock and merged them with gospel-tinged vocals of people like Otis Redding and Aretha Franklin to produce what we now call soul. So, there is history, geography, and a sometimes divine providence to the development of music. Motown's music was no different.

The word "Motown" was a shortened version of Motortown, Detroit, being the crucible of America's automobile industry. Henry Ford's Model-T went into large-scale mass production in 1909. The Great Migration, in which about 6 million African Americans from the rural Southern states moved to the urban, industrialized Northeast and Midwest started in 1916. Gordy's parents moved from Milledgeville, Georgia, in 1922. His father bought a grocery store and ran other businesses in a thriving industrial city where there was no shortage of work and, hence, disposable income. About a million people moved to Detroit during the boom years. "The new residents brought their customs with them, including the rich, musical traditions passed down through generations in the South," wrote Brian McCollum for *USA Today* (February 9, 2021).

Berry Gordy's early work experience included a spell on the production line at the Mercury-Lincoln plant. Here he got a close-up view of how a series of workers and machines in a factory were able to work progressively in unison to produce a succession of identical items, in this case cars. Gordy was not only a quick learner but a lateral thinker: if a motor company could turn out products that looked good, worked well, and sold not just to niche but to mass markets around the world, why couldn't he apply similar principles of production and distribution to music and get comparable results? The Gordy family's mutual benefit system involved all members contributing to a money pot, which could be drawn on when the occasion demanded. One such occasion arrived when Berry decided he wanted to start a record label. He took $800 from the family fund.

Vivian and James Bracken, in the 1950s, started Vee-Jay records in Gary, Indiana, onetime home of the Jackson family. Their records catered mainly to the blues, gospel, and doo-wop markets (doo-wop referred to close harmony vocals). There were other labels specializing in music either played by or popular with African Americans, known as "race music"; the records were cataloged separately, reflecting the social segregation that legally divided the United States until 1964. After this, civil rights and race music seemed an incongruous juxtaposition.

Prominent race music labels included OKeh, based in New York, and the celebrated Chess label in Chicago, which issued records by Etta James, Willie Dixon, and Muddy Waters, among other notable artists. But Gordy's interest lay outside the "race music" market. He would resist making "black music for black people," and remind anybody who would listen of this time and again over the years. Gordy avoided direct associations with blues or jazz, both genres closely associated with black musicians. The then emergent rhythm 'n' blues of artists such as Chuck Berry and Bo Diddley, both on the Chess label, was growing in popularity, especially in the UK, but Gordy was selective. His version of r'n'b was polished, well-rehearsed, and less muscular than other variants.

The Chess label was responsible for the Gordy family's introduction to the music business: Berry's sister Anna was a local distributor for Chess records and, in 1958, with her sibling Gwen started Anna Records. At this time, Berry was concentrating on composing, one of his best songs being "Reet Petite (The Finest Girl You Ever Want to Meet)," which was recorded by Jackie Wilson. The royalties from this provided Gordy with enough money to rent a small studio. When, in Chapter 19, I wrote of fortuitous meetings, I might have including Gordy's with William "Smokey" Robinson, who sang for a group called the Matadors, later to become the Miracles. The world would be poorer musically had they never met in the late 1950s. Together they wrote "Way over There," recorded by the Miracles and released in early 1960 on Gordy's label, then called Tamla, after the popular fictional white girl "Tammy" Debbie Reynolds played in a series of romcoms.

Gordy recruited the help of family, friends, and anyone who would help in packing boxes, making calls, and doing anything they could to push the records out. He took out a paid advertisement in *The Cash Box*, a music trade magazine, dispensing with false modesty by describing himself as "one of the young driving geniuses of the music business today." That was July 23, 1960. He even hawked copies of the records around radio deejays. "Way over There" eventually sold 60,000 copies, not a major success, but enough to demonstrate the fledgling operation's ability to take a record through all phases of manufacture and sales independently of a major corporation.

* * *

Gordy's enterprise started at a house, 2648 West Grand Boulevard, Detroit. Outside the house, he stuck a sign "Hitsville USA." After converting the house into a studio, Gordy recruited writers and producers and matched them with groups of singers, whom he schooled in dancing, dressing, and presentation. This was no art school, where aspiring musicians bumped into each, convened to someone's home, and spontaneously came up with music: Gordy presided over a small industry, complete with a quality control department. Just before he started his project, in 1958, Gordy recorded one of his own compositions, "Everyone Was There," with his brother Robert, as "Bob Kayli with Barry Gordy orchestra." (That's how it appeared on the Carlton Records label.) Sales were impressive and so "Bob Kayli" went out on a promotional tour. No sooner did he hit the road than sales dropped off. "The problem then became clear," said Gordy. "This white-sounding record did not go with his black face. Bob Kayli was history . . . When that happened, I realized this was not just about good or bad records, this was about race." It must have reminded him of his childhood newspaper selling.

This was probably why Gordy was so particular about the appearance of his artists: artists were dressed by professional stylists and choreographed by members of a department known as Artist Development. This was a critical part of Gordy's operation and central to his vision of breaking into the mainstream. One of the key members of Artist Development was former tap dancer Cholly Atkins, whose particular skill was in teaching singers not only to dance but to breathe in a way that didn't adversely affect their singing. No detail was neglected. This was quite a departure from the approach of Chess, OKeh, and others, which were more narrowly focused on records. Motown's acts were not just well-presented: they were packaged. Gordy had learned from the Kayli experience. And from selling newspapers in a white neighborhood.

One of the early releases on the nascent Tamla label was "Money (That's What I Want)," sung by Barrett Strong with Gordy and Janie Bradford credited as writers. It was cataloged as "Tamla 54027" to give the impression the label was long-established. It flopped, but was re-released after a year, in 1960, on Anna's label. This time, it had more success, though in the United States' r'n'b charts, which comprised African American artists' records. Gordy didn't know it at the time, but this song was to become enormously valuable when it was covered, along with two other Motown numbers, by the Beatles for their second album, *With the Beatles*, released in 1963.

A concert tour went on the road along eastern seaboard, North to South for three months in 1962. Called the Motortown Revue (not Motown) the show featured the Miracles, the Marvelettes, and Mary Wells, among others. Wells was a formidable talent: at seventeen, she recorded her own composition "Bye Bye Baby" for the label. At the time of the tour, she had major international success with Smokey Robinson's composition "Two Lovers" and would go on to have even greater success in 1964 with "My Guy," also written by Robinson, which reached number one in the charts despite competition from six cover versions, including one by Aretha Franklin. Wells also became one of Gordy's first artists to express discontent with the label's distribution of payments, as we will discover later.

There were grisly and chastening episodes of violence across the Southern states as civil rights gained momentum and white supremacists, including the Ku Klux Klan, made their prejudices known. The Motortown Revue tour bus was fired at by a mob in Birmingham, Alabama, where, five years earlier, a black man named Judge Edward Aaron was beaten with an iron bar, castrated, and had "KKK" scored into his skin, by a gang of whites. Gordy was aware the race issue in the South was apocalyptic compared to the North, though Detroit was the scene of a major episode in 1967. But he decided to continue the tour and, for the revue's New York date, introduced a twelve-year-old prodigy named Little Stevie Wonder. The newcomer's first three singles were released in 1962, but made no impact. Then came a live performance of a two-part song "Fingertips": this single launched an epic career spanning five decades.

The Tamla label's first *Billboard* Hot 100 number one record was "Please Mr. Postman" by the Marvelettes, an all-girl group. The Beatles were among several artists who covered this track (there are eighty-two covers to date), written by a five-person team of composers, including singer Georgia Dobbins Davis, who had left the group by the time the single reached the top of the charts in September 1961 (a play *Now That I Can Dance*, written by Rick Sperling tells the story of the band). Gordy opted not to feature the group on the cover of its album, opting instead for a picture of a mailbox with "The Marvelettes" across it. "I didn't have pictures of black artists on the record covers until they became big hits," he explained to *Vanity Fair*'s Lisa Robinson in 2008.

The Marvelettes couldn't replicate the success and were replaced as the label's premier female group by Martha and the Vandellas, which consisted of Martha Reeves and two interchangeable backing singers. Reeves had actually started work as a secretary before Gordy realized she could sing. By the summer of 1964, Martha and her group had registered two top hits. In July, the Civil Rights Act came into force, ending decades of overt discrimination and disenfranchisement. It was the result of seven years of rallies, marches, sit-ins, and civil disobedience, much of it inspired by Martin Luther King. Equal measures of serendipity and zeitgeist contributed to the release in the same month of Martha's "Dancing in the Streets," in which themes and motifs reverberating around America were echoed. The connection between the song, composed by Mickey Stevenson, Marvin Gaye, and Ivy Jo Hunter, and the politics of race might have been coincidental, but that didn't lessen its power. "Calling out around the world, are you ready for a brand new beat?" sang Martha.

"This track's pounding, liberating, yet wholesomely inclusive carnival of 'the street' could have been put together only in Gordy's Motown music factory, with its relentlessly cross-racial-sounding production palette," wrote sociologist William Site. "Yet the song also channeled an urban moment—what might be called a preriot urban imaginary—that would soon be swallowed up by quite different visions and sounds of the city." Detroit erupted into riot in 1967.

The song became the unintentional soundtrack to those who were jubilant over civil rights and those who remained frustrated and took notice of Malcolm X, who, in June, famously declared, "We will get our rights by any means necessary." However people interpreted its message, the tune resonated, and its commercial success established Martha and the Vandellas as Motown's leading act. Having a Tamla song adopted as a civil rights anthem wouldn't have been in Gordy's vision for his label (he'd actually sent one of his early compositions to Doris Day for her consideration), but he must have been buoyed by the record's resounding success. Reeves too was delighted, at least initially. She too grew discontented.

* * *

"I think I was the first person to ask where the money was going," Reeves told Gerri Hirshey in 1994. Her request to examine the royalty accounts was received by Gordy as a challenge, and from that point the search was on for the label's top female singer. Reeves's question about money set off a succession of inquiries. After Reeves left the label, Mary Wells followed, lured by a more lucrative contract with 20th Century Fox, which her husband encouraged her to accept. Gordy objected but Wells prevailed. She had been only seventeen when she signed her contract with Motown.

She transferred to Fox, but without success comparable to that she'd achieved with Motown: only "Use Your Head" made the Top 20. She subsequently changed labels again, to Atlantic in 1966. Her fortunes further descended when she was diagnosed with throat cancer in 1990. She died in 1992.

Singers were, in a sense, replaceable. After all, Gordy's production system all but guaranteed a fresh supply of them. But they needed original material, so, when, in 1967, Gordy's prodigious writing trio Brian Holland, Lamont Dozier, and Eddie Holland (or HDH, as they were known) asked Gordy to release them from their contract, with one year remaining, a catastrophe loomed. The songwriters suspected they were being shortchanged. When they left, Gordy sued for $4 million and they countersued for a then-staggering $22 million (about $175 million today). The abrasive legal dispute persisted until 2004, much of the wrangle centering on the legal ties between the composers and Gordy's publishing company. Gordy realized the value of music publishing early on and set up Jobete, a company that held the rights to his own compositions and those of several artists, including Robinson and Gaye as well HDH. In time, it became a valuable catalog of Motown music. As I pointed out in Chapter 18, publishing was and is a major source of revenue in the entertainment industry. Gordy sold Jobete in stages starting 1992, at first to EMI Music Publishing, later controlled by Sony, for about $320 million.

By the time of Eddie and Brian Holland and Lamont Dozier's acrimonious departure, Motown was established as a global label, its success resting on Gordy's vision and attention to detail, not neglecting good fortune in signing two of the twentieth century's major artists. Stevie Wonder (the "Little" prefix was dropped) could do little wrong. As an eleven-year-old, he signed his first contract with Gordy; it was a standard four-year recording deal with a few additional clauses that obliged him to pay production costs. He also had a management agreement with Gordy and his compositions would go into the Jobete catalog. The contract also had provision for a four-year extension when it expired. Wonder signed an improved deal in 1966. This came up for renewal in 1971, when Wonder was still only twenty-one, but already a very valuable commodity, having scored an international hit with a cover of "For Once in My Life," which had already been recorded by Motown artists, the Temptations, the Four Tops, and many other artists besides. Wonder was able to negotiate much more creative control than other Motown artists. It worked like a charm: he produced four virtuoso albums between 1972 and 1974, all of which sold impressively. They were *Music of My Mind, Talking Book, Innervisions*, and *Fulfillingness' First Finale* and their brilliance amply justified Gordy's faith in Wonder.

Diana Ross was in high school, she was asked to join the Primettes, an all-female counterpart to a male group called the Primes. The group consisted of Ross, Florence Ballard, Mary Wilson, and Barbara Martin, who later dropped out. They made a couple of records for the Detroit-based Lu-Pine label, "Pretty Baby" and "Tears of Sorrow" in 1960. In 1961, Gordy signed them, but insisted on changing their name to the Supremes. Their first half-dozen singles flopped, but the breakthrough "When the Lovelight Starts Shining Through His Eyes" climbed to 23 on the *Billboard* top 100 in 1963; though it was when the group began to work more closely with HDH that it realized its full potential. In 1964, the Supremes reached the top of the charts with "Where Did Our Love Go." They followed with four straight number ones, making them Motown's most successful group.

Increasingly, Ross's relationship with Gordy became intimate and introduced tensions. In 1967, there were the first signs of fracture when Gordy fired Ballard after a series of personal disputes over her drinking. This was a crucial moment in the group's and Motown's history. Ballard had, with Ross, shared lead vocals and her replacement Cindy Birdsong was a backing singer. Ross moved into focal position and Gordy incorporated her name into the band's. Diana Ross and the Supremes came into being in 1967. To emphasize the lead vocalist, the group dispensed with their traditional matching ensembles, allowing Ross to dress in more distinct outfits for performances. Wilson later disclosed that, in her view, Ross was covetous, manipulative, and hellbent on elevating herself above the others in the group.

Within two years, Ross went solo, releasing her first studio album in 1970 together with the international hit single "Reach Out and Touch (Somebody's Hand)." After this, Ross released a rearranged version of a Nick Ashford and Valerie Simpson composition she'd recorded two years before as part of a Supremes-Temptations collaboration: "Ain't No Mountain High Enough." This was the song that cemented her status as one of the world's foremost singers. She pivoted into acting in 1972, playing Billie Holiday in *Lady Sings the Blues*, a role for which she was Oscar-nominated. Her performance in *The Wiz*, in 1978, was, as I mentioned in the previous chapter, received less rapturously. Pop stars were never asked to sing the national anthem at Super Bowls, but, after Ross sang in 1982, they became regulars. In 1996, she returned for the halftime show. She triumphed—unlike Janet Jackson in 2004 (as we noted in Chapter 11). The only reverse in her post-*Wiz* career was in 2000 when a Supremes-reunion tour was canceled after a disappointing start. By that time, original member Florence Ballard had died from a bloodclot, aged thirty-two (in 1976) and Mary Wilson refused, because she was offered, on her account, at most a fifth of Ross's fee (thought to be between $15 and 20 million).

Wilson, who died in 2021, had recognized what she believed to be the unfavorable terms of her early recording contracts and fought to obtain access to Motown's financial records. She was dismissed by Motown in 1980. Added to the money-related grievances of Martha Reeves and Mary Wells and the disputatious departure of Dozier and the Hollands, this seemed to expose a faultline across the smooth Motown surface. Between 1964 and 1968, HDH wrote sixteen straight singles for the Supremes, including ten number ones. The Four Tops' best period, 1964-7, owed much to HDH songs, and the team was responsible for most of Martha and the Vandellas's material. So, in terms of prolificity, HDH was up there with Lennon and McCartney. It was an extraordinary parting of the ways when they left what was at the time one of the most celebrated and successful record labels in history. There were other withdrawals from Motown, mostly unnoticed. Barrett Strong, who had recorded Tamla's first release, followed by Brenda Holloway ("Every Little Bit Hurts"), Kim Weston, the Isley Brothers, the Miracles, the Temptations, Gladys Knight and the Pips, Jimmy Ruffin, Eddie

Kendricks, and the Four Tops. Years later, Gordy owned up to the probable reason his artists fled. "Perhaps stubbornly, I would not always pay what it would take to get them to stay. That might have been a mistake," he wrote in his 1994 autobiography, *To Be Loved*. No artist was indispensable for Gordy. To him, they were like products of an assembly line and there was always more raw material ready to be processed.

*   *   *

Florence Ballard and Mary Wilson both had beefs with Gordy and left Motown. But, during their years of friendship, they did him an inestimable favor: they introduced him to Bobby Taylor. Bobby who? You may well ask. But follow the footprints. One night, Ballard and Wilson heard Taylor performing with his band the Vancouvers and were impressed enough to recommend them to Gordy. He duly signed Taylor and the band. In 1968, Taylor and the Vancouvers released a modestly successful song titled "Does Your Mama Know about Me." The lyric concerned a black man enquiring about his white girlfriend's family. It was covered in the same year by Diana Ross and the Supremes and, in 1973, by Jermaine Jackson. Taylor may not register as a major Motown name and, after leaving the label, he went to mainland China and then to Hong Kong, where he died in 2017, after suffering from leukemia. But he left an appreciable endowment.

"Bobby Taylor called up and asked me to come down to his apartment, he wanted me to see something. I said no," recalled Suzanne de Passe, who would become an executive at Motown and president of Motown Television, but at the time was on a lower echelon, having only recently started work at the label, in 1968. She eventually relented and went to Taylor's apartment. "OK everybody, this is Suzanne de Passe and she works for Berry Gordy and you need to sing for her because she can get you an audition," announced Taylor. De Passe saw "these kids sort of strewn across his living room." They were in fact five brothers: Jackie, Jermaine, Tito, Marlon, and Michael, who was nine years old at the time. Taylor had seen them at the Apollo Amateur Night, in New York City, and persuaded them and their father to drive over 600 miles to Detroit. "They sang and I was blown away," de Passe told *Vanity Fair*'s Lisa Robinson.

The next day, de Passe called Gordy and suggested he sign the brothers for Motown. "I don't want any kids," replied Gordy with scarcely a moment's thought. "You know how much trouble it is with Stevie Wonder and the teachers, and when you're a minor you have to have a special chaperone, and court approval of the contract." But de Passe persisted and Gordy agreed to watch an audition. This was July 1968, a month before Michael's tenth birthday. Video clips of the audition are still viewable at: https://bit.ly/3cpKB8M and appear to show six performers, the drums probably played by Johnny Porter Jackson, a cousin who didn't continue with the band and eventually died in 2006.

Although Gordy had reservations about "kids," Jackie was nineteen, Tito seventeen, Jermaine fifteen, and Marlon thirteen. And, while Motown's typical demographic was probably older than the band's average age, fifteen, Gordy no doubt realized the adolescent market was a fertile one. He agreed to sign the band to Motown negotiating with the boys' father Joe, the group's manager. Part of the negotiation involved ownership of the name the Jackson 5. The Jackson 5 were introduced to the public by Diana Ross on August 11, 1968, at a Beverly Hills function. The contract was eventually finalized the following March.

Gordy assigned to the band songwriters and musicians who could steer them into the mainstream. "Surely the coupling, of this group with the Motown production staff is one of the most fortuitous events in the recent history of pop music," wrote Jon Landau, of *Rolling Stone* in 1971. The impact was tangible: between 1969 and 1970 the band's first four singles all went to number one in the charts. "I Want You Back" started the run. The song was written by a team known as The Corporation, which comprised Gordy, Alphonso Mizell, Freddie Perren, and Deke Richards, and released on October 7, 1969. Michael was eleven.

According to Matthew Delmont, "Most Americans learned about the talented brothers from Gary, Indiana when they performed on *The Ed Sullivan Show* for the first time in December 1969." Delmont, an American Studies professor, emphasizes the enormous impact of exposure on television, especially on Sullivan's prestigious show, which had featured Elvis (in 1955), the Beatles (1964), the Rolling Stones (1964), and Marvin Gaye (1966). The Jackson 5 had built their reputation on the concert circuit, but Sullivan's show was regularly watched by millions. Seventy-three million saw the Beatles' appearance. It wasn't the band's first appearance on tv; that was five months earlier on Miss Black America Pageant; they performed the Isley Brothers' "It's Your Thing." But the Sullivan show appearance was timed perfectly with the release of the album *Diana Ross Presents the Jackson 5*, the title implying that Ross had somehow discovered the band. "Bobby Taylor Presents the Jackson 5" just wouldn't have had the same impact. (Taylor was credited as producer.)

As the 1960s reached an end, Gordy was already strategizing the next phase of Motown: he planned to move the entire operation to Los Angeles. Gordy asked Joe Jackson to relocate the band and, by implication, the entire family—there were nine children and his wife to consider—from Indiana to California. Joe agreed and moved everyone to the West Coast, where he put his other children on stage, with daughters Rebbie, LaToya, and Janet performing in Las Vegas in the 1970s, along with the family's youngest son, Randy. Remember, several members of the family, including Michael, were school-age (in California, people between six and eighteen years of age are subject to compulsory full-time education); so performances were limited.

Delmont believes the brothers' television presence was crucial: they became regulars on variety shows and their appearances helped promote record sales.

Being a medium that "thrives on consistency," as Delmont puts it, the Jackson 5 was perfect: performances were always well-choreographed, with consistent vocals and nothing unexpectedly controversial at a time in America's history when unforeseen events were becoming a feature. While Delmont doesn't provide a backdrop, he might have mentioned the mounting protest against the Vietnam War expressed through marches in Washington, DC, and, in one infamous incident, an incident at Kent State University in which four students were killed by National Guardsman. The murders of Sharon Tate and Leno LaBianca, in 1969, by Charles Manson and his followers were executed in a way that seemed erroneously to implicate the Black Panthers, a militant political organization set up to campaign for black rights. One such Black Panther, Bobby Seale was, in 1968, arrested while protesting at the Democratic National Convention in Chicago and later sentenced to four years in prison for contempt of court. LA band Buffalo Springfield delivered mood music with "For What It's Worth," a song that warned, "There's battlelines being drawn / Nobody's right if everybody's wrong."

This was a volatile period in America's history and, though Delmont doesn't argue the Jacksons applied a salve, I do. The televised exhibition of five young well-groomed, well-behaved African Americans, with no grievances, no known views on any social or political event and an interest solely in the provision of entertainment, could have been designed to soothe an uneasy conscience. The Jackson family offered rhetoric, not remedies: they had no policy, nor vision, just comfort. While segments of society challenged and confronted, provoking and often outraging, the Jacksons reassured audiences America was at one with itself.

Other black artists who became television figures in the period included comedian Flip Wilson, who hosted his own variety show, Diahann Carroll, who played the eponymous *Julia* on television between 1968 and 1971, and Dick Gregory, who was, in several ways, an exception, highlighting poverty, and civil rights in his satirical comic routines. Gregory was not an emollient presence on tv. The Jackson 5 most decidedly were. It was as if the brothers had sprung fully formed from the cartoon world, loudly dressed in primary colors, and radiating family values. So why not make an actual cartoon series?

The Jackson 5ive was brought into life by ABC television and shown on Saturday mornings between 1971 and 1972. Animated and voiced with fidelity to the Jacksons, the series avoided stereotypes, depicting the brothers with some elasticity but not caricature. Gordy set up Motown Productions and *The Jackson 5ive* was the new company's first tv series. De Passe was involved in the creation of the series and kept a watchful eye. Motown had power to veto material it considered unsuitable. "Executives at Motown Productions made sure that *Jackson 5ive* series steered clear of racist caricatures of African Americans," wrote Richard M. Breaux in his 2010 article for the *Journal of Pan African Studies*. Breaux contended that the series "signaled the commodification and popular adaptation of Civil

Right and Black Power Movement ideologies," though he never developed this.

America, a country that once prided itself on its political radicalism, was turning inward in the early 1970s. Jarring reminders that Americans were not comfortable with the war, with bigotry, or with the war on bigotry formed a counterpoint to the reassuring aides-memoires from television and other parts of the entertainment industry. Comedy, enlightenment, and wish-fulfillment seemed neatly packaged in the media. The Jacksons' cartoon was never going to depict a historical lynching, or Klansmen attacking buses of Freedom Riders, or the brothers wearing leather jackets in the manner of the Black Panthers. *The Jackson 5ive* offered a version of the black experience that was witty, stylish, and inventive, but without dramatizing grisly complexities. It was a cartoon in the *Yellow Submarine* tradition rather than the *Waltz with Bashir* or even *South Park* mold (animation director Bob Balser had earlier worked on the Beatles' 1968 film). In other words, it was a product that was easily consumed with little to challenge the intellect or trouble the morality: it was a commodity, and, as if to underline this, each episode featured two tunes by the animated counterparts. So Jackson hits such as "ABC" and "I'll Be There" were incorporated into plotlines, sung by the brothers themselves (though they didn't voice the characters in the show).

But the show was sophisticated enough to reflect the times. In one episode, for example, Marlon and Michael are drafted into the military and get their lush afros shaved off. Afros were the fashionable coifs originating in the Black Power movement in the 1960s, but favored by practically every socially and fashionably aware African American, male or female. In another somewhat clairvoyant episode, Michael falls unconscious on a roller coaster and dreams he is in a Wonderland theme park. So, while there was no violence, there were themes that were clever enough to make the series relevant, though not for long. The animated show ran for two seasons, or twenty-three episodes, between 1971 and 1972, with re-runs in 1984 (in the "Jackson Era").

By the end of the second series in October 1972, Michael had released two solo studio albums, both in 1972, within seven months of each other. Today, an album is typically supported with a promotional tour and a marketing budget, so they arrive in cycles of three years, or longer. In the 1970s, Michael's first two efforts were closer to what we'd today call sideprojects, albums made by one or more people known for their work in a band. There was never any whiff of a suspicion that Michael would leave the band. His single "Ben," from the film of the same name, was an international success in 1972, though the song was initially intended for Donny Osmond, who must have been a source of some concern to Gordy in the early 1970s.

*   *   *

In 1981, a journalist from the British weekly *New Musical Express* was briefed before an interview with the Jacksons: avoid two subjects. One was astrology: as Jehovah's Witnesses, the brothers considered the study of celestial bodies' influence on human affairs ungodly. The other was the Osmonds. After all, the teen idol boy band seemed to be a white mirror image of the Jacksons. The Osmonds were innocent, wholesome, and righteous, being Mormons from Utah. Brothers Alan, Wayne, Merrill, and Jay Osmond had been appearing on television since 1962, when the Jackson 5 was no more than Joe Jackson's daydream. The youngest Osmond was three and eldest nine. The foursome did regular spots on NBC's *The Andy Williams Show*.

Sam Phillips, the owner of Sun Records, is supposed to have told anybody within listening distance, "If I could find a white boy who could sing like a black man, I'd make a million dollars." He was speaking in the early 1950s, just before he ran into Elvis. A similar thought must have crossed the mind of several people as they watched the rise of the Jackson 5 from 1969. Record producer Rick Hall could have been one of them. So, in 1970, when he was presented with the Osmond Brothers, by then inflated to a quintet by youngest brother Donny and called the Osmonds, he must have remembered Phillips's speculation. And, when he discovered the song he'd been given to record had actually been written for but rejected by the Jackson 5, he must have thought Elohim was looking down kindly on him. "One Bad Apple" went to the top of the charts in November 1970, spurring the kind of euphoria among fans, especially teenage fans, previously associated with only the Beatles. Osmondmania, as it was called, for a while outshone enthusiasm for the Jacksons. The Utah boys seemed to mimic the Jacksons, with Donny the white equivalent of Michael, occasionally splintering off to do solos and, in time, releasing his own records. His single "Sweet and Innocent" was released in July 1971, when he was thirteen, and became part of a string of successful records. For a while during 1972–3, there was an animated series; so even the cartoon Jacksons had white counterparts.

Then the copied became copiers. Within a month of the release of Donny Osmond's single, Gordy met Joe Jackson to discuss a solo path for Michael. By October 1971, thirteen-year-old Michael had a solo single, "Got to Be There." Its success encouraged further releases and Michael's solo career was effectively wrapped inside that of the group: he appeared on stage with his brothers and the Jackson 5 made records but the band became a culture for Jackson's solo career, helping him grow and mature as an individual performer.

Pop rivalries are never a bad thing: the Beatles and the Rolling Stones in the 1960s; fellow Brits Oasis and Blur in the 1990s; Taylor Swift, Katy Perry, Kanye West, Nicki Minaj, Miley Cyrus, and others at various times. Not one of them incurred lasting damage to their careers and, mostly, the adversaries profited from the exposure media typically offer celebrity squabbles. Gordy probably grinned when he saw the Osmonds steal the Jacksons' thunder; they went on to sell 100 million records. He probably knew his group was more than a match for the Osmonds musically. And, as the Jacksons grew older, he no doubt realized their afro'd hair and pimped-up clothes would resonate with fans. Yet he also knew he had nothing in his armory to combat the Osmond's whiteness. Even fast-forwarding to the 1990s, the search for white artists to challenge preeminent blacks still had momentum: MC Hammer saw off many contenders, including Vanilla Ice ("Ice, ice, baby"). Gordy himself had a promising white artist, R. Dean Taylor, from Canada, who worked closely with HDH and had success in 1967–8. Taylor's work was released on a Motown-owned label called Rare Earth Records intended for white acts, including a band called Rare Earth and Kiki Dee, the Brit singer whose "Love Makes the World Go Round" was released in 1970. Gordy was a pragmatist: he was compassed by practical considerations— how the world was, not how he wanted it to be. This is probably why he was prepared to upset Motor City traditionalists and move west.

The transfer to LA was officially completed in June 1972, when the Detroit offices closed for good; the studios stayed open for longer. The move was not an unqualified success for Gordy. While the Jacksons had no affinity with Detroit, many other Motown artists had and several of them felt betrayed. New artists joined the label but the success of the first phase wouldn't be duplicated. In its first ten years of operation, Tamla-Motown had created a musical identity, but Gordy wanted to pursue film projects. The first of these was *Lady Sings the Blues* in which Diana Ross would play Billie Holiday. Her romance with Gordy at an end, Ross continued to have a professional relationship with him, but only until 1981 when she left the label, signing a $20 million deal with RCA. Gordy also launched MoWest, a label designed for new West Coast talent. It had a successful single, "What the World Needs Now Is Love" by Tom Clay, but the label ceased after two years. By the time the transition was finalized, the Jackson 5 had joined Ross, Wonder, and Gaye in Motown's vanguard. Wonder released his acclaimed *Music of My Mind* in 1972. The year before, Gaye released *What's Going On,* which is still regarded as a musical lodestar. His *Let's Get It On* followed in 1973. Gaye would die in 1984, at the hands of his father.

Gordy had plotted Ross's career carefully and separating her from the Supremes in the mid-1960s was a masterstroke—for her, at least. He booked her into the Copacabana and Vegas with aim of conquering the white middle-class market. But the Jackson 5? They were popular with teenagers and youths, not the dinner club set. Joe disagreed. What's more, he was, if necessary, prepared to defy Gordy. He was the band's manager, after all. In 1974, with Michael approaching sixteen, the group appeared at the MGM Grand Hotel, Las Vegas. Janet and LaToya made guest appearances too. This may not have been the Gordy's first disagreement with Joe Jackson, but it was the most serious to date and it definitely wasn't the last. Gordy also canceled a British tour after Jackson released details to the media in spite of an embargo. After four years with Motown, "Their [the brothers'] father, Joe, went from being quietly behind the scenes to having many complaints and demands," Gordy wrote in his autobiography. "It was everything from wanting a say in how they were produced, what songs they did or didn't do, to how they were being promoted and booked."

Gordy was not wide of the mark: Joe did have complaints and demands in all these areas. But Gordy had a kind of Motown method that had worked and saw no reason to change it to meet the demands of one grumbling manager. Years later, Jackie Jackson told the *Financial Times*, "we thought it was time for us to start writing some of our own songs." There was probably a good artistic reason for this. There was definitely a financial reason too.

Gordy described the Jackson 5 as "the last stars I would develop with the same intensity and emotional investment as I had with the earlier Motown artists." But Joe may have thought otherwise: interest in the band was fading and sales reflected this. Joe was especially upset when Michael's fourth solo album, *Forever Michael*, made only 101 in the album charts, eight places lower than the 1973 *Music and Me* album, which was considered a failure. Gordy seemed to believe the formula he'd used for all Motown artists was tried-and-tested and allowed the brothers no room to write or produce their own material.

So it wasn't a huge surprise when, in July 1975, the band announced its decision to leave Motown. Gordy first heard the news through Jermaine Jackson, who was by then his son-in-law, having married his daughter Hazel. Jermaine told him the rest of the band was intending to sign with CBS, even though there was a year of the Motown contract to run. Joe Jackson and his business partner Richard Arons had been exploring options with other labels for some months before. CBS already had an arrangement with Kenny Gamble and Leon Huff, of Philadelphia International Records (as I noted in Chapter 19). CBS had subsidiary label known as Epic, run by Ron Alexenburg and this looked a likely home for the Jackson 5.

"We left Motown because we look forward to selling a lot of albums," Tito Jackson was quoted by the *New Yorker*, "Motown sells a lot of singles. Epic sells a lot of albums." In retrospect, it looked a terrific deal for both the brothers and CBS: the Jackson 5 had been schooled in the entertainment industry by one of the best establishments around. The Motown years were more than an apprenticeship: they were an induction into the higher orders of the record business. But Ross apart, Motown's successes were record by record. CBS had the resources not only to produce but to market and merchandise in a continuing cycle. And yet, CBS was taking a gamble when it offered a $750,000 advance and $350,000 guaranteed per album against royalties. The royalty rate was significantly different from that negotiated at Motown. Randy Taraborrelli's calculations suggest, "In terms of income, this new deal was worth about five hundred times more than the one the group had at Motown." Skeptics might have called this over-generous. Record sales suggested the public might have grown bored of the super-talented childstar, now a young man, and his competent but unspectacular brothers: neither Michael nor the group was shifting records as they were in the early years of the Motown contract.

Gordy didn't fight Joe tooth-and-nail to keep the brothers at Motown. He did, however, insist on keeping the name. On leaving Motown the Jackson brothers would no longer be the Jackson 5. Gordy owned the name and intended to use it on compilation albums and previously unreleased material. In any case, one brother was missing: Jermaine Jackson. He could still have left, but opted to stay with Motown and pursue a solo career. His decision served to alienate him from his father. Jermaine had great success with a Stevie Wonder/Lee Garrett composition, "Let's Get Serious," in 1980. He would leave Motown in 1983, rejoining the Jacksons for the *Victory* tour in 1984 (as covered in Chapter 14). His younger brother Randy became a member of the post-Motown band, which became known as The Jacksons.

There was the familiar legal melee: most artists who left Motown did so in rancorous circumstances. The Jacksons dispute was no different; in fact, it seemed ritualistic. Gordy sued the Jackson 5 and CBS. The Jacksons countersued, claiming unpaid royalties. Gordy raised the damages sought from $5 million to $20 million after an old picture featuring Jermaine was used to advertise a CBS television series. "In the end, we owed them nothing," reflected Gordy, "and we were paid a settlement of $100,000."

Gordy would sell Motown to MCA for $61 million in 1988. Five years later, Motown was sold on to PolyGram. Gordy would retire, aged eighty-nine, in 2019.

*   *   *

Walter Yetnikoff was only a few weeks into his job as president of CBS when the Jackson deal was finalized. He must have had doubts: the Jacksons were struggling to shake off their image as cute young boys and the *Jackson 5ive* cartoon series was still recent enough to linger in its audience's minds. A mere name-change was not going to convince people that the Jacksons were now a grownup band. A couple of albums produced by Gamble and Huff might. The producers wrote the majority of the tracks for the band's first album on Epic, *The Jacksons*, released in November 1976. Michael wrote one ("Blues Away," his first songwriting credit) and co-wrote another with Tito. The album was certified gold (500,000 units sold), mainly because of the success of two spinoff singles, "Enjoy Yourself" and "Show You the Way to Go," the latter a Gamble and Huff composition that went to number one in the UK.

Gamble and Huff also worked on the next Epic album a year later. *Goin' Places* also relied on the popularity of single spinoffs, in particular the title track. But it wasn't a promising start. Gamble and Huff were not involved in the third Epic album *Destiny*. This featured two tunes, "Blame It on the Boogie" and "Shake Your Body (Down to the Ground)," that presaged Michael's transition to a full-fledged artist. Joe Jackson entered into a business arrangement with two co-managers, both, like Arons, whom they replaced, white. Gordy had loaded his senior executive team with whites without feeling it necessary to explain his decisions—as he probably would have to today. Gordy, remember, was a pragmatist. So too was Joe. As manager and father of an African American band that didn't seem to be progressing as he'd hoped, he presumably shared some of Gordy's earlier concerns. To prevent black acts being ghettoized by a music industry dominated by whites, a few white negotiators nudging and pushing in the right places might be needed. It was a common tactic in the 1960s and 1970s and maybe still is.

The Jacksons' next album, *Destiny*, signaled a change in fortunes: it sold 2 million copies, making it the most commercially successful of the Epic records to date. The brothers took a greater share of the writing and producing of the work. The only track not written by the Jacksons was "Blame It on the Boogie." There is quite a story behind this song. Mike Atkinson, an A&R man at Epic, brought the tune to the attention of Epic executive Bobby Colomby in 1978. It was co-written and recorded by a white Englishman named Mick Jackson (no relation, of course), as I mentioned in Chapter 19. The Jacksons released their single after his, and in advance of their next album. A third version by Norwegian singer Inger Lise Rypdal soon followed; and a fourth by Italian Rita Pavone shortly after. The song has been covered over forty times. Jermaine Jackson released a solo version in 2011.

The Jacksons' cover was, by far, the most memorable and set up interest perfectly for the full album *Destiny*, which was released in December 1978. On reflection, this was a key single for the Jacksons: none of their previous singles had made much impression and while "Blame It on the Boogie" reached only fifty-four on the *Billboard* chart, it broke the top ten of several other countries and primed interest in *Destiny*. Michael was at the center of this album, taking lead vocals of most of the songs, including "Blame It on the Boogie" and "Shake Your Body (Down to the Ground)," which was also single. The yelps, whoops, and falsetto that would become familiar features of his solo career were apparent. It was the first Jacksons album to officially go platinum, denoting US sales of 1 million. It meant that, after a lean start to the Epic period, they had re-established themselves as a chart force. In 1978, Jackson was twenty and had been making solo albums since he was thirteen. While his first two attempts were modestly successful, his third and fourth projects were not. The failure of *Forever Michael* in 1975 must have hung over him like a cloud.

Two months before *Destiny* appeared in shops, the film *The Wiz* went on general release. Mercilessly hammered by critics, it was an artistic and commercial disaster. Jackson's decision to pitch for the role of the Scarecrow in 1977 was a masterstroke. Not because it was a great part or because he distinguished himself as a true thespian in an otherwise campy mishmash of artists doing their best to keep a straight face. On the film's set, Jackson met someone who was to change the course of his music and, by implication, his life.

The original 1966 lineup: The Jackson Five Plus Johnny (the "y" seems to have peeled off the drumskin). Johnny Porter aka Johnny Jackson was an occasional player with the brothers. He was stabbed to death in 2006.

21

In This Good Land of Ours

By an ironic twist, the incident will ultimately accomplish some good—for it has focused national publicity on the fact that a gentleman of outstanding character and talent may not travel with freedom and safety in prejudice-ridden areas of the country. The magnitude and brazenness of the incident shocks decent people thru out the land—in the North and the South. It is to be hoped that the incident will not merely be deplored, but will trigger some logical thinking among governmental and community groups who have been apathetic for too long a period. In the show business, just as in any business in this good land of ours, we must hew to fundamentals. It is shameful that they must be repeated, but it would be even more shameful were they not. Character, accomplishment, decency and honor are the traditional measures of a man.

The editorial in the April 21, 1956, issue of the entertainment magazine *Billboard* was reacting to an attack on Nat "King" Cole nine days before in Birmingham, Alabama, about 85 miles from Montgomery, where he was born. Cole (1919–65) was appearing on the first of two sets at the Municipal Auditorium: the early show was for a white audience, the late performance for blacks. The practice of segregating black-and-white populations was known as Jim Crow and, while a 1954 Supreme Court ruling had outlawed segregation in public education at state level, it would remain until 1964. Even a performer of Cole's stature was helpless in the face of segregation. Already, the most successful black artist in history, he had huge international hit records with "Unforgettable," "Mona Lisa," and "Autumn Leaves," and was due to launch his own television show with NBC—a new experience for a black artist.

During the first performance in Birmingham, four men clambered over the stage's footlights and rushed at Cole, dragging him to the floor. Police intervened and, later, charged six men, at first with intent to murder, later downgraded to conspiracy to commit a misdemeanor. Cole was injured and too shook up to continue the show. "I just came here to entertain you," Cole told the audience. "I thought that was what you wanted. I was born here." He later reflected to reporters: "I can't understand it . . . I have not taken part in any protests. Nor have I joined an organization fighting segregation. Why should they attack me?" Cole's lack of militancy drew criticism from the NAACP, though he later became a member of the organization and joined the historic March on Washington, which culminated in Martin Luther King's "I Have a Dream" speech in 1963. Cole's four attackers were sentenced to 180 days imprisonment each. "This good land of ours," as *Billboard* called it, offered inspiration because the country's founding ideas—like freedom and the American dream—were and still are so bewitching.

A little over two years after the incident, Michael Jackson was born. Not in the Deep South but in the Midwest city of Gary, Indiana, a company town built in 1906 on the shores of Lake Michigan, about 25-miles southeast of Chicago. The culture here was not as intimidating as it was further South, but it was no idyll for African Americans either. Southern blacks had migrated in the 1940s and 1950s, drawn by the prospect of decent paying jobs in the mills. Joe Jackson was originally from Fountain Hill, Arkansas, but moved to Oakland, California, aged twelve, after his parents separated. He was born in 1928. His father was a schoolteacher who took Joe to Oakland, while his mother went to East Chicago, Indiana.

Joe moved to East Chicago when he was eighteen. He boxed as an amateur and competed in the United States' national championships, the Golden Gloves. He met seventeen-year-old Katherine Scruse and they decided to marry in November 1949. Joe was twenty-one; it was his second marriage. The couple moved into a house in Gary, Indiana, where Joe took a job as a crane operator at US Steel, the largest employer in the area and the company responsible for creating the town. The couple had their first child, Rebbie, in 1950. By 1957, Joe and Katherine had four sons: Jackie, Tito, Jermaine, and Marlon. Joe had retired from boxing, but had ambitions in music: he and his brother, Luther, played in a band called the Falcons. Michael and Randy arrived in 1958 and 1961 respectively. Janet was born in 1966. Another child died shortly after birth in 1957.

After Marlon was born, when Joe had given up his dream of showbusiness and seemingly adjusted to a more humdrum life in heavy manufacturing, a rare, renegade talent appeared on his and everyone else's television. He was Frankie Lymon, from Harlem. Even in the context of entertainment industry, Lymon was remarkable. At thirteen, the New Yorker co-wrote and recorded a single that became a major hit in both the United States and United Kingdom. "Why Do Fools Fall in Love" featuring pubescent Lymon and his band, the Teenagers was released in January 1956, the same month as Elvis's "Heartbreak Hotel." The band had three African American and two Puerto Rican members. But Lymon was unquestionably the main attraction. He wrote, sang, and moved like a mature performer. He was also precocious in other ways: at fourteen, he started a romantic relationship with Zora Taylor, four years his senior, and a singer with the Platters. They eventually married in 1965. Taylor was the first of Lymon's three wives, or at least one of three women who claimed to be his wife and contested a share of his posthumous royalties.

Joe Jackson, like every other American and Brit, would have known of Lymon, who was as inescapable as it was possible to be in the late 1950s, a time when television was still an exciting new medium. (There is still footage of Lymon's first tv appearance here: https://bit.ly/2Q0IBuA.) Lymon and the Teenagers made another four records, all successful, and toured. But their showbiz life was short. When Lymon danced with a white girl on ABC television in 1957, "The Big Beat Show," as the show was called, was canceled amid the furor. He split from the band and went solo, but with only modest success. Lymon was also using heroin, aged fifteen, a habit that hastened his physical decline. He died in 1968 from an overdose, aged twenty-five. Diana Ross recorded a version of "Why Do Fools Fall in Love" in 1981.

It would be unusual if Joe Jackson hadn't been influenced in some way by Lymon's experience: his ascent meteoric but his stay at the top short-lived; the mixed blessing of being celebrated by white audiences, yet scrutinized and held to account for lapses that could be ruinous; the casualness of drugs use in showbusiness, particularly among musicians in Harlem that made for a hazardous environment. Louis Armstrong, Miles Davis, Billie Holiday, and Charlie Parker were among the many, many musicians who played or lived in Harlem, and acquired drugs habits. What if Lymon had been nurtured with more care? Managed in a firmer, more disciplined way that allowed him to expand his extraordinary talent, and in contexts that supported and guided rather than exposed him to the rebarbative elements of the entertainment industry? Remember, he was thirteen when he first broke through, the same age as Stevie Wonder when "Fingertips" was released in 1963. Wonder, at the time of writing, is in his seventies and still creating music.

*   *   *

In 1963, Jackie, Tito, and Jermaine (at nine, the youngest) got together with friends Ronnie Rancifer on keyboards and Milford Hite on drums and began to play, primarily for their own amusement. Joe, perhaps vicariously living out his own frustrated showbiz ambitions, sensed an opportunity and underwrote the boys' expenses for equipment, but only in exchange for hard work. Any residual lightheartedness in the boys' musical endeavor was quickly replaced by industry. This was no longer a playful collaboration of schoolkids entertaining themselves: once Joe got involved, he governed rehearsals as he might have expected his old boxing coach to oversee his training schedule. Daily three-hour practice sessions were the norm; five-hour spells were not unheard of. Added to this was homework, meaning the boys rarely got to bed before 2:00 a.m. The two younger brothers, Marlon and Michael, were allowed to watch the others rehearse with a view to incorporating themselves into the act in due course. The Jackson Brothers, as Joe called them, were made to hone their act so they'd be ready for the then-popular talent competition circuit.

Joe didn't spare his belt when it came to making his point: if the brothers deviated from his instructions, there were consequences. But he worked for this authority. Not only did Joe supervise rehearsals and make bookings, he drove his sons and their equipment in his Volkswagen to venues, often to the despair of mother Katherine, a Jehovah's Witness. There was another purpose for the road trips: Joe had a series of extramarital dalliances that he discreetly kept from the boys' mother, but which eventually came into the open. The brothers were probably too terrified to tell their mother, anyway. Years later, it was discovered Joe had fathered a child named Joh'Vonnie Jackson, who was born in 1974, her mother being Cheryle Terrell, who had a 25-year-long affair. Joh'Vonnie was Joe's youngest child; unlike the other children, she was allowed to call him daddy.

Years later, eldest son Jackie told the *Guardian*'s Simon Hattonstone, "He [Joe] was real disciplined. And the reason he was tough with us was because we had gangs in the neighbourhood and he didn't want us to fall into them, so he kept us busy. We worked all the time, whether it was on our music or just moving bricks in the backyard from one spot to another spot." The brick-moving was one of Joe's punishments for his boys. Hell hath no fury like a father pushing his sons to succeed where he failed as a musician. Well-meaning, unorthodox, deluded, perhaps, but Joe met criticism of his parenting methods with a shrug, explaining that hitting his children with a switch or belt didn't count as "beating" them.

At eight, Michael was more than ready to step up. Already a slick mover, he had a voice that had the fragility of youth, yet the strength that typically comes through age. So, in 1966, he and brother Marlon were added to the lineup. Rancifer disappeared and Hite was replaced by Johnny Porter, who became known as Johnny Jackson. He was a childhood friend of the brothers, having grown up near them in Gary. He drifted away from the band during the period with Steeltown Records and later played with a band called White Dove. Johnny was an occasional player with the ensemble but the five brothers were permanent and Joe retitled them the Jackson Five, or sometimes, when Johnny was playing, Jackson Five Plus Johnny. Joe continued to chauffeur them to talent shows, presumably in the expectation that somebody from a record label's A&R department would spot them. That's exactly what happened. (Johnny Jackson was stabbed to death in 2006, aged fifty-four.)

As with any musical prehistory, there are competing versions of events. One is that Joe Jackson was parading his sons regularly but without much sign of a recording contract. It's possible that another local band of family members known as The Five Stairsteps, which bore similarity to the Jackson 5, and recorded a single in 1966, "Don't Waste Your Time/You Wasted Your Time," stole the Jackson thunder. The Five Stairsteps may have been the primary target for the labels at the time. Certainly, the band made a few records between 1966 and 1970, including a twelve-inch LP, as Long-Playing records were called, on the Windy C label.

Another possibility is that there was lively competition to sign the Jackson band. Musician-cum-record label owner Gordon Keith definitely agreed a contract with Joe in 1967. He also arranged a recording session at his studios in Chicago. The most notable tune to come out of the session was "Big Boy." Keith had, in 1966, started Steeltown Records. He was one of five partners, their studio being on the South Side of Chicago. South Side is only about half-hour's drive from Gary. Keith noticed posters advertising the Jackson Five Plus Johnny and became interested enough to discover Joe's phone number. Joe invited him to meet the boys and watch them perform at the family home. Keith was impressed enough to offer a recording contract immediately. Michael was nine at the time and Keith later described him as "superhuman," to Susie An, of WBEZ Chicago.

The deal with Keith was complicated slightly by a couple of agreements Joe had made with radio deejays. Pervis Spann and E. Rodney Jones worked for WVON, a station that served the Chicago area and is still operating. Spann had seen the Jackson 5 compete in a talent contest and liked them enough to offer his services—as manager. Joe already occupied that role, but Spann remained interested. Jones also saw potential in the boys and, on some accounts, spent thousands of dollars of his own money promoting them, but without much success. Before Keith decided to enter an agreement with Joe Jackson, he apparently cleared it with both deejays. The band's first recording session took place at the Morrison Sound Studio, owned by Sunny Sawyer, who also sound-engineered the session. Tito played guitar, Jermaine bass, and Johnny Jackson drums. Keith also brought in rhythm, lead and bass guitarists and two additional percussionists. Keith himself sang backup harmonies with a number of others. The session produced four songs: "Big Boy," "You've Changed," "We Don't Have to Be over 21," and "Some Girls Want Me for Their Lover (Michael the Lover)."

It seems reasonable to call the Jackson 5 a working band at this stage: the talent contests were showcases, but Joe had secured a regular gig at Mr. Lucky's, a nightclub in Gary, and the boys made paid appearances at other clubs, such as Burning Spear and the Confidential Club. When the first single from the recording session "Big Boy" was released in January 1968, Joe sold copies at his boys' gigs. At the time, independent record labels struggled with distribution. It was a long time before the 360-degree deals of today, in which any revenue stream (from digital sales, merchandise, endorsements, and so on) are integrated into a single contract, so the artist receives substantial frontend payments and the entertainment company (such as a record label or promoter) receives income as it's earned. So Keith struck a distribution deal with the more established and much better-known Atlantic Records. "Big Boy" went on sale on the Atco label, as it was called. It looked a promising linkup with a company that boasted the likes of Aretha Franklin, Otis Redding, and several English rock bands. Sales began to pick up and the Steeltown's deal with Atlantic seemed to have worked like a dream. In fact, the first verse of "Big Boy" contained the line, "I don't enjoy fairy tales and wishful dreams," but the record itself brought both of these.

* * *

In Chapter 20, I reproduced Suzanne de Plasse's memory of the night she heard from Bobby Taylor. Taylor, she recalls, had seen the Jacksons perform at New York's Apollo. The *Chicago Reader*'s Jake Austen, who seems to have done exhaustive research into the early history of the band, suggests the performance Taylor witnessed took place nearer to home: possibly the Burning Spear club or maybe the Regal, both in Chicago. It would be a much shorter drive to Detroit from Chicago (about 280 miles, compared to 600 from New York). There's agreement about the rest of the story: Taylor brokered an audition and Gordy, despite his initial doubts, signed the band to Motown.

Again, discrepancies in the narrative arise: "I Want You Back," the Jacksons' first release with Motown and their first number one, was released in November 1969, almost a year and a half after Taylor had first seen them perform. It doesn't seem an inordinately long period of time, given Motown's striving for perfection and its insistence on well-choreographed routines to accompany a tune. But still a little longer than might be expected, considering Steeltown had released "Big Boy" twenty-two months before in January 1968.

Gordon Keith claimed his contracts with the Jacksons and Atlantic were valid and Atlantic tied Motown up in court before the band was free to release another record. Keith and Steeltown Records seem to have been marginalized in the case, which was like a hornet's nest: once kicked, claimants flew out and started stinging. Keith himself argued he was the band's manager; so did the two deejays, Spann and Jones; a police officer also reckoned he was the band's rightful manager. More credibly perhaps, Richard Arons, the New York lawyer mentioned in Chapter 20, reportedly struck a deal with Joe Jackson when the band appeared at Harlem's Apollo in May 1968; Etta James was on the same bill; it was a return visit to the famous theater after the band won an amateur night the previous year (in either February or August—again accounts differ). Arons scouted for live gigs, while Joe Jackson focused on a record deal.

"After he got squeezed out, Keith says, he just tried to grab what he could," wrote Austen, explaining how a kind of parallel reality came into being shortly after the Jacksons' move to Motown. While "I Want You Back," "ABC," and "I'll Be There" stormed the international charts and sent audiences into raptures in 1969 and 1970, other singles from their Steeltown session went on sale. Keith understood the dollars-and-cents of the record industry and knew Motown, by then a globally recognized commodity, would be reaping the benefits of the Jackson 5's surging popularity. Something similar happened with the Beatles: after "Love Me Do" was released in the UK in October 1962, reproductions of material they recorded earlier in Hamburg as Tony Sheridan and the Beat Brothers circulated, "My Bonnie" being the most notable. In 1970, Keith released "We Don't Have to Be Over 21," adding strings to resemble the band's Motown sound. It was completely eclipsed by the band's Motown output. So Keith shortened the title and licensed "Some Girls Want Me for Their Lover" to Dynamo Records in New York, his idea presumably being that distribution in the New York market would enhance sales. According to Austen's research, there were other recordings that were somehow excavated, one by an English record dealer who produced an acetate (a disk coated with cellulose acetate that used to be used for rough recordings) purporting to contain early Jacksons songs. In the event, it was found that the band was called Magical Connection and the song "Girl Why Do You Want to Take My Heart." Actually, the confusion is understandable: the sound resembles early Jacksons.

In 1972, in what seemed a desperate attempt to capitalize on his increasingly tenuous link with the Jackson 5, Keith put out a single on Steeltown by a band called (on the label) The Ripples and Waves Plus Michael. The song was "Let Me Carry Your School Books" and it sounded a lot like early Jackson 5, with "Michael Rogers," the vocalist, evidently doing his best impersonation. The confusion surrounding The Ripples and Waves Plus Michael actually deepened when, in 2000, twelve years after Gordy had sold Motown to MCA, seven years after MCA had sold it to PolyGram, and two years after PolyGram was acquired by the Universal Music Group, Universal released a compilation album with the title *Ripples and Waves: An Introduction to the Jackson 5*. This "prompted Keith and his nephew Elvy Woodard (a Ripple) to sue the Jacksons for infringement on the Ripples & Waves name," wrote Austen, who was assured by Keith that the suit was settled in part by some of the Jackson brothers, though not Michael, offering to issue an apology on DVD, a popular format in the early part of this century.

Keith had in 1989, with the "Jackson era" approaching an end, made a belated bid to exploit his then-historical association with the family by releasing an album entitled *Jackson 5 featuring Michael Jackson & Johnny—The beginnings 1968–1969*, comprising twelve tracks and a spoken monologue. The origins of the raw material—and some of it was very raw—

are uncertain. The Steeltown recordings are recognizable, but other tracks do not seem to have been intended for public consumption. The album still sells on vinyl, cd, and mp3 formats.

Old recordings of rehearsals bounced back in when a New York label released *Pre-History: Lost Steeltown Recordings*. The title was actually clever: Jackson's *HIStory: Past, Present and Future, Book I* went on sale in June 1995 and the *Pre-History* release appears to be around the same time. It's still available. With all "lost" recordings found and, in some cases enhanced, the Jackson family catalog would seem to have been complete. More than complete perhaps. Not quite: Austen's investigation took him down one more labyrinthine corridor of the Jackson citadel.

Steeltown's "Big Boy," released in January 1968, was for long accepted as the earliest commercially available Jackson 5 recording. Even the so-called lost Steeltown material seems to have emanated from the Chicago studio session arranged by Gordon Keith and engineered by Sunny Sawyer. Yet Jake Austen's sleuthing revealed an even earlier recording of "Big Boy" from mid-1967, when Michael was eight years old.

One-derful Records was set up in Chicago by brothers George and Ernie Leaner in March 1962. Its specialty was soul, the then-popular music incorporating gospel and rhythm 'n' blues, with an emphasis on impassioned vocals. Some of the artists mentioned earlier in this book came to fame as soul singers. Aretha Franklin was called the Queen of Soul. James Brown the Godfather of Soul. One-derful didn't have heavyweight like Franklin or Brown. Its first release, "The Town I Live In" by McKinley Mitchell, was moderately successful at a time when independent labels proliferated and before the market was dominated by media giants. It was also among a small number of labels owned by African Americans. Gordy has started Tamla three years before. Perhaps One-derful's most notable record was "Shake a Tail Feather" by the Five Du-Tones. First released in 1963, it was covered by dozens of artists, including Tina Turner, Ray Charles, and Tommy James & the Shondells.

According to Austen, Joe and Michael Jackson were spotted with an unknown other at One-derful's studio. Michael sang John D. Loudermilk's "Tobacco Road" a cappella. George Leaner concluded that Michael had talent, but was, at only eight years old, too young. It was 1966. About a year later, according to another remembrance collected by Austen, Michael returned to the studio, this time with his brothers. Presumably, Johnny Jackson would have been with them too. This time, Leaner was impressed enough to want to sign the band and develop them as an act. For five months, the boys and father Joe—and sometimes, mother Katherine—drove straight from school in Gary to the One-derful studio and practice harmonies, chord progression, and other features of vocal performance. Leaner was satisfied the band progressed quickly enough for him to offer a contract, but there was a prohibiting factor: their ages. Jackie, the eldest brother, was fifteen.

Gordy, remember, was also hesitant initially about signing the band. Leaner hesitated, leaving Keith free to sign the band to Steeltown.

So is the phantom recording of "Big Boy," or "I'm a Big Boy Now," as it's sometimes called, just that—a phantom? Steeltown, according to Austen, definitely made its own version with Sawyer in the studio. An earlier version, perhaps recorded at One-derful's studio, could have been heard and possibly used as a template. Leaner died in 1990 and One-derful went through many changes, disposing of much of its assets, including records. Austen asked Ernie Leaner to search for old tapes and he came up with a warped, discolored, and badly deteriorated reel dated July 22, 1967, labeled "Jackson 5 band tracks" but another, in better condition, bearing the label "Jackson Five—I'm a Big Boy Now."

But Austen is not Conan Doyle and the mystery didn't have a Sherlock-style denouement. The tape could hold the voice of Michael Jackson from beyond the grave but doubts remain. For all his painstaking efforts, Austen couldn't provide a conclusive resolution. Paradoxically, this is probably the most fitting resolution of all. Jackson's mystique—his surrounding aura of mystery, awe, and secrecy—was enhanced rather than diminished, as it might have been with a concrete answer. We're left with a fascinating possibility: somewhere, there could be one last Michael Jackson recording, perhaps the very first. We may never know for sure.

The word "icon" is overused, but, in Jackson's case, it is appropriate. At some point, he ceased to be just the world's most popular entertainer and became a symbol, worthy of veneration. Whether he was ever comfortable with that status we can only ponder. This ten-foot icon of Jackson was unveiled in 2006 in Las Vegas. There are countless similar representations of him all over the world.

22

Close to the Threshold of Hell

On June 25, 2009, paramedics arrived at Michael Jackson's home at 100 North Carolwood Drive, Beverly Hills, at 12:24 p.m. They were responding to a 911 call from Jackson's security staff. After finding Jackson wasn't breathing, the paramedics attempted CPR on him, compressing his chest and delivering mouth-to-mouth ventilation until, after forty-two minutes, he exhaled. The paramedics looked at each other in relief. "Let's get him to the hospital. Now!" They then rushed the still unconscious-but-breathing Jackson to the Ronald Reagan UCLA Medical Center, with fractured ribs and internal bleeding (from the vigorous cardiopulmonary resuscitation), but no apparent brain damage.

After several minutes, three surgeons emerged and addressed a group of journalists who had congregated at the hospital. For a few moments, the unusually subdued journalists and everyone else in the hospital's reception area turned toward the three arrivals. The media workers were still clueless and confused but captivated. They'd heard Jackson had been taken to the hospital, but for what? Was he still alive? Was he conscious? Was it an illness, an accident, an attack, a suicide attempt? All were equally plausible. Jackson had been creating headlines for thirty years and for a bewildering range of reasons. He continued to baffle everyone, as he had done for years, even as he lay in a hospital bed. As always, he gave no answers, allowing others to draw their own conclusions. On this occasion, the medics were in charge of the relevant information. One surgeon half-smiled and said they expected a complete recovery. She kept the address brief, describing how Jackson had been admitted, breathing but unconscious, and that he was now comfortable. More than that she wouldn't say. The journalists, no longer subdued, let fly with a volley of questions. There were no replies.

After twelve days, the fifty-year-old Jackson left hospital unassisted. Journalists were gathered but there were no opportunities for questions. Jackson, wearing fedora, sunglasses, facemask, pajamas, and an overcoat, waved but didn't speak. He was driven away in a Mercedes-Benz 500 SEL, cameras recording every second. As he left, an aide confirmed that Jackson had made a full recovery, though without specifying the cause of the problem, and that he appreciated their wishes. This sounded odd and ritualistic; there hadn't been any wishes. Within three days, Jackson resumed rehearsals for his fifty-show comeback concerts, *This Is It*, at London's 20,000 capacity O2 Arena. All seats to the concerts had long since sold. The concerts were due to start in only three days, so there was an understandable delay.

Critics doubted if he was capable of recapturing the spell he held in the late twentieth century; they pointed out that his lack of activity had hurt his already failing status. Enthusiasts thought the opposite: inactivity primed greater anticipation. Jackson's return to a British stage for the first time in twelve years came at a time when established performers were outdoing their younger counterparts: Madonna's 2008 *Sticky and Sweet* tour was the highest grossing tour by a solo artist that year. The Police's reunion tour brought in $340 million; and among 2007's biggest concerts were standouts from Bruce Springsteen and Bon Jovi. In the event, Jackson's hospitalization cranked up even greater interest in his concerts. Jackson completed thirty-nine of the scheduled events, taking a scheduled break from October to December and an unscheduled week's break for an unspecified reason. Canceled concert ticket owners were promised their money back, but, curiously, few took up the option, preferring instead to hold on to the tickets, perhaps as some kind of validation of their relationship with Jackson. That was probably worth more than the £50 they paid for the ticket.

Neither Randy Phillips, of promoters AEG Live, nor any of Jackson's team, would reveal exactly how much Jackson earned from the concerts. North of $80 million, according to most estimates. And, as if to remind the world, he happened to be in the right part of the universe at the right time in history, sales of his albums picked up. Jackson had sold somewhere in the region of 500–750 million records worldwide before the concerts. He'd declined to record any new material for the concerts. So, in the absence of a new studio album, fans bought digital or physical copies of his existing records, even though most had probably already got copies in their collections. Again, there was some sort of validation at work: as if fans wanted to affirm their loyalty, affection, and perhaps love for Jackson.

They probably thought he needed it. After all, it had been four years since Jackson had been cleared in court of charges of sexual abuse, but, even as an innocent man, he had never shrugged the innuendo that had existed since as far back at 1993 when he faced imputations. Since then Jackson had been abused, not by logic or evidence, but by allusive rumors or disparaging hints; undertones, insinuations, or whispers about Jackson had circulated for about sixteen years and Jackson had no magic powerful enough to make them disappear.

As a consequence Jackson had existed in a kind of semi-organized pandemonium: more than any popular entertainer in history, his life was in tumult and had been for years. If he wasn't in court, he was in front of cameras, at one point in 2003 appearing as if he was determined to annihilate his own reputation. He had children, though not by conventional means, then, as if to underline his unfitness to be a parent, held one of them over a hotel balcony. He turned on his record label, accusing key personnel of racism. Then at last, out of the commotion, he promised stability, the stability of a long residency in London, where he would just sing, dance, and enchant the world as he had done in the 1980s and 1990s. Jackson emerged triumphant after a stupendous series of concerts in London, released a live album of the show, featured in a documentary concert film and made two studio albums full of new material over the next ten years.

By 2019, Jackson had become a virtual recluse. He was rarely seen outside Neverland and, while his occasional podcasts kept him in touch with fans, he ceased to be a relevant figure in showbusiness. In his sixtieth year, Jackson was rich again and, while the studio albums he released after the O2 dates were politely but not rapturously received, he seemed to be settling for a sedentary-type of semi-retirement. The likes of Billie Eilish, Taylor Swift, and Ed Sheeran had moved up to the level Jackson once occupied. His status was much like that of his peer Madonna, the best-selling female artist in history, who, at a similar age, swapped stadiums and arenas for more intimate settings when performing her *Madame X* concerts in 2019–20.

And then the stories returned to torment him again. A television documentary produced by HBO and the UK's Channel 4 and directed by Dan Reed was released after all manner of legal obstacles were overcome. The documentary featured James Safechuck and Wade Robson, both of whom claimed that they were sexually abused from their childhood into their teen years. The documentary renewed suspicions about Jackson. He denied the allegations as he had done many times before, and tried to stop transmission. To no avail. Jackson wasn't prepared to let the tv documentary go unchallenged: he couldn't stop the broadcast, but he could counter it. Deluged with requests for a reaction, he responded to as many as humanly possible, resolutely denying the claims of his two accusers. It was like a Vegas card player's methodology: keep repeating the same thing over and over and you eventually cheat chance. As well as his blazing denials, he set his legal team about dismantling Safechuck and Robson, as well as Reed. Robson, the lawyers pointed out, testified under oath in Jackson's defense when the performer faced charges of child molestation, first by Jordan Chandler in 1993 then in 2005 by Gavin Arvizo. But it made no difference. Pop stars can withstand infamy and, in many cases, profit from it; but Jackson's stain was, by then, indelible.

None of this happened, of course. The paramedics actually arrived at 12:26 p.m. by which time Jackson appeared lifeless. "When I picked him up, his legs were quite cool," Richard Senneff, an LA paramedic remembered. "His eyes were quite dry," Senneff was quoted by CNN's Alan Duke. The ambulance team couldn't detect a pulse and the heart monitor indicated that Jackson was flatlining as he lay on his bedroom floor. Senneff estimated that Jackson had stopped breathing for at least twenty minutes before he and other members of crew arrived at North Carolwood Road. Jackson was eventually pronounced dead at 2:26 p.m.

*   *   *

In yet another parallel universe, Jackson retired in 1975 at the age of seventeen. This improbable, but artful scenario was suggested by Ludovic Hunter-Tinley, of the *Financial Times* in 2003, six years before Jackson's death. "Suppose Michael Jackson were a trim, middle-aged man with a greying Afro hairstyle and some gold discs hanging on his wall as mementoes of his childhood stardom," Hunter-Tinley pitches his idea. When Joe Jackson decided to move his sons away from Motown and toward Epic, Michael stepped back from the front line and left his brothers to develop their showbusiness careers without him. In 2003, Michael still got calls from journalists, but only when they were writing those "Where are they now?" stories.

In Hunter-Tinley's scenario, *Off the Wall* and *Thriller* would never have materialized. Nor would Neverland; Jackson wouldn't have been able to afford it. A lot of lawyers and plastic surgeons in Southern California would be less wealthy. And the tabloids would have missed out on one of their most dependable sources of outlandish stories. But musically, would the world be different? Hunter-Tinley thinks not. Elvis and the Beatles forced a paradigm shift—a complete transformation in which the entire grammar of popular music was replaced by something new. Jackson's music didn't have a comparable effect.

This is a fair point, though Jackson's impact went far beyond music and was often oblique. Hunter-Tinley hinted at this when he observed, "While his [Jackson's] skin colour has lightened over the years (a pigment disorder, he claims), popular culture has become blacker, African-American music, fashion and slang are crucial elements of youth culture worldwide." This was not the case in 1982, when Jackson was, as we noted in Chapter 16, the first black performer to get rotation airplay on MTV. "He led the transition from a racially segregated music market to a more fluid one," concluded Hunter-Tinley, speculating that Jackson's imagined early retirement would have left someone else to take the lead. Prince or Whitney Houston shaped up as possibles.

Yet it remains a paradox of his life. Did he help persuade America that race no longer mattered? Or did he remind America that it mattered so much he wanted to wipe it out of his life? When, in 1969, Jackson first appeared, barely eleven years old, with a hit record, no one would have anticipated the impact he would make. He might have been just another flash in the pan kiddie pop singer: cute, but destined to vanish the moment "I Want You Back" was displaced at the top of the charts by Shocking Blue's "Venus" on February 7, 1970. Yet nothing like that happened: Jackson hardly struggled to find his place in the landscape. He fitted right in: a perfect compatibility of biography and history.

The preternaturally talented young Jackson appeared at a time in history when the terra firma was unsettled and civil rights promised to change what had previously been concrete certainties of American life. Jackson was a familiar and comforting figure: a gifted black child, who could sing and dance and would probably do no more than this. His role was to entertain people. And by people, I mean mainly whites. Jackson had no resemblance to Malcolm X, Bobby Seale, Martin Luther King, or any of the other African Americans who had shaken the foundations of American society. Or rather, he *did* have a resemblance. That was the point. He was a black person who inspired good feelings rather than dread, not by persuading America that the struggle was over but by inviting them not to think about it.

At this stage, Jackson's life could have been an update of the sociologist Jan Nederveen Pieterse's thesis. "The black male's access to the white man's world is conditional," wrote Pieterse in his book *White on Black*, which presents illustrations from history to show how black people, men in particular, have been allowed to become successful, as servants or entertainers on the condition they don't rock the boat. "A desexualized figure," like a child star, was perfect, as was a minister or a scholar, or even "a brainless athlete or super-stud." These characters conformed to racial stereotypes, so they could easily be assimilated into the white mentality. Blacks were permitted to manifest excellence in two realms, sports and the entertainment industry—both areas where they performed for the amusement and delectation of white audiences. They still do, of course. Historically, the fears of slave rebellions and anxiety over civil rights were assuaged by flamboyantly talented entertainers who were too grateful to be concerned with bucking the system. Whites were able to exorcise their trepidation by rewarding a few blacks with money and status way beyond the reach of the majority. The young Jackson had barely begun to reap his rewards and could, at a different time in history, have disappeared in a vapor trail. But, at the time, the world was agreed: Jackson was a true talent, perhaps the truest talent of the 1960s and 1970s, that decisive interregnum between slavery's offspring, segregation, and the first stirrings of civil rights.

Unbeknown to everyone, Jackson was already rehearsing for another role. A star in his own right by the time the Jackson 5 left Motown (in 1975) and became the Jacksons, Michael came into his own as an individual at Epic, particularly after his epoch-launching album *Off the Wall*. Even at twenty-one, he seemed mature enough to be able to reimagine the African American experience through the prism of upwardly mobile achievers rather than ghetto dwellers or combative radicals. Was he peddling facts or fables? It didn't matter. Again, his timing was perfect. He was black and he was successful and, even more importantly, he was visible. The civil rights movement had given way to Black Power, but now both were giving way to the black bourgeoisie: cool, urbane, sophisticated, ambitious, and seemingly unencumbered by racism. An emblem of a new age. The firebrands were still vocal, the fury was still in the streets, blacks were still being beaten and killed. But this was a time before Black Lives Matter when considerations like these were pushed into a background narrative. The vision of the historical moment was white-suited 24-year-old Jackson, as he appeared on the cover of *Thriller* (1982).

Praising Jackson was respectable: it meant whites could persuade themselves that the specter of historical racism was gone and that they were contributing to a fair and more righteous society in which talented African Americans could rise to the top. It seems strange that Jackson was influential in encouraging this belief and, in the process, animating a mainstream enthusiasm for black popular music even as his own skin shade became mysteriously fairer and his face, particularly his nose, altered dramatically. Or perhaps it isn't so strange. It's possible that Jackson's global acceptance as an entertainer was at least partly because he was a black person with the world at his feet, and could have anything he wanted apart from the thing he seemed to desire most. He wanted to be white. The consummate purveyor of a cool funk that made his African American roots audible in every note, Jackson was so evidently uncomfortable in his own skin that he wanted to shed it.

"I am a black American . . . I am proud of my race," proclaimed 35-year-old Jackson in a 1993 television interview with Oprah Winfrey. But it sounded implausible. For years, he seemed to be trying to escape his blackness; since 1979 in fact, when he had an accident during rehearsals and had plastic surgery that left him with a narrower nose. It was the first of several procedures: his lips lost plumpness and his chin acquired a cleft. Combined with his chemically treated hair, his blanched skin, and the signs of dermal fillers, the overall impression he gave was of a man trying to discard his natural appearance and replace it with that of a white man.

*   *   *

No one knew it at the time, but Jackson was still rehearsing for future roles: self-possessed emblem of a new age he might have been, but he was on his way to notoriety, stopping en route for a period as eccentric-genius popstar. In the 1980s, Jackson's hygienic spotlessness was taken for granted. No one whiffed malevolent intent. Even when evidence of Jackson's idiosyncrasies began to appear, he was no less serviceable as a representation, but of something other than a new age. Jackson was like a genetically modified chameleon that changed color not to blend into its environment but to stand out. Many of his quirks seem to be contrived, perhaps. Jackson knew all about the benefits of publicity. But, for all his ingenuity, Jackson surely didn't design all his own peculiarities. More likely, he was genuinely peculiar. And that was the beauty of it all.

Jackson was spectacularly successful, copiously rich, an overachiever without parallel. And he was black. And odd. Arguably odder than any artist in history. Any number of stars had booze and drugs tendencies. Several had puzzling allegiances to doctrinaire cults; Tom Cruise was one of a number of adherents to Scientology, for example. Some stars had weirdly uncommon dress senses: Lady Gaga wore a dress made of raw beef to the 2010 MTV Awards. Elvis had a gargantuan appetite, consuming about 10–12,000 calories per day shortly before his death, and a diet that would horrify gourmets; he especially liked peanut butter, bacon and banana sandwiches. But Jackson had no peers when it came to idiosyncrasies.

Critics and disciples alike accepted Jackson was unusual. Extremely unusual. They interpreted his unusualness differently, but they were agreed on his character. He was a black man who had grown and developed from a childstar to a grownup icon and was, by twenty-four, one of the world's preeminent entertainers. He had the world at his feet. *He was a black man* with the world at his feet. So, what did he do? Become even more spellbinding. He became funny, ostensibly, and unwittingly, as when he was pictured in a hyperbaric tank or had befriended a monkey, not as a pet but as a companion. Then there were unsettling stories about his attempt to purchase the skeleton of the Elephant Man; it was a ghoulish and puzzling bid of £1 million (rejected by London Hospital Medical College in 1987, according to Associated Press). Why not spend his money on a Learjet 75 Liberty at $9.9 million, or a case of Goût de Diamants champagne at $1.5 million a bottle, or even a 59.60-carat Pink Star diamond ring, which could be picked up at auction for about $70 million? Or just squander it. These are the kinds of questions he never answered. His silence made him even more like an unputdownable book.

The allegations that emerged in 1994 made him even more compulsive reading. Accused of abuse, Jackson, then thirty-five, settled out of court. It seems unlikely that any star today would be treated as leniently by the public as Jackson. Combined with proliferating stories of his eccentricities and the secretive goings-on at his well-protected Neverland estate, the Jackson mystique could have taken on a thoroughly unwholesome character. In the event, this rumor-within-rumors became the single most compelling reason for his lasting attractiveness.

In many entertainers, moral or character deficiencies can be ruinous. But not in Jackson's case: he appears to have operated untrammeled as a serial child abuser, often with the tacit, if unwitting, complicity of parents. The reason it didn't damage him is that audiences, especially white audiences, found his flaws reassuring. Here was a manchild with blessings in abundance and arguably more adulation than any other entertainer: he could have reaped the wonder of the world. But he was defective, grotesquely so. And, in a black man, this made him more of a comfort than a menace. Once a celestial being who flashed across cultural heavens, only to crash spectacularly and devastatingly to earth, Jackson was a reminder that black men, even those gilded in virtuosity, can be deceptively dangerous. But reassuringly, they will instigate their own destruction.

There is a reason why the ruination of black stars is satisfying and again, the clues lie in Pieterse's theory. Jackson was a singer, a dancer, an idiosyncratic collector, a quirky obsessive, a sexual enigma, and many other things besides. He didn't fight racism or position himself as an icon of black endeavor. Yet he lived and played in a violent, tribal, conflict-torn society trying to rid itself of its most stubborn demon. Maybe Jackson didn't conform to established stereotypes, but he evolved into a screwball amalgam. That was his value: fabulously talented, worshiped by millions, had enough money to make the world go round in any direction he chose. And yet he was a mass of foibles, flaws, quirks, and assorted idiosyncrasies that made him, to use a word I've avoided so far in this book, wacko. (Vigilant readers will remember I used it but in quotation marks when referring to British media depictions in Chapter 12.)

* * *

Who created Michael Jackson? We all did. Jackson possessed singular gifts but at a cost to his full humanity. Like every other black entertainer in history, Jackson was playing in a white psychodrama. His role was a tightly defined one: play music and amuse people. Amusement can take many forms, but as long as audiences were agreeably distracted and interested in the foibles that characterized Jackson's latter years, everything was fine. Inadequacies or deficiencies were more than fine. Jackson's shortcomings demonstrated that, even with status and money, a black man would still fail. Not because of racism, or anything in the outside world, but because of *inherent vice*, this being a natural characteristic that makes things liable to damage. It's an inborn defect, in other words. There is nothing so accommodating to a racist than to witness the rise and rise of a black figure to a position of seemingly unassailable prominence and prestige, only for him or her to self-destruct.

And the world did see Jackson self-destruct; he did it in full view. The *Living with Michael Jackson* documentary in 2003, was Jackson's own initiative: he actually wanted to appear on tv and reveal that he, a 44-year-old man, was having children for sleepovers, sometimes in his bedroom. There has never been such visible slaughter in showbusiness. Everyone was left to wonder where Jackson's motivation came from. Some sacrificial imperative, perhaps. A desire to create chaos. Whatever he was trying to do, the bloodletting started in 2003 and never stopped. Jackson's death just opened up a new artery.

A hopelessly flawed Jackson, wracked with anxiety and discontent, demonstrably unhappy with his physical appearance, and probably uncomfortable with his ethnicity, was a much more appealing prospect than the confident and stylish sophisticate who stood astride the world in the 1980s. The urbane Jackson was a great reminder of the strides America had made in ridding itself of racism, but the latter-day Jackson was notice that genuine equality was never going to happen.

I've argued that Jackson's secondary meaning was as a symbol. I'm presuming his primary meaning was as an entertainer, but perhaps the two are one and the same thing. At a vital time in the post-civil rights period, when America needed assurance it was changing in the direction it was supposed to, Jackson heaved into view as both a shiny representative and unmistakable evidence of newly aspirational blacks. He demonstrated how a black man could be one of the greatest entertainers in history, holding his own alongside Elvis, Sinatra, and the Beatles.

Now reader, stop reading for ten seconds and think of five African Americans who have earned widespread social approval over the past forty years. Michael Jordan will probably be on most readers' lists. Barack Obama too, even though his presidential tenure revealed fallibility that was once considered unthinkable. Oprah Winfrey would surely appear on most lists. Beyoncé, like Jackson an aspirational singer whose dreamlike rise was followed by a generation, will feature too. George Floyd might crop up, not so much for what he did, but for launching an unprecedented global movement. Probably not Michael Jackson. Yet his achievements compare favorably with those of the others, he is as relevant and challenging as any of them, and he will certainly be remembered as vividly. But probably for his decline rather than ascent or plateau. (The years 1970–83 would roughly be his ascent, 1984–90 his plateau, and 1991 onward his descent, at first gradual, then shifting steeply downward from 2003 and plummeting, of course, after his death.)

No relevant and challenging figure ever gets complete approval. Jackson clearly never will. Many of his onetime fans turned on him, some, like Wesley Morris, in the *New York Times*, wondering, "what if his outward self became some semiconscious manifestation of a monster that lurked within?" The condemnation wasn't unanimous either. "I believe with all my heart that Michael Jackson was not only a beautiful gift from God, but perhaps a Messenger from Him," wrote Bridget Rowley in Lorette C. Luzajic's 2010 collection of essays. Whether he is a monster or a divine gift will remain a matter of perspective. There will never be agreement on Jackson, his importance, or his legacy. He will continue to splinter opinion and defy categorization; as do most significant characters in history. The more Jackson is monstered, the more his worshipful apostles will be convinced he was crucified—for what, no one is sure.

Once iconized, Jackson seemed to find reality a disagreeable place and decided to wander away from it. Perhaps his christening of his Californian home Neverland was a clue we all missed. Jackson became not just untouchable, but unreachable, unrecognizable, and unreal. But none of this mattered: when he stopped enchanting people, he began to trouble them. And that, in essence, was Jackson's life: once a shining symbol of a post-civil rights land of new opportunity, he seemed to demonstrate the American dream was alive, but that it was a bad dream. Black people can rise as far as their talent and capacity for hard work will take them, in Jackson's case, to the very apex of society. But even those who stand astride the world and have everything they could possibly want can't resist damaging themselves. Some whites do it. But most blacks do. They want more and more and never quite understand what the world is telling them: all this is yours—you have wealth, fame, and an abundance of every constituent of the good life, but you can still destroy yourself and everybody watching will help you, so go ahead. Jackson did exactly that. He took every opportunity on offer and still wasn't satisfied. When he started the destruction, he found there was no shortage of people willing to assist.

There is a confusing moral in his destruction. Confusing that is, unless we keep remembering Jackson was black. No matter how lighter or Caucasian-like he became, he was still a black man, as Don King had reminded him in blunter terms, early in his career. And this is precisely why he remained such a compelling character, long after his popularity had transitioned into notoriety. In this sense, Jackson represented America and its values more faithfully than any of the usual figures. Neil Armstrong, the astronaut; JFK, whose vision guided America through the Cold War; Betsy Ross, the flag-making patriot; and Elvis, the handsome trailblazer who ended up a bloated, burned-out caricature of himself. They all seem inadequate representatives compared to Jackson: in his life we see the true America, its liberal hypocrisy, and tarnished utopianism barely disguising a racism that refuses to disappear.

Years after his death, Jackson draws the admiration and perhaps respect of an unknown legion of devotees, music aficionados, and perhaps cynics who have witnessed black men symbolically emasculated many times before. For them, he is a falsely disparaged hero. He also incenses a sharp-clawed public who believe they were taken in by his depraved subterfuge; they will denounce him as an unforgivably malfeasant villain. In his afterlife, Jackson will be a fugitive soul destined to remain in a shadowland, some distance from heaven and perhaps close to the threshold of hell.

Maybe he was cursed after all.

Destruction and Creation: KeyPlayers

Family

JOE JACKSON 1928–2018. Father, manager, and patriarch of the family

KATHERINE JACKSON B. 1930. Mother and costume designer

REBBIE JACKSON-BROWN B. 1950. Eldest sister

JACKIE JACKSON B. 1951. Eldest brother

TITO JACKSON B. 1953. Continues to perform with the band.

JERMAINE JACKSON B. 1954. *Let's Get Serious* was his 1980 million-selling album

LATOYA JACKSON B. 1956. Singer, songwriter, reality tv star, and sometime critic of Michael

MARLON JACKSON B. 1957. Closest in age to MJ (1½ years apart); the two shared lead vocalist roles as the Jackson 5's lead singers

STEVEN RANDY JACKSON B. 1961. Youngest brother; performed with the group since he was eight

JANET JACKSON B. 1966. One of the most successful recording artists of the late twentieth century with seven number one albums on the *Billboard* charts

Jackson's Children

MICHAEL JOSEPH "PRINCE" JACKSON JR. B.1997. Jackson's first child; the most reclusive of the three children, he does work in the entertainment industry

PARIS JACKSON B. 1998. Jackson's only daughter and the biological child of Debbie Rowe, who signed over custody of Paris to Jackson, following the couple's divorce in 1999; now a model and actor

BIGI JACKSON II B. 2002. Formerly known as Prince Michael "Blanket," his biological mother, a surrogate, is not known; he is also under the guardianship of Katherine

Friends

ELIZABETH TAYLOR 1932–2011. Born in London, moved to the United States as a child and became world-renowned star of *Cleopatra*, *Giant*, and *Cat on a Hot Tin Roof*; her tempestuous affair and two marriages with Richard Burton was the source of one of the biggest scandals of the twentieth century; Taylor was a stalwart supporter of Jackson, dismissing his oddities and defending him against abuse accusations.

DIANA ROSS B. 1944. Born in Detroit, she was already an established star at Motown when the Jackson 5 signed for the iconic label; she was lead singer with the Supremes, then a solo artist; she duetted with MJ and stood by him when he was accused of abuse; some say MJ idolized her; he made his solo debut in 1971 on a Diana Ross tv show.

URI GELLER B. 1946. Born in Israel, he served in the Six Day War in 1967, was wounded and became a nightclub entertainer; his purported psychic powers earned him a reputation and he became internationally known for his spoon-bending; he settled in England; after befriending Jackson, he asked him to be best man at a ceremony to renew his wedding vows; he put Jackson in touch with Martin Bashir, who made the fateful documentary on Jackson; in 2015, he announced he was leaving England to return to Israel. **HIT LIST**

AL SHARPTON B. 1954. New Yorker, was ordained a minister in the Pentecostal church at ten, and became engaged politically as a teenager; he led several protests at what he considered racial injustice before damaging his reputation by being involved in the Tawana Brawley case in 1987; a longtime friend of the Jackson family, he supported Michael in his attempt to expose his record company as racist; in 2020, Sharpton spoke at the memorial for George Floyd and led the wake for Daunte Wright in 2021.

DEBBIE ROWE B. 1958. Native of Spokane, Washington, she met MJ while working for the dermatologist, Dr. Arnold Klein, who was treating MJ for vitiligo. She had first married in 1982 and divorced six years later. She married MJ in 1996 and had two children; they divorced in 1999; she received $8 million and a Beverly Hills home and gave full custody of the children to MJ. In 2001, Rowe went to a private judge to have her parental rights for the two children terminated. In 2004, after Jackson was charged with child abuse, she tried to reverse the decision. A series of lawsuits followed. She was diagnosed with breast cancer in 2016.

DIANA, PRINCESS OF WALES 1961–97. Met MJ only once in 1988 but remained a friend until her death; her famous tv interview with Martin Bashir in 1995 enhanced her public image and influenced MJ's decision to let Bashir interview him; Diana's ambiguous relationship with media was comparable with Jackson's. She died following a horrific car crash in Paris on August 31, 1997, when fleeing from paparazzi. Although an inquest jury concluded that the chasing paparazzi and Diana's driver were both to blame for her death, conspiracy theories around her death continued to circulate for years.

SHMULEY BOTEACH B. 1966. Born in LA, he is an American Orthodox Jewish rabbi, who, at twenty-two, was sent to Oxford, England, where he served for eleven years; during this time he befriended Uri Geller; on returning to the United States, he built a following as a tv show host; became a friend and perhaps spiritual adviser of Jackson in the 1990s; in 2001, he became involved in MJ's charity Heal the Kids, aka Time for Kids; MJ fell out with him shortly after; after Jackson's death, Boteach published transcripts of conversations with Jackson; he also said he believed Jackson's accusers. HIT LIST

LISA MARIE PRESLEY B. 1968. Only child of Elvis Presley, she married MJ at a secret ceremony in the Dominican Republic in 1994, twenty days after her divorce from Danny Keough, whom she had married in 1988 and with whom she had two children. In January 1996, she filed for divorce, citing irreconcilable differences. Years later, she told Oprah, "He [MJ] was conditioned to get himself where he needed to go for his career, and he became very good at making and creating and puppeteering."

BRETT BARNES B. 1982. He was only five when he first met MJ after writing him a fan letter; at nine, he began visiting Neverland, both with and without his parents; when, in 1993, Jordan Chandler made claims against MJ, Barnes defended MJ; saying he "kissed you like you kiss your mother"; he testified in support of MJ at the 2005 trial; he didn't appear in *Leaving Neverland*; it's believed he moved to Australia.

Accusers

THOMAS W. SNEDDON 1941–2014. LA-born district attorney; he served in Vietnam, 1967–9; on his return joined the DA's office in Santa Barbara and became DA in 1983; twice tried to convict Jackson on child molestation charges; first in 1993 but the case collapsed when the family of Jordan Chandler accepted a settlement and declined to testify against him; a decade later he led a second investigation and the jury cleared Jackson. HIT LIST

JAMES SAFECHUCK B. 1978. Born in Simi Valley, CA; was nine or ten years old when he met MJ and became a companion, touring on the *Bad* concert tour; originally defended MJ and claimed he was never assaulted, but in 2014 he filed a lawsuit against MJ's estate claiming that therapy helped him realize he was sexually abused when he was ten; he was one of the main accusers in *Leaving Neverland*.

JORDAN CHANDLER B.1980. Introduced to MJ when he was twelve and visited Neverland regularly; in 1993, the LA police launched an inquiry into Jackson after Chandler alleged abuse against him; no criminal evidence was found by the police after a search; the Chandler family sued Jackson for $30 million; in January 1994, the case was settled for $25 million and from February to April, the grand juries declined to indict Jackson. Later that year, Chandler said he would not testify; he was reportedly given a new identity after the settlement.

WADE ROBSON B. 1982. Australian dancer and choreographer; became a companion of MJ after winning a dance contest in Brisbane; testified at MJ's trial in 1993, saying he didn't abuse him, but later, in 2015, changed his claim and accused MJ of abusing him when he was seven; like Safechuck a key character in *Leaving Neverland*.

GAVIN ARVIZO B. 1989. Suffered from cancer when he was a child, and first met Jackson, aged ten, in one of the hospitals where he was being treated; came to prominence in the 2003 tv documentary *Living with Michael Jackson*; in 2003, he claimed Jackson molested him, and a few months later, Jackson was charged with partaking in lewd and lascivious acts with a child under the age of fourteen; in 2005 Jackson was cleared of charges.

Professional Associates

BERRY GORDY B.1929. Influential founder of Motown, Jackson 5's second label, he was the first African American music entrepreneur (and songwriter/producer) to create a record label designed for mainstream, not just black markets. His label began as Tamla Records in 1959, adopting the name Motown the following year. He sold the company for $61 million in 1988. The Jackson 5 spent the formative years of their professional life at Motown. When they left in 1975, he retained the name, obliging the brothers to continue as the Jacksons.

QUINCY JONES B. 1933. Born in Chicago, Jones played trumpet for Lionel Hampton's band as well as Count Basie, Cannonball Adderley, Dizzy Gillespie, and other big names who came to prominence after the swing era (ending mid-1940s). In the 1960s, he became an A&R man for Mercury Records, his forte being jazz. He recovered from a life-threatening brain aneurism in 1974. Working on the soundtrack of *The Wiz*, he met MJ and this led to a collaboration that yielded *Off the Wall* (1979), *Thriller* (1982), and *Bad* (1987). He also wrote several film scores, worked as a cultural ambassador and continued to record. His *Q: Soul Bossa Nostra* was released in 2010.

WALTER YETNIKOFF B. 1933. Brooklyn lawyer-turned-record executive, he was president and ceo of CBS Records when it was bought by Sony for $2 billion in January 1988. Sony needed content for its groundbreaking hardware, including the Walkman and, eventually, the cd. MJ described him as "a friend and a true believer. In my years with CBS, he's encouraged me to be my own man and to do the things that had to be done the way I had to do them." Initially skeptical about the *Thriller* video, he backed Jackson in what, at first, seemed an outlandish venture.

GORDON KEITH 1939–2020. "The man who discovered the Jacksons," as he often claimed, was the co-owner of a record label Steeltown Records, based in Chicago. He signed the Jackson 5 to his then fledgling label in 1967 after seeing them play at their own home. Steeltown released the single "Big Boy" in early 1968. Later in the year, Motown took an interest in the band, but, even after a court case, Keith could not hold on to the band and he didn't profit from his early insight.

ANTHONY PELLICANO B. 1944. Private investigator who played an important role in MJ's 1993 negotiations with Evan Chandler, whose son accused Jackson of molestation; he had several other highprofile clients, including Roseanne Barr, Tom Cruise, and Sylvester Stallone; was convicted of seventy-eight charges of wiretapping, racketeering, conspiracy, and wire fraud in 2008, and sentenced to fifteen years, released in 2019.

FRANK DILEO 1947–2011. Became MJ's manager in 1984, previously VP at Epic Records; helped negotiate the historic 1982 deal with PepsiCo, reputedly worth $10 million. Parted in 1989 after MJ was disappointed with sales of *Bad*; he reunited with MJ shortly before his death in 2009.

TOMMY MOTTOLA B. 1949. Onetime singer from New York, who, in 1974, started his own music management company; was appointed president of CBS Records/ Sony Music (US) in 1988; left Sony in 1993; his working relationship with Jackson went sour in 2001 after the release of *Invincible;* Jackson accused him of racism and of being part of a recording company conspiracy against black artists; Al Sharpton defended Mottola against the criticism, while maintaining concerns about the industry generally; Mottola married Mariah Carey in 1993. She later revealed that he had a control over her; she called their estate in New York "Sing Sing" after the local prison as she felt she was monitored by cameras and "armed guards." They divorced in 1998. HIT LIST

THOMAS MESEREAU B. 1950. Criminal lawyer, an alumnus of Harvard and the LSE, he successfully defended Jackson against charges of child abuse, in 2004–5; he came to prominence in 2003 when he represented actor Robert Blake on a murder charge; he also worked for Mike Tyson and rap mogul Suge Knight; in 2017 he was hired to defend Bill Cosby and was replaced two years later after Cosby was convicted of felony sexual assault.

CONRAD MURRAY B. 1953. Born in Grenada in the Caribbean, he studied medicine in Texas and Tennessee; practiced in Las Vegas; he first met Jackson when treating one of his children in 2006 and, in 2009 was appointed his personal physician for the planned London concerts; a Los Angeles jury found him guilty of the involuntary manslaughter of Jackson in 2011 and he served two years of a four-year sentence; he continues to appeal his conviction (see Chapter 3).

MYUNG-HO LEE birthdate unknown. US-educated South Korean lawyer, he was a business adviser to MJ, who said Jackson hired him in the late 1990s to put his finances in order; in 2003, he claimed in a law suit that Jackson owed him $12 million and was near-bankruptcy; the suit alleged Jackson had $200 million loans in a single year and continued to spend lavishly in order to maintain his extravagant lifestyle; in his suit, he claimed Jackson was a "ticking financial time bomb waiting to explode at any moment"; a confidential out-of-court settlement was reached in 2003, thus preventing Jackson's financial situation from becoming known.

ABDULLAH BIN HAMAD BIN ISA AL-KHALIFA B. 1976. A member of the Bahrain royal family, he invited MJ and his family to stay with him in 2005, immediately after Jackson was cleared at trial; on his account, he loaned Jackson money to pay legal fees; an expensive but ill-fated musical project ended with al-Khalifa claiming Jackson owed him $7 million in 2008, they reached an out-of-court settlement.

Cultural Figures

NAT KING COLE 1919–65. Singer and pianist born in Montgomery, Alabama, who became arguably the first African American to cross into entertainment's mainstream when he hosted a short-lived tv variety show in 1956–7. He struggled to find a position in the civil rights movement: despite being attacked by racists in 1956, he wasn't supportive, at least initially, maintaining, as an entertainer, he had no role to play. Later, in the 1960s, he joined other black performers in boycotting segregated venues and aligned himself with the NAACP and supported the March on Washington in 1963.

SAMMY DAVIS JR. 1925–90. Inspirational black entertainer who was a symbol for the civil rights movement, Davis was criticized in his early career for his close associations with whites, particularly Sinatra and the Rat Pack; but later acknowledged for his importance as one of the first black entertainers to achieve mainstream popular acceptance. MJ affirmed a personal debt at Davis's sixtieth birthday tribute, when he sang an unreleased co-composition with the lyric, "You were there before we came / You took the hurt / You took the shame / They built the walls to block your way / You beat them down / You won the day."

MARTIN LUTHER KING 1929–68. Atlanta-born civil rights leader, who was assassinated six months before *I Want You Back* jumped to the number-one-singles spot; MJ was just ten; MLK's civil rights movement was instrumental in legislation that ended racial segregation in 1964/65.

EMMETT TILL 1941–55. Chicago-born African American victim of a racist murder in Money, Mississippi, where he allegedly made a flirtatious remark to a white woman; he was beaten by two white men, who gouged out an eye, shot him in the head, tied him to a cotton gin with barbed wire and threw his body in the Tallahatchie River; he was fourteen; two men were arrested and acquitted by an all-white jury; the trial brought the brutality of segregation in the American southern states into relief and was a spur to what became the civil rights movement; the murder and subsequent trial remain historical landmarks, reminders of the habitual violence occasioned on blacks in the twentieth century, over ninety years after the abolition of slavery.

BILL COSBY B. 1937. Philadelphia-born comedian-actor who was praised for his innovative tv show in the 1980s and damned for his sex offenses in the twenty-first century; a genuine pioneer in tv (he was the first black actor to play a straight lead in a tv show, *I Spy*), Cosby, in the mid-1980s, was hailed for his innovative creation; he was part of the same changing cultural landscape as Jackson; later,

Cosby became a conservative campaigner, urging blacks to stabilize their families and become responsible parents; this alienated him from parts of the African American population; in 2015, he was charged with sexual assault in relation to a 2004 incident and later imprisoned, leading many to conclude he betrayed black Americans.

GLORIA ALLRED B. 1941. Educated at NYU and Loyola Law School; attorney who briefly represented Jordan Chandler in 1993 and subsequently became a severe critic of Jackson; in 2002, she asked California's Department of Social Services County to determine whether it had jurisdiction to investigate MJ for child endangerment after he dangled his child from a balcony; much of her career was spent fighting sex equality cases; she represented the family of Nicole Brown Simpson during the 1995 O. J. Simpson trial and several accusers of Bill Cosby as well as others who accused Donald Trump of sexual harassment.

HIT LIST

O. J. SIMPSON B. 1947. San Francisco-born football star, then actor, in 1995 he was at the center of one of the most famous legal cases in history, when he, an African American, was acquitted of the murder of his wife Nicole, a white woman, and her friend Ronald Goldman; his globally publicized trial started in January 1995, only four months after molestation charges against Jackson were dropped; in February 1997 Simpson was found liable at a civil trial for the wrongful deaths of his wife and Goldman and ordered to pay their families $33.5 million; he later spent nearly nine years in prison for armed robbery and kidnapping, released on parole in 2017.

MADONNA B. 1958. Born in Bay City, Michigan, full name Madonna Louise Ciccone, she vied with Jackson as the world's premier entertainer in the MTV era (c.1981–2000), often provoking outrage with her deliberately controversial videos. More than any other artist of her time, she realized the potential of scandal as a valuable resource rather than a shameful experience. By 1991, she had sold 70 million albums, putting her in the same class as Jackson. She closed a $60 million deal with Time Warner, though her 2007 deal with Live Nation eclipsed this, being valued at $120 million. Complementing her musical career with film, she played in several movies and directed others, including her own biopic.

WHITNEY HOUSTON 1963–2012. Born in Newark, NJ, she started out in a gospel choir before Clive Davis signed her to Arista in 1983; by 1990, she had three best-selling albums; in 1992, she acted in *The Bodyguard* and released the single "I Will Always Love You" to establish herself as one of the world's leading singers; a turbulent marriage and drugs habit precipitated her decline and she died of accidental drowning in a bathtub with drug paraphernalia nearby.

RODNEY KING 1965–2012. Born in Sacramento, CA, he became an unwitting symbol of civil rights when, in 1991, he was beaten by LAPD officers after a highspeed chase; the incident was captured on video and the officers indicted. But after a three-month trial, the officers were cleared, inflaming citizens and prompting riots in LA. On the third day of unrest, he made a public appearance, making his now-famous plea: "People, I just want to say, can't we all get along?" He was found dead at the bottom of a swimming pool in Rialto, California.

HIT LIST An unsubstantiated inventory of people Jackson suspected were trying to destroy him and on whom he intended to wreak vengeance.

Destruction and Creation: Playlist

This playlist can be found at the following spotify link: https://spoti.fi/3wji2C3

Scream
Michael Jackson, Janet Jackson

We Are the World
USA for Africa

Got To Be There
Michael Jackson

Sweet and Innocent
Donny Osmond

Ben
Michael Jackson

One Bad Apple
The Osmonds

When Doves Cry
Prince

Girlfriend
Michael Jackson

I Want You Back
Jackson 5

Say It Loud—I'm Black and I'm Proud
James Brown

Big Boy
The Jackson 5

I Never Loved a Man (the Way I Love You)
Aretha Franklin

Dancing in the Street
Martha and the Vandellas

Georgia on My Mind
Ray Charles

Why Do Fools Fall in Love
Frankie Lymon & The Teenagers

Cross Road Blues
Robert Parker

Stranger in Moscow
Michael Jackson

Billie Jean
Michael Jackson

I Will Always Love You
Whitney Houston

You Rock My World
Michael Jackson

Don't Be Cruel
Otis Blackwell

All Shook Up
Otis Blackwell

Don't Be Cruel
Elvis Presley

All Shook Up
Elvis Presley

To Be Young, Gifted and Black
Bob and Marcia

Ode to Billie Joe
Bobbie Gentry

American Skin (41 shots)
Bruce Springsteen

Heal the World
Michael Jackson

Candle in the Wind 1997
Elton John

Interlude: Pledge
Janet Jackson

Rhythm of the Night
DeBarge

Control
Janet Jackson

Paparazzi
Lady Gaga

Free Xone
Janet Jackson

Tonight's the Night
Janet Jackson

Together Again
Janet Jackson

Rock Your Body
Justin Timberlake

Remember the Time
Michael Jackson

Black or White
Michael Jackson

Like a Prayer
Madonna

Justify My Love
Madonna

Peggy Sue
Buddy Holly

That'll be the Day
Buddy Holly and the Crickets

Lawdy, Miss Clawdy
Lloyd Price

Lawdy, Miss Clawdy
Elvis Presley

Tutti Frutti
Pat Boone

Ain't That a Shame
Pat Boone

This Is America
Childish Gambino

Beat It
Michael Jackson

Superfreak
Rick James

U Can't Touch This
MC Hammer

Electric Avenue
Eddy Grant

She Works Hard For the Money
Donna Summer

Rock Around the Clock
Bill Haley & His Comets

Thriller
Michael Jackson

State of Independence
Donna Summer

Girlfriend
Wings

The Girl Is Mine
Michael Jackson, Paul McCartney

Say, Say, Say
Paul McCartney, Michael Jackson

Ain't No Stopping Us Now
McFadden & Whitehead

If You Don't Know Me By Now
Harold Melvin & The Blue Notes

Shake, Rattle and Roll
Big Joe Turner

Love Me Do
The Beatles

Robin Hood
Dick James

Hey Jude
The Beatles

Revolution
The Beatles

All You Need Is Love
The Beatles

When I'm Sixty-Four
The Beatles

Let It Be
The Beatles

Come Together
The Beatles

Help!
The Beatles

The Long and Winding Road
The Beatles

Dreams
Fleetwood Mac

This Note's For You
Neil Young

It's Now or Never
Elvis Presley

You Make Me Feel (Mighty Real)
Sylvester

Dance, Dance (Yowsah, Yowsah, Yowsah)
Chic

Hey Now Hey (The Other Side of the Sky)
Aretha Franklin

Off the Wall
Michael Jackson

Blame It on the Boogie
Mick Jackson

Blame It on the Boogie
The Jacksons

Shake Your Body (Down to the Ground)
The Jacksons

Who's Lovin' You
The Miracles

Who's Lovin' You
The Jackson 5

Reet Petite (The Finest Girl You Ever Want To Meet)
Jackie Wilson

Way over There
The Miracles

Everyone Was There*
Bob Kayli. *YouTube Music:*

Money (That's What I Want)
Barrett Strong

Money (That's What I Want)
The Beatles

Bye Bye Baby
Mary Wells

Two Lovers
Mary Wells

My Guy
Mary Wells

My Guy
Aretha Franklin

Fingertips, parts 1 and 2
Stevie Wonder

Please Mr. Postman
The Marvelettes

Please Mr. Postman
The Beatles

Use Your Head*
Mary Wells. *YouTube Music:*

For Once in My Life
Stevie Wonder

For Once in My Life
The Temptations

For Once in My Life
The Four Tops

Pretty Baby
The Primettes

Tears Of Sorrow
The Primettes

When the Lovelight Starts Shining Through His Eyes
The Supremes

Where Did Our Love Go
The Supremes

Reach Out and Touch (Somebody's Hand)
Diana Ross

Ain't No Mountain High Enough
Diana Ross & The Supremes, The Temptations

Ain't No Mountain High Enough
Diana Ross

Every Little Bit Hurts
Brenda Holloway

Does Your Mama Know about Me
Bobby Taylor & The Vancouvers

It's Your Thing
The Jackson 5

For What It's Worth
Buffalo Springfield

ABC
The Jackson 5

I'll Be There
The Jackson 5

Ice Ice Baby
Vanilla Ice

Love Makes the World Go Round
Kiki Dee

What the World Needs Now Is Love
Tom Clay

Let's Get Serious
Jermaine Jackson

Blues Away
The Jacksons

Enjoy Yourself
The Jacksons

Show You the Way to Go
The Jacksons

Unforgettable
Nat King Cole

Mona Lisa
Nat King Cole

Autumn Leaves
Nat King Cole

Heartbreak Hotel
Elvis Presley

Why Do Fools Fall in Love
Diana Ross

Don't Waste Your Time/You Wasted Your Time
The Five Fairsteps

You've Changed
The Jackson 5

Some Girls Want Me for Their Lover (Michael the Lover)
The Jackson 5

My Bonnie
Tony Sheridan and the Beat Brothers

We Don't Have to Be Over 21
The Jackson 5

Girl Why Do You Want to Take My Heart
Magical Connection

Let Me Carry Your Schoolbooks**
The Ripples & Waves plus Michael. *YouTube Video*

Let Me Carry Your Schoolbooks*
The Jackson 5. *YouTube Music*:

The Town I Live In
McKinley Mitchell

Shake a Tail Feather
The Five Du-Tones

Tobacco Road
John D. Loudermilk

Venus
Shocking Blue

*Available on YouTube Music
** Available on YouTube Video

BIBLIOGRAPHY

Abramovitch, Seth (2021) "THR Icon: Quincy Jones Reflects on Career, Michael Jackson and Why He Wouldn't Work With Elvis," *The Hollywood Reporter* (May 20). Available at: https://bit.ly/3fEUm3c. Accessed: May 2021.

Abt, Vicki and Seesholtz, Mel (1994) "The Shameless World of Phil, Sally and Oprah: Television Talk Shows and the Deconstructing of Society," *Journal of Popular Culture*, vol. 28, no. 1, pp. 171–191.

Adams, William Lee (2008) "Michael Jackson Settles Out of Court with Sheik," *Time* (November 24). Available at: https://bit.ly/2uLy9wP. Accessed: February 2020.

Amnesty International (2009) "Another Year, Another Unarmed Black Man Killed by Police," *Amnesty International* (January 7). Available at: https://bit.ly /39xkQyy. Accessed: May 2021.

An, Susie (2009) "Record Label Founder Remembers Jackson," *WBEZ Chicago* (June 26). Available at: https://bit.ly/3mvGSKa. Accessed: April 2021.

Andersen, Christopher (1994) *Michael Jackson: Unauthorized*, New York: Simon & Schuster.

Anderson, Kyle (2014) "Janet Jackson's 'Rhythm Nation 1814': Still Dancing and Dreaming 25 Years Later," *Entertainment* (September 19). Available at: https:// bit.ly/2yTJWv8. Accessed: June 2020.

Anderson, John (1897) "Elizabeth Taylor Sells Mystique With a Passion," *Chicago Tribune* (September 27). Available at: https://bit.ly/2Ac5CDo. Accessed: June 2020.

Andrews, David L. and Silk, Michael L. (2010) "Basketball's Ghettocentric Logic," *American Behavioral Scientist*, vol. 53, no. 11, pp. 1626–1644.

Arango, Tim (2008) "Before Obama, There Was Bill Cosby," *New York Times* (November 7). Available at: https://nyti.ms/3yszFQK. Accessed: May 2021.

Associated Press (1987) "Hospital Refuses To Sell Elephant Man Skeleton To Pop Star" (June 18). Available at: https://bit.ly/3eqfKIO. Accessed: April 2021.

Austen, Jake (2009) "The Jackson Find," *Chicago Reader* (September 10). Available at: https://bit.ly/3cSQRpC. Accessed: April 2021.

Baldoni, John (2019) "Should We Still Admire Ronald Reagan?," *Forbes* (August 1). Available at: https://bit.ly/3nWDqIw. Accessed: December 2020.

Baldwin, James (2010; originally 1964) "The White Problem," in *The Cross of Redemption: Uncollected Writings by James Baldwin*, edited by Randall Kenan, New York: Pantheon.

Banfield, Ashleigh, Marx, Tracey and Peduto, Sabrina (2011) "Dr. Conrad Murray Was Talking on Phone to Waitress as Michael Jackson Was Dying, Prosecutors Say," *ABC News* (February 3). Available at: https://abcn.ws/3yLAbJQ. Accessed: May 2021.

Barber, Lynn (2001) "Interview: The Magic Touch," *Observer* (December 9). Available at: https://bit.ly/2VGBWH9. Accessed: February 2020.

Bastin, Giselle (2009) "Filming the Ineffable: Biopics of the British Royal Family," *a/b: Auto/Biography Studies*, vol. 24, no. 1, pp. 34–52.

BBC Home (No date) "1984: Michael Jackson Burned in Pepsi Ad," *On This Day, 1950–2005* (January 27), Available at: https://bbc.in/2Wkpts5. Accessed: July 2020.

BBC News Channel (2009) "In Quotes: The Jackson Memorial," (July 7). Available at: https://bbc.in/2UryAqH. Accessed: February 2020.

Becerra, Hector (2005) "Jackson Finds a New Home in Bahrain," *Los Angeles Times* (October 21). Available at: https://lat.ms/3c9oYrd. Accessed: February 2020.

Bennett, Joy T. (2007) "Michael: The Thrill is Back," *Ebony* (December 7). Available at: https://bit.ly/2ugXHld. Accessed: February 2020.

Blistein, Jon (2019) "Michael Jackson Estate Releases Concert Film During 'Leaving Neverland' Premiere," *Rolling Stone* (March 4). Available at: https://bit.ly/3854zSm. Accessed: June 2020.

Bonnell, Rick (2020) "Exclusive: Michael Jordan on Racism, Education and $100 Million for Social Justice," *Charlotte Observer* (June 5). Available at: https://bit.ly/2X1fTdw. Accessed: January 2021.

Boteach, Rabbi Shmuley (2013) "Martin Bashir Has More Apologizing to Do," *Observer Media* (November 19) Available at: https://bit.ly/38cdL5E. Accessed: February 2020.

Boshoff, Alison (2008) "Michael Jackson - The Man Who Blew a Billion. The Mind-Boggling Spending of the World's Wackiest Pop Star," *Daily Mail* (November 24) Available at: https://dailym.ai/39uPatT. Accessed: February 2020.

Brackett, David (2012) "Black or White? Michael Jackson and the Idea of Crossover," *Popular Music and Society*, vol. 35, no. 2 (May), pp. 169–185.

Brady, Jim (2002) *Boxing Confidential*, Lytham, England: Milo Books.

Breaux, Richard M. (2010) "'I'm a Cartoon!' The Jackson5ive Cartoon as Comodified [*sic*] Civil Rights & Black Power Ideologies, 1971–1973," *Journal of Pan African Studies*, vol. 3, no. 7 (March), pp. 79–99.

Brown, Mick (2016) "Berry Gordy: The Man Who Built Motown," *Daily Telegraph* (January 23). Available at: https://bit.ly/2PBHYYr. Accessed: March 2021.

Byrne, Bridget (1987) "Michael Jackson: An Eccentric Makes Marketing a Tricky Proposition," *Los Angeles Times* (October 11). Available at: https://lat.ms/3ivtvaj. Accessed: July 2020.

Calligeros, Marissa (2009) "Michael Jackson's Children 'Not His'," *Brisbane Times* (June 29). Available at: https://bit.ly/2VzyfBn. Accessed: April 2020.

Campbell, Duncan and Branigan, Tania (2003) "Jackson Sick (Literally) of Being Sued and May Be Facing Bankruptcy," *Guardian* (May 28). Available at: https://bit.ly/2xburh1. Accessed: March 2020.

Capretto, Lisa (2017) "Berry Gordy Explains How A Childhood Lesson On Race Influenced His First Few Motown Albums," *Huffington Post* (December 6). Available at: https://bit.ly/2NT3jMD. Accessed: March 2021.

Caputi, Jane (1999) "The Second Coming of Diana," *NWSA Journal*, vol. 11, no. 2, pp. 103–123.

Carlson, Jennifer (2016) "Moral Panic, Moral Breach: Bernhard Goetz, George Zimmerman, and Racialized News Reporting in Contested Cases of Self-Defense," *Social Problems*, vol. 63 (January), pp. 1–20.

Carlson, Peter and Wolmuth, Roger (1984) "Tour de Force," *People* (May 7). Available at: https://bit.ly/308qVA1. Accessed: July 2020.

Carroll, Rory (2017) "OJ Simpson: An Eternal Symbol of Racial Division – Or Has America Moved On?," *Guardian* (October 1). Available at: https://bit.ly /2v1Q1Ui. Accessed: February 2020.

CBC Arts (2009) "Bill Cosby Gets Praise for Social Activism," *CBC News* (December 23). Available at: https://bit.ly/31FJhYG. Accessed: August 2020.

CBS News (2011) "Celebrity Plastic Surgery Disasters?," *CBS News* (January 4). Available at: https://cbsn.ws/3ufvzZR. Accessed: February 2021.

Cheal, David (2020) "George Benson: 'I Practise Every Single Day'," *Financial Times* (November 7). Available at: https://on.ft.com/3ujH1DS. Accessed: February 2021.

Cloud, Dana L. (1996) "Hegemony or Concordance? The Rhetoric of Tokenism in 'Oprah' Winfrey's Rags-to-Riches Biography," *Critical Studies in Mass Communication*, no. 13, pp. 115–137.

CNN.com (2004) "Toobin: Jackson Courtroom 'Like Nothing I've Ever Seen'," *Law Center* (January 16). Available at: https://cnn.it/2SMxNzr. Accessed: February 2020.

CNN.com (2005) "Jackson Jurors: Evidence 'Just Wasn't There'," *Law Center* (June 15). Available at: https://cnn.it/38Y8jF0. Accessed: February 2020.

Coleman, Miriam (2013) "Quincy Jones Sues Michael Jackson Estate," *Rolling Stone* (October 26). Available at: https://bit.ly/3qeZYFm. Accessed: February 2012.

Coleman, Ray (1998) *McCartney: Yesterday And Today*, London: Diane Books.

Collier, Gene (2020) "35 Years After Air Jordans, We're Still Killing Each Other Over Sneakers," *Pittsburgh Post-Gazette* (April 19). Available at: https://bit.ly /2L5QNaQ. Accessed: December 2020

Connelly, Christopher (1983) "The Year in Music: 1983," *Rolling Stone* (December 22). Available at: https://bit.ly/35O3lvN. Accessed: September 2020.

Cragg, Michael (2019) "Janet Jackson at Glastonbury 2019 Review – Pop's Elder Stateswoman in Full Control," *Guardian* (June 29). Available at: https://bit.ly /2XIQeHF. Accessed: June 2020.

Dagbovie, Sika Alaine (2007) "Star-Light, Star-Bright, Star Damn Near White: Mixed-Race Superstars," *Journal of Popular Culture*, vol. 40, no. 2, pp. 217–237.

Dart, John (1987) "Jackson Out of Jehovah's Witnesses Sect," *Los Angeles Times* (June 7). Available at: https://lat.ms/2M7PVU1. Accessed: January 2021.

Davis, Matthew (2005) "Jackson Counts the Cost of Freedom," *BBC News* (June 15). Available at: https://bbc.in/33inI1m. Accessed: May 2021.

D'Agostino, Ryan (2020) "Macaulay Culkin Is Not Like You: The 39-Year-Old— Call Him 'Mack'—Has Been Liberated Longer Than You Realize," *Esquire* (February 11). Available at: https://bit.ly/2SXUDEt. Accessed: February 2020.

Deans, Jason (2003)"Granada Stands by Bashir," *Guardian* (February 6). Available at: https://bit.ly/3tnort1. Accessed: May 2021.

Delmont, Matthew (2010) "Michael Jackson and Television Before Thriller," *Journal of Pan African Studies*, vol. 3, no. 7, pp. 64–78.

Dougherty, Steve and Gold, Todd (1989) "All Bad Things Come to An End as a Tearful Michael Jackson Bids Bye-Bye to the Highway," *People* (February 13). Available at: https://bit.ly/3ev3e9S. Accessed: June 2020.

Duerden, Nick (2005) "Gwen Stefani: Beyond Doubt," *Independent Magazine* (August 28), pp. 12–14. Available at: https://bit.ly/3uCxGWJ. Accessed: June 2021.

Duke, Alan (2011) "Paramedic on Michael Jackson Call: Doctor's Story 'Didn't Add Up'," *CNN* (January 6). Available at: https://cnn.it/3mGwKOT. Accessed: April, 2021.

Durkee, Cutler (1987) "Unlike Anyone, Even Himself," *People* (September 14). Available at: https://bit.ly/3fb07UJ. Accessed: July 2020.

Dwyer, Jim (2019) "The True Story of How a City in Fear Brutalized the Central Park Five," *New York Times* (May 30). Available at: https://nyti.ms/2JFt3WI. Accessed: April 2020.

Ellis-Petersen, Hannah (2016) "Urban Myths Director Defends Casting of White Actor as Michael Jackson," *Guardian* (January 10). Available at: https://bit.ly /2TDRR6o. Accessed: March 2020.

Entman, Robert M. and Rojecki, Andrew (2000) *The Black Image in the White Mind: Media and Race in America*, Chicago, IL: University of Chicago Press.

Fast, Susan (2010) "Difference that Exceeded Understanding: Remembering Michael Jackson (1958–2009)," *Popular Music and Society*, vol. 33, no. 2, pp. 259–266.

Fettmann, Eric (2202) "Al's Jackson Problem," *New York Post* (July 10). Available at: https://bit.ly/3aTTTpS. Accessed: March 2020.

Finn, Natalie (2019) "Inside the Outrage Over *Leaving Neverland* and Michael Jackson's Complicated Legacy," *E! News* (January 29). Available at: https://eonli .ne/2y0jDTE. Accessed: May 2020.

Fischer, Mary A. (1994) "Was Michael Jackson Framed? The Untold Story," *GQ* (October). Available at: https://bit.ly/3fqGCbA. Accessed: May 2020.

Fong-Torres, Ben (1971) "The Jackson 5: The Men Don't Know But the Little Girls Understand," *Rolling Stone* (April 29). Available at: https://bit.ly/3eitLZV. Accessed: July 2021.

Friedman, Devin (2006) "Where's Michael?," *GQ* (April 5).

Friedman, Roger (2003) "Michael Jackson's Unacceptable Behavior Revealed," *Fox News* (February 7). Available at: https://fxn.ws/2PHa4ys. Accessed: March 2020.

Friedman, Roger (2005) "Jacko in Exile With 20-Year-Old Protégé," *Fox News* (August 8). Available at: https://fxn.ws/2HVducY. Accessed: February 2020.

Fuller, Jennifer (2010) "Branding Blackness on US Cable Television," *Media, Culture and Society*, vol. 32, no. 2, pp. 285–305.

Gabler, Neal (1998) *Life: The Movie – How Entertainment Conquered Reality*, New York: Vintage Books.

Gabler, Neal (2009) "Tiger-Stalking: In Defense of Our Tabloid Culture" (Also Titled "The Greatest Show on Earth")," *Newsweek* (December 11). Available at: https://bit.ly/2vVXFA4. Accessed: March 2020.

Gardner, Eriq (2017) "The Brash Plan to Defend Bill Cosby:'Rehabilitate His Reputation' at Trial," *The Hollywood Reporter* (April 26). Available at: https:// bit.ly/3kH6WRc. Accessed: August 2020.

Gates, Henry Louis Jr. (1998) "Net Worth: How the Greatest Player in the History of Basketball Became the Greatest Brand in the History of Sports," *The New Yorker* (June 1). Available at: https://bit.ly/3nzH2Qp. Accessed: December 2020.

Gerdau, Richard and Hoffman, Lee (2009) "Debbie Rowe: Why She Had Jackson's Children," *ABC News* (July 7). Available at: https://abcn.ws/3bmqy7B. Accessed: March 2020.

Goldberg, Michael (1992) "Michael Jackson: The Making of 'The King of Pop'," *Rolling Stone* (January 9). Available at: https://bit.ly/2ULmEPS. Accessed: June 2020.

Goldberg, Michael and Connelly, Christopher (1984) "Michael Jackson: Trouble in Paradise," *Rolling Stone* (March 15). Available at: https://bit.ly/2Oo4boX. Accessed: July 2020.

Goldberg, Michael and Handelman, David (1987) "Is Michael Jackson For Real," *Rolling Stone* (September 24). Available at: https://bit.ly/3edRtDV. Accessed: July 2020.

Goldman, John J. (2000) "4 White Officers Are Acquitted in Death of Diallo," *Los Angeles Times*, (February 26). Available at: https://lat.ms/2UjGoKA. Accessed: March 2020.

Goleman, Daniel (1984) "Psychologists Examine Appeal of Michael Jackson," *New York Times* (July 9) (Section C), 13.

Gollner, Philip (1989) "Even in Disguise, Michael Jackson Gets Attention," *Los Angeles Times* (May 3). Available at: https://lat.ms/30JUDMf. Accessed: June 2020.

Gómez-Barris, Macarena and Gray, Herman (2006) "Michael Jackson, Television, and Post-Op Disasters," *Television and New Media*, vol. 7, no. 1 (February), pp. 40–51.

Gomstyn, Alice and Connelly, Chris (2011) "Michael Jackson's Secret World: Willing Doctors, Hospital-Grade Sedatives," *ABC News* (November 4). Available at: http://abcn.ws/1wknOR8 Accessed: May 2020.

Gordy, Berry (1994) *To Be Loved: The Music, The Magic, the Memories of Motown*, London: Headline.

Grizzuti Harrison, Barbara (1989) "The Importance of being Oprah," *New York Times Magazine* (June 11), pp. 28–30; 46–48; 54; 130; 134–136. Available at: https://nyti.ms/2LNcInl. Accessed: January 2021.

Guerrasio, Jason (2019) "'Leaving Neverland' Director Explains Why He Didn't Interview Macaulay Culkin for His Brutal Michael Jackson Documentary," *Business Insider* (March 4). Available at: https://bit.ly/3epKNp1. Accessed: July 2021.

Gundersen, Edna (2001) "Michael in the Mirror," *USA Today* (December 14). Available at: https://abcn.ws/2IQbvXT Accessed: March 2020.

Harris, Dan (2009) "Was Michael Jackson a Shrewd Businessman or Underhanded Friend?," *ABC News* (June 28). Available at: https://abcn.ws/3fFfMwA. Accessed: November 2020.

Harris, Ellen T. (1997) "Twentieth-century Farinelli," *The Musical Quarterly*, vol. 81, no. 2, pp. 180–189.

Hasen, Jeff (1984) "Michael Jackson Hospitalized after Fireworks Mishap on Set of Pepsi Commercial," *UPI Archives* (January 29). Available at: https://bit.ly/331tpC1. Accessed: July 2020.

Helligar, Jeremy (2019) "What Happened to the Black Queer Music Revolution That Frank Ocean Almost Started?," *Variety* (June 20). Available at: https://bit.ly/3gLgUyW. Accessed: June 2020.

Henderson, Eric (2003) "Review: Janet Jackson, *Control*," *Slant* (October 30). Available at: https://bit.ly/2B0QlWf. Accessed: May 2020.

Hilburn, Robert (1990) "Janet Jackson Finally Learns to Say 'I'," *Los Angeles Times* (April 15). Available at: https://lat.ms/3dWpw3Z. Accessed: June 2020.

Hirshey, Gerri (1994) *Nowhere to Run: The Story of Soul Music*, New York: Da Capo Press.

Hoffman, Jordan (2019) "Yair Netanyahu Tells Boteach in NYC His Father Saves Jews 'From Annihilation'," *Times of Israel* (November 7). Available at: https://bit.ly/2wrrngj. Accessed: March 2020.

Holden, Stephen (1979) "Off the Wall," *Rolling Stone* (November 1). Available at: https://bit.ly/3tP3M2i. Accessed: February 2021.

Holland, Steve (2009) "Obama has Tough-Love Message for African-Americans," *Reuters* (July 17). Available at: https://reut.rs/36EbrGv. Accessed: July 2021.

Hoskyns, Barney (1996) *Waiting for the Sun: The Story of the Los Angeles Music Scene*, London: Viking.

Howard, Greg (2018) Al Sharpton, Reconsidered," *New York Times* (March 9).

Hunt, Dennis (1979) "Michael Jackson's 'Off the Wall'," *Los Angeles Times* (October 14). Available at: https://lat.ms/3adE1RA. Accessed: February 2021.

Hunter, James (1995) "HIStory: Past, Present, Future, Book I," *Rolling Stone* (August 10). Available at: https://bit.ly/2V67mWC. Accessed: April 2020.

Hunter, James (2001) "Invincible," *Rolling Stone* (December 6). Available at: https://bit.ly/2Iz2HFy. Accessed: March 2020.

Hunter-Tilney, Ludovic (2003) "A Better Kind of Stardom in a Jacko-less World," *Financial Times* (December 24).

Hunter-Tilney, Ludovic (2016) "Motown Stories," *Financial Times* (March 18). Available at: https://on.ft.com/2ObguZc. Accessed: April 2021.

Hunter-Tilney, Ludovic (2018) "Michael Jackson at the National Portrait Gallery -- All Thriller, No Filler," *Financial Times* (June 28). Available at: https://on.ft.com/3fC4D1E. Accessed: April 2021.

Hutchinson, Earl Ofari (2014) "Is Bill Cosby Still the Darling of Conservatives?," *Chicago Tribune* (November 17). Available at: https://bit.ly/3g4ri3d. Accessed: August 2020.

Ingram, Billy (no date) "A Short History of the Tabloids: 55+ Years of the National Enquirer," (Online only). Available at: http://bit.ly/-IngramTabloids. Accessed: June 2020.

Inniss, Leslie B. and Feagin, Joe R. (1995) "The Cosby Show: The View From the Black Middle Class," *Journal of Black Studies*, vol. 25, no. 6 (July), pp. 692–711.

Jackson, LaToya (with Romanowski, Patricia) (1991) *Growing Up in the Jackson Family*, New York: Dutton.

Jancelewicz, Chris (2017) "Michael Jackson Jury Members Recall Child Molestation Trial, Why They Found Him Not Guilty," *Global News* (July 26). Available at: https://bit.ly/2PmuE7d. Accessed: February 2020.

Jefferson, Alphine W. (1986) "Black America in the 1980s: Rhetoric vs. Reality," *The Black Scholar: Journal of Black Studies and Research*, vol. 17, no. 3, pp. 2–9.

Jefferson, Margot (2018; first pub. 2006) *On Michael Jackson*, London: Granta.

Jefferson, Margot (2019) "Was I in Denial? Margo Jefferson on Michael Jackson's Legacy," *Guardian* (June 7). Available at: https://bit.ly/2wxP6vd. Accessed: March 2020.

Jeffries, Mark (2020) "Michael Jackson's Blood-Stained IV Drip is Being Auctioned by Family Member," *Daily Mirror* (September 24). Available at: https://bit.ly/3hL6t1j. Accessed: May 2021.

Jhally, Sut and Lewis, Justin (1992) *Enlightened Racism: The Cosby Show, Audiences, And The Myth Of The American Dream*, Boulder CO: Westview Press.

Johnson, Angella (1995) "Jackson Angers Ex-Beatles," *Guardian* (November 6). Available at: https://bit.ly/39flQLj. Accessed: November 2020.

Jones, Jeffrey M. (2003) "Fifty-Four Percent of Americans Believe Allegations Against Jackson: Public Views 'King of Pop' Unfavorably," *Gallup News Service* (December 17). Available at: https://bit.ly/2uPmM7r. Accessed: February 2020.

Johnson, Robert E. (1984) "The Michael Jackson Nobody Knows," *Ebony* (December), pp. 155–162. Available at: https://bit.ly/3mwDPAK. Accessed: December 2020.

Kareem Little, Nadra (2020) "How MTV Handled Accusations of Racism and Became More Inclusive," *liveaboutdotcom* (January 14). Available at: http://bit.ly/-MTVandBlackMusic.

Kashner, Sam (2011) "Elizabeth Taylor's Closing Act," *Vanity Fair* (November). Available at: http://vnty.fr/1x3O9zB Accessed: October 2014.

Kashner, Sam (2011) "Elizabeth Taylor, Michael Jackson, and Marlon Brando Star in . . . *Escape From New York*," *Vanity Fair* (May). Available at: https://bit.ly/2TGQIe7. Accessed: March 2020.

Kiersh, Edward (1992) "Mr. Robinson vs. Air Jordan: The Marketing Battle for Olympic Gold," *Los Angeles Times Magazine* (March 22), p. 28. Available at: https://lat.ms/3qJzJHI. Accessed: December 2020.

Klein, Naomi (2001) *No Logo*, London: Flamingo.

Knoedelseder, William Jr (1985) "Michael Jackson Pays $40 Million for ATV Music: Beatles Song Catalogue Acquired," *Los Angeles Times* (August 15). Available at: https://lat.ms/3fKR4Ly. Accessed: November 2020.

Knopper, Steve (2016) "Behind the Scenes of *The Wiz* With Michael Jackson," *Time* (December 3). Available at: https://bit.ly/3jFjY1u. Accessed: February 2021.

Kron, Joan (2009) "Michael Jackson's Dermatologist and Former Plastic Surgeon Talk," *Allure* (August 12). Available at: https://bit.ly/2N9oCcr. Accessed: February 2021.

Lapham, Lewis H. (1997) "Fatted Calf," *Harper's*, vol. 295 (November), pp. 11–14.

Lawrence, Greg (2011) *Jackie as Editor: The Literary Life of Jacqueline Kennedy Onassis*, New York: Macmillan.

Leonard, David J. (2004) "The Next M.J. or the Next O.J? Kobe Bryant, Race, and the Absurdity of Colorblind Rhetoric," *Journal of Sport and Social Issues*, vol. 28, no. 3, pp. 284–313.

Levy, Emanuel (2021) "Director Lee Daniels on The United States vs. Billie Holiday," *Financial Times* (January 27). Available at: https://on.ft.com/3fFbpmR. Accessed: June 2021.

Lister, David (2003) "Bashir Makes Fly-on-the-Wall Documentary on Michael Jackson," *Independent* (January 21). Available at: https://bit.ly/2T9F4cx. Accessed: February 2020.

Lupica, Mike (1991) "The Sporting Life," *Esquire*, part 115 (March 3), pp. 52-54.

Macintosh, Jeane (2002) "Jacko Got Off-Tracko, Rev. Al Says," *New York Post* (July 8). Available at: https://bit.ly/39LY5YD. Accessed: March 2020.

McCollum, Brian (2021) "Soulful Sounds from the South Were Polished for the Masses in Motown," *USA Today* (February 9). Available at: https://bit.ly /3v1I9gP. Accessed: March 2021.

McDonell-Parry, Amelia (2019) "Michael Jackson Child Sexual Abuse Allegations: A Timeline," *Rolling Stone* (January 29). Available at: https://bit.ly/3cKMBpT. Accessed: May 2020.

McDougal, Dennis (1985) "The Thriller of 'Victory': Snatching Profit from the Agony of the Biggest, Splashiest and Most Troubled Rock Concert Tour in History," *Los Angeles Times* (January 6). Available at: https://lat.ms/2P2RXT0. Accessed: July 2020.

Macias Jr., Martin (2020) "Quincy Jones' $9 Million Win in Michael Jackson Royalties Suit Wiped Out on Appeal," *Courthouse News Service* (May 5). Available at: https://bit.ly/3bb2HdS. Accessed: March 2021.

Manasan, Althea (2010) "'Michael had Feelings for Me': Man Claims He was Michael Jackson's Gay Lover," *National Post* (April 30). Available at: https://bit .ly/2SS1dhX. Accessed: May 2021.

Mankiewicz, Josh (2004) "New Details About 1993 Jackson Case," *Dateline NBC* (3 September). Available at: https://nbcnews.to/3fvzDxJ. Accessed: May 2020.

Mankiewicz, Josh (2010) "Michael Jackson: A Mother's Story," *NBC News* (June 26). Available at: https://nbcnews.to/3j32lZb. Accessed: January 2021.

Marchese, David (2018) "In Conversation: Quincy Jones," *Vulture* (February 7). Available at: https://bit.ly/3cG4CbD. Accessed: February 2021.

Meyersohn, Jon, McFadden, Cynthia and McCarthy, Tom (2009) "Why Did Michael Jackson Go So Far to Alter His Appearance?," *ABC News* (July 1). Available at: https://abcn.ws/3prXaU4. Accessed: February 2021.

Miller, Jim (1980) "Jim Miller on Pop Music: Migraine Heaven," *New Republic* (June 19). Available at: https://bit.ly/3dagJht. Accessed: February 2021.

Miller, Julie (2015) "Infamous Dermatologist, Dies at 70," *Vanity Fair* (October 23). Available at: https://bit.ly/3gjet68. Accessed: July 2020.

Morley, Paul (2019) *The Awfully Big Adventure: Michael Jackson in the Afterlife*, London: Faber & Faber.

Morris, Wesley (2019) "Michael Jackson Cast a Spell. 'Leaving Neverland' Breaks It," *New York Times* (February 28). Available at: https://nyti.ms/3xg3Vxk. Accessed: April 2021

Mottola, Tommy (2013) *Hitmaker: The Man and His Music*, New York: Grand Central Publishing.

Moynihan, Colin (2020) "Setback for Quincy Jones on Payment for Michael Jackson Film," *New York Times* (May 5). Available at: https://nyti.ms/3ar1s9Z. Accessed: February 2021.

Moynihan, Daniel (1965) *The Moynihan Report: The Negro Family -- The Case for National Action*, Washington, DC: US Department of Labor. Available at: https://bit.ly/38YoHVl. Accessed: February 2020.

Murray, Conrad (2016) *This Is It! The Secret Lives of Dr. Conrad Murray and Michael Jackson*, Pennsauken, NJ: BookBaby.

Neimark, Jill (1995) "The Culture of Celebrity," *Psychology Today* (May/June), pp. 54–7; 87–90.

Newfield, Jack (1995) *Only in America: The Life and Crimes of Don King*, New York: William Morrow & Co.

Newsweek Staff (1983) "Michael Jackson: The Peter Pan of Pop," *Newsweek* (January 9). Available at: https://bit.ly/3ysPCWY. Accessed: May 2021.

Newsweek Staff (1984) "1984 Michael Jackson Tour," *Newsweek* (July 15). Available at: https://bit.ly/2Digz7y. Accessed: July 2020.

Newton, Jim and Nazario, Sonia (1993) "Police Say Seized Tapes Do Not Incriminate Jackson," *Los Angeles Times* (August 27).

Obama, Barack (2006) *The Audacity of Hope: Thoughts on Reclaiming the American Dream*, New York: Crown Publishing.

O'Brien, Timothy L. (2006) "What Happened to the Fortune Michael Jackson Made?," *New York Times* (May 14). Available at: https://nyti.ms/2SIBuEU. Accessed: February 2020.

O'Connor, John J. (1985) "TV Reviews: Bill Cosby's Triumph," *New York Times* (May 9). Available at: https://nyti.ms/2DsSwU9. Accessed: August 2020.

O'Connor, Roisin (2017) "Michael Jackson Film Announced after Sky Pulls Joseph Fiennes Portrayal in Urban Myths," *Independent* (January 16). Available at: https://bit.ly/2TrkW62. Accessed: March 2020.

O'Malley Greenburg, Zack (2014) "Infographic: Michael Jackson's Multibillion Dollar Career Earnings, Listed Year By Year," *Forbes* (May 29). Available at: https://bit.ly/2GSLENN. Accessed: February 2020.

Orth, Maureen (1994) "Nightmare in Neverland," *Vanity Fair* (January 1). Accessed: January 2020.

Orth, Maureen (2003) "Losing His Grip," *Vanity Fair* (April 1). Accessed: January 2020. Available at: https://bit.ly/2RVenXo

Orth, Maureen (2004) "Neverland's Lost Boys," *Vanity Fair* (March 1). Available at: https://bit.ly/2HhGlYz. Accessed: February 2020.

Owens Patton, Tracey and Snyder-Yuly, Julie (2007) "Any Four Black Men Will Do: Rape, Race, and the Ultimate Scapegoat," *Journal of Black Studies*, vol. 37, no. 6 (July), pp. 859–895.

Page, Clarence (1989) "The '80s Have Been A Mixed Bag For African Americans," *Chicago Tribune* (November 29). Available at: https://bit.ly/3gulTCF. Accessed: August 2020.

Palmer, Robert (1984) "Pop: 'Victory' Album Echoes Jacksons' Tour," *New York Times* (July 7). Available at: https://nyti.ms/2P5lgEz. Accessed: July 2020.

Pareles, Jon (1984) "Michael Jackson at 25: A Musical Phenomenon," *New York Times* (January 14). Available at: https://nyti.ms/33EaL1T. Accessed: September 2020.

Pareles, Jon (2001) "A Cautious Return to His Throne, With Air Kisses for Loyal Subjects," *New York Times* (September 10). Available at: https://nyti.ms /3aw08jt. Accessed: March 2020.

Parkes, Christopher (2005) "Michael Jackson Cleared of All Charges", *Financial Times* (June 13). Available at: https://on.ft.com/2PflzwX. Accessed: February 2020.

Parry, Ryan (2009; updated 2012) "Michael Jackson Exclusive: Blanket Jackson's Surrogate Mother is a Mexican Nurse Named Helena," *The Mirror* (August 12). Available at: https://bit.ly/3p9CpxX. Accessed: March 2020.

Peck, Janice (1994) "Talk About Racism: Framing a Popular Discourse of Race on Oprah Winfrey," *Cultural Critique*, no. 7, pp. 89–126.

Perpetua, Matthew (2011) "Doctor: Michael Jackson Was Dependent on Demerol," *Rolling Stone*, (October 28). Available at: https://bit.ly/383teGe. Accessed: February 2020.

Petrides, Alexis (2001) "Normality Play," *Guardian* (October 26). Available at: https://bit.ly/2TP1grD. Accessed: March 2020.

Petrides, Alexis (2018) "Joe Jackson was One of the Most Monstrous Fathers in Pop," *Guardian* (June 27). Available at: https://bit.ly/3dF7ZhR. Accessed: April 2021.

Pew Research Center (2015) "Use of Spanking Differs Across Racial and Education Groups," *Pew Research Center* (December 14). Available at: https://pewrsr.ch /2UmFLCK. Accessed: July 2021.

Pieterse, Jan Nederveen (1992) *White on Black: Images of Africa and Blacks in Western Popular Culture*, New Haven: Yale University Press.

Posner, Gerald (2009) "The Jackson-Liz Drug Link," *Daily Beast* (June 7). Available at: http://thebea.st/1yY01rc. Accessed: October 2014.

Queenan, Joe (2007) "Vinyl Word: How Billie Jean Changed the World," *Guardian* (July 12). Available at: https://bit.ly/3gTi0HE. Accessed: September 2020.

Revesz, Rachael (2016) "Don King drops N-word in a Church while Introducing Donald Trump to the Stage," *Independent* (September 21). Available at: https:// bit.ly/2BWxTPu. Accessed: July 2020.

Rich, Katey (2016) "The Michael Jackson, Marlon Brando, Elizabeth Taylor Story Gets Even Crazier Thanks to Casting," *Vanity Fair* (January 27). Available at: https://bit.ly/2VMuwSw. Accessed: March 2020.

Ritz, David (1998) "Sex, Sadness and the Triumph of Janet Jackson," *Rolling Stone* (October 1). Available at: https://bit.ly/3ciOclr. Accessed: May 2020.

Robinson, Lisa (2008) "It Happened In Hitsville," *Vanity Fair* (December 13). Available at: https://bit.ly/3w0i3u5 Accessed: March 2021.

Rogers, Ibram (2008) "Putting Barack Obama's Candidacy in Historical Perspective," *Diverse Issues in Higher Education*, vol. 25, no. 18, pp. 15–17.

Rowley, Bridget (2010) "Be Like Mike," pp. 37–43 in Luzajic, Lorette (ed.) *Michael Jackson for the Soul: A Fanthology of Inspiration and L.O.V.E.*, San Bernadino, CA: Handymaiden Books.

Ryan, Harriet (2012) "A-List Doctor's Star Has Faded," *Los Angeles Times* (January 1). Available at: http://lat.ms/1gtu82F. Accessed September 2015).

Ryan, Joal (2002) "Whitney Comes Clean (Sort Of)," *E! News* (December 3). Available at: https://eonli.ne/2SsGPRY. Accessed: February 2020.

Sanders, Charles L. (1979) "The Jacksons: Famed Brothers Are No Longer Little Boys," *Ebony* (September), pp. 33–38; 40.

Saperstein, Pat (2009) "Michael Jackson Dies at 50: Pop Icon Suffers Suspected Heart Attack in L.A.," *Variety* (June 25). Available at: https://bit.ly/3wDcNM7. Accessed: July 2021.

Scobie, William (1986) "Pepsi Bests Millions on Jackson's Comeback," *Chicago Tribune* (June 5). Available at: https://tinyurl.com/y8g3cm2y Accessed: July 2020.

Scriven, Darryl (2010) "Michael Jackson &The Psycho/Biology of Race," *Journal of Pan African Studies*, vol. 3, no. 7 (March), pp. 100–105.

Seal, Mark (2012) "The Doctor Will Sue You Now," *Vanity Fair* (March). Available at: http://vnty.fr/1otBiaW Accessed: October 2014.

Serwer, Adam (2018) "How Cosby's 'Pound Cake' Speech Helped Lead to His Downfall," *The Atlantic* (April 26). Available at: https://bit.ly/3gMewrk. Accessed: August 2020.

Sharkey, Jacqueline (1997) "The Diana Aftermath," *American Journalism Review*, vol. 19, no. 9, pp. 18–25.

Sharpton, Al (2013) *The Rejected Stone: Al Sharpton & the Path to American Leadership*, New York: Cash Money Content.

Shelden, Michael (2001) "The Man Who Made Michael Jackson," *Daily Telegraph* (April 2). Available at: https://bit.ly/2ZsvLHb. Accessed: February 2021.

Simpson, Dave (2010) "Why Someone in Whitney Houston's Condition Shouldn't Be on Stage," *Guardian* (February 24). Available at: https://bit.ly/2SwhJ4u. Accessed: February 2020.

Simpson, Tyrone R. III (2002) "Hollywood Bait and Switch: The 2002 Oscars, Black Commodification, and Black Political Science," *Black Camera*, vol. 17, no. 2, pp. 6–7, 11.

Sisario, Ben (2009) "In Death as in Life Michael Jackson Sets Music Sales Records," *New York Times* (July 1). Available at: https://nyti.ms/2SvvAa6. Accessed: February 2020.

Sites, William (2012) "Is This Black Music? Sounding Out Race and the City," *Journal of Urban History*, vol. 38, no. 2, pp. 385–395.

Skow, John (1978) "Cinema: Nowhere Over the Rainbow," *Time* (October 30). Available at: https://bit.ly/3tUHsEu. Accessed: February 2021.

Smith, Rupert (2003) "The Kid's Not Alright," *Guardian* (February 4). Available at: https://bit.ly/3hHkdKb. Accessed: July 2021.

Sperling, Nicole (2019) "Michael Jackson Documentary *Leaving Neverland* Stuns at Sundance," *Vanity Fair* (January 26). Available at: https://bit.ly/38koqwi. Accessed: February 2020.

Spiegel, Claire and Ellis, Virginia (1994) "3 Doctors Cited in Taylor Drug Case: Medicine: The Physicians Receive Reprimands for Prescribing Excessive Medication to Treat the Actress's Pain. Their Attorneys Say the Decision is an Exoneration," *Los Angeles Times* (August 11). Available at: https://lat.ms /34AsLuJ. Accessed: May 2021.

Stanley, Alessandra (2003) "A Neverland World of Michael Jackson," *New York Times* (February 6). Available at: https://nyti.ms/3cs7HJE. Accessed: March 2020.

Staples, Brent (2018) "The Racist Trope That Won't Die," *New York Times* (June 17). Available at: https://nyti.ms/34eqbd2. Accessed: April 2020.

Steele, Shelby (1990) *The Content of Our Character: A New Vision of Race in America*, New York: HarperCollins.

Sternig, Barbara and Duffy, David (1993) "Michael Jackson's Secret Family – A Millionaire's Wife and Her Two Kids," *National Enquirer* (May 25). Reproduction Available at: https://bit.ly/3dcudWj. Accessed: June 2020.

Storey, Kate (2019) "Inside Michael Jackson's 2005 Trial Featured in *Leaving Neverland*," *Esquire* (March 3). Available at: https://bit.ly/32hfSnK. Accessed: February 2020.

Swash, Rosie (2009) "Michael Jackson to Announce London Shows," *Guardian* (March 3). Available at: https://bit.ly/394INxk. Accessed: February 2020.

Taraborrelli, J. Randy (2009) *Michael Jackson: The Magic, the Madness, the Whole Story, 1958-2009*, New York: Grand Central Publishing.

Teather, David (2009) "Michael Jackson Dies Owing Up to $500m," *Guardian* (June 26). Available at: https://bit.ly/31zupgf. Accessed: June 2020.

TMZ (2019) "Michael Jackson Jewelry Shopping for James Safechuck in '80s Surveillance Footage," *TMZ News* (March 13). Available at: https://bit.ly/3esNYwh. Accessed: July 2021.

Touré (2014) "Michael Jackson: Black Superhero," *Rolling Stone* (June 26). Available at: https://bit.ly/37SKNZm. Accessed: February 2020.

Tourni, Habib (2006) "Jackson Settles Down to His New Life in the Gulf," *Gulf News* (January 23), Available at: https://bit.ly/38qwdZf. Accessed: February 2020.

Trow, George W. S. and Kincaid, Jamaica (1975) "Leaving Motown," *New Yorker* (July 14). Available at: https://bit.ly/3cEpOhE. Accessed: April 2021.

UPI News Service (2005) "Michael Jackson's Family Flying to Bahrain for Drug Intervention," *Reality TV World* (December 7). Available at: https://bit.ly/2HWG11K. Accessed: February 2020.

Vineyard, Jennifer (2003) "Former Friend of Jackson's Regrets Suggesting TV Documentary," *MTV News* (November 26). Available at: https://on.mtv.com/2PFI4LK. Accessed: March 2020.

Vogel, Joseph (2014) "The Nation That Janet Jackson Built," *The Atlantic* (September 15). Available at: https://bit.ly/3d4z4tn. Accessed: May 2020.

Williams Patricia, J. (2007) "The Audacity of Oprah," *The Nation* (December 24), p.8.

Willman, Chris (1991) "Michael Jackson's 'Dangerous'," *Los Angeles Times* (November 24). Available at: https://lat.ms/37HLlBW. Accessed: June 2020.

Wilson, Scott (1997) "The Indestructible Beauty of Suffering: Diana and the Metaphor of Global Consumption," *Theory and Event*, vol. 1, no. 4. Available at: http://bit.ly/-WilsonIndestructible. Accessed: April 2020.

Wyman, Bill (2012) "The Pale King: Michael Jackson's Ambiguous Legacy," *The New Yorker* (December 17). Available at: https://bit.ly/3jQHfN1. Accessed: September 2020.

Wyman, Bill (2013) "Did 'Thriller' Really Sell a Hundred Million Copies?," *The New Yorker* (January 4). Available at: https://bit.ly/321Gn2e. Accessed: July 2020.

Film and Television

Living With Michael Jackson (2003) Director, Julie Shaw. Granada Television (UK).

The Michael Jackson Interview: The Footage You Were Never Meant to See (2003) Producer, Marc Schaffel. Brad Lachman Productions (USA).

Louis, Martin & Michael (2013) Director, Will Yapp. BBC Films (UK). Available at: https://bbc.in/2I44guT. Accessed: February 2020.

Michael Jackson's Journey from Motown to Off the Wall (2016) Director, Spike Lee. Optimum Productions, Sony Legacy and 40 Acres and a Mule Filmworks (USA).

Leaving Neverland (2019) Director, Dan Reed. Amos Pictures, Channel 4 (UK) and HBO (USA).

The Last Dance (2020) Director, Jason Hehir. ESPN Films, NBA Entertainment, Mandalay Sports Media (MSM), Netflix, Chicago Bulls, ESPN, Jump 23 (uncredited) (USA).

INDEX